The Mass Ornament

...

Siegfried Kracauer, late 1920s

THE MASS ORNAMENT

WEIMAR ESSAYS

■ ■ ■

SIEGFRIED KRACAUER

Translated, Edited, and with an Introduction by
Thomas Y. Levin

Harvard University Press
Cambridge, Massachusetts
London, England
1995

LIBRARY OF CONGRESS CATALOGING–IN–PUBLICATION DATA

Kracauer, Siegfried, 1889–1966.
 [Ornament der Masse. English]
 The mass ornament : Weimar essays / Siegfried Kracauer ;
translated, edited, and with an introduction by Thomas Y. Levin.
     p.   cm.
 Originally published as: Das Ornament der Masse: Essays, by
Suhrkamp Verlag, c1963.
 Includes bibliographical references and index.
 ISBN 0–674–55162–1. — ISBN 0–674–55163–X (pbk.)
 I. Levin, Thomas Y.   II. Title.
AC35.K64613   1995
081—dc20   94–47397
               CIP

For Theodor W. Adorno

...

Contents

■ ■ ■

CONTENTS

∎∎∎

Illustrations

. . .

Translator's Note

■■■

This translation is based on the second edition of *Das Ornament der Masse: Essays* (Frankfurt: Suhrkamp Verlag, 1977), which, as the editor Karsten Witte explains in his afterword, is essentially identical to the first edition that Kracauer himself supervised in 1963. Aside from the correction of typographical errors and bibliographic data, the only substantive change made in the later, posthumous edition was the reinsertion of a number of passages that had figured in the original versions of the essays published in the *Frankfurter Zeitung* but that Kracauer had for some reason excised from the 1963 edition. The translation follows Witte's philological lead and reinstates all passages, titles, emphases, and text breaks from the original publications, marking them as such in the notes. Indeed, as already suggested by the slightly modified subtitle *Weimar Essays*, the various editorial additions all attempt to compensate for the irreducible temporal and linguistic distance of the texts from their original historical and intellectual context. Thus, the annotations serve not only to articulate thorny or especially rich translative moments and to provide bibliographic and filmographic data for cited works and passages, but also to elucidate the wide range of cultural references from the Weimar period that are embedded in Kracauer's prose. The constellation of photographs from the Weimar period is intended to have a similarly evocative function. The decision to include them was motivated by a comment Kracauer made upon rediscovering the early essays that would eventually make up *Das Ornament der Masse*. In a letter to Adorno on October 1, 1950, conveying the news of his find, Kracauer expressed the wish that these Weimar texts be published in a book-length collection "which could include drawings" (cited in *Marbacher Magazin* 47 [1988]: 110). The minimally intrusive location of the photographs between,

■ x ■

rather than within, the individual essays is meant to signal that their function is more emblematic than illustrative. All notes, except where specified otherwise, have been added by the translator.

■■■

"Reality is a construction": this oft-cited phrase from Kracauer's study *Die Angestellten* is equally true for the reality of a translation project such as this one. Among my many co-constructors, I would like to thank above all Lindsay Waters and Alison Kent of Harvard University Press for their generous encouragement and heroic editorial patience; Miriam Hansen, who introduced me to Kracauer during my graduate work at Yale and encouraged me to undertake this translation; Karsten Witte for his untiring assistance and friendship at every stage in this project; Eric Rentschler and Evi and Walter Levin for their careful readings and comments on the entire volume; Jerry Zaslove and the Institute for the Humanities at Simon Fraser University for their magnanimous support of translation reviews of a number of the essays by Michael Mundhenk; Ingrid Belke and the superb staff at the Deutsches Literaturarchiv in Marbach am Neckar for their help during my research in the Kracauer papers over the years; the J. Paul Getty Foundation and the Princeton University Committee for Research in the Humanities for stipends that subsidized both research and production costs; and the German Academic Exchange Service (DAAD), which sustained this project at various stages from its beginning to its completion. Among the many friends, colleagues, and fellow Kracauer scholars who were generous with comments, suggestions, and critiques, I would like to express particular gratitude to Edward Dimendberg, David Frisby, Karsten Harries, Anton Kaes, Thomas Keenan, Michael Kessler, Evonne Levy, Leyla Mayer, Klaus Michael, Inka Mülder-Bach, Gerhard Richter, D. N. Rodowick, Heide Schlüpmann, Andreas Volk, and Judith Wechsler. Maria Ascher's meticulous and astute editorial scrutiny has been a pleasure and an enormous help, not least in ridding the translation of residual teutonicisms in both vocabulary and style. Although Kracauer's often poetic theoretical prose presents a special challenge to the translator, any infelicities that remain here are entirely my responsibility.

Introduction

■ ■ ■

Thomas Y. Levin

> Today, access to truth is by way of the profane.
> —Siegfried Kracauer, "The Bible in German"

Among the many refugees gathered in Marseilles in August 1940, hoping to flee the tightening grip of collaborationist France, were two German Jewish cultural critics: Walter Benjamin and Siegfried Kracauer. These long-time friends had corresponded with each other for many years, worked on similar issues, published in many of the same venues, and written about each other's work.[1] Both were now hoping to reach New York, where they were awaited by friends and former colleagues at the Institute for Social Research—Theodor Adorno, Max Horkheimer, Leo Löwenthal, Meyer Schapiro, Richard Krautheimer—who had signed affidavits and arranged for their travel to, and employment in, the United States. Weeks went by during which the two met almost every day. In late September, after Spain suddenly announced that it would no longer issue transit visas to people without passports, Benjamin attempted to cross the border illegally by way of a difficult mountain path through the Pyrenees. Carrying the same papers as Kracauer, he was detained at the border and, in desperation, took his life. Only days later Kracauer and his wife Lili attempted the same route and were also forced to turn back, ending up in Perpignan. Though likewise close to despair, they continued to wait; and in February 1941, after a few agonizing months, they were finally able to get across Spain to Lisbon, whence they embarked for America. Here, after eight hard years of exile in France, the fifty-one-year-old immigrant and his wife had to start over once again.

Forced to learn yet another new language, Kracauer was nevertheless able to eke out a living in New York as a freelance writer, publishing articles in a wide range of journals (including the *Nation, Commentary,* the *New Republic, Harper's Magazine, Public Opinion Quarterly,* and the *New York Times Book Review*), as well as preparing commissioned but largely unpublished "reports" for various government and research agencies such as the Experimental Division for the Study of War Time Communications (in Washington, D.C.), UNESCO, the Voice of America, and the Bureau of Applied Social Research at Columbia University.[2] Grants from the Rockefeller, Guggenheim, Chapelbrook, and Bollingen foundations also enabled him to pursue his own research, first as "special assistant" to Iris Barry, curator of the film library at New York's Museum of Modern Art, and subsequently as an independent scholar. Though he was often interrupted by other income-producing work, such as his obligations as consultant to the Bollingen and the Old Dominion foundations, it was during these difficult last twenty-five years of his life that Kracauer also produced the books which made his reputation in the English-speaking world: his polemical history of Weimar cinema *From Caligari to Hitler* (Princeton University Press, 1947), his *Theory of Film* (Oxford University Press, 1960), and a meditation on the philosophy of history published posthumously as *History: The Last Things before the Last* (Oxford University Press, 1969).

Kracauer was able to reach the New World, whereas Benjamin was not. Curiously, however, the opposite is true of their writings from the Weimar period. Unlike Benjamin's oeuvre, which is well known and increasingly available in translation, Kracauer's successful emigration to the Anglo-American realm effectively delayed the English-language reception of the fascinating corpus of early writings which had built his reputation as one of Weimar Germany's most incisive political and cultural critics. Indeed, Anglo-American readers generally know only the many works Kracauer produced in English during his exile in the United States and his "social biography" of Jacques Offenbach, which he wrote and published during his years in France.[3] They remain largely unaware of the nearly two thousand articles he published in the *Frankfurter Zeitung* during the 1920s and 1930s.[4] This disproportionate emphasis on Kracauer's exile production has certainly played a key role in the reductive categorization of his work as "realist" film theory, a misperception in urgent need of revision. An exposure to his early writings, such as those collected here, will foster such a rereading, bringing to light the epistemological foundations, the philosophy and theology of history, the sociological sensibility, and the political motivations that inform, in various and constantly shifting ways, Kracauer's turn to cinema and its relation to his other writings. Furthermore, by locating Kracauer's pioneering film criticism from the 1920s within the larger project of his cultural criticism, these early texts reveal that Kracauer was, as he himself once insisted, not exclusively "a film person but rather a cultural philosopher, or a sociologist, and a poet as well . . . (So far as film is concerned, it was never anything but . . . a means of making certain sociological and philosophical points.)"[5]

It is thus no accident that in the collection of his Weimar writings which Kracauer himself edited in 1963 under the title *Das Ornament der Masse (The Mass Ornament)*, the few—albeit crucial—texts on photography and film are surrounded by allegorical meditations and scholarly essays on everything from Kafka, Benjamin, Weber, Scheler, and Simmel to the Buber-Rosenzweig translation of the Bible, historical biography, boredom, urban arcades, and more. These texts present a very different Kracauer, one formally, thematically, and epistemologically reminiscent of the Benjamin of *Einbahnstraße (One Way Street,* 1928) and *Illuminationen (Illuminations,* 1961), the Bloch of *Spuren* (1930) and *Erbschaft dieser Zeit (Heritage of Our Times,* 1935), and the Adorno of *Minima Moralia* (1951). It is here that one finds, for example, an explicit anticipation of Adorno and Horkheimer's "dialectic of enlightenment" thesis, but inflected in a way that leads to a refreshing rehabilitation of popular culture and "distraction" in defiance of polemically dismissive accounts of mass culture. In their relentless interdisciplinarity, and as an exemplary articulation of aesthetics and politics, these early essays shed an important new light not only on Kracauer's own later work, but also on the Frankfurt School (and especially its analysis of mass culture), on the genealogy of film theory and cultural studies, on Weimar cultural politics and, not least, on the exigencies of intellectual exile.

If we consider their journalistic origins (twenty-one of the twenty-four texts reprinted in *Das Ornament der Masse* were first published in the daily newspaper *Die Frankfurter Zeitung*), Kracauer's Weimar writings are astonishing not only in the freshness and relevance of their arguments, but above all in their decidedly philosophical character. For whereas the contemporary daily newspaper with its editorial constraints and inflexible production schedule is only rarely a forum for sustained theoretical writing, such substantive sociocritical reflection was the staple of the continental tradition of feuilleton journalism for which the *Frankfurter Zeitung* was renowned. Founded in 1856 as a trade and finance newspaper by the Jewish banker and politician Leopold Sonnemann, the *Frankfurter Zeitung* quickly became one of the leading and internationally acclaimed organs of the liberal bourgeois press, highly regarded in economics and business circles. Its politics were close to those of the liberal Deutsche Demokratische Partei, with some leanings toward the Social Democrats. Explicit in its support of the Weimar constitutional democracy, it favored the signing of the Versailles treaty and advocated nationalization of major branches of the economy of the new republic. Although it never had the circulation of any of the other competing bourgeois papers, all of which were located in Berlin, it was a highly visible publication, appearing daily in no less than four editions (three local and one national), each with numerous special supplements. Once described by Joseph Roth as "a microcosm of Germany," the *Frankfurter Zeitung* complemented its political and economic coverage with an equally prestigious feuilleton—somewhat equivalent to today's arts and culture section—which was featured prominently on the lower third of the cover and subsequent pages in every issue. It was here, "below the line" (a reference to the graphic marker which served to separate the section devoted to cultural criticism from the remainder of the paper), that Kracauer published the vast majority of his work.

The feuilleton as a genre had existed since the nineteenth century as a site for belletristic excursions of all sorts, but it began to play an important role in Germany only in the wake of World War I, at a moment when the inherited cultural vocabulary seemed particularly inadequate to the reality of the nascent republic. Indeed, as evidenced in the prescient journalistic writings of feuilleton editors such as Joseph Roth and Siegfried Kracauer, one could say that in the Weimar era the feuilleton took on an avant-garde function as the locus of a concerted effort to articulate the crisis of modernity. Its transformation from a belletrist forum into a site for diagnostic analyses of contemporary phenomena is perhaps best exemplified in Kracauer's very popular dissection of the new employee class of white-collar workers, first published serially in the feuilleton of the *Frankfurter Zeitung*, and subsequently in book form as *Die Angestellten*.[6] Through the combined efforts of the regular feuilleton authors, many of whom Kracauer himself engaged—including Alfons Paquet, Friedrich Sieburg, Wilhelm Hausenstein, Soma Morgenstern, Bernard von Brentano, Theodor Adorno, Walter Benjamin, Ernst Bloch, and Joseph Roth—the *Frankfurter Zeitung* feuilleton assumed a new shape in response to the rapidly changing social and cultural character of modernity. Here, Kracauer and others examined the Weimar Republic in the way that, as Adorno recalled in an intellectual portrait of his friend, Kracauer had taught him to approach philosophy—that is, "as a kind of coded text from which one could read the historical situation of the spirit [*Geist*], with the vague expectation that in doing so one could acquire something of truth itself."[7]

It was Kracauer who, in a programmatic insight, perhaps best captured the new orientation of the feuilleton: "We must rid ourselves of the delusion that it is the major events which have the most decisive influence on us. We are much more deeply and continuously influenced by the tiny catastrophes that make up daily life."[8] Besides presenting book reviews, conference reports, and other analyses of the state of intellectual and cultural life in the republic, the feuilleton was thus the realm of the quotidian—unemployment offices and arcades, travel experiences and dance troupes, bestsellers and boredom, neon-light displays and mass sports events—which became the focus of philosophical and sociological analyses very much in the tradition of Kracauer's teacher Georg Simmel (about whom he wrote a book-length monograph in the early 1920s).[9] To explain this new cultural landscape, the feuilleton now practiced a sort of physiognomic essayistics, a minute decoding of the surface phenomena of modernity as complex historical ciphers. The polemical stakes in Kracauer's deployment of such philosophical micrologies (Simmel called them *Momentbilder,* snapshots) may be less evident today in light of the ubiquity of "thought-images" (*Denkbilder,* to use Benjamin's term for the genre), as popularized, for example, by Roland Barthes' *Mythologies.*[10] At the time, however, the feuilleton of the *Frankfurter Zeitung* effectively provided Kracauer with a laboratory in which he and others could experiment with such new forms along the lines of the "material theory of knowledge" that he had proposed in 1920 and whose theoretical contours he had articulated in his 1922 study *Soziologie als Wissenschaft (Sociology as Science).*[11]

Kracauer joined the *Frankfurter Zeitung* as a salaried writer in August 1921, abandoning an unfulfilling career as a trained architect in order to pursue, as a journalist, his double passion for sociology and philosophy. During the first years his assignments consisted mostly of reports on local Frankfurt events and topics: lectures, conferences, architecture, city politics, and films, as well as short notices on new books (especially in philosophy, the social sciences, and architecture) and occasional essayistic pieces, many written under pseudonyms. Benno Reifenberg's appointment as head of the feuilleton staff in 1924 strengthened Kracauer's position at the paper: he became a full editor with his own office, a promotion that allowed him to delegate much of his local reporting duties and to expand his writings on cinema into a regular column, in which he effectively pioneered the genre of sociological film criticism. However, as Kracauer's feuilleton contributions became more polemical and ideologically critical in the wake of political developments in the late 1920s, they were increasingly at odds with the new financial and political allegiances of the *Frankfurter Zeitung.* The economic crisis in the 1920s and structural transformations in the advertising market following World War I were having dire consequences for many newspapers in Weimar Germany, and the *Frankfurter Zeitung* was no exception.

Max Beckmann, Editorial office of the *Frankfurter Zeitung;* pencil sketch, 1924

"Saved" from financial insolvency in 1929 by an infusion of laundered capital, which, as later became clear, stemmed from the chemical conglomerate I. G. Farben, the paper subsequently began to manifest signs of editorial bankruptcy in its newfound, decidedly pro-industry orientation.[12] This was dramatically evident in a series of politically motivated personnel changes, especially among the altogether too-critical feuilleton staff. Though Heinrich Simon remained in charge as chief editor, Reifenberg was replaced by a Swiss lawyer, Friedrich Traugott Gubler, and the liberal editor of the Berlin bureau, Bernhard Guttmann, was replaced by the more cooperative and conservative Rudolf Kirchner, provoking the bitter resignation of Bernard von Brentano, the *Frankfurter Zeitung*'s cultural correspondent in Berlin.

The change in the paper's ownership had important consequences for Kracauer as well. Instead of becoming Reifenberg's successor, as expected, he was sent to run the Berlin feuilleton, a lateral move that was less a promotion than the first in a series of indignities whose final (and ultimately successful) aim was to eliminate a highly outspoken, well-known, and excessively left-wing editor. According to Kracauer's own account in his autobiographical novel *Georg*,[13] during the Berlin years the paper's new, increasingly conformist regime repeatedly rejected or severely cut his articles, drastically reduced his pay without any reduction of responsibilities, and even threatened to "sell" him to the enemy, negotiating behind his back in 1931 for him to be engaged by the state film conglomerate UFA, which could thereby silence one of its most biting critics. In the wake of the Reichstag fire in early 1933, what had been latent became explicit: after eleven years as an editor at the *Frankfurter Zeitung*, Kracauer—who had fled to France in the meantime and had hopes of becoming the Paris correspondent—was summarily fired, the paper obviously counting on the fact that in Nazi Germany an emigrated Jew would have no legal recourse. When Kracauer nevertheless sued for severance pay through a Berlin lawyer, the *Frankfurter Zeitung* cited as grounds for his dismissal the fact that he had published a text in Leopold Schwarzschild's unacceptably leftist journal *Das neue Tagebuch* without the paper's prior approval.

By the early 1930s, Kracauer had become a highly respected voice in the Weimar public sphere and might well have capitalized on his renown in order to make a career as a freelance writer. In light of this fact, it is important to understand what might have motivated his decision to stay at the *Frankfurter Zeitung* despite its increasingly unacceptable editorial politics and the rapidly degenerating work environment. It could hardly have been the financial security of being a salaried editor (which ultimately turned out to be short-lived) that kept Kracauer from accepting one of the repeated offers to write for a more ideologically sympathetic but less widely read paper such as the *Weltbühne*. Rather, Kracauer's decision to stay with the increasingly conservative *Frankfurter Zeitung* was surely informed by strategic political considerations. A move to another forum would have dramatically changed the makeup of Kracauer's reading public just when—given the growing political influence of the right, and of the National Socialists in particular—it was more crucial than ever for him to maintain his contact with the bourgeois class that constituted the majority of the *Frankfurter Zeitung*'s readership. Thus, instead of writing for a more "engaged," left-wing publication during the last years of the Weimar Republic, Kracauer deliberately channeled his polemical editorial energies into the *Frankfurter Zeitung* feuilleton, publishing a series of critical exposés of "conservative-revolutionary" developments, such as his 1931 analyses "Bestsellers and Their Audience" and "Revolt of the Middle Classes," the latter an ideological unmasking of the conservative journal *Die Tat*.

The political imperatives and sense of responsibility that informed Kracauer's self-conception as an engaged intellectual during the crucial final years of the Weimar Republic are articulated quite clearly in his essay "Über den Schriftsteller" ("On the Writer"), which also dates from 1931. The task of the journalist, Kracauer writes, has always been to "attack current conditions in a manner that will change them."[14] However, in the wake of recent pressures (state censorship, the resulting self-censorship, and the increasingly dire financial circumstances of an ever more conservative bourgeois press), newspapers might no longer offer the best site for this sort of critical social practice. Instead, as Kracauer observes (recasting the then-prevalent juxtaposition of the politically concerned journalist and the more indulgently autonomous "writer"),[15] the traditional responsibility of the journalist has begun to fall more and more to "a new type of writer." According to Kracauer, himself the author of the quite popular anonymously published novel *Ginster* (1928), there is a new breed of writers who, "instead of being contemplative, are political; instead of seeking the universal beyond the particular, they find it in the very workings of the particular; instead of pursuing developments, they seek ruptures." Although he resisted doing so until he had no other choice, Kracauer himself ultimately opted for what he had already foreseen in 1931 as the inevitable consequence of this logic: "to do justice to his duty as a journalist [by] joining the ranks of the writers." With his dismissal from the *Frankfurter Zeitung* and the beginning of his life-long exile, Kracauer's journalistic voice had to seek new sites and forms of expression. Nevertheless, the book-length studies that became Kracauer's primary mode of production during the following decades should be seen, despite their differences in scope, tone, and focus, as continuing to stand in some sort of relation to the project of his earlier political and cultural criticism.[16]

Kracauer's commitment to journalism as a vehicle for engaging the public sphere was certainly also motivated by the fact that only a newspaper could allow him to write in rapid succession about a wide spectrum of topics, ranging from film, circus, and radio to reviews of literary, sociological, and philosophical works, to architecture, urban planning, political commentary, and sociopolitical analysis. Such eclecticism, often dismissed as an unavoidable feature of the trade, became a theoretical and political imperative for Kracauer during the socioeconomic crisis of the late 1920s. The responsible intellectual in the late Weimar Republic, he argued, "did not feel called upon to serve the interests of the 'absolute,' but rather felt duty-bound to articulate for himself (and for a wider audience) a sense of the current situation."[17] This meant abandoning the unavoidable myopia of "expert-culture," whose tendency to disregard the larger (social) picture was particularly irresponsible in a period of political turmoil. "Instead of disappearing behind clouds of idealist fog or barricading himself within his specialty, which in truth is no specialty at all, [the expert] must, particularly in times of crisis, bring the difficulties that arise within his professional enclave into confrontation with the more overarching social difficulties and draw his conclusions in this way."[18] Anticipating many of the insights that have recently fostered calls within the contemporary academy for greater "interdisciplinarity," Kracauer insisted that if expert-culture was to remain meaningful, it would have to integrate the particular objects of its research into a more inclusive general model informed by those particulars. For him, this meant detailed investigations of a wide range of concrete phenomena shaping the contemporary Weimar landscape— phenomena that he read as symptoms of larger sociopolitical developments. Considered as an ensemble, the seemingly disparate cultural analyses that Kracauer published in the *Frankfurter Zeitung* thus appear as a consistent, interdisciplinary attempt to articulate the material construction of a historically specific social reality.

Kracauer devoted at least five hours a day to his writing for the

Frankfurter Zeitung. Despite his political commitment to the medium, as an author he felt an understandable frustration with journalism's limited posterity. As he put it in a letter to Adorno, "I sacrifice my energy for articles and essays, most of which will never have a life beyond the paper. And I'm incapable of dashing off these sorts of things effortlessly, but rather compose them with the same love as I do my novels."[19] Indeed, it was the care he lavished on the style and argumentation of his journalistic writing, together with the incisiveness of his political analyses, that became the hallmark of Kracauer's work in the *Frankfurter Zeitung.* Moreover, although unavoidably eclectic, Kracauer's journalism tended nevertheless to concentrate on a number of specific issues, as he himself recognized as early as 1930: "Despite the amount of time I have to spend working for the paper, I'm not unsatisfied. A significant portion of the newspaper articles focus on a consistent set of concerns and in this way transcend their merely quotidian existence."[20] It is thus not surprising that Kracauer already envisioned a book-length collection of his journalistic texts while he was still working at the paper. In 1933, almost exactly three decades before the volume finally appeared in print, Kracauer submitted a proposal to the publisher Bruno Cassirer for what he called his *Straßenbuch (Street Book)*, an anthology of forty-one texts from the *Frankfurter Zeitung* divided into three sections: "Auf der Straße" ("On the Street"), "Neben der Straße" ("Beside the Street"), and "Figuren" ("Figures").[21]

Kracauer's desire to publish a volume of his *Frankfurter Zeitung* essays coincided almost precisely with the National Socialists' rise to power and the beginning of his permanent exile—a simultaneity that tempts one to read the idea for the anthology as Kracauer's memorial to what was in fact the end of his relationship with the paper. The publication of a collection of texts which, as Kracauer himself put it, "considered as a whole, already produce a nicely destructive effect"[22] was just as impossible in the now officially Nazi Germany as any future association between its author and that paper. As a result, the project remained buried in his files until 1950, when he stumbled upon the bulky folder of yellowed newspaper articles in New York and decided to pursue it once again. As he wrote to Adorno at the time, "Even now a small book of this sort wouldn't be bad; the essays have retained their freshness."[23] It was not until 1956, however, that the first step toward realizing this project took place: negotiations with the Hamburg publisher Rowohlt produced contracts for a number of Kracauer's works in German, including the film books, *Die Angestellten,* and "a volume comprising my cultural and political essays in the *Frankfurter Zeitung.*"[24] In the end, however, Rowohlt brought out only one of them: a tendentiously edited and politically subdued translation of *From Caligari to Hitler* that appeared in 1958.[25] On May 25, 1963, Kracauer announced the imminent publication of what he referred to as his "collected essays," and it was ultimately thanks to Suhrkamp Verlag, the publisher of Adorno and Benjamin, that these finally did appear, in two volumes. The first, dedicated to Adorno and with a cover drawing by Josef Albers, was *Das Ornament der Masse: Essays* (1963); the second, a year later, was titled *Straßen in Berlin und anderswo (Streets in Berlin and Elsewhere).* Together they marked the beginning of a lengthy publishing relationship culminating in the multivolume edition of Kracauer's works that is currently nearing completion.

Das Ornament der Masse and *Straßen in Berlin und anderswo* are the only collections of Kracauer's early texts which he edited himself.[26] As such, the makeup of their contents is worth examining in some detail. Both volumes are composed almost entirely of essays from the *Frankfurter Zeitung,* nearly all of them taken from "below the line"—from the feuilleton section on the front page. Furthermore, their publication dates (which range from 1921 to 1933) correspond generally to the dates of the Weimar Republic, and specifically to the very period during which Kracauer was employed by the paper. Indeed, the two books can be read together as a chronicle of Kracauer's production for the *Frankfurter Zeitung,* with *Das Ornament der Masse* weighted more toward the Frankfurt years (through 1930) and *Straßen in Berlin und anderswo,* as indicated in its title, more toward the Berlin period (1930–1933).[27] Virtual barometers of the shifting intellectual climate during the turbulent development of the republic, both collections also map a crucial period in Kracauer's own writing, during which his thinking underwent a number of important and quite dramatic transformations. However, since the texts are arranged not chronologically but in a series of suggestive constellations (in *Das Ornament der Masse* these are "Lead-In: Natural Geometry," "External and Internal Objects," "Constructions," "Perspectives," "The Movies," and "Fadeaway: Toward the Vanishing Point"), it is all the more essential for the contemporary reader to have a general idea of Kracauer's theoretical development during those Weimar years in order to make sense of the widely divergent theoretical presuppositions which inform the various essays.

In marked contrast to Kracauer's concerns in his essays of the late 1920s and early 1930s, which focused primarily on the empirical reality of the Weimar Republic, his work through the early 1920s is generally marked by a resigned and even lapsarian metaphysical tone. This melancholic perspective is a product of Kracauer's understanding of the historical process—namely, as an evacuation of meaning, a bifurcation of being and truth that has culminated in a modernity bereft of unity and substance. Unlike many of his intellectual contemporaries, Kracauer initially viewed the early Weimar Republic not as a promising new beginning but rather as the final stage in a process of "decay." His essays from this period are thus a series of variations on the consequences of the modern emancipation from the world view and institutions of the Christian Middle Ages, or, in other words, on the effects of so-called secularization. Kracauer's highly romanticized vision of a utopian Middle Ages, which he describes as a "unified culture" that was "saturated with meaning,"[28] forms a striking contrast to his reading of modernity, which he considers above all in terms of its spiritual lack, indicting it for its estrangement from the absolute and its want of a master narrative. Kracauer's seemingly nostalgic invocation of the then popular opposition between organic community *(Gemeinschaft)* and technological-functional society *(Gesellschaft),* for example, is less a sociological than a metaphysical distinction which attempts to mark, respectively, the presence and absence of meaning *(Sinn)*. Indeed, Kracauer's essays up to the mid-1920s can be read as various attempts to map what he calls, echoing Lukács, the "transcendental homelessness" of this age, offering a material phenomenology of the "vacuum of faithlessness" which, as Kracauer argues in his 1921 essay "Catholicism and Relativism," characterizes the modern world.[29]

Critical of "short-circuit" responses attempting to escape this uncomfortable condition by prematurely embracing practices that seem to fill the void, Kracauer reads the intensity of various types of fanaticism—messianic, anthroposophic, and aesthetic (such as the circle around Stefan George)—as the flip side of the same "homelessness," an index of a repressed metaphysical *Angst*. Instead of such pseudo-solutions, Kracauer suggests (in a move similar to Heidegger's valorization of *Gelassenheit*) that the alternative to both utter relativist skepticism (Weber) and a new devoutness (Steiner) is a strategic waiting, a longing for an absolute which can come about only when *everything* changes. But the consequence is not simply a resigned cultural pessimism; rather, as Kracauer explains in his essay "Those Who Wait," it is a new relationship to daily life, a "hesitant openness," which also implies a sensitivity to "the world of *reality* and its domains." This purposive ambivalence, a simultaneous "yes" and "no" to modernity, is described as a "hesitant affirmation of the civilizing trend"—that is, a careful, critical, but decidedly committed concern with the compromised domain of the quotidian. This, Kracauer insists in "Travel and Dance" (his pivotal 1925 reading of the rage for sightseeing and new types of social dancing as indices of mechanization and rationalization), is at once "more sober than a radical cult of progress" and "more realistic than the condemnation by those who romantically flee the situation into which they have been thrust." Without abandoning entirely the metaphysical schema that informed his earlier position, Kracauer's lapsarian lens has here begun to focus on the impoverished but potentially revelatory landscape of daily life. For it is only by carefully scrutinizing, interpreting, and cataloguing all facets of this surprisingly unfamiliar present that, according to Kracauer, one can hold open the possibility of a transcendence of this very destitution.

During the transitional years 1922–1925, Kracauer's choice of the detective novel as the subject for an extended "philosophical tractate" is thus highly symptomatic.[30] Even while he reads the genre as an allegory of lack (a perspective reminiscent of that of his earlier texts), it is nevertheless an artifact of popular culture that he chooses as a means of exposing that lack. For Kracauer, the specificity of the detective novel lies in the way it stages a world completely dominated by a blind rationality and entirely alienated from any kind of meaning. The process of deduction in a detective novel—which privileges method over content in a manner reminiscent of both systematic philosophy and the logic of legal reasoning—is a purpose unto itself. Since the crimes are committed merely as a pretext for the detective's complex reconstructive logic, the solutions turn out to be rather banal. In the formal organization of the detective novel, Kracauer argues, "thoroughly rationalized" contemporary culture can recognize itself as in a distorted mirror. What is significant in this structural homology, of course, is the status Kracauer accords a work of so-called "low culture," insisting that such cultural objects reflect "the face of de-realized society more purely than any other means by which one can catch a glimpse of it."[31] He thus reads the mass-cultural artifact as an encrypted historico-metaphysical figure whose cultural marginality warrants its truth value.

The assumption that informs this shift—heavily indebted to Lukács' *Theory of the Novel,* which Kracauer reviewed enthusiastically on more than one occasion[32]—is that aesthetic form is particularly suited to express the truth of an alienated historical era and render it readable: "The more life deteriorates, the more it needs the work of art, which unlocks life's impenetrability and organizes its elements to such a degree that these elements, which are strewn helter-skelter, suddenly become meaningfully related."[33] But whereas Lukács granted privileged status to the realm of the aesthetic, Kracauer ascribes it to marginal, quotidian phenomena. According to his methodology, which reminds us of Morelli's proleptic articulation of Freud's logic of the parapraxis, it is the very *insignificance* of such quotidian artifacts that allows them to serve as reliable indices or symptoms of specific historical conditions.[34] As Kracauer explains in the methodologically programmatic opening section of his 1927 essay "The Mass Ornament":

> The position that an epoch occupies in the historical process can be determined more strikingly from an analysis of its inconspicuous surface-level expressions than from that epoch's judgments about itself. Since

these judgments are expressions of the tendencies of a particular era, they do not offer conclusive testimony about its overall constitution. The surface-level expressions, however, by virtue of their unconscious nature, provide unmediated access to the fundamental substance of the state of things. Conversely, knowledge of this state of things depends on the interpretation of these surface-level expressions. The fundamental substance of an epoch and its unheeded impulses illuminate each other reciprocally.

What has changed in the mid-1920s such that the domain of empirical reality—and in particular its superficies, previously dismissed as a realm of emptiness and lack—can suddenly assume such a central role in Kracauer's interpretive schema?

The significant factor behind this shift is a major transformation in Kracauer's philosophy of history. In the wake of an intensive reading of Kierkegaard and the early Marx, in the mid-1920s Kracauer replaces his essentially static model of history as fall or decline with a dynamic conception of history as a process of disenchantment *(Entzauberung)* or demythologizing (*Entmythologisierung,* a synonym he uses to mark a decided distance from the will-to-myth that characterizes pre-Fascist critiques of the Enlightenment). Kracauer now articulates the historical process as a struggle between the blind forces of nature and the force of reason *(Vernunft)*—a struggle in which mankind gains an unprecedented independence from the imperatives of nature. However, the achievements of such "progress" are in no way guaranteed and must be constantly secured anew. In the present era, according to Kracauer, a crisis has occurred in the process of "demythologizing" because modern rationality, whose role in this project is a function of its negative and analytic force, has been unable to exert itself fully. Forced under the "rationalizing" yoke of the increasingly intractable capitalist relations of production, this rationality has been robbed of its progressive potential. The *"Ratio"* specific to capitalism is thus a "murky" reason which, as *abstract* rationality, has once again taken on mythic traits. While the "false concreteness" of mythical thinking has here been transformed into its unmediated opposite, a false abstraction, the latter nevertheless still bears the hallmark of myth in that it treats the products of its own historical action—that is, the capitalist relations of production and the conditions of life that result from them—as if they were unchangeable nature. As a result, capitalist *Ratio* poses a threat to the continued process of disenchantment and the reign of reason *(Vernunft)*.

So far this conception of history is thoroughly compatible with the earlier model of history as decline: whether envisioned as a fall from an anterior plenitude or as a process of disenchantment, both consider the work of history as an operation of destruction or desubstantiation. But whereas in his earlier writings Kracauer resigned himself to this decay as an unfortunate but irreversible process, in his later writings he enthusiastically endorses the same disintegration as a necessary—albeit negative—step along the way to a "breakthrough" of reason. This in turn casts the crisis of modernity in an entirely new light: the problem is not the advanced state of disenchantment but rather the fact that this disenchantment has not advanced far enough. The alienation of *Ratio* here becomes an intermediate stage in the process of liberation from myth; the danger stems from the fact that the process seems to have come to a halt and that this stagnation is not recognized as such. Only if *Ratio* continues to be subjected to the interrogation of reason can the project of disenchantment—which Kracauer here conceives as the self-transcendence *(Selbstaufhebung)* of *Ratio*—be fully realized.

This is the context for Kracauer's famous polemical claim in "The Mass Ornament" that capitalism "rationalizes not too much, but rather too *little*." Avoiding the pitfalls inherent in both the New Objectivity's often facile endorsement of capitalist conditions and in a culturally conservative anticapitalism, Kracauer calls for even more rationalization, hoping that this supplement will be sufficient to liberate *Ratio*'s latent analytical and critical potential such that it can then overcome itself. Indeed, it is this drama of enlightenment—the wavering between utopian possibility and apocalyptic threat—that structures the title essay of *The Mass Ornament* and, by extension, the entire book. As Kracauer points out, the ornamental patterns produced by groups of dancers (and echoed in the increasingly popular stagings of vast stadium spectacles of rhythmic gymnastics) are "the aesthetic reflex of the rationality to which the prevailing economic system aspires." In both, production becomes

the work of an anonymous mass whose individual members each per-
form specialized tasks; but these tasks take on meaning only within the
abstract, rationalized totality that transcends the individuals. While Kracauer notes the formal analogy between the patterns of stadium spectacles and the conditions of assembly-line production ("The hands in the
factory correspond to the legs of the *Tiller Girls*"), he does not simply
reduce the mass ornament to a superstructural reflection of the prevailing mode of production, as would a traditional Marxist analysis of
ideology. Rather, he reads the geometry of human limbs as an ambivalent historico-philosophical allegory, insisting that they are also a mise-
en-scène of disenchantment. The mass ornament, he argues, manifests
progressive potential as the representation of a new type of collectivity
organized not according to the natural bonds of community but as a
social mass of functionally linked individuals. Yet these very formations
are still in some sense opaque, composed as they are according to the
dictates of a *Ratio* that sacrifices meaning for the sake of an abstract
unity of reified elements. As such, they regress into myth, and in the
process expose the gulf between capitalist *Ratio* and reason. Suspending
the traditional opposition of (merely decorative) applied ornament and
functional structure (a discussion familiar to him from his ten-year stint
as an architect), Kracauer here casts the geometry of the mass of Tiller
Girls as both an ornamentalization of function and a functionalization of
ornament.

The essays in *The Mass Ornament* map the return of myth across a
wide spectrum of high and low culture, in the renaissance of religiosity,
in youth movements and body cults, in philosophy, and in cultural criticism. Carefully avoiding the pitfalls of both "pure" philosophy and hard
core social science, the socially informed philosophical writing in this collection occupies a force field that is characteristic of Frankfurt School
critical theory. It is thus not surprising that Kracauer was not only a
member of the wider circle of the Institut für Sozialforschung (Institute
for Social Research), as has often been noted, but, although not institu-
tionally affiliated, arguably one of its central theorists on questions of film
and mass culture.[35] In "The Mass Ornament," as well as in essays such
as "Those Who Wait," "The Revolt of the Middle Classes," and "Bore-

dom," one can clearly observe Kracauer's striking anticipation in a Webe-rian vocabulary of all the essential components of Adorno and Horkheimer's thesis of the "dialectic of enlightenment," twenty years prior to the publication of the book by that name.[36] As Adorno noted in 1933, concerning the man thirteen years his senior who had guided him through his first encounter with Kant, Kracauer "was the first of any of us to seriously tackle once again the problems of the enlightenment."[37] Indeed, some have argued that the critique of enlightenment in Krac-auer's essays is epistemologically more fundamental than the one put forth in the *Dialectic of Enlightenment,* which has been faulted for falling back into the same myth that it analyzes.[38] As Heide Schlüpmann has shown, Kracauer's careful reading of Kant already anticipates and counters in the very form of its theoretical apparatus the critique of Kant as the paradigmatic figure of the enlightenment moment.[39] The essays of *The Mass Ornament* also reveal the important differences in these two "dialectics of enlightenment": whereas Adorno and Horkheimer, con-fronted with the threat of Fascism, see only the bleak prospects of his-torical regression, Kracauer, while in no way naïvely utopian, still holds open the possibility that the enlightenment could overcome its own paral-ysis and rescue itself from the petrification of *Ratio.* Unlike some of his Frankfurt colleagues who insisted that autonomous art offered the sole remaining preserve for the enlightenment project, Kracauer held almost exactly the opposite position, insisting that "the path leads directly through the center of the mass ornament, not away from it."

It is thus in the context of a struggle between *Ratio* and reason that the status of the surface took on new significance. In Kracauer's earlier work the surface was a locus of loss, the hallmark of a world lacking the meaning which alone could give it substance. Kracauer invoked it only to damn it and dismiss it in the name of a lost absolute. From the perspective of a new philosophy of history, however, that same surface domain, though still a site of lack, suddenly acquires new meaning. Once the historical process is conceived not as an irreversible and lamen-table decline but as a salutary negation of myth in the service of what could turn out to be the reign of reason, then even the poverty of a world of surface retains a hidden potential. For only by thoroughly

examining the very superficiality of the surface, by looking at the alienation of *Ratio* as directly as possible, can one maintain the possibility of
a negation of this negativity. Hence the surface, though still situated
within a terrain mapped by the idealist oppositions of essence/appear-
ance and truth/empirical reality, becomes a cipher, a sur-face subject to
a variety of physiognomic readings. Indeed, the attention to that surface
takes on a striking urgency. As Kracauer puts it, employing a resonant
(and quite popular) image for the "disenchanted world" which was the
realm of surface, "America will disappear only when it discovers itself
fully."[40]

The phenomenology of the surface in Kracauer's writings after the
mid-1920s thus undertakes a serious exploration of superficies of cultural
ephemera and marginal domains—hotel lobbies, dancing, arcades, bestsellers—in order, however, ultimately to transcend them. The focus on
scorned quotidian realms, artifacts, and practices, the interpretive atten-
tiveness to the castoffs from the storm of progress (which motivated Benjamin's description of Kracauer as a "rag-picker"), and the voyage of
discovery to the "new world" of modernity which informs nearly every
one of the essays in *The Mass Ornament:* these are all part of a strategy—
Kracauer calls it a "trick"—whose goal is to move beyond that surface
realm. Echoing a rhetoric of hyperbolized negativity which was rather
widespread during the Weimar era (evident, for example, in Benjamin's
notions of "revolutionary nihilism" and "positive barbarism"), Kracauer
insists on the possibility of a utopian—or even messianic—moment in
what he calls the "revelation of the negative."[41]

Kracauer's revaluation of quotidian superficiality also explains his
early and sustained interest in the representational practices that display
an elective affinity with the surface—namely, photography and film. Disregarding the debates as to their artistic status, Kracauer focused instead
on their diagnostic value as social facts, reading photography and film
(prior to any specific content) as material expressions of a particular historical condition. Contrary to the almost canonical misreading of Kracauer in histories of film theory as a "naïve realist,"[42] what photographic
and cinematic "objectivity" arrests is the reality of the world as a metaphysical void. Although Kracauer's turn to these mass media in the mid-

1920s was thus certainly overdetermined by the evidentiary quality of the photograph and photogram (that is, their iconic and indexical semiotic specificity), the "realist vocation" common to both resided in their unstaged depiction of the "real" negativity of the metaphysics of modernity. As Kracauer makes clear in his pathbreaking essay "Photography" (which should be read as a counterpart to "The Mass Ornament," published only a few months earlier), the photographic image is like the geometric limbs of the Tiller Girl formations in that it, too, serves to map the current ambivalent stage of the dialectic of enlightenment: "The photograph captures the remnants that history has left behind . . . The same mere nature that appears in the photograph is thriving in the reality of the society created by capitalist *Ratio*." On the one hand, the prosthetic vision of the photograph extends our grasp of the material world beyond the constraints of our sensory and cognitive apparatus, affording access to what Benjamin would later call the "optical unconscious."[43] Yet despite this "redemptive" moment, the photograph's materialism captures a spatial continuum devoid of both time and meaning. What an old photograph conveys, Kracauer writes, is not "the knowledge of the orig-

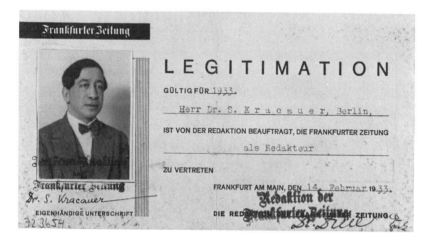

Siegfried Kracauer's journalist identification card from the *Frankfurter Zeitung*, 1933

inal but the spatial configuration of an instant; it is not the person who stands forth in his or her photograph, but the sum of that which can be abstracted from him or her. The photograph annihilates the person by portraying him or her." Photography stages nature as the negativity of history. As such, the hegemony of photography speaks the truth of the alienation of *Ratio* even as it reveals a previously invisible residuum of nature which holds open the possibility of a new, emancipated relationship between reason and nature. In other words, the "go-for-broke game of history" which Kracauer sees being played out in the turn to photography is the drama of the dialectic of capitalism—and of enlightenment.

Cinema also plays a central role in Kracauer's sociometaphysical diagnosis, since it combines, at the level of its syntax, the historically ambivalent photogram with another symptomatic index of lack: the fragmentation facilitated by cinematic montage. In the "creative geography" of the specifically cinematic syntagm or sequence, Kracauer recognizes a staging of the relationless jumble that is the signature of modernity. Instead of dismissing it, however, he welcomes this confusion as an emphasis on the external that could potentially reveal the actual, desubstantialized metaphysical condition. This insight, in turn, is cast as the condition of possibility of the transformation of that present condition: only once the current state of things is revealed as provisional (that is, not nature) can the question of their *proper* order arise. Kracauer thus sees cinema's radical superficiality as both its revolutionary responsibility and its promise: "The fact that these shows convey precisely and openly to thousands of eyes and ears the *disorder* of society—this is precisely what would enable them to evoke and maintain the tension that must precede the inevitable and radical change" ("Cult of Distraction"). In its insistence on the superficial, the cinematic spectacle also exposes the anachronistic aesthetic politics of the relics of bourgeois culture which mask the reality of the disintegration of contemporary culture through what Benjamin would later describe as a fraudulent invocation of the "aura."

Pseudo-authenticity of various stripes is deconstructed in great detail throughout *The Mass Ornament*, for example in Kracauer's critiques of historical biography and of the Buber-Rosenzweig translation of the Bible. The cinema was of course not immune to the pressures of such reactionary aesthetic politics, as is evident in genres such as the art film or historical film drama, whose closed and linear structures attempted to reinstate (as did much of Hollywood narrative cinema) the very features of classical drama which the new medium had rendered obsolete. But in contrast to these cinematic practices, for which he had nothing but scorn, Kracauer insisted on the importance of a cinema of distraction "that exposes disintegration instead of masking it" ("Cult of Distraction"). Like the circus (about which Kracauer wrote enthusiastically on numerous occasions), the anarchy of lowbrow cinematic forms such as the slapstick of a Harold Lloyd or a Mack Sennett had a corrective and revelatory function. Here, Kracauer insisted, "this emphasis on the external has the advantage of being *sincere*. It is not externality that poses a threat to truth. Truth is threatened only by the naïve affirmation of cultural values that have become unreal." In short, Kracauer privileged photography and film because of their capacity to stage not the world as such but what he once described elsewhere as a "revolutionizing negativity,"[44] a nihilism for the sake of the positive.

While one could indeed argue that such productive negation is a formal potential of the cinematic medium, by 1926 Kracauer had recognized that the majority of films being screened in the Weimar Republic were serving not to expose the metaphysical void but rather to deny the growing sociopolitical crisis. Just as it had been his theory of history that had motivated the turn from the realm of more traditional philosophical topics to the domain of mass culture, it was now the latter's increasingly problematic political function that motivated Kracauer to replace his theologico-messianic and philosophical reading of mass media with an analysis centered on their ideological function. In the changing political conditions of the Weimar Republic, the foremost question for Kracauer was no longer whether cinema unveiled the metaphysics of a fallen world, but rather to what extent film production revealed the sociopolitical contradictions and conditions of the reigning order. The responsibility of a progressive cinema (such as he saw manifest, for example, in Eisenstein's *Potemkin*) was now "to look the dire situation straight in the eye." In what is effectively a political inflection of his earlier argument about the progressive and revelatory potential of film's metaphysical negativity, Kracauer now held out great hope for a politically "concerned" cinema: "Were it to depict things as they really are today and the way they try to be, moviegoers could get uneasy and begin to have doubts about the legitimacy of our current social structure."[45]

As a film critic, Kracauer was well aware that very few German commercial films of the later 1920s were critical and analytical in character. At best, most of them conveyed repressed wishes and daydreams, but in an alienated form that simultaneously reproduced their denial. In such a situation, as Kracauer himself explained in his programmatic 1932 essay on film criticism, the role of the marginalized progressive film also necessarily became that of the responsible critic. The latter, he wrote, "can be conceived only as a social critic. His mission is to expose the social conceptions and ideologies hidden in average films and thereby to subvert the influence of these films themselves everywhere it is necessary."[46] These objectives are evident both in Kracauer's ideological analysis of the illusionist studio wizardry in various UFA films (published under the title "Calico-World") and in his essay "The Little Shopgirls Go to the Movies," in which he catalogued the various means by which the culture industry has recast political and social exploitation into the more appealing forms of adventure, romance, and triumph. In his readings here, Kracauer objects not to the status of these films as fantasies—which he defends as an important vehicle for the articulation of desires—but to the way they disfigure the actual social and political situation. Yet this move does not depend upon a facile split between reality and representation. Rather, Kracauer's methodological strategy in these analyses (evident in much of his Weimar film writings and also in *From Caligari to Hitler* almost two decades later) is to grasp a film's ideological reconfiguration of the world as itself a socially symptomatic—and thus in an important sense "real"—political fact. According to Kracauer, "Stupid and unreal film fantasies are the *daydreams of society*, in which its actual reality comes to the fore and its otherwise repressed wishes take on form . . . The more incorrectly they present the surface of things, the more correct they become and the more clearly they mirror the secret mechanism of society" ("The Little Shopgirls Go to the Movies"). Anything but a facile positivist, Kracauer here demonstrates that there is a significant psychosocial dimension to his conception of the "real." Wherever, as in these readings of films, reality is equally manifest in the mechanisms of repression and what is repressed, access to the "real" is possible only in and through its contradictions. There is thus an important structural analogy between the methodology of Kracauer's critical social theory and the practice of montage, which he championed as a cinematic technique. In both, as Miriam Hansen has shown, a practice of constellation enables issues of contemporary politics to appear, as it were, "between the lines," since in both (as Kracauer remarked in a famous line from *Die Ange-stellten*), reality itself is a construction.[47]

Unlike much of the contemporaneous German theoretical writing on film, which was primarily concerned with establishing the medium's aesthetic, metaphysical, and discursive specificity,[48] Kracauer's work on the cinema during the later Weimar years was inflected more toward sociopolitical issues of production (analyses of the UFA studios), reception (the study of the architecture of Berlin cinema palaces), regulation (polemical attacks on government censorship), and the development of a critical public sphere through the practice of a responsible film criticism. As such it was among the earliest to make what has since come to be called the important transition from film theory to cinema theory, the latter understood as a practice that is both more historically reflexive and more sensitive to larger institutional factors.[49] Indeed, one could argue that as a collection *The Mass Ornament* documents one of the first sustained attempts at cinema theory, intricately embedding the discussion of film within a much broader spectrum of cultural theory. This is perhaps most evident in Kracauer's focus on questions of cinematic spectatorship, a concern that grew out of his work on the emerging culture of white-collar workers in Berlin and the transformations in the forms of their subjectivity, leisure, and class.[50] For it is in this study that Kracauer established the important correlation between the psychosocial conditions peculiar to that class (lack of roots, isolation, emotional vulnerability, a general feeling of insecurity) and the new social obsession with consumption and conspicuous, compensatory leisure (cafés, dance halls, illustrated magazines, cabarets). Taking up the question explored in his analysis of bestselling novels, Kracauer asked whether the same audience that has long had a reactionary relationship to reading could adopt a progressive stance toward the cinema. His affirmative answer grows out of a detailed analysis of the historical transformation in the nature of attention, along lines later taken up in Benjamin's essay "The Work of Art in the Age of Its Technological Reproducibility" and again by more recent theorists.[51]

Anticipating by more than half a century the important discussion of cinema's "subject effect," a methodological schema that developed out of the psychoanalytically informed semiotic film theory of the 1970s, Kracauer argues that the site of intelligibility which cinema constructs for its spectators is no longer that of the coherent and self-identical bourgeois subject. Instead of the immersed and contemplative concentration characteristic of this now outmoded paradigm of stable subjectivity and its equally anachronistic, "stabilizing" spectacles, it is "distraction" that now becomes the defining characteristic of cinematic spectatorship. Stripped of its pejorative connotation, this category is here recast as the signature of a nonbourgeois mode of sensory experience. In his prescient essay "Cult of Distraction," Kracauer locates the emancipatory potential of a distracted mode of reception in its capacity to retool perceptual and motor skills for the new sensorial economy of modernity, whose most salient characteristics are its speed and abrupt transitions—the very hallmark of cinema as the school of "shock," which Benjamin would celebrate almost a decade later as one of the medium's most progressive features.[52] Distraction further serves as both a lived critique of the bourgeois fiction of the coherent self-identical subject and as a barometer of the current state of mankind's alienation from itself. As such, it speaks the truth of modernity: "Here, in pure externality the audience encounters itself; its own reality is revealed in the fragmented sequence of splendid sense impressions. Were this reality to remain hidden from the viewers, they could neither attack nor change it; its disclosure in distraction is therefore of *moral* significance." It is thus in the potential of the audience as collective, in the possibility that cinema could provoke a structural transformation of the public sphere such that it would itself become a site of enlightenment, that Kracauer ultimately locates the emancipatory moment of a truly mass-cultural aesthetic politics.

The status of the subject (and of the concomitant category of experience) in modernity, so crucial to Kracauer's discussion of cinema, is in fact one of the key issues of this entire volume. The attempt to trace the transformation of subjectivity and of the contours and limits of experience is evident not only in Kracauer's radical theory of boredom, in his analysis of "those who wait," and in his discussion of "the group as the bearer of ideas," but indeed in some sense in virtually every one of these essays. Beyond its extensive thematic treatment, this problematic is also manifest in the curious mixture of subjectivity and objectivity which is one of the hallmarks of Kracauer's style. His frequent and often disarming alternation between the impersonal voice of abstract theoretical discourse and utterances in first person is only the most visible rhetorical indication of the fact that his theoretical analyses are almost always at some level also a reflection of his own experience. One sees the same imbrication of experience and critique, for example, in the "spiritual homelessness" which Kracauer ascribes to both white-collar workers and intellectuals (such as himself), or in the shopgirls' reactions to the movies, which are, in fact, as Adorno and others have noted, a barely concealed rehearsal of Kracauer's own spectatorial experience. To some extent this was a function of Kracauer's willingness to acknowledge the proximity of his own class position to that of the employees he studied as a virtual "participant-observer." However, as Adorno pointed out, the question of experience also served Kracauer as a sort of litmus test for the validity of his theoretical constructs: "The medium of his thought was experience, not that of the empiricist and positivist schools, which distill experience itself down to its general principles and make a method out of it. He pursued intellectual experience as something individual, determined to think only what he could fill with substance, only what had become concretized for him about people and things."[53] This struggle is evident throughout *The Mass Ornament*, whose essays can be read profitably as an autophenomenology of subject formation in the modern era and as a case study in the methodological and discursive consequences for the practice of cultural theory of such an attention to the particularity of experience.

Like other contextualizing rereadings of canonical figures in the history of film theory such as Sergei Eisenstein and André Bazin,[54] *The Mass Ornament* plays a key role in the revisionist assessment of Kracauer that is currently under way. Just as it is most profitable to approach his *Theory of Film* and the study *From Caligari to Hitler* as a two-volume textual dialectic, so too must each of these inquiries be located in relation to his diverse Weimar writings. Like the *Theory of Film*, which, as new scholarship has shown, can be properly understood only against the background of Kracauer's much earlier work (as well as his unpublished draft of a film theory written in Marseilles in 1940), *From Caligari to Hitler* must also be read as an inflection of arguments and analyses made in the corpus of film and cultural criticism prior to Kracauer's exile in 1933. Such a prism opens up the possibility of interpreting the *Caligari* book not only in terms of its controversial psychosociological central thesis but also, for example, as a sort of follow-up study of the gentrification and manipulation of the distraction that Kracauer analyzed in his earlier writings.[55] It also complicates the often reductive recourse to the "epistemological shift" between the "two" Kracauers, a periodization of his career that contrasts his early micrological and sociopolitical Weimar writings with the more systematic, ostensibly apolitical pieces he wrote during his exile in the United States.[56] His early writings further reveal the need for a careful reconsideration of the Frankfurt School debates on modernity and mass culture, with Kracauer taking up a much more central position in the terrain previously circumscribed exclusively by Adorno and Benjamin.[57]

In the context of more general methodological discussions, *The Mass Ornament* has been heralded as a reorientation of film theory away from its long-standing and fertile engagement with French models and more toward a German philosophical and sociological discursive tradition. As a model of theoretical practice that resists totalizing systemic tendencies, as a reconciliation of phenomenology and semiotics in the form of a materialist phenomenology of daily life, and in its insistence on the critical analysis of both the sensorial/experiential and the institutional dimensions of social phenomena such as cinema, Kracauer's

Weimar essays serve as an early paradigm of what is now increasingly being called "cultural studies." Indeed, one can read *The Mass Ornament* in various ways as a voyage across historical and epistemological space: as a cultural tourist's philosophical diary of the Weimar Republic and as a flaneurial history of visual fascination, as a catalogue of the phenomena of disenchantment and as a critical phenomenology of the subject formations of modernity.

Besides *The Mass Ornament*'s incisiveness as a historical and cultural-theoretical document, its multifaceted analysis of the crisis of modernity retains an astonishing actuality. Nowhere was this more strikingly evident than in Berlin during the winter of 1993–94, as this introduction was being written. For it was there, in the epicenter of the "spiritual homelessness" called "reunified" Germany, that texts Kracauer had published during the Weimar years in the *Frankfurter Zeitung* began to reappear uncannily in the new capital's daily papers. Kracauer's 1930 analysis of Heinrich Tessenow's renovation of Friedrich Schinkel's Neue Wache, for example, was reprinted in the context of the monument's highly controversial refurbishing and re-inauguration in November 1993[58]—a reappearance which curiously confirmed that many of the issues surrounding the crisis of modernity had hardly vanished with the advent of "postmodernity." While the fault lines of the current re-mythologization are perhaps even more difficult to discern than they were sixty years ago, Kracauer's incisive critiques of the central role of German cultural-nationalist politics in that "crisis" are just as urgent today. But it was the subsequent republication in full of yet another Kracauer text which established beyond doubt the social and political contemporaneity of his critically diagnostic analyses. Here, in his 1930 allegorical reading of the architecture of unemployment offices, Kracauer elaborates a variation on the mass-ornament thesis: "Every typical space is created by typical social relations which are expressed in such a space *without the disturbing intervention of consciousness.* Everything that consciousness ignores, everything that it usually just overlooks, is involved in the construction of such spaces. Spatial structures are the dreams of a society. Whenever the hieroglyph of any such spatial structure is decoded, the foundation of the social reality is revealed."[59] In its deciphering of Weimar culture, in its readings of the work of history through the reconfiguration of metropolitan topography (the case of the "new" Linden mega-mall being perhaps the most dramatic signifier of the violence of "transition"), *The Mass Ornament* not only reveals that the complexities of a modernity in crisis are scarcely a thing of the past; it also gives the contemporary reader a set of tools with which to render that landscape readable in all of its contradictions.

···

LEAD-IN
NATURAL GEOMETRY

Bullfight in the arena at Nîmes, France

Lad and Bull

A Study in Movement

• • •

Aix-en-Provence, Mid-September, 1926

"A lad kills a bull." This sentence out of a school primer appears in a yellow ellipse in which the sun is boiling. Everyone is gazing down into the oval from the stands and trees, where the locals hang like overripe bananas. The bull careens through the arena in a stupor. Facing the drunken mass, the lad stands alone.

He's an orange point with a pinned-up braid. Thirteen years old, with the face of a boy. Other youths his age sweep across the prairie in magnificent costumes and rescue the white squaw from a martyr's death. Confronted with a bull, they'd have run away. The lad stands there and smiles ceremoniously. The animal succumbs to a marionette.

The marionette goads the gale according to the rules of the ritual that magnifies it. Even a little puppet could dangle the red cape that the bull recognizes as its counterfetish. It tries to assault it, but the cape floats away, transformed into an arabesque by the little puppet. A thing of nature could be gored, but powers wane when confronted with the weightlessness of the flowing pleats.

The marionette turns into an orange lass, who lures the oafish creature. She approaches it with swaying steps, her hands hoisting two small colorful lances. The upright heroine's theatrical laugh announces the start of the love battle. The bull falls into the snare of the cleverly calculated rhythm. But the web is elastic, and before you know it the tiny wizard has thrust the small lances into its flanks. Three pairs of lances adorn the patch, knitting needles in a ball of yarn, with waving ribbons. The bull tries to shake them off, but in vain: the geometry is firmly set in the bulges.

The lad unfolds a cloth as red as a cock's comb. The dagger he conceals behind the curtain is so long that he could use it to climb up into the air. The characteristics of the plane and the line indicate that the end is drawing near. The marionette makes the cloth scintillate and draws ever narrower circles with the dagger. The bull is seized by a trembling in the face of the ornaments' power. Those who earlier hovered about like rings of smoke and then struck it in numerous places now close in upon it ever more threateningly, so that it will expire on the scene.

Up to this point, it is still a game. The dagger could still pull back; the redness would not necessarily have to encounter itself in blood. It is a single stab, a rapid stabbing sparkle, that surges through the barrier. The dagger darts forth from the marionette; it was not the lad who wielded it. The astonished element recoils and glares. The curving of the sinking mass triumphs over the line of the dagger. Now colors and sweeping movements dominate the scene.

Caps and bags fly into the air as the miniature victor runs a lap, bouquets of jubilation. The sun glows in the ellipse. The lad stands there and smiles ceremoniously.

The quay of the old harbor in Marseilles, France, late 1920s

Two Planes

∎∎∎

The Bay

Marseilles, a dazzling amphitheater, rises around the rectangle of the old harbor. The three shores of the square paved with sea, whose depth cuts into the city, are lined with rows of façades, each one like the next. Across from the entrance to the bay, the Cannebière, the street of all streets, breaks into the square's smooth luminescence, extending the harbor into the city's interior. It is not the only connection between the soaring terraces and this monster of a square, from whose foundation the neighborhoods rise like the jets of a fountain. The churches point to the square as the vanishing point of all perspectives, and the still-virgin hills face it as well. Rarely has such an audience ever been assembled around an arena. If ocean liners were to fill the basin, their trails of smoke would drift to the most remote houses; if fireworks were to be set off over the plane, the city would be witness to the illumination.

No ocean liners fill the bay, and no fireworks are coasting down; there are only yawls, motor launches, and pinnaces, resting lazily at the edges. During the sailfishing era, the harbor used to be a kaleidoscope dispatching moving patterns across the quays. They trickled off into the pores; the gratings of lordly mansions, set back from the shorefront, glistened. The splendor has lost its luster, and the bay has degenerated from the street of all streets into a rectangle. Its desolateness is shared by a side branch of water, a forgotten rivulet that does not mirror the stark houses.

The city keeps its fishing nets open. The catch is collected in the harbor's new basins, which, together with the coastline, describe a mighty trajectory. The arrival and departure of the ocean liners, aglow as they disappear over the horizon, constitute the poles of life. The bleakness of the bare warehouse walls is an illusion; their front side is what the fairy-tale prince would see. In the spongy depths of the harbor quarter the fauna of humanity is teeming, and in the puddles the sky is pristine. Outdated palaces are converted into brothels that outlive every ancestral portrait gallery. The mass of humanity in which the peoples of different nations blend together is flushed through avenues and bazaar streets. These define the borders of the districts into which the human tide disperses. In the shell-like windings of one of those districts rages the eternal mass of small-time tradespeople.

Unfrequented amid all this, the bay lounges about lazily. Its very existence prevents the arches from closing. The streets dead-end on its banks; it bends straight ones into curves. In its public space the obvious vanishes; its emptiness spreads to distant corners. The bay is so mute that it surges through the shrieks like a respite. The filled tiers of the amphitheater spread around a cavity. The upright audience turns its back on it.

The Quadrangle

Whoever the place finds did not seek it.[1] The alleys, crumpled paper streamers, are laced together without knots. Crossbeams traverse the soil wrinkles, rubbing against plaster, plummeting into the depths of basements, then ricocheting back to their starting point. A backstairs quarter, it lacks the magnificent ascending entrances. Grayish-green smells of sea waste come smoldering out of open doors; little red lamps lead the way. In the spaces that afford a view, one finds improvised backdrops: rows of flying buttresses, Arabic signs, stair windings. If one leaves them behind, they are torn down and reconstructed at a different site. Their order is familiar to the dreamer.

A wall heralds the square. It stands sleeplessly erect, sealing off the labyrinth. A gully accompanies it with canine obedience, plodding alongside every step of the way. Hatches have been blasted into the wall, small holes at large intervals that admit no light into the spaces behind. Other walls of equal length foreshorten like railway tracks; but not this one. Its vanishing points diverge, either because the gully drops down or because the crown of the wall steadily rises. Suddenly, next to the gully, the square unfolds.

It is a quadrangle which has been stamped into the urban tangle with a giant template. Blocks of barracks fall into formation around it, the rear wall painted red. An apron shoots out from the wall, stops, breaks off. The horizontal lines are drawn with a ruler, dead straight.

On the deserted square, something happens: the force of the quad-rilateral pushes the person who is trapped into its center. He is alone, and yet he isn't. Although no observers are visible, the rays of their gazes pierce through the shutters, through the walls. Bundles of them traverse the space, intersecting at its midpoint. Fear is stark naked, at their mercy. No bouquet of palm trees capable of swathing this bareness caresses the edges. On invisible seats around the quadrangle a tribunal is in session. It is the moment before the pronouncement of the verdict, which is not handed down. The sharpened arrow of the apron points to the one who is waiting, follows him, a moving indicator. The eyes of notorious portraits constantly follow the viewer in this way. The red rear wall is separated from the plane of the square by a crack from which a roadway rises, hidden by the apron.

In this tangle of pictorial alleys, no one seeks the quadrangle. After painstaking reflection, one would have to describe its size as moderate. But once its observers have settled into their chairs, it expands toward the four sides of the world, overpowering the pitiful, soft, private parts of the dream: it is a square without mercy.

Marianne Breslauer, Untitled; Paris, 1929

Analysis of a City Map

■ ■ ■

Faubourgs and the Center

Some of the Parisian faubourgs are giant shelters for all sorts of ordinary people, from low-level functionaries down to the workers, the tradespeople, and those who are called losers because others consider themselves winners. The way in which they have cohabited over the centuries is expressed in the form of these shelters, which is certainly not bourgeois but is not proletarian either, to the extent that the latter term evokes smokestacks, tenements, and highways. It is impoverished and humane at the same time. This humaneness results not only from the fact that existence in the faubourgs contains remnants of a natural life which give this existence some fulfillment. What is much more decisive is that this replete existence is slated for demolition.

■ ■ ■

On Saturday afternoons the avenue St. Ouan is a fairground. Not that the fair simply set itself up here like a traveling circus; rather, the avenue was pregnant with it and brings forth the fair from within itself. The need to lay in supplies for Sunday brings together a crowd that would appear to astronomers as nebulae. It jams together into dense clumps in which the tightly packed individuals wait, until at some point they are again unpacked. Between purchases they savor the spectacle of the constant disintegration of the complexes to which they belong, a sight that keeps them at the peripheries of life.

Were the Mediterranean lapping at the avenue's edges, the shops could hardly expose themselves in a more windowless fashion. They disgorge a stream of commodities that serves to satisfy creaturely needs; it climbs up the façades, is interrupted at street level, and then shoots with redoubled force up into the heights on the far side of the cross-current of passersby. Above the uncleared undergrowth of natural products which will later enliven the menu as hors d'oeuvres, the primeval forests of meat shanks are swaying their treetops. Next door the supply of household goods runs wild, with covers made of burlap on which a charming flora scatters flowers across everyday life.

Necessity brings objects into the sphere of human warmth. Out of the organic thicket of the grocery sections arises an apparatus made of glass and metal whose sharp sting could have been born only from an appetite for inflicting torture. Its gleam gives one the impression that the instrument would, just for the fun of it, be capable of stabbing the flourishing array of butchered meat, fish, and mussel ragouts in whose midst it has ensconced itself. It is an oil-dispensing apparatus which allows easily digestible yellow portions to drip out of its glass stomach into the customers' small receptacles. The needy character of the environment has put it in a friendly mood and has transformed a mechanical bee into a harmless house goblin that takes care of preparing the meals and is good to the children.

Although the fairground recalls a department-store catalogue in all its cosmic completeness, it is nevertheless only the popular edition of the big world. Whatever is on hand is limited and modest and somewhat vague, like bad photographs. It is no accident that the revolutions were spawned in the faubourgs. They are lacking in good fortune, in sensory splendor.

...

This splendor spreads out over the upper world of the boulevards in the city center. The crowds here are different from those further out. Neither a purpose nor the hour compels them to circulate; they trickle about timelessly. The palaces that have become darkened over time and continue to exist as images can hardly master the swarms of people and cars any longer through the power of their delicate proportions. No one invented the plan according to which the elements of the hustle and bustle scribble a jumble of lines into the asphalt. There is no such plan. The goals are locked in the individual little particles, and the law of least resistance gives the curves their direction.

Behind mirrored panes, necessary objects mix with superfluous ones, which would be more necessary if they didn't pour forth so abundantly. People of every class are free to lose themselves for entire afternoons, contemplating the jewelry, furs, and evening attire whose unambiguous magnificence beckons promisingly at the end of dime novels. The fact that one can estimate their cost makes such material objects even more unapproachable than they were before. Their spatial contiguity demands that one visit shop after shop to buy objects of every sort for the purpose of maintaining an inventory. But anyone whom they might have would be the last to possess them.

As dusk begins to fall, the lights go on at eye level. Undeflectable like the little balls on an abacus, the arc lamps prowl through the labyrinth of flaming arrows and Bengalese oscillations. In the centers of night life the illumination is so harsh that one has to hold one's hands over one's ears. Meanwhile the lights have gathered for their own pleasure, instead of shining for man. Their glowing traces want to illuminate the night but succeed only in chasing it away. Their advertisements sink into the mind without allowing one to decipher them. The reddish gleam that lingers settles like a cloak over one's thoughts.

Out of the hubbub rise the newspaper kiosks, tiny temples in which the publications of the entire world get together for a rendezvous. Foes in real life, they lie here in printed form side by side; the harmony could not be greater. Wherever Yiddish papers supported by Arabic texts come into contact with large headlines in Polish, peace is assured. But, alas, these newspapers do not know one another. Each copy is folded in on itself and is content to read its own columns. Regardless of the close physical relations that the papers cultivate, their news is so completely lacking in any contact that they are uninformed about one another. In the interstices the demon of absentmindedness reigns supreme.

Paris is not the only place where this holds true. All the cosmopolitan centers that are also sites of splendor are becoming more and more alike. Their differences are disappearing.

■ ■ ■

Wide streets lead from the faubourgs into the splendor of the center. But this is not the intended center. The good fortune in store for the poverty further out is reached by radii other than the extant ones. Nevertheless, the streets that lead to the center must be traveled, for its emptiness today is real.

EXTERNAL AND INTERNAL OBJECTS

Sasha Stone, Untitled; after 1932

Photography

■ ■ ■ ■

In the days of cock-a-doodle I went and saw Rome and
the Lateran hanging from a silk thread. I saw a man
without feet outrunning a swift horse and a sharp, sharp
sword cutting a bridge in two.
—The Brothers Grimm, "The Tale of a Cock-a-Doodle"

1

This is what the film diva looks like. She is twenty-four years old,
featured on the cover of an illustrated magazine, standing in front of the
Hotel Excelsior on the Lido. The date is September. If one were to look
through a magnifying glass one could make out the grain, the millions
of little dots that constitute the diva, the waves, and the hotel. The
picture, however, refers not to the dot matrix but to the living diva
on the Lido. Time: the present. The caption calls her demonic: our
demonic diva. Still, she does not lack a certain allure. The bangs, the
seductive position of the head, and the twelve eyelashes right and
left—all these details, diligently recorded by the camera, are in their
proper place, a flawless appearance. Everyone recognizes her with
delight, since everyone has already seen the original on the screen. It is
such a good likeness that she cannot be confused with anyone else, even
if she is perhaps only one-twelfth of a dozen Tiller girls.[1] Dreamily she
stands in front of the Hotel Excelsior, which basks in her fame—a being
of flesh and blood, our demonic diva, twenty-four years old, on the
Lido. The date is September.

Is this what *grandmother* looked like? The photograph, more than sixty years old and already a photograph in the modern sense, depicts her as a young girl of twenty-four. Since photographs are likenesses, this one must have been a likeness as well. It was carefully produced in the studio of a court photographer. But were it not for the oral tradition, the image alone would not have sufficed to reconstruct the grandmother. The grandchildren know that in her later years she lived in a narrow little room with a view onto the old part of town and that, to amuse the children, she would make toy soldiers dance on a glass plate;[2] they also know a nasty story about her life, and two confirmed utterances which change a bit from generation to generation. One has to believe the parents—who claim to have gotten it from grandmother herself—that this photograph depicts the very same grandmother about whom one has retained these few details that may also in time be forgotten. Yet eyewitness accounts are unreliable. It might turn out after all that the photograph depicts not the grandmother but a friend who resembled her. None of her contemporaries are still alive. And the question of likeness? The ur-image has long since decayed. But the now-darkened appearance has so little in common with the traits still remembered that the grandchildren submit in amazement to the imperative of encountering in the photograph their fragmentarily recorded ancestor. All right, so it's grandmother; but in reality it's any young girl in 1864. The girl smiles continuously, always the same smile. The smile is arrested yet no longer refers to the life from which it has been taken. Likeness has ceased to be of any help. The smiles of plastic mannequins in beauty parlors are just as rigid and perpetual. This mannequin does not belong to our time; it could be standing with others of its kind in a museum, in a glass case labeled "Traditional Costumes, 1864." There the mannequins are displayed solely for the historical costumes, and the grandmother in the photograph, too, is an archaeological mannequin which serves to illustrate the costumes of the period. So that's how women dressed back then: chignons, cinched waists, crinolines, and Zouave jackets.[3] The grandmother dissolves into fashionably old-fashioned details before the very eyes of the grandchildren. They are amused by the traditional costume, which, following the disappearance of its bearer, remains alone on the battlefield—an external decoration that has become autonomous. They are irreverent, and today young girls dress differently. They laugh, and at the same time they shudder. For through the ornamentation of the costume from which the grandmother has disappeared, they think they glimpse a moment of time past, a time that passes without return. Although time is not part of the photograph like the smile or the chignon, the photograph itself, so it seems to them, is a representation of time. Were it the photograph alone that endowed these details with duration, they would not at all outlast mere time; rather, time would create images for itself out of them.

2

"From the early days of the friendship between Goethe and Karl August."—"Karl August and the 1787 coadjutor election in Erfurt."— "A visit of a Bohemian in Jena and Weimar" (1818).—"Recollections of a Weimar high school student" (1825 to 1830).—"A contemporary account of the Weimar Goethe celebration on November 7, 1825."—"A rediscovered bust of Wieland by Ludwig Klauer."—"Plan for a national monument to Goethe in Weimar."—The herbarium for these and other investigations is provided by the Goethe Society yearbooks, a series that in principle can never come to an end. It would be superfluous to ridicule the Goethe philology which deposits its specimens in these volumes, all the more so since it is as ephemeral as the items it processes. In contrast, the pseudo-luster of the numerous monumental works on Goethe's stature, being, personality, and so on has hardly begun to be questioned. The principle of Goethe philology is that of *historicist* thinking, which emerged at about the same time as modern photographic technology. On the whole, advocates of such historicist thinking[4] believe they can explain any phenomenon purely in terms of its genesis. That is, they believe in any case that they can grasp historical reality by reconstructing the course of events in their temporal succession without any gaps. Photography presents a spatial continuum; historicism seeks to provide the temporal continuum. According to historicism, the complete mirroring of an intratemporal sequence simultaneously contains the meaning of all that occurred within that time. Thus, if the connecting links of the Erfurt coadjutor election or the recollections of the Weimar high school student were missing in the presentation of Goethe, such an account would lack reality for the historicist. Historicism is concerned with the photography of time. The equivalent of its temporal photography would be a giant film depicting the temporally interconnected events from every vantage point.[5]

3

Memory encompasses neither the entire spatial appearance of a state of affairs nor its entire temporal course. Compared to photography, memory's records are full of gaps. The fact that the grandmother was at one time involved in a nasty story that is recounted time and again because people really do not like to talk about her—this does not mean much from the photographer's perspective. He knows every little wrinkle on her face and has noted every date. Memory does not pay much attention to dates—it skips years or stretches temporal distance. The selection of traits that it assembles must strike the photographer as arbitrary. The selection may have been made this way rather than another because dispositions and purposes required the repression, falsification, and emphasis of certain parts of the object; a virtually endless number of reasons determines the remains to be filtered. No matter which scenes an individual remembers, they all mean something relevant to that person, though he or she might not necessarily know what they mean. An individual retains memories because they are personally significant. Thus, they are organized according to a principle which is essentially different from the organizing principle of photography. Photography grasps what is given as a spatial (or temporal) continuum; memory images retain what is given only insofar as it has significance. Since what is significant is not reducible to either merely spatial or merely temporal terms, memory images are at odds with photographic representation. From the latter's perspective, memory images appear to be fragments—but only because photography does not encompass the meaning to which they refer and in relation to which they cease to be fragments.

Similarly, from the perspective of memory, photography appears as a jumble that consists partly of garbage.

The meaning of memory images is linked to their truth content. So long as they are embedded in the uncontrolled life of the drives, they are inhabited by a demonic ambiguity; they are opaque, like frosted glass which scarcely a ray of light can penetrate. Their transparency increases to the extent that insights thin out the vegetation of the soul and limit the compulsion of nature. Truth can be found only by a liberated consciousness which assesses the demonic nature of the drives. The traits that consciousness recollects stand in a relationship to what has been perceived as true, the latter being either manifest in these traits or excluded by them. The image in which these traits appear is distinguished from all other memory images, for unlike the latter it preserves not a multitude of opaque recollections but elements that touch upon what has been recognized as true. All memory images are bound to be reduced to this type of image, which may rightly be called the last image, since it alone preserves the unforgettable. The last image of a person is that person's actual *history*. This history omits all characteristics and determinations that do not relate in a significant sense to the truth intended by a liberated consciousness. How a person represents this history does not depend purely on his or her natural constitution or on the pseudo-coherence of his or her individuality; thus, only fragments of these assets are included in his or her history. This history is like a *monogram* that condenses the name into a single graphic figure which is meaningful as an ornament. Eckart's monogram is fidelity.[6] Great historical figures survive in legends that, however naïve they may be, strive to preserve their actual history. In authentic fairy tales, the imagination has intuitively deposited typical monograms. In a photograph, a person's history is buried as if under a layer of snow.

4

In his description of a Rubens landscape presented to him by Goethe, Eckermann notices to his surprise that the light in the painting comes from two opposing directions, "which is quite contrary to nature."[7]

Goethe responds: "This is how Rubens proves his greatness, and shows to the world that he stands *above* nature with a free spirit, fashioning it according to his higher purposes. The double light is indeed violent, and you could even say that it is contrary to nature. But if it is contrary to nature, I also say that it is *higher* than nature; I say that it is the bold hand of the master, whereby he demonstrates in a brilliant way that art is not entirely subject to natural necessity but rather has laws of its own." A *portrait painter* who submitted entirely to "natural necessity" would at best create photographs. During a particular period, which began with the Renaissance and may now be approaching its end, the "artwork" has indeed been faithful to nature, whose specificity has revealed itself more and more during this period. But by penetrating this nature, the artwork orients itself toward "higher ends." There is cognition in the material of colors and contours; and the greater the artwork, the more it approaches the transparency of the final memory image, in which the features of "history" converge. A man who had his portrait painted by Trübner asked the artist not to forget the wrinkles and folds on his face. Trübner pointed out the window and said, "Across the way, there's a photographer. If you want to have wrinkles and folds, then you'd better hire him—he'll put 'em all in. Me, I paint history."[8] In order for history to present itself, the mere surface coherence offered by photography must be destroyed. For in the artwork the meaning of the object takes on spatial appearance, whereas in photography the spatial appearance of an object is its meaning. The two spatial appearances—the "natural" one and that of the object permeated by cognition—are not identical. By sacrificing the former for the sake of the latter, the artwork also negates the *likeness* achieved by photography. This likeness refers to the look of the object, which does not immediately divulge how it reveals itself to cognition; the artwork, however, conveys nothing but the transparency of the object. In so doing, it resembles a magic mirror which reflects those who consult it not as they appear but rather as they wish to be or as they fundamentally are. The artwork, too, disintegrates over time; but its meaning arises out of its crumbled elements, whereas photography merely stockpiles the elements.

Until well into the second half of the nineteenth century, the practice of photography was often in the hands of former painters. The not yet entirely depersonalized technology of this transition period corresponded to a spatial environment in which traces of meaning could still be trapped. With the increasing independence of the technology and the simultaneous evacuation of meaning from the objects, *artistic photography* loses its justification: it grows not into an artwork but into its imitation. Images of children are Zumbusches,[9] and the godfather of photographic landscape impressions was Monet. These pictorial arrangements—which do not go beyond a skillful emulation of familiar styles—fail to represent the very remnants of nature which, to a certain extent, advanced technology is capable of capturing. Modern painters have composed their images out of photographic fragments in order to highlight the side-by-side existence of reified appearances as they manifest themselves in spatial relations. This artistic intention is diametrically opposed to that of artistic photography. The latter does not explore the object assigned to photographic technology but rather wants to hide the technological essence by means of style. The artistic photographer is a dilettante artist who apes an artistic manner minus its substance, instead of capturing the very lack of substance. Similarly, rhythmic gymnastics wants to incorporate the soul about which it knows nothing. It shares with artistic photography the ambition to lay claim to a higher life in order to elevate an activity which is actually at its most elevated when it finds the object appropriate to its technology. The artistic photographers function like those social forces which are interested in the semblance of the spiritual because they fear the real spirit: it might explode the material base which the spiritual illusion serves to disguise. It would be well worth the effort to expose the close ties between the prevailing social order and artistic photography.

5

The photograph does not preserve the transparent aspects of an object but instead captures it as a spatial continuum from any one of a number of positions. The last memory image outlasts time because it is unforgettable; the photograph, which neither refers to nor encompasses such a memory image, must be essentially associated with the moment in time at which it came into existence. Referring to the average film whose subject matter is the normal photographable environment, E. A. Dupont remarked in his book on film that "the essence of film is, to some degree, the essence of time."[10] If photography is a *function of the flow of time*, then its substantive meaning will change depending upon whether it belongs to the domain of the present or to some phase of the past.

Current-event photography, which portrays phenomena familiar to *contemporary* consciousness, provides access of a limited sort to the life of the original. In each case it registers an exteriority which, at the time of its reign, is a means of expression as generally intelligible as language. The contemporaneous viewer believes that he or she sees the film diva herself in the photograph, and not just her bangs or the pose of her head. Naturally, the viewer cannot gauge her on the basis of the photograph alone. But luckily the diva numbers among the living, and the cover of the illustrated magazine functions as a reminder of her corporeal reality. This means that present-day photography performs a mediating function: it is an optical sign for the diva, who is meant to be recognized. One may have doubts in the end as to whether her decisive trait is really the demonic. But even the demonic is not so much something conveyed by the photograph as it is the impression of the moviegoers who experience the original on the screen. They recognize it as the representation of the demonic—so be it. The image denounces the demonic not because of, but rather *despite* its likeness. For the time being, the demonic belongs to the still-vacillating memory image of the diva to which the photographic likeness does not refer. But the memory image drawn from the viewing of our celebrated diva breaks through the wall of likeness into the photograph and thereby lends the latter a modicum of transparency.

Once a photograph ages, the immediate reference to the original is no longer possible. The body of a deceased person appears smaller than the living figure. Likewise, an *old* photograph presents itself as the reduction of a contemporaneous one. The old photograph has been emptied of the life whose physical presence overlay its merely spatial configuration. In inverse proportion to photographs, memory images enlarge themselves into monograms of remembered life. The photograph is the sediment which has settled from the monogram, and from year to year its semiotic value decreases. The truth content of the original is left behind in its history; the photograph captures only the residuum that history has discharged.

If one can no longer encounter the grandmother in the photograph, the image taken from the family album necessarily disintegrates into its particulars. In the case of the diva, one's gaze may wander from her bangs to her demonic quality; from the nothingness of the grandmother, the gaze is thrown back onto the chignons. It is the fashion details that hold the gaze tight. Photography is bound to time in precisely the same way as *fashion*. Since the latter has no significance other than as current human garb, it is translucent when modern and abandoned when old. The tightly corseted dress in the photograph protrudes into our time like a mansion from earlier days that is destined for destruction because the city center has been moved to another part of town. Usually members of the lower class settle in such buildings. It is only the very old traditional dress, a dress which has lost all contact with the present, that can attain the beauty of a ruin. The effect of an outfit which was still worn only recently is *comical*. The grandchildren are amused by the grandmotherly crinoline of 1864, which provokes the thought that it might hide the legs of a modern girl. The recent past which claims to be alive is more outdated than the past that existed long ago and whose meaning has changed. The comic quality of the crinoline results from the powerlessness of its claim. In the photograph, the grandmother's costume is recognized as a cast-off remnant that wants to continue to hold its ground. It dissolves into the sum of its details, like a corpse, yet stands tall as if full of life. Even the landscape and all other concrete objects become costumes in an old photograph. For what is retained in the image are not the features envisaged by a liberated consciousness. The representation captures contexts from which such consciousness has departed—that is, it encompasses orders of existence that have shriveled without wanting to admit it. The more consciousness withdraws from natural bonds, the more nature diminishes. In old etchings whose fidelity is photographic, the hills of the Rhine look like mountains. As a result of technological development, they have in the meantime been reduced to tiny slopes, and the grandiosity of those aged views seems a bit ridiculous.

Ghosts are simultaneously comical and terrifying. Laughter is not the only response provoked by antiquated photography. It represents what is utterly past, and yet this detritus was once the present. Grandmother was once a person, and to this person belonged the chignon and the corset as well as the high-Renaissance chair with its turned spindles, ballast that did not weigh her down but was just carried along as a matter of course. Now the image wanders ghost-like through the present, like the lady of the haunted castle. Spooky apparitions occur only in places where a terrible deed has been committed. The photograph becomes a ghost because the costumed mannequin was once alive. The image proves that the alien trappings were incorporated into life as accessories. These trappings, whose lack of transparency one experiences in the old photograph, used to be inseparably meshed with the transparent aspects. This terrible association which persists in the photograph evokes a shudder. Such a shudder is evoked in drastic fashion by the pre–World War I films screened in the avant-garde "Studio des Ursulines" in Paris—film images that show how the features stored in the memory image are embedded in a reality which has long since disappeared. Like the photographic image, the playing of an old hit song or the reading of letters written long ago also conjures up anew a disintegrated unity. This ghost-like reality is *unredeemed*. It consists of elements in space whose configuration is so far from necessary that one could just as well imagine a different organization of these elements. Those things once clung to us like our skin, and this is how our property still clings to us today. Nothing of these contains us, and the photograph gathers fragments around a nothing. When the grandmother stood in front of the lens, she was present for one second in the spatial continuum that presented itself to the lens. But it was this aspect and not the grandmother that was eternalized. A shudder runs through the viewer of old photographs. For they make visible not the knowledge of the original but the spatial configuration of a moment; what appears in the photograph is not the person but the sum of what can be subtracted from him or her. The photograph annihilates the person by portraying him or her, and were person and portrayal to converge, the person would cease to exist. An illustrated newspaper recently put together photographs of famous personalities as children and as grown-ups and published them under the heading "The Faces of Famous People: This Is How They Once Were—and This Is How They Are Today!" Marx as a youth and Marx as leader of the Center party, Hindenburg as a lieutenant and as our Hindenburg. The photographs are set side by side like statistical reports, and one can neither guess the later image from the earlier one nor reconstruct the earlier image from the later. One has to take it on faith that the optical inventory lists belong together. The features of human beings are retained only in their "history."

6

The daily papers are illustrating their texts more and more. And what would a magazine be without pictures? The most striking proof of photography's extraordinary validity today is the increase in the number of *illustrated newspapers*. In them one finds assembled everything from the film diva to whatever is within reach of the camera and the audience. Infants are of interest to mothers, and young gentlemen are captivated by the legs of beautiful girls. Beautiful girls like to see sports and stage celebrities standing on gangways of ocean liners, embarking on voyages to distant lands. In distant lands there are battles of conflicting interests. Yet the focus of attention is not on them but on the cities, the natural catastrophes, the cultural heroes, and the politicians. In Geneva, the League of Nations is meeting; it serves as a pretext for showing Mr. Stresemann and Mr. Briand[11] conversing in front of the entrance of the hotel. The new fashions also must be disseminated, or else in the summer the beautiful girls will not know who they are. Fashion beauties attend chic events accompanied by young gentlemen; earthquakes take place in distant lands; Mr. Stresemann is seated on a terrace with potted palms; and for the mothers we have the little tots.

The aim of the illustrated newspapers is the complete reproduction of the world accessible to the photographic apparatus. They record the spatial impressions of people, conditions, and events from every possible perspective. Their method corresponds to that of the weekly newsreel, which is nothing but a collection of photographs, whereas an authentic film employs photography merely as a means. Never before has an age been so informed about itself, if being informed means having an image of objects that resembles them in a photographic sense. Most of the images in the illustrated magazines are topical photographs, which refer to existing objects. The reproductions are thus basically signs which may remind us of the original object that was supposed to be understood. The demonic diva. In reality, however, the weekly photographic ration does not at all mean to refer to these objects or ur-images. If it were offering itself as an aid to memory, then memory would have to determine the selection. But the flood of photos sweeps away the dams of memory. The assault of this mass of images is so powerful that it threatens to destroy the potentially existing awareness of crucial traits. Artworks suffer this fate through their reproductions. The phrase "lie together, die together" applies to the multiply reproduced original; rather than coming into view through the reproductions, it tends to disappear in its multiplicity and to live on as art photography. In the illustrated magazines, people see the very world that the illustrated magazines prevent them from perceiving. The spatial continuum from the camera's perspective dominates the spatial appearance of the perceived object; the resemblance between the image and the object effaces the contours of the object's "history." Never before has a period known so little about itself. In the hands of the ruling society, the invention of illustrated magazines is one of the most powerful means of organizing a strike against understanding. Even the colorful arrangement of the images provides a not insignificant means for successfully implementing such a strike. The *contiguity* of these images systematically excludes their contextual framework available to consciousness. The "image-idea" drives away the idea. The blizzard of photographs betrays an indifference toward what the things mean. It does not have to be this way; but in any case the American illustrated magazines—which the publications of other countries emulate to a large degree—

equate the world with the quintessence of the photographs. This equation is not made without good reason. For the world itself has taken on a "photographic face"; it can be photographed because it strives to be absorbed into the spatial continuum which yields to snapshots. Sometimes it is the fraction of a second required for the exposure of an object that determines whether or not a sportsman will become famous to the point where illustrated magazines commission photographers to give him exposure. The camera can also capture the figures of beautiful girls and young gentlemen. That the world devours them is a sign of the *fear of death*. What the photographs by their sheer accumulation attempt to banish is the recollection of death, which is part and parcel of every memory image. In the illustrated magazines the world has become a photographable present, and the photographed present has been entirely eternalized. Seemingly ripped from the clutch of death, in reality it has succumbed to it.

7

The series of pictorial representations of which photography is the last historical stage begins with the *symbol*. The symbol, in turn, arises out of the "natural community," in which man's consciousness was still entirely embedded in nature.

> Just as the history of individual words always begins with the sensuous, natural meaning and only progresses to abstract, figurative uses in the later stages of its development, one can observe the same progression from substance and matter to the spiritual and the intellectual in religion, in the development of the human individual and of mankind in general. Likewise the fundamental meaning of the symbols in which the earliest human beings customarily deposited their views of the nature of the world surrounding them is purely physical and material. Symbolism, like language, sat in nature's lap.[12]

This statement, by Bachofen, comes from his study of the rope-twisting Ocnus in which he shows that the spinning and weaving depicted in the image originally referred to the activity of the creative power of nature. As consciousness becomes more and more aware of itself and in the process the originary "identity of nature and man"[13] dissolves, the meaning of the image becomes increasingly abstract and immaterial. But even if, as Bachofen puts it, the image progresses to the point of designating "the spiritual and the intellectual," the meaning is nevertheless so much a part of the image that it cannot be separated from it. For long stretches of history, imagistic representations have remained symbols. So long as human beings need them, they continue, in practice, to be dependent on natural conditions, a dependence that determines the visible and corporeal expression of consciousness. It is only with the increasing domination of nature that the image loses its symbolic power. Consciousness, which disengages itself from nature and stands against it, is no longer naïvely enveloped in its mythological cocoon: it thinks in concepts which, of course, can still be used in an altogether mythological way. In certain epochs the image retains its power; the symbolic presentation becomes *allegory*. "The latter signifies merely a general concept or an idea which is distinct from it; the former is the sensuous form, the incorporation of the idea itself." This is how old Creuzer defines the difference between the two types of images.[14] At the level of the symbol, what is thought is contained in the image; at the level of allegory, thought maintains and employs the image as if consciousness were hesitating to throw off its cocoon. This schematization is crude. Yet it suffices to illustrate the transformation of representations which is the sign that consciousness has departed from its natural contingency. The more decisively consciousness frees itself from this contingency in the course of the historical process, the more purely does its natural foundation present itself to consciousness. What is meant no longer appears to consciousness in images; rather, this meaning goes toward and through nature. To an ever-increasing degree, European painting during the last few centuries has represented nature stripped of symbolic and allegorical meanings. This certainly does not imply that the human features it depicts are bereft of meaning. Even as recently as the days of the old daguerreotypes, consciousness was so imbricated in nature that the faces bring to mind meanings which cannot be separated from natural life. Since nature changes in exact correspondence with the particular state of consciousness of a period, the foundation of nature devoid of meaning arises with modern photography. No different from earlier modes of representation, photography, too, is assigned to a particular developmental stage of practical and material life. It is a secretion of the capitalist mode of production. The same mere nature which appears in photography flourishes in the reality of the society produced by this capitalist mode of production. One can certainly imagine a society that has fallen prey to a mute nature which has no meaning no matter how abstract its silence. The contours of such a society emerge in the illustrated journals. Were it to endure, the emancipation of consciousness would result in the eradication of consciousness; the nature that it failed to penetrate would sit down at the very table that consciousness had abandoned. If this society failed to endure, however, then liberated consciousness would be given an incomparable opportunity. Less enmeshed in the natural bonds than ever before, it could prove its power in dealing with them. The turn to photography is the *go-for-broke game* of history.

8

Although the grandmother has disappeared, the crinoline has nonetheless remained. The totality of all photographs must be understood as the *general inventory* of a nature that cannot be further reduced—as the comprehensive catalogue of all manifestations which present themselves in space, to the extent that they are constructed not out of the monogram of the object but from a natural perspective which the monogram does not capture. Corresponding to this spatial inventory is historicism's temporal inventory. Instead of preserving the "history" that consciousness reads out of the temporal succession of events, historicism records the temporal succession of events whose linkage does not contain the transparency of history. The barren self-presentation of spatial and temporal elements belongs to a social order which regulates itself according to economic laws of nature.

A consciousness caught up in nature is unable to see its own material base. It is the task of photography to disclose this previously unexamined *foundation of nature*. For the first time in history, photography brings to light the entire natural cocoon; for the first time, the inert world presents itself in its independence from human beings. Photography shows cities in aerial shots, brings crockets and figures down from the Gothic cathedrals. All spatial configurations are incorporated into the central archive in unusual combinations which distance them from human proximity. Once the grandmother's costume has lost its relationship to the present, it will no longer be funny; it will be peculiar, like an ocean-dwelling octopus. One day the diva will lose her demonic quality and her bangs will go the same way as the chignons. This is how the elements crumble, since they are not held together. The photographic archive assembles in effigy the last elements of a nature alienated from meaning.

This warehousing of nature promotes the confrontation of consciousness with nature. Just as consciousness finds itself confronting the unabashedly displayed mechanics of industrial society, it also faces, thanks to photographic technology, the reflection of the reality that has slipped away from it. To have provoked the decisive confrontation in every field: this is precisely the go-for-broke game of the historical process. The images of the stock of nature disintegrated into its elements are offered up to consciousness to deal with as it pleases. Their original order is lost; they no longer cling to the spatial context that linked them with an original out of which the memory image was selected. But if the remnants of nature are not oriented toward the memory image, then the order they assume through the image is necessarily provisional. It is therefore incumbent on consciousness to establish the *provisional status* of all given configurations, and perhaps even to awaken an inkling of the right order of the inventory of nature. In the works of Franz Kafka, a liberated consciousness absolves itself of this responsibility by destroying natural reality and scrambling the fragments. The disorder of the detritus reflected in photography cannot be elucidated more clearly than through the suspension of every habitual relationship among the elements of nature. The capacity to stir up the elements of nature is one of the possibilities of film. This possibility is realized whenever film combines parts and segments to create strange

constructs. If the disarray of the illustrated newspapers is simply confusion, the game that film plays with the pieces of disjointed nature is
reminiscent of *dreams* in which the fragments of daily life become jumbled. This game shows that the valid organization of things remains
unknown—an organization which would designate the position that the
remains of the grandmother and the diva stored in the general inventory
will some day have to occupy.

Laszlo Moholy-Nagy, "Berlin Radio Tower," 1925

Travel and Dance

■ ■ ■

But only those who leave for leaving's sake
are *travelers;* hearts tugging like balloons.
—Baudelaire, "The Voyage"

Today the society that is called "bourgeois" indulges in the desire to travel and dance with an enthusiasm far greater than that shown in any previous epoch for these sorts of profane activities. It would be all too facile to attribute these spatio-temporal passions to the development of transportation or to grasp them in psychological terms as consequences of the postwar period. For no matter how correct such indications might be, they explain neither the particular form nor the specific meaning that both of these manifestations of life have taken on in the present.

■ ■ ■

When Goethe traveled to Italy, it was to a country he sought with his soul.[1] Today the soul—or whatever it is that is meant by that word— seeks the change of environment offered by *travel.* The goal of modern travel is not its destination but rather a new place as such; what people seek is less the particular being of a landscape than the foreignness of its face. Thus the preference for the exotic, which one is eager to discover because it is completely different and not because it has already become an image in one's dreams. The more the world shrinks thanks to automobiles, films, and airplanes, the more the concept of the exotic in turn also becomes relativized. Though at present the exotic may still cling to the pyramids and the Golden Horn, someday it will designate any spot in the world whatsoever, to the extent that the spot appears unusual from the perspective of any other point in the world. This relativizing of the exotic goes hand in hand with its banishment from reality—so that sooner or later the romantically inclined will have to agitate for the establishment of fenced-in nature preserves, isolated fairy-tale realms in which people will still be able to hope for experiences that today even Calcutta is hardly able to provide. This is rapidly becoming the case. As a result of the comforts of civilization, only a minute part of the globe's surface remains *terra incognita* today; people feel just as much at home in their homes as they do elsewhere—or they do not feel at home anywhere at all. Which is why, strictly speaking, the travel that is so *à la mode* actually no longer enables people to savor the sensation of foreign places: one hotel is like the next, and the nature in the background is familiar to readers of illustrated magazines. Instead, travel is undertaken for its own sake. The emphasis is on the detachment as such that travel affords, not on the contemplation of this or that type of area which it makes possible. The significance of travel amounts to nothing more than that it allows people to consume their five o'clock tea[2] in a space that just happens to be less deadeningly familiar than the space of their daily affairs. More and more, travel is becoming the incomparable occasion to be somewhere other than the very place one habitually is. It fulfills its decisive function as a spatial transformation, as a temporary change of location.

Just as travel has been reduced to a pure experience of space, *dance* has been transformed into a mere marking of time. The waltz dream[3] has come to an end, and the minutely regulated gaiety of the Française is a thing of the past. What used to be signified by such danced ceremoniousness—pleasant flirtation, a tender encounter in the realm of the sensuous—is evoked today (if at all) only by the older generation. The modern social dance, alienated from the network of conventions governing the middle classes, tends to become a representation of rhythm as such. Instead of expressing specific ideas in time, its actual content is time itself. If in the earliest eras dance was a cult practice, today it has become a cult of movement; if rhythm used to be a manifestation of eros and spirit, today it is a self-sufficient phenomenon that wants to rid itself of meaning. The secret aim of jazz tunes, no matter how negroid their origins may be, is a tempo that is concerned with nothing but itself. These tunes strive to extinguish the melody and spin out ever further the vamps that signal the decline of meaning, in that they reveal and perfect the mechanization already at work in the melody. A shift has taken place here, away from movement that refers to a meaning and toward movement that is solely self-referential. This is further confirmed by the use of dance steps cut to measure by Parisian dance teachers. The progression of these steps is not determined by an objective and substantive law to which the music must conform. Rather, it arises freely out of the particular impulses of movement that develop in response to the music. An individuation perhaps, but one that is not at all oriented toward the individualistic. For jazz music, no matter how vital it may consider itself to be, leaves whatever is merely alive to its own devices. As a result, the movements it engenders (which obviously tend to get worn down to a meaningless shuffle) are hardly more than rhythmic offerings, temporal experiences whose ultimate joy is syncopation. Admittedly, as a temporal event dance in general can hardly do without the rhythmic component; yet there is a difference between experiencing something authentic by means of rhythm and experiencing rhythm itself as the inauthentic objective. The contemporary practice that makes jazz dance into a sport testifies to its lack of substantive meaning over and above that of disciplined movement.

Travel and dance thus have the dubious tendency to become formalized. They are no longer events that happen to unfold in space and time, but instead brand the transformation of space and time itself as an event. Were this not the case, their contents would not increasingly allow themselves to be determined by *fashion*. For fashion effaces the intrinsic value of the things that come under its dominion by subjecting the appearance of these phenomena to periodic changes that are not based on any relation to the things themselves. The fickle dictates of fashion, which disfigure the world, would be purely destructive in character if they did not confirm—in however low a realm—the intimate human connectedness that even things can effectively come to signify. The fact that nowadays the creation and selection of seaside resorts depend largely on the whim of fashion is just one more proof of how unimportant the actual travel destination is. Similarly, in the domain of the social dance, the arbitrary tyranny of fashion allows one to conclude that the favorite movements of the season are not especially saturated with substance.

As formal events, travel and dance have, of course, long been overburdened. The particular area and the steps an individual prefers may well be tied (like hairstyles) to the directives of that curious and profane anonymous entity whose caprices are blindly followed by trend-setting society. It almost seems as if what is being called for is the very activity of spatial and temporal indulgence as such. The adventure of movement as such is thrilling, and slipping out of accustomed spaces and times into as yet unexplored realms arouses the passions: the ideal here is to roam freely through the dimensions. This spatio-temporal double life could hardly be craved with such intensity, were it not the *distortion* of real life.

■ ■ ■

The *real* person, who has not capitulated to being a tool of mechanized industry, resists being dissolved into space and time. He certainly exists in this space here, yet is not utterly dispersed in it or overwhelmed by it. Instead he extends himself across latitudinal and longitudinal parallels into a supra-spatial infinity that should not in any way be confused with the endlessness of astronomic space. Nor is he circumscribed by time experienced as expiration or as measured by the clock. Rather he is committed to eternity, which is different from an endless extension of time. Even though he lives in this life here,[4] which appears to him and in which he appears, he does not live only in this life here; for, as anyone who has encountered death knows, it is both contingent and incomplete. How else is that which is passing away in space and time supposed to participate in reality, other than through the relationship of man to the indeterminate that lies beyond space and outside time? As one who exists, man is really a citizen of two worlds, or, more correctly, he exists between the two worlds. Thrust into a spatio-temporal life to which he is not enslaved, he orients himself toward the Beyond in which everything in the Here would find its meaning and conclusion. The dependence of the Here upon such supplementation manifests itself in the work of art. By giving shape to the phenomenal, art provides a form that enables it to be touched by a meaning which is not simply given along with it; it thus relates the phenomenal to a significance that goes beyond space and time, transforming the ephemeral into a construct. The real person has a real relationship to this significance, which in the work of art combines with the extant to form an aesthetic unity. Caught in the Here and in need of the Beyond, he leads, in the literal sense of the expression, a *double existence*. However, this duality cannot be split into two positions that could be occupied one after the other, because, when it is understood as man's participation (aroused by an inner tension) in both realms, it defies dissection. He suffers tragedy because he strives to realize the absolute *(Unbedingtes)* in the Here; he experiences recon-ciliation because he has the vision of perfection. He is always simulta-neously within space and at the threshold of a supra-spatial endlessness, simultaneously within the flow of time and in the reflection of eternity; and this duality of his existence is simple, since his being is precisely the tension from out of the Here into the There. Even if he were to travel or to dance, for him travel and dance would never be events whose meaning is self-contained. Like all endeavors, they receive their content and their form from that other realm toward which he is oriented.

The forces leading toward *mechanization* do not aim beyond space and time. They are blessed with an intellect that knows no mercy. Inasmuch as it is convinced that the world can be grasped on the basis of mechanistic presuppositions, this intellect frees itself from all rela-tions to the Beyond and renders pale the reality that man, extended across space and time, occupies. This detached intellect begets tech-nology and aims at a rationalization of life that would accommodate it to technology. But since such a radical flattening out of everything living can be achieved only by sacrificing man's intellectual *(geistigen)* con-stitution, and since it must repress man's intermediate spiritual *(see-lisch)* layers in order to make him as smooth and shiny as an automobile, one cannot easily ascribe any real meaning to the bustle of machines and people that it has created. Consequently, technology becomes an end in itself, and a world arises that, to put it in vulgar terms, desires nothing other than the greatest possible technologizing of all activities. Why? It does not know. It knows only that space and time must be conquered by the power of the intellect, and is proud of itself in its mechanistic domination. Radio, telephotography, and so forth—each and every one of these outgrowths of rational fantasy aimlessly serves one single aim: the constitution of a depraved omnipresence within calculable dimensions. The expansion of land, air, and water traffic is a final manifestation of this, and speed records are the most extreme of all. Rightly so, for if man is only a carrier of intellect and intellect alone, there remains nothing else for him to wish for: the successful surmounting of spatio-temporal barriers confirms his rational sovereignty. The more he tries to deal with things by means of mathematics, however, the more he himself becomes a mathematical given in space and time. His existence *(Dasein)* disintegrates into a series of organizationally dictated activities, and nothing would be more in keeping with this mechanization than for him to contract into a *point,* so to speak—into a useful part of the intellectual apparatus. Being forced to degenerate in this direction is already enough of a burden on people. They find themselves shoved into an everyday life that turns them into henchmen of the technological excesses. Despite or perhaps precisely because of the humane foundations of Taylorism, they do not become masters of the machine but instead become machine-like.

In a situation enveloped by mechanistic categories—one that summons up caricatured faces *à la* George Grosz to a surface that leaves nothing hidden—it is painfully difficult for people to lead a real double existence. If they attempt nevertheless to place themselves in reality, they run into the wall of those categories and tumble back into the spatio-temporal arena. They want to experience the endless and are points in space; they want to establish a relationship with the eternal and are swallowed up by the flow of time. Access to the sphere they seek is blocked, and thus their demand for reality can express itself only inauthentically.

■ ■ ■

Civilized people, so the claim would be, today discover in travel and dance a *substitute* for the sphere to which they have been denied access. Since they are confined to the spatio-temporal coordinate system and are unable to extend themselves beyond the forms of perception to the perception of the forms, they are granted access to the Beyond only through a change in their position in space and time. In order to assure themselves of their citizenship in both of the worlds, these people (who have been reduced to mere spatio-temporal points) must intermittently dwell in one place and then in another, must sometimes move at one tempo and other times at another. Travel and dance have taken on a *theological* significance: they are the essential possibilities through which those in the grip of mechanization can live (albeit inauthentically) the double existence that is the foundation of reality. As travelers, they distance themselves from their habitual location; going to an exotic place is their sole remaining means of showing that they have outgrown the regions of the Here that enslave them. They experience supra-spatial *endlessness* by traveling in an endless geographic space and, specifically, through travel as such. Such travel is of the sort that above all and most of the time has no particular destination; its meaning is exhausted in the mere fact of changing locations. This is to say that for them the inter-locking of reality, its in-one-another *(Ineinander)* quality has been reduced to a sequence, to an after-each-other *(Nacheinander)* structure. Whereas those who are attuned to the absolute are not only in space when they take up space, the people in the mechanized bustle are either at their normal place or somewhere else. For them, this either-or never becomes a simultaneity. They always bend apart the indissoluble dou-bleness into two separate spatial events.

The same holds for the experience of time. Dance provides those who have been raped by intellect with a possibility of grasping the *eternal.* For them, the double existence transforms itself into two kinds of behavior within time itself: it is only within the mortal that they grasp the immortal. This is why what is decisive also within the temporal medium is the formal transformation, an abandonment of the tempo-rality of the profane hustle and bustle for another temporality, which is that of rhythm itself and not that of what dance means. And in this medium, too, the point-like people cannot catch hold of the double existence in one breath, so to speak, like those people who really exist. Ripped out from the tension that receives the eternal within the temporal, they are not simultaneously here and there but rather first here and then at a different place—which is also here. For them, the distorted image of eternity emerges only out of the sequentiality of trustee board meetings and displays of dancing.

The manner in which special spatio-temporal events are currently being savored to the hilt is abundant confirmation that what is at stake in this very enjoyment is a distortion of an increasingly unavailable real existence. What one expects and gets from travel and dance—a liberation from *earthly woes*, the possibility of an *aesthetic* relation to organized toil—corresponds to the sort of elevation above the ephemeral and the contingent that might occur within people's existence in the relation to the eternal and the absolute. With the difference, however, that these people do not become aware of the limitations of this life Here but instead abandon themselves to the normal contingency within the limitations of the Here. For them, this life here has the same significance as the ordinary office environment: it encompasses in space and time only the flatness of everyday life and not all that is human as such (which of course includes travel and dance). And when they then renounce their spatio-temporal fixity during their breaks, it seems to them as if the Beyond (for which they have no words) is already announcing itself within this life here. Through their travels (and for the time being it doesn't matter where they are headed) the shackles are burst, and they imagine that infinity itself is spreading out before them. In trains they are already on the other side, and the world in which they land is a new world for them. The dancer also grasps eternity in the rhythm: the contrast between the time in which he floats about and the time that demolishes him is his authentic rapture within the inauthentic domain. Dance itself can readily be reduced to a mere step, since after all it is only the act of dancing that is essential.

∎ ∎ ∎

In his book *Justification of the Good*, Vladimir Solovyov states: "If it is necessary that in a given era people should invent and build all sorts of machines, dig the Suez Canal, discover unknown lands, and so on, then it is equally necessary for the successful realization of these tasks that not all people be mystics; yes, one could even say that it is necessary that not all people be sincere believers."[5] This uncertain, hesitant confirmation of the civilizing impulse is more realistic than a radical cult of progress, whether the latter be of rational lineage or aimed directly at the utopian. But it is also more realistic than the condemnations by those who romantically flee the situation they have been assigned. It awaits the promises without articulating them. It not only understands the phenomena that have freed themselves conclusively from their foundations as deformations and distorted reflections, but also accords them a few possibilities of their own which are, after all, rather positive.

The passionate swarming out into all dimensions also demands *redemption,* if its negativity is thought through to the end. It could be that the addiction to a mere change of place or tempo is a side effect of the imperative to master in every sense the spatio-temporal realms opened up by technology (albeit not by technology alone). Our conceptions of the lower nature of the world have expanded so abruptly that it may be quite some time before they are integrated into the realm of the empirical. We are like children when we travel, playfully excited about the new velocity, the relaxed roaming about, the overviews of geographic regions that previously could not be seen with such scope. We have fallen for the ability to have all these spaces at our disposal; we are like conquistadors who have not yet had a quiet moment to reflect on the meaning of their acquisition. Similarly, when we dance we also mark a time that previously did not exist—a time that has been prepared for us over the course of a thousand discoveries whose contents we cannot gauge, possibly because for the time being their unfamiliar scale strikes us as their content. Technology has taken us by surprise, and the regions that it has opened up are still glaringly empty . . .

Travel and dance in their present form would thus be simultaneously excesses of a theological sort and predecessors of a profane sort, distortions of real being and conquests in the (in themselves unreal) media of space and time. These may become filled with meaning once people extend themselves from the newly won regions of this life here to the infinite and to the eternal, which can never be contained in any life here.

Girls at a rehearsal, 1929

The Mass Ornament

■ ■ ■

The lines of life are various; they diverge and cease
Like footpaths and the mountains' utmost ends.
What we are here, elsewhere a God amends
With harmonies, eternal recompense, and peace.
　　—Hölderlin, "To Zimmer"

1

The position that an epoch occupies in the historical process can be determined more strikingly from an analysis of its inconspicuous surface-level expressions than from that epoch's judgments about itself. Since these judgments are expressions of the tendencies of a particular era, they do not offer conclusive testimony about its overall constitution. The surface-level expressions, however, by virtue of their unconscious nature, provide unmediated access to the fundamental substance of the state of things. Conversely, knowledge of this state of things depends on the interpretation of these surface-level expressions. The fundamental substance of an epoch and its unheeded impulses illuminate each other reciprocally.

2

In the domain of body culture, which also covers the illustrated newspapers, tastes have been quietly changing. The process began with the Tiller Girls.[1] These products of American distraction factories are no longer individual girls, but indissoluble girl clusters whose movements are demonstrations of mathematics. As they condense into figures in the revues, performances of the same geometric precision are taking place in what is always the same packed stadium, be it in Australia or India, not to mention America. The tiniest village, which they have not yet reached, learns about them through the weekly newsreels. One need only glance at the screen to learn that the ornaments are composed of thousands of bodies, sexless bodies in bathing suits. The regularity of their patterns is cheered by the masses, themselves arranged by the stands in tier upon ordered tier.

These extravagant spectacles, which are staged by many sorts of people and not just girls and stadium crowds, have long since become an established form. They have gained *international* stature and are the focus of aesthetic interest.

The bearer of the ornaments is the *mass* and not the people *[Volk]*, for whenever the people form figures, the latter do not hover in midair but arise out of a community. A current of organic life surges from these communal groups—which share a common destiny—to their ornaments, endowing these ornaments with a magic force and burdening them with meaning to such an extent that they cannot be reduced to a pure assemblage of lines. Those who have withdrawn from the community and consider themselves to be unique personalities with their own individual souls also fail when it comes to forming these new patterns. Were they to take part in such a performance, the ornament would not transcend them. It would be a colorful composition that could not be worked out to its logical conclusion, since its points—like the prongs of a rake—would be implanted in the soul's intermediate strata, of which a residue would survive. The patterns seen in the stadiums and cabarets betray no such origins. They are composed of elements that are mere building blocks and nothing more. The construction of the edifice depends on the size of the stones and their number. It is the mass that is employed here. Only as parts of a mass, not as individuals who believe themselves to be formed from within, do people become fractions of a figure.

The ornament is an *end in itself*. Ballet likewise used to yield

ornaments, which arose in kaleidoscopic fashion. But even after dis-
carding their ritual meaning, these remained the plastic expression of
erotic life, an erotic life that both gave rise to them and determined their
traits. The mass movements of the girls, by contrast, take place in a
vacuum; they are a linear system that no longer has any erotic meaning
but at best points to the locus of the erotic. Moreover, the meaning of
the living star formations in the stadiums is not that of military exer-
cises. No matter how regular the latter may turn out to be, that regularity was considered a means to an end; the parade march arose out of
patriotic feelings and in turn aroused them in soldiers and subjects. The
star formations, however, have no meaning beyond themselves, and the
masses above whom they rise are not a moral unit like a company of
soldiers. One cannot even describe the figures as the decorative frills of
gymnastic discipline. Rather, the girl-units drill in order to produce an
immense number of parallel lines, the goal being to train the broadest
mass of people in order to create a pattern of undreamed-of dimensions.
The end result is the ornament, whose closure is brought about by
emptying all the substantial constructs of their contents.

Although the masses give rise to the ornament, they are not involved
in thinking it through. As linear as it may be, there is no line that extends
from the small sections of the mass to the entire figure. The ornament
resembles *aerial photographs* of landscapes and cities in that it does not
emerge out of the interior of the given conditions, but rather appears
above them. Actors likewise never grasp the stage setting in its totality,
yet they consciously take part in its construction; and even in the case of
ballet dancers, the figure is still subject to the influence of its performers.
The more the coherence of the figure is relinquished in favor of mere
linearity, the more distant it becomes from the immanent consciousness
of those constituting it. Yet this does not lead to its being scrutinized by
a more incisive gaze. In fact, nobody would notice the figure at all if the
crowd of spectators, who have an aesthetic relation to the ornament and
do not represent anyone, were not sitting in front of it.

The ornament, detached from its bearers, must be understood *rationally*. It consists of lines and circles like those found in textbooks on
Euclidean geometry, and also incorporates the elementary components of

physics, such as waves and spirals. Both the proliferations of organic forms and the emanations of spiritual life remain excluded. The Tiller Girls can no longer be reassembled into human beings after the fact. Their mass gymnastics are never performed by the fully preserved bodies, whose contortions defy rational understanding. Arms, thighs, and other segments are the smallest component parts of the composition.

The structure of the mass ornament reflects that of the entire contemporary situation. Since the principle of the *capitalist production process* does not arise purely out of nature, it must destroy the natural organisms that it regards either as means or as resistance. Community and personality perish when what is demanded is calculability; it is only as a tiny piece of the mass that the individual can clamber up charts and can service machines without any friction. A system oblivious to differences in form leads on its own to the blurring of national characteristics and to the production of worker masses that can be employed equally well at any point on the globe.—Like the mass ornament, the capitalist production process is an end in itself. The commodities that it spews forth are not actually produced to be possessed; rather, they are made for the sake of a profit that knows no limit. Its growth is tied to that of business. The producer does not labor for private gains whose benefits he can enjoy only to a limited extent (in America surplus profits are directed to spiritual shelters such as libraries and universities, which cultivate intellectuals whose later endeavors repay with interest the previously advanced capital). No: the producer labors in order to expand the business. Value is not produced for the sake of value. Though labor may well have once served to produce and consume values up to a certain point, these have now become side effects in the service of the production process. The activities subsumed by that process have divested themselves of their substantial contents.—The production process runs its secret course in public. Everyone does his or her task on the conveyor belt, performing a partial function without grasping the totality. Like the pattern in the stadium, the organization stands above the masses, a monstrous figure whose creator withdraws it from the eyes of its bearers, and barely even observes it himself.—It is conceived according to rational principles which the Taylor system merely pushes to their ultimate conclusion. The hands in the factory correspond to the legs of the Tiller Girls. Going beyond manual capacities, psychotechnical aptitude tests attempt to calculate dispositions of the soul as well. The mass ornament is the aesthetic reflex of the rationality to which the prevailing economic system aspires.

Educated people—who are never entirely absent—have taken offense at the emergence of the Tiller Girls and the stadium images. They judge anything that entertains the crowd to be a distraction of that crowd. But despite what they think, the *aesthetic* pleasure gained from ornamental mass movements is *legitimate*. Such movements are in fact among the rare creations of the age that bestow form upon a given material. The masses organized in these movements come from offices and factories; the formal principle according to which they are molded determines them in reality as well. When significant components of reality become invisible in our world, art must make do with what is left, for an aesthetic presentation is all the more real the less it dispenses with the reality outside the aesthetic sphere. No matter how low one gauges the value of the mass ornament, its degree of reality is still higher than that of artistic productions which cultivate outdated noble sentiments in obsolete forms—even if it means nothing more than that.

3

The process of history is a battle between a weak and distant reason and the *forces of nature* that ruled over heaven and earth in the myths. After the twilight of the gods, the gods did not abdicate: the old nature within and outside man continues to assert itself. It gave rise to the great cultures of humanity, which must die like any creation of nature, and it serves as the ground for the superstructures of a *mythological* thinking which affirms nature in its omnipotence. Despite all the variations in the structure of such mythological thinking, which changes from epoch to epoch, it always respects the boundaries that nature has drawn. It acknowledges the organism as the ur-form; it is refracted in the formed quality of what exists; it yields to the workings of fate. It reflects the premises of nature in all spheres without rebelling against their existence. Organic sociology, which sets up the natural organism as the prototype for social organization, is no less mythological than nationalism, which knows no higher unity than the unison of the nation's fate.

Reason does not operate within the circle of natural life. Its concern is to introduce truth into the world. Its realm has already been intimated in genuine *fairy tales,* which are not stories about miracles but rather announcements of the miraculous advent of justice. There is profound historical significance in the fact that the *Thousand and One Nights* turned up precisely in the France of the Enlightenment and that eighteenth-century reason recognized the reason of the fairy tales as its equal. Even in the early days of history, mere nature was suspended in the fairy tale so that truth could prevail. Natural power is defeated by the powerlessness of the good; fidelity triumphs over the arts of sorcery.

In serving the breakthrough of truth, the historical process becomes a *process of demythologization* which effects a radical deconstruction of the positions that the natural continually reoccupied. The French Enlightenment is an important example of the struggle between reason and the mythological delusions that have invaded the domains of religion and politics. This struggle continues, and in the course of history it may be that nature, increasingly stripped of its magic, will become more and more pervious to reason.

4

The *capitalist epoch* is a stage in the process of demystification. The type of thinking that corresponds to the present economic system has, to an unprecedented degree, made possible the domination and use of nature as a self-contained entity. What is decisive here, however, is not the fact that this thinking provides a means to exploit nature; if human beings were merely exploiters of nature, then nature would have triumphed over nature. Rather, what is decisive is that this thinking fosters ever greater independence from natural conditions and thereby creates a space for the intervention of reason. It is the *rationality* of this thinking (which emanates to some extent from the reason of fairy tales) that accounts—though not exclusively—for the bourgeois revolutions of the last one hundred fifty years, the revolutions that settled the score with the natural powers of the church (itself entangled in the affairs of its age), of the monarchy, and of the feudal system. The unstoppable decomposition of these and other mythological ties is reason's good fortune, since the fairy tale can become reality only on the ruins of the natural unities.

However, the *Ratio* of the capitalist economic system is not reason itself but a murky reason. Once past a certain point, it abandons the truth in which it participates. *It does not encompass man.* The operation of the production process is not regulated according to man's needs, and man does not serve as the foundation for the structure of the socioeconomic organization. Indeed, at no point whatsoever is the system founded on the basis of man. "The basis of man": this does not mean that capitalist thinking should cultivate man as a historically produced form such that it ought to allow him to go unchallenged as a personality and should satisfy the demands made by his nature. The adherents of this position reproach capitalism's rationalism for raping man, and yearn for the return of a community that would be capable of preserving the allegedly human element much better than capitalism. Leaving aside the stultifying effect of such regressive stances, they fail to grasp capitalism's core defect: it rationalizes not too much but rather *too little*. The thinking promoted by capitalism resists culminating in that reason which arises from the basis of man.

The current site of capitalist thinking is marked by *abstractness*. The predominance of this abstractness today establishes a spiritual space that encompasses all expression. The objection raised against this abstract mode of thought—that it is incapable of grasping the actual substance of life and therefore must give way to concrete observation of phenomena—does indeed identify the limits of abstraction. As an objection it is premature, however, when it is raised in favor of that false mythological concreteness whose aim is organism and form. A return to this sort of concreteness would sacrifice the already acquired capacity for abstraction, but without overcoming abstractness. The latter is the expression of a rationality grown obdurate. Determinations of meaning rendered as abstract generalities—such as determinations in the economic, social, political, or moral domain—do not give reason what rightfully belongs to reason. Such determinations fail to consider the empirical; one could draw any utilitarian application whatsoever from these abstractions devoid of content. Only behind the barrier of these abstractions can one find the individual rational insights that correspond to the particularity of the given situation. Despite the substantiality one can demand of them, such insights are "concrete" only in a derivative sense; in any case they are not "concrete" in the vulgar sense, which uses the term to substantiate points of view entangled in natural life.—The abstractness of contemporary thinking is thus *ambivalent*. From the perspective of the mythological doctrines, in which nature naïvely asserts itself, the process of abstraction—as employed, for example, by the natural sciences—is a gain in rationality which detracts from the resplendence of the things of nature. From the perspective of reason, the same process of abstraction appears to be determined by nature; it gets lost in an empty formalism under whose guise the natural is accorded free rein because it does not let through the insights of reason which could strike at the natural. The prevailing abstractness reveals that the process of demythologization has not come to an end.

Present-day thinking is confronted with the question as to whether it should open itself up to reason or continue to push on against it without opening up at all. It cannot transgress its self-imposed boundaries without fundamentally changing the economic system that constitutes its infrastructure; the continued existence of the latter entails the continued existence of present-day thinking. In other words, the unchecked development of the capitalist system fosters the unchecked growth of abstract thinking (or forces it to become bogged down in a false concreteness). The more abstractness consolidates itself, however, the more man is left behind, *ungoverned* by reason. If his thought midway takes a detour into the abstract, thereby preventing the true contents of knowledge from breaking through, man will once again be rendered subject to the forces of nature. Instead of suppressing these forces, this thinking that has lost its way provokes their rebellion itself by disregarding the very reason that alone could confront such forces and make them submit. It is merely a consequence of the unhampered expansion of capitalism's power that the dark forces of nature continue to rebel ever more threateningly, thereby preventing the advent of the man of reason.

5

Like abstractness, the *mass ornament* is ambivalent. On the one hand its rationality reduces the natural in a manner that does not allow man to wither away, but that, on the contrary, were it only carried through to the end, would reveal man's most essential element in all its purity. Precisely because the bearer of the ornament does not appear as a total personality—that is, as a harmonious union of nature and "spirit" in which the former is emphasized too much and the latter too little—he becomes transparent to the man determined by reason. The human figure enlisted in the mass ornament has begun the *exodus* from lush organic splendor and the constitution of individuality toward the realm of anonymity to which it relinquishes itself when it stands in truth and when the knowledge radiating from the basis of man dissolves the contours of visible natural form. In the mass ornament nature is deprived of its substance, and it is just this that points to a condition in which the only elements of nature capable of surviving are those that do not resist illumination through reason. Thus, in old Chinese landscape paintings the trees, ponds, and mountains are rendered only as sparse ornamental signs drawn in ink. The organic center has been removed and the remaining unconnected parts are composed according to laws that are not those of nature but laws given by a knowledge of truth, which, as always, is a function of its time. Similarly, it is only remnants of the complex of man that enter into the mass ornament. They are selected and combined in the aesthetic medium according to a principle which represents form-bursting reason in a purer way than those other principles that preserve man as an organic unity.

Viewed from the perspective of reason, the mass ornament reveals itself as a *mythological cult* that is masquerading in the garb of abstraction. Compared to the concrete immediacy of other corporeal presentations, the ornament's conformity to reason is thus an illusion. In reality the ornament is the crass manifestation of inferior nature. The latter can flourish all the more freely, the more decisively capitalist *Ratio* is cut off from reason and bypasses man as it vanishes into the void of the abstract. In spite of the rationality of the mass pattern, such patterns simultaneously give rise to the natural in its impenetrability. Certainly man as an organic being has disappeared from these ornaments, but that does not suffice to bring man's basis to the fore; on the contrary, the remaining little mass particle cuts itself off from this basis just as any general formal concept does. Admittedly, it is the legs of the Tiller Girls that swing in perfect parallel, not the natural unity of their bodies, and it is also true that the thousands of people in the stadium form one single star. But this star does not shine, and the legs of the Tiller Girls are an abstract designation of their bodies. Reason speaks wherever it disintegrates the organic unity and rips open the natural surface (no matter how cultivated the latter may be); it dissects the human form here only so that the undistorted truth can fashion man anew. But reason has not penetrated the mass ornament; its patterns are *mute*. The *Ratio* that gives rise to the ornament is strong enough to invoke the mass and to expunge all life from the figures constituting it. It is too weak to find the human beings within the mass and to render the figures in the ornament transparent to knowledge. Because this *Ratio* flees from reason and takes refuge in the abstract, uncontrolled nature proliferates under the guise of rational expression and uses abstract signs to display itself. It can no longer transform itself into powerful symbolic forms, as it could among primitive peoples and in the era of religious cults. This power of a language of signs has withdrawn from the mass ornament under the influence of the same rationality that keeps its muteness from bursting open. Thus, bare nature manifests itself in the mass ornament—the very nature that also resists the expression and apprehension of its own meaning. It is the *rational and empty form* of the cult, devoid of any explicit meaning, that appears in the mass ornament. As such, it proves to be a relapse into mythology of an order so great that one can hardly imagine its being exceeded, a relapse which, in turn, again betrays the degree to which capitalist *Ratio* is closed off from reason.

The role that the mass ornament plays in *social life* confirms that it is the spurious progeny of bare nature. The intellectually privileged who, while unwilling to recognize it, are an appendage of the prevailing economic system have not even perceived the mass ornament as a sign of this system. They disavow the phenomenon in order to continue seeking edification at art events that have remained untouched by the reality present in the stadium patterns. The masses who so spontaneously adopted these patterns are superior to their detractors among the educated class to the extent that they at least roughly acknowledge the undisguised facts. The same rationality that controls the bearers of the patterns in real life also governs their submersion in the corporeal, allowing them thereby to immortalize current reality. These days, there is not only *one* Walter Stolzing singing prize songs that glorify body culture.[2] It is easy to see through the ideology of such songs, even if the term "body culture" does indeed justifiably combine two words that belong together by virtue of their respective meanings. The unlimited importance ascribed to the physical cannot be derived from the limited value it deserves. Such importance can be explained only by the alliance that organized physical education maintains with the establishment, in some cases unbeknownst to its front-line supporters. Physical training expropriates people's energy, while the production and mindless consumption of the ornamental patterns divert them from the imperative to change the reigning order. Reason can gain entrance only with difficulty when the masses it ought to pervade yield to sensations afforded by the godless mythological cult. The latter's social meaning is equivalent to that of the Roman *circus games*, which were sponsored by those in power.

6

Among the various attempts to reach a higher sphere, many have been willing to relinquish once again the rationality and level of reality attained by the mass ornament. The bodily exertions in the field of *rhythmic gymnastics*, for example, have aims that go beyond those of personal hygiene—namely, the expression of spruced-up states of the soul—to which instructors of body culture often add world views. These practices, whose impossible aesthetics can be ignored entirely, seek to recapture just what the mass ornament had happily left behind: the organic connection of nature with something the all too modest temperament takes to be soul or spirit—that is, exalting the body by assigning it meanings which emanate from it and may indeed be spiritual but which do not contain the slightest trace of reason. Whereas the mass ornament presents mute nature without any superstructure whatsoever, rhythmic gymnastics, according to its own account, goes further and expropriates the higher mythological levels, thereby strengthening nature's dominance all the more. It is just one example among many other equally hopeless attempts to reach a higher life from out of mass existence. Most of these depend in a genuinely romantic way on forms and contents that have long since succumbed to the somewhat justified critique of capitalist *Ratio*. In their desire to once again give man a link to nature that is more solid than the one he has today, they discover the connection to the higher sphere, not by appealing to a still unrealized reason in this world but by retreating into mythological structures of meaning. Their fate is *irreality*, for when even a glimmer of reason shines through at some point in the world, even the most sublime entity that tries to shield itself from it must perish. Enterprises that ignore our historical context and attempt to reconstruct a form of state, a community, a mode of artistic creation that depends upon a type of man who has already been impugned by contemporary thinking—a type of man who by all rights no longer exists—such enterprises do not transcend the mass ornament's empty and superficial shallowness but flee from its reality. The process leads directly through the center of the mass ornament, not away from it. It can move forward only when thinking circumscribes nature and produces man as he is constituted by reason. Then society will change. Then, too, the mass ornament will fade away and human life itself will adopt the traits of that ornament into which it develops, through its confrontation with truth, in fairy tales.

Werner Mantz, Sinn Department Store, Gelsenkirchen, 1928

On Bestsellers and Their Audience

■ ■ ■

1

The series of articles that appeared in the book review section of the *Frankfurter Zeitung* under the title "What Makes a Book a Bestseller?" has created quite a sensation among readers and in publishing circles. So far the series has had essays on best-selling works by Richard Voβ, Stefan Zweig, [Erich Maria] Remarque, and Frank Thieβ; Jack London was also included, although he does not really belong in this company.[1] The series might well be continued, and I could imagine, for example, that it might provide a context for a discussion of the popularity of biographical works[2] or for an investigation of the grounds for the enthusiastic reception enjoyed by certain novels that have appeared in illustrated newspapers. At any rate, it seems to me that the handful of reviews mentioned above should suffice to elucidate the motives behind the series. The point of view that links all these articles has, however, occasionally been misunderstood. It therefore seems appropriate to detach it from the material and examine it separately. The conclusions developed in the published analyses will be of help in the presentation of this shared point of view.

2

The purpose of the series is already indicated by the very *selection* of the bestsellers. A number of such books—instances of either obvious or disguised dime novels *[Kolportage]*—were excluded from the outset. Dime novels have undoubtedly always enjoyed wide circulation but for reasons that are invariable and that hardly serve to illuminate the present situation. They convey significant contents in distorted form and respond to tendencies that are as unchanging as their compositional structure. Just as the success of dime novels is tied to the satisfaction of long-lasting instincts and deep-seated expectations, the success of other bestsellers is linked to their relationship to sensational events that captivate the general consciousness at the moment. Such literary hits, whose relevance is limited to their topicality, were also excluded from the series. Equally little consideration was given to publications aimed from the start at specific interest groups—that is, works with a marked political slant or books that achieved their effect by making special concessions to the Catholic perspective, for instance, or to the concerns of the proletariat. The reason for the huge sales figures of such works is obvious. In principle, the success of books that do not belong to any of the abovementioned genres could be attributed to the plenitude of their authentic and generally convincing contents. If this were the case, an analysis would merely have to bring these contents to light in order to explain the fame of the works. The fact is, however, that the contents resemble the stars, in that the light which emanates from them may reach us only decades later. There have been times in human history during which many of these stars seemed to have been definitively discovered and therefore did not need to be searched for. But today the heavens are obscured, and who knows if one could even spot them with a giant telescope. Some of Franz Kafka's works have failed to sell even a thousand copies. The popularity of certain literary products must therefore be attributable to causes other than just their encapsulated contents. On the contrary: the more veins of gold they conceal in their depths, the more readily they are generally despised by the masses, which prefer browsing to dowsing.[3] Once the process of erosion has done its work, then everyone can easily grasp—or at least name—the contents that have emerged in the meanwhile . . .

If the success of the works that concern us here cannot in fact be deduced from the meanings they convey, then from what sources does it arise? The question as to what these sources are is all the more justified since it also stumps those who are most interested in the answer. Despite or perhaps because of their routine, experienced professional readers and publishers refrain from predicting the fate of books. They usually remark that popular success cannot be calculated, and if they venture to make a forecast it is no less problematic than a meteorological deliberation about the weather. The case of Remarque is a particularly striking indication of the degree to which experts are at a loss when faced with climatic variations in the sphere of literature. The manuscript of his novel received the most disdainful rejections from distinguished publishers who undoubtedly would have welcomed a smash hit to restore their financial soundness. When finally, after a long voyage, Remarque's novel successfully docked in the Ullstein harbor,[4] even their port inspectors by no means recognized its quantitative value right away. Occasionally the soothsayers become bold and try to generate the weather patterns themselves. I know of a book whose subsequent success may have been due to the push it was given when it was launched. It was meant to come out just after the September elections and was ready for shipping before they took place. But because of the election results the book was withheld, and a few sections that might have offended the apparently strongly nationalist masses were quickly modified. Not only do these events confirm once again that the size of the print run is no standard of value, but they also give an indication of what the real basis for a major book success is. It is the *sign of a successful sociological experiment*, proof that elements have once again been blended in such a way as to correspond to the taste of the anonymous mass of readers. The success of a particular book can be explained only by the needs of these readers, who greedily devour certain components while decisively rejecting others. The success of a particular book cannot be explained by the qualities of the work itself—or if so, only to the extent that they satisfy those needs. And should these qualities perchance contain real traces of substance, they secure the book its fame not in their capacity as contents but rather as responses to widespread social tendencies. The success of a book as a commodity ultimately depends upon the book's ability to satisfy the demands of a broad social stratum of consumers. These demands are much too general and constant for their direction to be determined by private inclinations or mere suggestion. They must be based on the *social conditions* of the consumers.

What is the social standing of the audience that is the vehicle for successful books? Such successes are by no means attributable to proletarian consumers. The proletariat primarily reaches for books whose contents have been given a stamp of approval, or else it reads up on what the bourgeoisie has already read. It is still the *bourgeoisie* that accords certain authors dubious fame and indubitable wealth. But the bourgeoisie is no longer the relatively self-contained class it was before; it has become a multiplicity of strata that extend from the high bourgeoisie down to the proletariat. These strata are a new development that has emerged over the last fifty years and is still undergoing radical transformation. What do we know about them? The fact that we know nothing or next to nothing about them easily explains why it is impossible to ascertain the chances of a book's success in advance. We do have a sort of class instinct, but even that is faulty. As a result, every literary creation that becomes marketable is like a winning number in a lottery.

3

The current *structural transformations in the economic sphere* have above all affected the former middle class, including the petite bourgeoisie. This class, formerly the carrier of bourgeois culture and the mainstay of the reading public, is currently on the verge of dissolution. Among the events that led up to this state of affairs, one might name the inflation and the resulting impoverishment of the small stockholders, the concentration of capital, and the increasing rationalization, not to mention the crisis that has led to further destruction of resources. As a result of all of these factors, those who now occupy the position of the middle class lack certain features—such as limited independence, a modest pension, and so on—which characterized the former middle class. The new middle class has become dependent and has sunk down to a "proletarianoid" existence. My study *Die Angestellten* (The Employees)[5] attempted to document this proletarianization and, furthermore, to demarcate the entire space occupied by the children and grandchildren of the smaller, prewar middle class. From an economic point of view, it is hardly more than a step from them to the workers. Of course, the transformed conditions of production also have an effect on the haute bourgeoisie. Part of this class now consists of employees or civil servants and is in the midst of a reorganization whose effects are hard to gauge.

The structural transformations to which I am referring have given rise, incidentally, to tendencies that for the time being must remain in disguise because they are at odds with outdated but still reigning notions. At issue here are those tendencies that correspond to our factual situation and are already trying to realize themselves everywhere but that are not entirely compatible with the fundamental principles of private enterprise. For example, civil law is increasingly invading the individual sphere and seizing wider authority; the thought of social obligation has become so concrete in reality that it can no longer be effaced; both town and country planning transcend individual egotism; the collectivization of life is increasing. Yet, for the time being, these currents—which take into account both social reality and material imperatives—are far from determining the system in which they are developing. They appear incognito, as it were, so that even if they actually do materialize they do not gain acceptance for what they are, because the prevailing consciousness is accustomed to things being otherwise.

There would be plenty of room available for these currents, however, since many of the *contents of bourgeois consciousness* have been just as *dismantled*[6] as their carriers. Robbed of their economic and social foundations, they can no longer survive. I am thinking of the way in which people have become less and less conscious of social standing—a decline manifest in numerous circles of bureaucrats and employees; of the way in which people have abandoned an individualistic stance, to an extent often clearly visible in practice; and especially of the way in which leading figures in the economy display an *absence of illusion*. It is precisely at the top that a strong disenchantment has set in, and ideas which used to drive the economy are now rhetorical ornaments in ceremonial speeches. The renunciation of contents now dethroned by current conditions is an indication that those threatened with spiritual impoverishment do have a certain sense of realism. But only few people see beyond the tips of their noses. Most of them venerate ideals in art, science, politics, and so on which they have long since seen through in their very own fields.

Is the unmasking of certain ideologies (which many people do not even clearly acknowledge) an indication of the weakening of bourgeois consciousness? In any case, the fact that the higher strata have fallen silent contributes to the radicalization of the younger generation. You can't live on bread alone, particularly when you don't even have any. Even right-wing radicals have partially freed themselves from a bourgeois mindset which they feel does not serve them well. But theirs is an emancipation in the name of irrational powers that are capable of reaching a compromise with the bourgeois powers at any time. The larger masses of the middle class and the intellectuals do not, however, participate in this mythical rebellion, which rightly strikes them as a regression. Rather than allowing themselves to be forced by the spiritual void (which reigns in the upper regions) to break out of the corral of bourgeois consciousness, they instead use all available means to try to preserve this consciousness. They do this less out of real faith than out of fear—a fear of being drowned by the proletariat, of becoming spiritually degraded and losing contact with authentic aspects of culture and education. But where does one find reinforcements for the threatened superstructure? The latter now lacks various material props, and the newly emerged strata that consider themselves part of the bourgeoisie are not its obvious supporters. They do not have any idea where they belong, and are merely defending privileges and perhaps traditions. The important question then is: How are they fortifying their position? Since under the present conditions they cannot simply adopt the inventory of bourgeois consciousness as such, they have to resort to all kinds of alternatives in order to make it seem as if they still wield their former spiritual/intellectual power.

4

In my essay on Frank Thieß I wrote, "Analyses of widely read books are an artifice to investigate social strata whose structure cannot be determined by a direct approach."[7] Indeed, our earlier analyses have already afforded decisive insights into the behavior of the bourgeois classes, which are currently in ferment, and particularly into the (largely unconscious) *measures which they are taking for their own protection.* For it can certainly be assumed that books which are hugely successful are precisely those which either represent or support such measures.

Strong *individualism* guarantees sizable prospects. Consider the following description of the heroes in Richard Voß's novel: "As two mature individuals, they provide moral support for the protest against the tendencies toward collectivization that are becoming increasingly evident today. They are at odds with large parts of the German *Volk* . . . In any case, the popularity of the novel indicates that 'personalities' of the stature of Judith and Father Paulus have at least the same drawing power as portrayals of the man in the street."[8] Both Frank Thieß and Stefan Zweig also focus on the individual. Wherever the individual appears, *tragedy* is inevitable. Such tragedy embeds bourgeois existence in the depths of metaphysics and is therefore very appealing to readers, even in its distorted form, or precisely because of this form. As was remarked of Zweig's novellas, "The worried, fearful person of today, and particularly the person from the upper classes, almost always has to keep his feelings under wraps in the often futile struggle to maintain his standard of living. Such a person grasps . . . eagerly for such stories, because in them the passions play themselves out in an admittedly improbable but therefore all the more magnificent and unrestrained manner. In these stories, the fate of the private individual triumphs even in catastrophe."[9] Since the middle classes undoubtedly perceive their intermediate position as a calamity but nevertheless want to maintain that position under all circumstances, they naturally tend to elevate all calamities into tragic events. The individual who perishes tragically for the sake of an idea is also a constitutive part of an idealist world view, and thus the favorite texts understandably take on a certain *idealism.*

Not authentic idealism, which is a thing of the past, but rather its blurred afterimages. A close reading of Stefan Zweig's prose in fact reveals that some of his sentences unquestionably "have an irresistible effect on many contemporary readers, who want to maintain a faded idealism at any price."[10] This is primarily true, however, of the upper classes, which demand both style and distance. It is the tone that makes the music; and Zweig, as we can see in his novellas, strikes the very tone that resonates among the more cultivated circles, which are haunted by taste, culture, and education. Rather than expensive reserve, the middle class and the impoverished masses in general demand heart, which costs nothing. When people lack all else, *feeling* is everything. It humanizes tragedy without abolishing it and obscures any criticism that might threaten the preservation of outdated contents. Voß tries to make up for the loss in suspense by employing a style that is probably in large part responsible for the book's appeal. It is brimming with the kind of sentimentality (devoid of any literary form) that appeals to the anonymous masses. Remarque also achieves his effect by knowing how to be touching: "This touching quality," explains the essay on his novel, "points . . . sociologically to those classes on whom it had the strongest effect and who determine the success of the book. It is the expression of an intermediate position between acceptance and rebellion—a position that corresponds to a middle-class attitude."[11]

Often the contents that need to be stabilized are not invoked explicitly. Instead, the author will make an attempt to preserve them indirectly; that is, he will avoid encountering them by taking *flight* into some distant realm. If one leaves them alone, they do not crumble so easily. So they are put under a glass cover, and then the ladies and gentlemen go out for a drive. One of the most tempting destinations for such excursions is and remains the realm of the erotic. Concerning Thieß, who goes there often, one reads the following comment: "I believe that many readers are enticed by the erotic sultriness, which is worked in with such abundance. Moreover, one cannot make the slightest substantive objection to it, since it is completely appropriate as a means of presenting the underlying attitude."[12] To some extent, certainly, *geographic adventures* are likewise popular because they distract attention from the spiritual/intellectual ones. Not least among the authors who provide free home delivery of such adventures is Jack London. Analysis of his work shows, however, that what is decisive in his case is his intimate relationship with *nature*. As is proven by the bestsellers, nature is the great refuge for which the masses of readers yearn. Were they to entrust themselves to reason *[Ratio]*, which is not synonymous with nature, the constructs of their consciousness might possibly be threatened, whereas when they retreat into nature they avoid all problematic issues. It matters little whether nature is tragic or demonic—in either case, it is a soft pillow for those who do not want to be awakened. "The heroes in Zweig's novellas run amok.[13] They are mad, bewitched, or enchanted people who, while not responsible for their actions, nevertheless want to demonstrate something through them—something undetermined and secret."[14] In fact, nature in Jack London's works has the best intentions toward people; it is an ideal nature whose call he can follow without concern. He has survived all possible dangers, "but there is no demon that chases him and drives him to the edge of the abyss, like Hamsun's vagabonds; he merely follows his 'nature.' "[15] Unfathomable, this nature is ultimately the limit of all justification. Moreover, it is *mute*—an advantage that just about guarantees its success, for the fans of huge bestsellers, driven by their instinct for self-preservation, desire nothing more fervently than to see embarrassing questions sink into the abyss of silence. Since they rightly or wrongly fear the answers, they insist that barriers be erected far forward, to hinder the advance of knowledge. Their demand reads: *indifference*. It is certainly indifference that is at the root of Remarque's success among the international petite bourgeoisie. As the analysis of his novel explains, "The only discussion of the war in the book gives evidence of this . . . indifference, which is content to state that 'it is even better to have no war at all.' Outrage manifests itself, if anywhere, against low-level authority, and hatred is directed only against self-motivated patriotic civilians—for example, a teacher, who is brutally taken to task for encouraging unfit individuals to enlist voluntarily."[16]

Our analyses thus yield a quite comprehensive picture of the structure of the consciousness of the new bourgeois classes. The latter are

engaged in attempts to prop up certain contents that today lack sufficient support. Using every conceivable means, they strive to avoid the
confrontation of outdated ideals with contemporary social reality, a
juxtaposition they evade by taking flight in all directions and into every
hideout. They prefer to lie in the bosom of nature, where they can
renounce language and defend themselves against reason *[Ratio]*, whose
aim is the eradication of mythological institutions and surviving forms
of consciousness.

5

Those who want to change things must be informed about what needs
to be changed. The use value of the articles we published in our series
lies in their ability to facilitate intervention into social reality.[17]

Germaine Krull, Woman and car, mid-1920s

The Biography as an Art Form of the New Bourgeoisie

■■■

If prior to World War I the biography was a rare work of erudition, today it is a widespread literary product which has been adopted as a form of expression by the literati, the prose artists. In France, England, and Germany these writers are portraying the lives of the few remaining public figures that have not already been dealt with by Emil Ludwig.[1] Indeed, soon there will be scarcely any major politician, general, or diplomat who has not been commemorated by a more or less ephemeral monument. Poets, however, are more likely to remain available as subjects for such commemoration, since they are not nearly as much in favor as those names which have played a decisive role in the course of history. This is a striking shift in comparison with earlier preferences; whereas formerly it was biographies of artists that flourished in cultivated circles, today's heroes are for the most part taken from history, and their biographies are printed by belletristic publishers en masse for the masses.

There have been attempts to simply dismiss as a mere fashion the growing popularity of biography as a genre—a tendency that has been taking root in Western Europe for some time now. It is no more a fashion than war novels were. Instead, its unfashionable foundations lie in the events of world history during the past fifteen years. I use the expression "world history" reluctantly, because it easily induces a state of intoxication that is at best appropriate only when world history really becomes the history of everybody's world. On the radio, for example, when people hear the oft-repeated announcements "This is Paris" or

"This is London," the mere mention of such cosmopolitan cities serves the same function as cheap booze. Nevertheless, it cannot be denied that the world war, the political and social changes it engendered, and not least the new technological discoveries as well have indeed shaken up and transformed the daily life of so-called cultured people. These developments have had the same effect on the domain at issue here as the theory of relativity has had in physics. Just as, thanks to Einstein, our spatio-temporal system has become a limit concept, the self-satisfied subject has become a limit concept thanks to the object lesson of history. In the most recent past, people have been forced to experience their own insignificance—as well as that of others—all too persistently for them to still believe in the sovereign power of any one individual. It is precisely this sovereign power, however, which is the premise of the bourgeois literature produced during the years preceding the war. The unified structure of the traditional novel form reflects the supposed unity of character, and its problematic is always an individual one. Today the creative artist has once and for all lost faith in the objective meaning of any one individual system of reference. But when this fixed coordinate grid disappears, all the curves plotted on it lose their pictorial form as well. The writer can no more appeal to his self than he can depend on the world for support, because these two structures determine each other. The former is relativized, and the contents and figures of the latter have been thrown into an opaque orbit. It is no accident that one speaks of the "crisis" of the novel. This crisis resides in the fact that the reigning compositional model for the novel has been invalidated by the abolition of the contours of the individual and its antagonists. (This is not to say, however, that the novel has become an artistic genre of the past. It might conceivably be resurrected in a new form appropriate to the confused world, which means that confusion itself would acquire epic form.)

In the midst of this world which has become blurred and ungraspable, the passage of *history* becomes a primary element. The same history that has gotten us into such a mess emerges as solid land in a sea of amorphousness and unrepresentability. For the contemporary writer, who neither can nor wants to tackle it directly like the historian, history is condensed in the lives of its highly visible heroes. These heroes become the subject of biographies not because there is a cult of hero worship but because there is a need for a legitimate literary form. Indeed, the course of a life that has had an effect on history seems to contain all the component parts that make it possible under present conditions to construct a work of prose. The existence that it captures is a crystallization of the work of history, whose inviolability is beyond doubt. And isn't the objectivity of the representation guaranteed by the historical significance of the actual figure? Literary biographers believe that this historical figure ultimately provides the support they had been seeking in vain elsewhere, the valid frame of reference that absolves them from subjective arbitrariness. Its binding character is very obviously due to its factual nature. The central character in a biography really did live, and there is documentary proof of all aspects of this life. The gist of a prose work, which used to be provided by the invented narrative, is now regained through an authenticated fate. This fate also functions simultaneously as the guarantor of the compositional form. Every historical figure already contains its own form: it begins at a specific moment, develops through its conflicts with the world, takes on contours and substance, draws back in old age, and passes away. Thus, the author is not obligated to come up with an individual formal schema, since he is given one delivered right to his door that is as obligatory for him as it would be for anyone else. This is attractive not so much because it makes things easy but because it relieves the author's conscience, if we assume that this is not one of those biographies produced in assembly-line fashion to make a lot of money. For today the biography can compete with the novel only because—unlike the latter, which is free floating—it deals with materials that determine its form. The moral of the biography is that, in the chaos of current artistic practices, it is the only seemingly necessary prose form.

It is a prose form of the established *bourgeoisie,* which of course has to deny any knowledge and all problems of form that threaten its continued existence. The bourgeoisie feels the power of history in its bones and is all too aware that the individual has become anonymous. Yet these insights, which impose themselves on the bourgeoisie with the force of physiognomic experiences, do not lead it to draw any conclusions capable of illuminating the current situation. In the interest of self-preservation, the bourgeoisie shies away from confronting that situation. The literary elite of the new bourgeoisie makes no serious attempt to penetrate the materialist dialectic; neither is it willing openly to face the impact of the lowly masses or to dare take even a single step in any direction beyond the border it has reached, out into the other world of class. Yet it could only touch ground at all if, stripped of all protective ideological covering, it were to place itself at the breaking point of our societal construct and, from this advanced position, tackle the social forces that embody reality today. It is here and nowhere else that one can glean the insights which could perhaps guarantee a true art form. For the validity that this art form requires can be ascribed solely to the expression of the most advanced consciousness, which can develop only here. It is out of such an advanced consciousness and the support it provides that a literary form can arise. Then again, it may not, in which case literary creation would simply be denied to us at present. (If it was claimed above that confusion itself might be able to gain epic form, it should now be added that this can occur only on the basis of the most advanced consciousness, which sees through that confusion.) As the literary form of the new bourgeoisie, the biography is a sign of *escape* or, to be more precise, of evasion.[2] In order not to expose themselves through insights that question the very existence of the bourgeoisie, writers of biographies remain, as if up against a wall, at the threshold to which they have been pushed by world events. Instead of crossing this threshold, they flee back into the bourgeois hinterlands, a fact that can be demonstrated through an analysis of a cross-section of biographies. Although such biographical works do contemplate the workings of history, they get so lost in their contemplation that they can no longer find their way back to the present. Their choice of subjects from among the great figures of history is hardly discriminating and in any case does not grow out of an understanding of the current situation. They want to get rid of all the psychology that was so characteristic of prewar prose; but despite the seeming objectivity of their subject matter, they still employ to some extent the old psychological categories. They throw a suspect individualism out the back door, and then escort officially endorsed individuals through the main entrance back into the bourgeois house. They thereby also achieve a second objective: the unarticulated rejection of an authority that arises out of the depths of the masses. The literary biography is a borderline phenomenon that stays behind the border.

It is also more than simply escape. As surely as the bourgeoisie today finds itself in a period of transition, so too every one of its achievements has a double meaning. The very achievements by which the bourgeoisie aims to defend its existence unintentionally confirm that this transition has taken place. Like emigrants gathering up their personal belongings, bourgeois literature gathers the effects of a household that will soon have to vacate its current site. The motif of escape, to which the majority of biographies owe their existence, is eclipsed by the motif of *redemption*. If there is a confirmation of the end of individualism, it can be glimpsed in the museum of great individuals that today's literature puts on a pedestal. And the indiscriminate manner in which this literature seizes on any and all statesmen is evidence both of an inability to make correct period-specific selections and, equally, of the redeemer's hurry. The task is to provide pictures for an exhibition space where a type of memory, for which each picture has the same value, can indulge itself. No matter how questionable one or another biography might be, the shimmer of departure lingers upon their community.

So far as I can see, there is only one biographical work that is fundamentally different from all other remaining biographies: *Trotsky's*.[3] It violates the conditions imposed on the literary biography. Here the description of the life of the historical individual is not a means to evade an understanding of our situation; rather, it serves only to reveal that situation. This is why, in this self-portrayal, the individual who takes shape is different from the one aimed at in bourgeois literature. It is a type of individual which has already been superseded, in that it does not claim to have a reality of its own but becomes real only through its transparency with regard to reality. This new type of individual stands outside the haze of ideologies: it exists only to the degree that, in the interest of pressing and generally recognized imperatives, it has sublated itself.

Erich Comeriner, "Berlin, Friedrichstraße," ca. 1930

Revolt of the Middle Classes

AN EXAMINATION OF THE *TAT* CIRCLE

■ ■ ■

1

The journal *Die Tat*[1] has a significant readership today, particularly among intellectuals of the middle classes. This can be explained not only by the fact that the *Tat* Circle consciously advocates the practical and ideological interests of these classes, but also by the very manner of its confrontation. Its format is of a sort to which the German intelligentsia has become unaccustomed.

"Listen to the youth that follows the National Socialists or the Communists today. It is the best human material Germany has ever had."[2] This sort of statement demonstrates that the articles published in *Die Tat* are based on an authentic and broad-based experience of the solidarity of the destitute German people. In this respect they are different from numerous other analyses of the contemporary situation, which are dominated now by party-line imperatives and interest-group preferences, now by theoretical constructions that fail to take into account the particular obligations of daily existence. Building on their fundamental experience, the staff of *Die Tat* also attempts to become concretely aware of the concrete situation. And no matter how questionable Fried's[3] interpretations of the economic situation might be, it is healthy ordinary fare (though lacking even the slightest nutritional value) compared to the idealistic ostentation still being served to the younger generation in books and lecture halls. The will to renounce idealism and get involved with the things themselves ultimately gives rise to attempted solutions that go beyond the mere treatment of tactical problems and seek to grasp the situation more or less strategically, based on an overall position. It still remains to be seen whether these solutions are really solutions. What is certain, however, is that a great many people who see the material and ideational decline occurring in front of their very eyes feel that they can take heart from *Die Tat*'s current views.

In light of the seriousness and consequences of *Die Tat*, an examination of this journal is doubly urgent, in the interest of its readers as well as in the interest of those who write for it. From the outset, however, I will refrain from giving central importance to Fried's economic positions and to the special program which, as is well known, demands that Germany adopt, among other things, a particular form of planned economy, autarchy, an orientation toward southeast Europe, and the support of Soviet Russia.[4] Much more decisive is an analysis of the stance that gives rise to the various thoughts and proposals, since the coherence of the results is tied to the coherence of that stance itself. In one of his essays Zehrer[5] writes, "There has never been a new movement that was not driven *ad absurdum* in its early phases by the seeming rationality of an old language serving the interests of the conservative and traditional powers."[6] This observation is entirely appropriate if it is meant to ward off objections that claim to strike at the heart of a movement by criticizing its conceptual expressions. It should not be used, however, to exonerate the language of *Die Tat*, whose fluent formulations are anything but the helpless babbling that, according to Zehrer, is supposedly characteristic of every new movement. For better or for worse, we will have to accord this language quite a bit of importance . . . Unfortunately, it is equally impossible to avoid bringing *Die Tat*'s views into confrontation with reason, something the *Tat* Circle does not hold in great esteem. I believe, however, that one can safely expose oneself to the dangers involved in the employment of such reason: on the one hand because argumentation is possible only if the rights of reason are acknowledged, and on the other hand because whether intentionally or unintentionally even *Die Tat* not infrequently has recourse to, and even expressly calls upon, the very faculty of reason it so disparages.

Let us anticipate some of the principal conclusions of the following analysis, which is based on the journal's output during this past year. The guiding ideas of the *Tat* Circle are the precise reflection of the difficult situation of the middle classes. They point to a stance that is essentially unreal and full of contradictions. Because of their unproductive confusion, these ideas do not provide any kind of a solution at all.

2

Experience provides *Die Tat* with the concept of the *Volk*, which it postulates as an irreducible conceptual foundation. One minute there is talk of "the *völkisch* thought of totality," and the next minute public institutions are inspected to determine their "proximity to the *Volk*." According to this romantically employed concept, the *Volk* seems to be something that has arisen organically and is thus opposed to all theories which are liberal in the broadest sense, meaning that they posit the individual as the basis of the community. On the other hand, it is equally opposed to the modern concept of the masses: "We think not . . . in terms of masses but in terms of people and *Völker*."[7] Just what is at stake in the reference to "people" will be explored later on.

In light of this initial orientation, the important role played by the concept of space is hardly surprising. A *Volk* presents itself physically in space. This explains the barely concealed satisfaction behind the remark that "today the world is disintegrating into individual, closed, national spaces";[8] thus the programmatic call for autarchy. The notion of space dominates *Die Tat* so thoroughly that Zehrer even breaks down the overall space of the *Volk* into subdivisions, to which he, like Nadler, attributes formative power.[9] As Zehrer explains, "We affirm the landscape as a self-contained space that has its own very particular type of existence and is tied to blood, earth, and destiny."[10] The smallest geographic cell is without doubt the family home. In any case, the concept of space expresses a will to the organic which is directly opposed to the atomizing tendency of liberalism and its type of internationalism.

In temporal terms, the *Volk* asserts itself as a state. It manifests itself, as in Hegel, as the "total state"—a concept adopted by Carl Schmitt which obviously draws its pathos from its rejection of the "night-watchman state."[11] According to the demands of *Die Tat*, the *Volk* and its organizations are to be "integrated into" this total state. In Fried's formulation, what is at issue is "the shift from the primacy of economy to the primacy of the state."[12] At another point, one finds the following claim about professions: "For us a profession is a life's task which itself encompasses in a surveyable space . . . the imbrication of the individual and the state."[13] Similarly, the federalist principle is realized only "when individual statehood is a true means of integration into the whole."[14] These stipulations all posit the ideal state not as a constructive, rational unity but as an irrational living unity whose elements join together to constitute it, so to speak, on their own. This is a romantic conception of the state that strongly emphasizes the organic element.

What is being aspired to here is an order of things that is almost the exact opposite of the sort demanded by the Enlightenment. At the very least, it is extremely antiliberal. Anyone who, like the *Tat* Circle, considers it "calamitous" to have even a single "drop of liberalism in one's blood"[15] naturally must also hate the intellect, since, after all, it too is identified with reason, depending on one's needs. The intellect is considered to be liberalism's chief weapon and, since *Die Tat* rightly fears that it would come off badly if it tried to combat liberalism with its own weapons, it prefers to use other, more violent ones. "One can oppose this reason," writes Zehrer, "first of all, only with a new faith, and faith can never encounter its opponent dialectically, since, if it follows the opponent into his terrain, it will always be the weaker."[16] But how does a faith that refuses to explain itself establish itself in the real world? Zehler's primitive answer is: "The only argument that does not fit into the framework of the liberalist system of reason and discussion is the sword. The sword and the fist!" In a word, *Die Tat*'s agents *[Täter]* are arming themselves against reason, lowering their visors in order to avoid, at all costs, catching a glimpse of their arguments, and seeking salvation in barbarism. In their blind rage, they succeed in making reason responsible for events in which it is innocent of all involvement.

"Reason!" Zehrer cries. "In the name of this reason millions of people have died." A closer investigation would presumably reveal that the very forces of unreason [*Unvernunft*] which Zehrer himself invoked were responsible for unleashing the world war.

Still, if *Die Tat* is not fighting under the sign of reason, it is nevertheless following some other guiding star. Zehrer gives the following definition: "A new faith, a new myth will replace the liberal system." The concept of myth, which is emphasized in the publications of the *Tat* Circle as strongly as the idea of a planned economy, emerges from the waters of *Lebensphilosophie* and is developed with reference to Sorel.[17] The great significance accorded the concept of myth is evidently due to the fact that people no longer have confidence in the restraining effects of rational knowledge, but feel compelled to replace it with resplendent images that are constituted in some secret manner out of irrational forces. But then, instead of revealing any of these images, Zehrer unfortunately restricts himself merely to calling for them. Indeed, the only thing that is certain is simply that Zehrer views the middle classes as an outstanding medium for the myth that he has been proclaiming: "These classes cannot experience their solidarity with the larger community, with the *Volk* and the nation, by means of a union, club, class, or any other kind of organization. They can experience this solidarity only through the ideal that is, in myth." One might perhaps add that this myth has to be a national one. In an unambiguous reference to this imperative, Zehrer explains that the task of the future is "to create a new *Volk*-community under the aegis of the myth of a new nation."[18]

Volk, state, myth—these thoroughly interrelated concepts refer to a substantive reality. By virtue of its orientation toward this material reality, *Die Tat* is also qualified to undertake a substantive critique of the reigning conditions. Indeed, it turns away from the extant state of things only because it is essentially unbearable. To me, it seems beyond doubt that the influence which the *Tat* Circle has gained is not least due to this critique of its time. As might be expected, given the way this stance has been characterized here, it is directed first and foremost against the material poverty [*Substanzarmut*] that is becoming increasingly widespread under the current regime. I leave it open as to whether the presentation of that poverty necessarily has to proceed by means of the common denominator of the abovementioned concepts, or whether it could not do at least as well starting out with other concepts, such as that of class. For the moment, what is important is only that by using its own categories, *Die Tat* was able to diagnose significant deficiencies. I am thinking not only of Fried, who forces contemporary distortions of capitalist management into his alfresco paintings in an admittedly very violent manner, but also of statements of lesser scope that strike at the heart of current conditions. These correct, for example, the vulgar, overly optimistic notion of profession, expose the powers that are flourishing behind a protective federalist façade, and accurately analyze the situation of some of the parties. Probably the most profound of *Die Tat*'s critiques, however, is its perpetual protest against uncommitted thinking. Yet it does harm to its own position because it often goes astray and charges into battle under the wrong flag. How irresponsible is its formulation of the claim that Jewish intelligence is lacking in constructive skills. How malicious, how utterly malicious, is the following line: "Einstein, the advertising genius of modesty, dodders resolutely around the world, using the weapon of relativity theory to fight for conscientious military objection and Zionism."[19] Besides such lapses—which are unworthy of a serious journal—there is also the constant confusion of this thought with "liberalist reason," or even with reason as such, with which it really has nothing in common. The language of *Die Tat*, which Zehrer justifies in advance as a product of extenuating circumstances, is not helpless but imprecise: the actual object of its attack merely shimmers obscurely through the haze which it itself has produced. This object is *Ratio*, which denies its origins and no longer recognizes any limits, as opposed to reason in general and "liberalist reason" in particular, which is, after all, based on faith in humanity. This unleashed *Ratio*, which, moreover, cannot simply be designated as intellect, has so little in common with reason that, like a demon of nature *[Naturdämon]*, it overpowers everything reasonable. And it is precisely this powerlessness of reason which enables *Ratio* to prevail so unrestrainedly today. Blind *Ratio:* it is this that inspires profit-lust to undertake its transactions, that produces the irresponsibility of a certain type of yellow journalism, that is to blame for the precipitancy of the process of rationalization and for all those calculations of a degenerate economy which take every factor into account except man. Just as it has unthinkingly created a technological apparatus which we face like the sorcerer's apprentice, unable to exorcise its enchanted elements, it is also *Ratio* that has corroded the bonds that formerly maintained the cohesion of society. I have tried to sketch the terrible consequences of this *Ratio*-induced disintegration, above all for the middle classes, in my book *Die Angestellten (White-Collar Workers)*.[20] Having been emptied of all substance, these classes are now no longer subject to anything other than the binding neutrality of contentless thought. It is into the muteness of such thinking that the severely shaken economic and social system in which we currently live has taken refuge.

3

Die Tat turns its back on the conditions it criticizes. Does it go beyond critique? Can it do justice to the substantial reality aimed at by its fundamental concepts?

The answer to all these questions is no. For the way *Die Tat*'s contributors constantly refer to the *Volk*, state, myth, and so forth clearly shows that what are at issue are not substantialities that they have experienced but ones that they are yearning for. As is demonstrated by the use to which these substantialities are put, they are not being presupposed but are instead being called for: they are not the point of departure but rather the objective that must be achieved. In other words, the reality that means so much to *Die Tat* does not exist at all, except perhaps as a goal. But talk of substantive contents is meaningful only if these can be shown to exist. To proclaim them as some sort of plan to be brought about by mere exertion of will is to make a demand which is doomed to be unfulfilled from the start. A substantiality either exists or it does not. Someone who employs the concept of such a substantiality without actually having it in hand does not thereby gain that substantiality by means of the concept, but instead reveals something else entirely—namely, that the concept is a pure reaction. All the positively charged concepts employed by

Die Tat are little more than reactions to the negatively marked system which *Die Tat* subsumes under the general term "liberalism." Strictly speaking, these concepts are unreal, which is to say that they do not correspond to a reality that, after all, would have to exist if one were to appeal to it legitimately. The significance of these concepts is fully exhausted in their status as symptoms of a countermovement that one can without doubt describe as romantic.

The fact that the *Tat* Circle does not count on the appearance of a leader *[Führer]* but instead puts its hopes in the creative capacities of a spiritual *[geistige]* elite, which it believes really exists, bespeaks a certain thoughtfulness. It is quite likely that, above all, it considers itself part of the very elite that it wishes for, and indeed the *Tat* Circle really is the cream of the German youth. Still, it does not refrain from glorifying the eventual leader right now. Zehrer dreams of the awaited one as follows: "The yearning for this individual has smoldered among the *Volk* for more than a decade. Let's not delude ourselves: the moment the first sharp but just word of command from a really personal will hits the German *Volk*, people will fall into line and close ranks . . . and this *Volk* will breathe a sigh of relief because it will once again know where it is going."[21] The German *Volk* will certainly not do any of these things because—and so long as—good political will discharges itself in the yearning for a leader. The emergence and endurance of this leader depend entirely on a correct and constructive understanding of the situation: if such a leader relies solely on his status as leader, without grasping the situation (Clemenceau, Lloyd George, and so on),[22] he will disappear again. Yet instead of trying to create (insofar as this is possible) the conditions necessary for a leader to appear in the first place, Zehrer glorifies the leader as such in advance. This is a very widespread strategy, which obviously arises out of an aversion toward the parliamentarianism of liberal democracy but does not achieve anything whatsoever. On the contrary! By spending one's time singing hymns to the leader before he has even arrived, one neglects precisely to prepare the way for him and might even fall prey to charlatans. Anticipating a leader does not hasten his advent but instead prevents him from approaching. The only thing that might possibly facilitate his arrival is a constant inquiry into what would need to take place for it to happen. And it is only the already apparent leader and not the anticipated one who can aspire to enter into the consciousness of the *Volk* as an image. The haloed image of Lenin is the end and not the beginning of a leader's career, the product of actions based on knowledge.

Even the concept of myth, under whose sign the new state-*Volk* is meant to constitute itself, is also a powerless counterconcept. Born of the rebellion against a denatured liberalism, it wants to establish a more effective force in place of reason, which has supposedly failed. But myth cannot be established. It is, according to Bachofen, "nothing other than the representation of the experiences of a *Volk* in the light of religious faith."[23] Or, as Carl Albrecht Bernoulli remarks in the annotations to his Bachofen edition, "Myth is either valid or invalid, depending on whether or not it proves effective for us. In any case, whether it 'is' or 'is not' depends on our emotional world."[24] This is only apparently contradicted by Mussolini's speech prior to his march on Rome—a speech in which he credited Fascism with having *created* the myth of "the nation." Indeed, even Carl Schmitt, who—not without sympathy—cites this passage from the speech in his book *The Crisis of Parliamentary Democracy*, calls the events to which it was linked "an example of the irrational power of the national myth."[25] It still remains to be established to what degree the so-called fascist myth is not simply the ideological superstructure of specific material and social relations and whether it could survive solely on the basis of its own irrational strength. At one point Zehrer himself unintentionally reveals how weak the foundation is on which the *Tat* Circle's myth program is based. Regarding Communism he writes, "One must not, however, underestimate its position either. It has a myth—the alleged model of Russia—that is . . . independent of Communism's theoretical content and that functions exclusively to gather the masses and to take power."[26] We will ignore entirely the frivolousness with which the relationship between theory and subsequent practice, between the slogan and its realization, is trivialized here by this worshiper of the irrational. The question we must raise is: What factors does Communism cite as being responsible for engendering its myth? The answer: the very theory that Zehrer so despises. It is only through the power of their theoretical insights that the Russian Communists were able to make Russia into that which the *Tat* Circle—but not Communism itself—considers to be a myth. And even if, as Carl Schmitt (in accordance with Sorel) explains in his previously mentioned book, national energies were responsible for the victory of the Russian Revolution, it was not these that were invoked; rather, what was—and still is—being appealed to is socialism. From which it follows that perhaps even today a myth can still arise out of the realization of insights, but that the straightforward demand for myth is meaningless. One can thus characterize *Die Tat*'s appeal to myth as a reaction without content.

The same holds true for the concept of space. For example, Zehrer's claim that the spiritual elite must necessarily gather in the countryside elevates an incidental feature into a determining factor. For although it is true that a new doctrine—which is the sole means to define an elite—spreads easily among neighbors, this hardly makes neighborly relations a precondition for the creation of this elite. According to similar logic, *Die Tat* consistently treats space as something of great importance in itself, whereas in reality it acquires meaning only through the substantialities that are realized within it and that this space can of course preserve, transform, and preclude. This is a cult of space that is quite obviously directed against a type of thinking—not uncommon in liberal circles—which tends toward internationalism, without also establishing fully characteristic spatial features. By setting up space as an absolute, however, this countermeasure largely over-shoots its goal and creates an inflated, hollow concept that makes space into a bugbear. I cannot resist giving an example of Fried's space-art, an example taken from an essay in the May issue titled "The Restructuring of the World": "The capitalist Occident . . . will probably also lose its hold on South America and Australia, where the nationalist movement is pushing more and more toward isolation, disengagement from the world economy, and autonomy. It seems possible that South Africa will then also drop out. In North America, the ripening conflict between the debt-ridden farmers in the West and the industrial and financial powers in the East will ultimately lead to an economic symbiosis similar to the one between central Europe and Russia. As a result, all of North America (including Canada) is sure to become completely self-sufficient and will shut itself off from the rest of the world. This leaves etc. . . ."[27] The unreality of this billboard architecture is patently obvious. It brands the economy that manifests itself in a space as simply a function of this space and misrepresents the need for customs boundaries as a virtue of autarchy.

Most frightening of all is *Die Tat*'s reaction to the meaningfulness that liberalism—and not only liberalism—ascribes to events. As much as I can understand the tendency to turn away from a situation that seems to have lost all meaning, the way in which Fried moves into the void of barbarism—fully aware of what he is doing—strikes me as unacceptable. He, too, claims to be searching for meaning (albeit not the meaning of what *should be* but rather the meaning of what *is*), yet this explanation does not prevent him from citing with approval the following line by Spengler: "World history is the world court: . . . it has always sacrificed truth and justice to might and race, and has condemned to death men and peoples for whom truth was more important than deeds and justice more essential than power."[28] It would be easy to refute Spengler's statement with examples (the Dreyfus trial comes to mind) that prove precisely the opposite. What is of interest here, however, is only the fact that by adopting this thesis Fried betrays the same impoverished sense of reality that *Die Tat* manifests whenever it makes claims about the new reality. For the line he puts forth as reality—the one claiming that throughout world history, truth and justice have always fallen victim to might and race—does not in fact arise from a contemporary relation to reality, but is much more the fruit of a purely historical perspective. It is the same perspective that *Die Tat* refers to elsewhere in the following quite justified terms: "Very basically, from an ethical point of view, one could ask whether the historical perspective is not at its very root unhistorical, in that it refuses to enter the dialectic of history and thereby become truly 'historical.' "[29] Were Fried to enter into the dialectic of history, he would recognize that might and race regularly triumph only when in the service of those doctrines that also embody truth and justice. He would also recognize, by contrast, that might and race are doomed to fail if all they seek is to wield power as such. Fried extricates himself from this dialectic. As a result of such unrealistic behavior, he takes a dubious historical meditation as a maxim for action, and exaggerates the natural presuppositions of substantive behavior into a substance in its own right. His position is nothing but opposition to every sort of meaningfulness, and is itself as devoid of content as only unilluminated nature can be.

Die Tat thus does not counter liberalism's reality by constructing a different, more substantial one; instead it only makes demands for a reality that cannot be demanded. If one were malicious, one could enlist one of the *Tat* Circle's idols in the fight against it: I'm thinking of Spengler. He has written somewhere that the Nordic soul, having exhausted its inner capacities to the point that it retained only "the drive, the creative passion, a spiritual mode of existence without substance," had to at least pretend that its activity had some content. "Ibsen called it the lie of life," Spengler continues, "and there is an element of that in all the spiritual activity of Western European civilization, to the extent that it orients itself toward a religious, artistic, philosophical future, an immaterial goal, a third *Reich*, though all the while in the uttermost depths there is a dull feeling that insists on being heard, a feeling that all this activity is an illusion, the desperate self-deception of a historical soul . . . *Bayreuth* is based on this lie of life in its desire to be something, in contrast to Pergamon, which really *was* something."[30] Spengler actually made these observations (whose substance as observations cannot be examined here) in reference to socialism, but they describe much more accurately the conceptual realm of *Die Tat*. It, too, wants something that once really was something and that, I should add, cannot really become something so long as it is the goal of an act of will.

4

If only the concepts of the *Tat* Circle were simply unrealistic—but they also suffer from the affliction of contradiction. Not the unavoidable sort of contradiction that arises at the limits of every closed system, where its presuppositions lie, but rather the type that dissolves the system from within. There are good reasons why, like exorcists chasing witches, *Die Tat*'s staffers are suspicious of liberalism everywhere, counting the number of calamitous drops that people have of it in their blood. *Die Tat* considers conservatism and socialism to be completely contaminated. And what is Russian Bolshevism? "It is liberalism in Marxist clothing!"[31] Fascism is likewise accused of trafficking with this evil and must put up with the reputation of being infested with a host of liberal ideas. In short, *Die Tat* wants to be more Catholic than the pope, assuming that one is even allowed to mention him in the context of Fascism. The manic need to harass and chase liberalism into the most remote recesses allows one to conclude indisputably that this is, in psychoanalytic terms, something like a symptom of repression. People pursue liberalism with such hatred because it is something they discover within themselves. And indeed *Die Tat* unconsciously contains so much of it that it spews forth from all sides. It will not allow itself to be hidden: the liberalism turned away at the front gate is always graciously invited to enter through the back door. And even if it slips in under a different name, there is no way to mistake it. Its presence within a realm of thought hostile to it is, however, just further evidence of the latter's powerlessness.

At decisive points, the concept of the individual appears in formulations that are at odds with the conscious position of the *Tat* Circle. For example, what is aspired to in the struggle against Americanism and capitalism is not only a revival of the notion of profession but also the construction of a "new culture of personality." In the essay "Where Are We Headed?"—the same text that contains *Die Tat*'s program—one also finds the following italicized sentence: "*What is at issue is the person. And the decision as to where we are headed and how long it will take will be made by each individual person and nowhere else!*"[32] What domain do these stipulations come from, and how have they ended up here? They stem from an individualism of an idealistic sort, bourgeois concepts if you like, which in any case cannot under any circumstances be united with the demands of an "integral nationalism" and a "total state." For the realization of the latter is at the very least tied to the unity of the general and the subjective will. But since, as was stated explicitly, the decision depends only on the individual and on nothing else, then the will of the state is thereby excluded from the outset—and this holds even where the model of the state is articulated in organic terms. This autonomous individual is much more likely to be the bearer of the old liberal system than of an autarchy. Liberalism's ability to capture the place of honor in a thoroughly antiliberal conceptual framework thus testifies to the power of inherited liberal ideas. As we learned from the drastic example provided by Russia, what is necessary in order for people to be "integrated into" the sovereign state is precisely the suspension of the individual's autonomy. And although *Die Tat*'s people accuse the Soviet Union of liberalism, the Soviets understand much better than they that the construction of a national state economy cannot tolerate a "culture of personality." To call openly for such a culture of personality and simultaneously to develop the concept of the total state is in any case nonsense.

Die Tat does not limit itself simply to shifting the locus of decision to the individual. It also develops a rather clearly defined picture of the individual's future existence: "He will have less to do than he does currently, since he will no longer be employed eight hours a day. As a result, he will have more time than he does now. He will be able to lie in the sun and in the open air. He will have more peace and quiet, and more security. And he may once again take pleasure in occupying himself with material of serious spiritual value, for which he today has neither the peace and quiet nor the time."[33] Who is this person, behind whom is a weekend house shimmering in the distance? It is the individualist petit bourgeois who grew up under liberalism, who leaves the state be, and who is certainly less suited than anyone to create the new order *Die Tat* desires. Zehrer himself says outright that this individual lacks vigor. Speaking elegiacally of the Russians, he states at one point that "the actual driving force of this new economic state is at its core a great revolutionary vigor, which, however, we can no longer copy from the Russians, for we are at the end of this liberal vigor. Do we still believe in technology? Do we still believe in the machine? Do we still believe in the ecstasy of the great freedom that takes hold of a person freed from all constraints and thrown into the present? No—we do not believe in these things any longer. We have become tired of them!"[34] I admit that after all this I can no longer even imagine the birth of a new myth. It is preposterous to assign to the individual something approaching a metaphysical significance and in the same breath to extol a myth that leaves no space whatsoever for the individual. Furthermore, when this individual is defined as a tired petit bourgeois who lacks not only liberalist vigor but also, apparently, any drive whatsoever, then the myth that this individual will supposedly bring about becomes utterly unthinkable. Spengler, too, speaks of the fatigue of Western man. But he is incomparably more logical than *Die Tat:* he attributes this fatigue to the Caesarist form of domination, whose presuppositions include neither a state *Volk* nor a myth.[35] By invoking myth and nevertheless maintaining the concept of the individual, *Die Tat* is guilty of a contradiction that could hardly be more complete.

The individual—the centerpiece of authentic liberalism—is also the vehicle by which reason makes its entrance into *Die Tat*'s world picture. Despite their best intentions to beat it back with the sword, they not only successfully employ reason on certain occasions in the essays devoted to critique, but even go so far as to demand that it prove itself effective. Having established (in *Die Tat*'s November issue) that the terrain would soon be available "for a new reconstruction and a throwing off of chains," Zehrer continues as follows: "We have an enemy that is not prepared for this moment, that is busily struggling to maintain its own cadres but lacks all theoretical preparation."[36] Theoretical preparation—what better way to promote this than through the use of reason? Indeed, reason is all the more essential since the program envisages a state-controlled planned economy. Here contradiction penetrates to the very core, for the concept of planning is utterly at odds with that of growth. Thus, if *Die Tat* on the one hand is advocating a state that arises through organic growth, yet on the other hand wants to achieve a kind of socialism by means of a planned economy, it is aiming at something that is simply impossible. It throws reason out of the temple of the *Volk*'s state and simultaneously invites it into the offices of the state economy. This is not *one* but two movements, and they are going in opposite directions. The first, the primary movement, is the reaction against liberalism; the second, which aims at a planned economy that can be realized only by means of rational organization, marks the appearance of the principle of reason, which is all too reductively designated "liberalist." I have shown above that *Die Tat*'s people constantly confuse today's uncommitted thinking (which really cannot be called liberal) with reason itself. One of the many consequences of this confusion is that they believe they can dismiss the Soviet regime as liberal. The basis for this confusion, however, is that they are not only protesting against liberalism but are also attempting to repudiate the *logos*. In the end, what one sees in *Die Tat* is nature rebelling against spirit. And it is only thanks to the indecision of the rebels that they tangle themselves in contradictions and, despite their retreat into the domain of the natural, repeatedly allow the individual and reason to gain entrance.

5

It is the dispossessed middle classes that are rebelling. "The Key Position of the Middle Classes" is the headline of the first section of an essay by Horst Grüneberg that opens with the following explanation: "No one can overlook the decisive fact that there can be no government without the old and the new middle classes."[37] And *Die Tat* adopts the concerns of these middle classes so fully that it orients all its principal concepts toward them. It derives the call for myth, as I have mentioned, from the same middle-class imperatives that also provide it with a foundation for its model of the ideal state. As formulated in the essay just cited, "Positive middle-class politics can only be a will to a new order, and a will to the state."[38] I should note, incidentally, that since the *Tat* Circle has such clear insight into the affiliation of certain programs with certain social strata, it should easily be able to recognize the legitimacy of the concept of class.

In economic terms, the middle classes today are to a great extent proletarianized; in conceptual terms, they are homeless. During the current crisis, this proletarianization has exacerbated their resentment of capitalism. Grüneberg even remarks explicitly that "without a basically anticapitalist stance, we will never be able to awaken the positive forces of the middle classes."[39] But this economic anticapitalism in no way leads to a commitment to proletarian socialism. On the contrary: in order to assure its own survival, the middle class adamantly insists on clearly differentiating itself from the proletariat. The experiences I recorded in my book *Die Angestellten* already confirm the fact that even the worst-paid white-collar worker under no circumstances wants to be a wage laborer. In *Die Tat*'s September issue, Ernst Wilhelm Eschmann makes essentially the same point: "The growing self-awareness of the middle classes not only makes the construction of a proletarian socialism impossible, but also makes these middle classes into essential factors of the nascent national economy."[40] The middle classes thus refuse, out of a vital interest in their own continued survival, to declare their solidarity with the proletariat. This raises the question of what means remain available to them for escaping their ideational homelessness—a homelessness stemming from the fact that they feel unable to find refuge in the liberal system so shaken by economic crisis but are also unwilling to take shelter within Marxism.

They are standing in a void and have no choice but to try to develop a new consciousness that will provide the ideational framework for their social survival. This explains the desperate battle on the part of the intermediate strata represented by *Die Tat*—a battle against the liberalism that is their heritage—as well as their glorification of state, space, and myth. It has become obvious that these concepts do not refer to any homeland *[Heimat]* but are a *fata morgana* in the desert. The middle classes may not be conscious of just how unreal these concepts are, but it is a fact, and they undoubtedly have a vague sense of it. In any case, this ideational abandonment alone accounts for their continued vacillation between two extremes. One extreme is an appeal to brute violence, which arises from the feeling that this is their only means to stay alive. The spiritual battle being waged by *Die Tat* does in fact threaten again and again to degenerate into an unspiritual revolt: it calls the sword an argument, lets blood triumph over money, and undeniably tends to set the heroized chthonic powers against all consciously formed life. In all the concepts it supplies to the middle classes, one feels the stirring of brute nature as well. The other extreme is the very liberal position which has been abandoned. For if the middle class that has rejected Marxism wants to assure itself of its own consciousness—in the absence of a nonbourgeois and nonproletarian consciousness—it will in the end always stream back to the obsolete bourgeois tradition and its inherited intellectual property. The drainage outlets of its consciousness are plugged: it either dries up or backs up, and then is forced to flow back to its point of origin. This and nothing else can explain the sudden appearance in *Die Tat* of the concepts of the individual and of reason, which are so at odds with the journal's actual tendencies.

The publications of the *Tat* Circle consequently mirror this very disintegration of the dispossessed middle class (caused by the material and ideational situation), which flees into romanticism and is tossed about between violence and reason. This also means, however, that these publications are unable to offer any alternatives, but are capable only of displaying the current situation. If *Die Tat* cannot go beyond such display, then the revolt will either fail because of its ideological confusion or will be taken over by forces with a more robust constitution. If I am not completely mistaken, there are three dangers to which the *Tat* Circle is primarily vulnerable. The first is that capital will exploit it against its will as an advance attack cadre in capital's struggle against Marxist socialism, only to then hurl it overboard like so much excess ballast, if necessary, once it has served its purpose. This wouldn't be the first time something like this happened, and in the process middle-class socialism would be liquidated. The second danger is that, because of the hopelessness of *Die Tat*'s attempts to impose its utterly unrealistic and contradictory program, it will tend more and more toward a barbarism that is already manifest in latent form, wielding its sword with its right hand. As the guardian of cultural traditions, the middle class stands to suffer the most from this. The third danger is that the people of *Die Tat* would suffer the same fate as the German Romantics did: in the end, they would take refuge in religion. The moment they learn through praxis that their concepts fail to correspond to any reality, they will still be able to throw themselves head over heels into the reality of religious faith. Already we can see that they have a certain tendency toward radical protestantism. It betrays itself, for example, in the statement that "what is at issue today is above all a major spiritual transformation, which is in the process of taking place and which once again takes as its focus man in his totality."[41] If faith were being fully deployed, the word "totality"—also used frequently in other contexts— would take on the weight assigned it here. But the political activity of *Die Tat* would thereby have come to an end.

6

The present inquiry was prompted by a worry about the fate of the irreplaceable forces present in the middle classes. Its sole purpose is to reveal the situation in which *Die Tat* finds itself. It is also offered in the interest of the concerns represented by *Die Tat*, for the sake of every concern that is of concern.

As far as I can tell, *Die Tat*'s concerns are based on the profound experience of the unity of the *Volk*, discussed above. It is precisely the middle class, because of its intermediate position, that is able to experience this unity. Indeed, I know of no better articulation of it than the following sentences by Zehrer: "The conservative whose nature, tradition, blood, and character prevent him from ever recognizing today's system, and the contemporary person on the left who has been thrashed by—and ejected from—today's system, have more in common than they realize; they are closer to each other than they think. The way of the future is to bring together the person on the right with the person on the left, and vice-versa."[42] To this, one must also add the experience of the damage done by today's system, an experience that leads to the legitimate revolt against unleashed *Ratio*. It, too, is linked to insights that the middle class above all has made during the crisis.

The task of making the middle class's substantive experiences fruitful is, however, by no means synonymous with narrow-minded middle-class politics. For although these experiences do stem from the middle class, they do not simply aim to perpetuate this class in its socially intermediary position. Were the *Tat* Circle to remain content with such a mission, it would definitely be a dead end with no outlet, would fail due to its unrealistic concepts and its inner contradictions and could hardly hope to avoid the dangers noted above. But in fact, *Die Tat* did not set itself this goal after all, choosing instead another one which extends beyond strictly middle-class concerns. The practical aspects of solving this latter task cannot be discussed here. What must be established is simply that tackling this task presupposes a revision of the *Tat* Circle's position in two important respects.

First of all, I believe that the *Tat* Circle will not be spared from having to amend its concepts of the leader and the state—to purge both of them of their reactionary significance. In an essay in the September issue, Eschmann writes: "We oppose Marxism here not for ideological reasons . . . but because it renders enormous energies unproductive by determining them according to a dogma, thereby precluding the proper decisions."[43] But by concocting conceptual chimera that at most raise up the middle class without being able to support it, *Die Tat* also determines a host of energies that could be implemented with incomparably greater productivity. It wants to bring together people on the right with people on the left, but it really functions no differently from the "Red Company-Cell Newspapers" *[Rote Betriebszellenzeitungen]*. These are described by Christian Reil in the April issue as having a rather limited influence beyond the circle of their own party members, "since they consist largely of articles criticizing the labor unions and since the Communists seem to lack completely, for the time being at least, the appropriate language, which has to be specifically pitched at the level of the white-collar workers in order to be effective."[44] It is in just this manner that the *Tat* Circle fails with regard to the working classes. Instead of penetrating the reality that it is concerned with, *Die Tat* gets lost in the pseudo-reality of the images of state and of myth, which it portrays as an alternative to the arch-devils of Marxism and Liberalism painted on the wall. Its oppositional concepts lead it to reduce the left to a mere concept. But in order to get a sense of the experience of the *Volk*, *Die Tat* would have to go to the proletariat and include it as well.

Such an endeavor would, however, presuppose that *Die Tat* allow itself to be led not by emotional reactions but by knowledge. And this brings me to the second aspect of the *Tat* Circle's position that needs to be amended. I believe that in the service of its proper task, *Die Tat* will have to restore the dignity of reason. The rebellion that has been instigated against reason, while perhaps understandable as a desperate act on the part of a threatened middle class, is under no circumstances the proper means to keep the ravages of uncontrolled *Ratio* in check. On the contrary! The latter, unrestrained type of thinking detached from all creaturely needs has been able—in the postwar world—to ignore with impunity all limits in fields such as economics and politics. And this *Ratio* has a much greater affinity with barbarism than with reason, including liberal reason. *Ratio* is, to repeat a previously articulated point, the advocate of blind forces of nature, and nothing would be more absurd and hopeless than to want to combat it with the help of the same bare nature that manifests itself in this very *Ratio*. Only reason can restrain this boundless *Ratio*—a reason whose characteristics include an awareness of its own limitations. At one point a passage in *Die Tat* states, "We admired the French as enemies during the war. During trips to France, many of us later came to know the lifestyles of the French petite bourgeoisie and peasants and we understood their static, conservative mentality."[45] Now this certainly admirable mentality belongs to a *Volk* that at one time accorded reason divine honors and candidly acknowledged its rule. The *Tat* Circle, too, should no longer yield to the fruitless rancor against reason, which only deflects it from its true goals. In the November issue Erwin Ritter explains, "We are striving to . . . make the intellect more modest again."[46] The modest intellect: this, after all, is what reason is—reason that in today's increasingly urgent situation is more necessary than ever. For without the full deployment of reason, without the clear and terse rejection of the dark forces of antispirit/anti-intellect *[Wiedergeist]*, the circle of people gathered around *Die Tat* will never have what is so dear to them and what they have been dreaming of: a new economy, which can only be the work of knowledge, and a new *Volk*, composed of left *and* right.

Sasha Stone, "Kaiser Wilhelm Memorial Church," Berlin, ca. 1929

Those Who Wait

■ ■ ■

There are a lot of people these days who, although unaware of each other, are nevertheless linked by a common fate. Having eluded the profession of any particular faith, they have acquired their share of the cultural and educational wealth generally available today and tend to live with an alert sense of their time. These scholars, businessmen, doctors, lawyers, students, and intellectuals of all sorts spend most of their days in the loneliness of the large cities. And since they are sitting in offices, receiving clients, directing negotiations, and attending lectures, they quite often forget their actual inner being in the din of the hustle and bustle and fancy themselves free of the burden that secretly weighs upon them. But when they do pull back from the surface into the center of their being, they are overcome by a profound sadness which arises from the recognition of their confinement in a particular spiritual/intellectual [geistige] situation, a sadness that ultimately overruns all layers of their being. It is this metaphysical suffering from the lack of a higher meaning in the world, a suffering due to an existence in an empty space, which makes these people companions in misfortune.

■ ■ ■

In order to answer the question of what gave rise to the *emptying out* of people's spiritual/intellectual space, one would have to pursue the centuries-old process during which the self tears itself away from its attachment to God and the theological world, and slips away from the constraints of a community established by church authority, tradition, statutes, and dogma. One would have to retrace in detail how this self develops in its struggle to attain autonomy; how, after its fall from a temporality encompassing the eternal and into the rapid succession of

historical epochs, the self contracts into the timeless rational self
[*Vernunft-Ich*] of the Enlightenment; how it then rounds itself out into
the highly expressive, unique personality of Romanticism, and how,
later, in the age of materialism and capitalism, it both becomes ever
more atomized and increasingly degenerates into an arbitrary chance
construct. One would furthermore have to show that, corresponding to
these transformations of the self, there are transformations of the outside object-world, of reality, which is gradually robbed of its substance
and compressed to a point where its structure depends on the self. One
would also have to consider the social developments and a hundred
other lines of development that ultimately lead to the present chaos; yet,
in the end, one still wouldn't have really answered the question (that is,
in its metaphysical sense) but instead would have given a historical
derivation encumbered with all the inadequacies peculiar to such der-
ivations.

In this context, however, it is less essential to go into historical
problems than it is to elaborate the spiritual [*seelische*] situation in
which the people at issue here find themselves. At core they are suffering from their *exile* from the religious sphere; that is, they are suffering from the enormous alienation prevailing between their spirit/
intellect and the absolute. They have lost their faith—indeed they have
almost lost the capacity for faith—and for them religious truths have
become colorless thoughts which they are now at best only capable of
thinking. Yet, for the most part, they already have extricated themselves
from the exclusiveness of a world view determined purely by the natural
sciences. They recognize very clearly, for example, that some of the
intellectual contradictions which emanate from a rational mentality can
be resolved only by shifting into a religious frame of mind, or that a soul
which is not anchored in the absolute lacks stability. All in all, after
lengthy suffering, they have nearly reached the point from which the
religious realm actually begins to be accessible. But the gate through
which they wish to enter does not open for them, and, stalled in the
intermediate realm just in front of it, they are tortured by their inability
to believe.

In addition, these people are struck by the curse of *isolation and
individuation*. Tradition has lost its power over them. From the outset,

for them community is not a reality but merely a concept; they stand outside form and law, somehow holding their ground as tiny splintered-off particles in a temporal stream that is trickling away. Constrained by an excess of economic relations, they live unattached and lonely in a spiritual/intellectual world dominated by the principle of *laissez-aller,* a world in which every major trans-individual agreement has long since been blown apart and in which, as a result, the I can bridge the gap to the Thou (if at all) only by virtue of a revocable personal decision.

The alienation from the absolute and the isolation and individuation both leave their mark in a *relativism* that has been pursued to the extreme. Since these people lack ties and firm ground *[Halt und Grund],* their spirit/intellect drifts along without direction, at home everywhere and nowhere. They traverse the infinite variety of spiritual/intellectual phenomena—the world of history, of spiritual events, of religious life—as isolated individuals who no longer stop for anything, equally close to and equally far from all circumstances. Equally close, since they easily submerge themselves in any essentiality *[Wesenheit],* because there is no longer any faith that would bind their spirit/intellect and thereby prevent it from being somehow consumed by any and all phenomena. Equally far, since they never consider any insight as the ultimate one—that is, they have never penetrated an essentiality to such an extent that they could enter its depths permanently and, so to speak, never leave it. Their restless wandering is only an indication that they live at the greatest remove from the absolute and that the spell which envelops the self and which renders the essence of things unambiguous has been broken.

Typical of this spiritual/intellectual situation is the philosophy of *Georg Simmel,* who ultimately believed he could conquer relativism (and indeed, at the very least, clearly grasped its problematic issues) by positing "life" as the last absolute—life, which releases from its womb ideas and forms that subjugate life for a length of time but that are only to be in turn themselves devoured by life. But this doctrine recognized life-transcending norms and values only for the time being, so to speak, and destroyed the absolute in the very act of making the ebb and flow that is indifferent to value—in other words, the process of life—into an absolute. It was an act of desperation on the part of relativism, which, in its search for a solid foundation, ultimately came upon groundless and rootless life and thereby landed with itself—or perhaps did not land at all . . .

Horror vacui—fear of emptiness—governs these people. And one can easily understand in which directions their yearning extends. Everything in and around them urges them toward renewed being within the religious sphere and simultaneously toward redemption from unrestrained permissiveness, both of these to be achieved by entering into a community bound by form. Consciously or unconsciously, they seek to reconstruct the shattered world from the perspective of a higher meaning in which they believe, to suspend their flawed individuality, and awaken an order superior to them in which they can find their place. As for the rest, their desire to reenter the domain of religious life is by no means always compatible with the other desire—namely, that religious contents and the community held together from above by religious forms will take shape. The great variety of approaches being pursued today is evidence of the gaping divergence of the demands of the soul.

■ ■ ■

It is important to shed some light on at least a few of the approaches that are supposed to lead to a new homeland of the soul. One can hardly ignore *anthroposophic* doctrine,[1] since the honest need and yearning of numerous adherents depend upon it. Steiner's sizable following can be largely explained as a function of his claim—based on his insight into the untenability of our spiritual/intellectual situation—to have a scientifically verifiable method that allegedly will enable people to perceive supersensory realities as well as fathom human destiny; he gives the deceptive impression that his method establishes secure connections to the absolute. Now, isn't it tempting to set foot on this *illusory bridge* spanning the gap between science and religion and thereby be permitted without *sacrificium intellectus* to believe in and, yes, even understand a good many miraculous things? The groundswell in the movement is certainly also due to the fact that, sociologically, crucial aspects of the Steiner community represent the model of the church, thereby enabling it to reassuringly embrace the isolated individual and give him a feeling of safety and security. One can understand why many people fall prey to such a temptation, which, however, for a number of very sound reasons, is not a temptation for a reflective person but rather a distorted image of an authentic participation in the absolute.

There are other approaches, however, that at the very least ought not to be described as misleading paths. Take, for example, the *messianic Sturm und Drang* types of the communist persuasion who inhabit a world of apocalyptic notions and await the coming of a messiah who will proclaim the reign of God on earth. They oppose the treacherousness of a mere existence bereft of meaning with shining visions of fulfillment and of the overcoming of our frail wanderings. A merciless age gives rise to these chiliastic dreamers, who break out of the vacuum in *tempo furioso* in order to take certain ultimate religious positions by storm. In their fixation on the desired utopian community, however, they completely trample everything reminiscent of form and law, since they consider these to be merely preliminaries of a lower order.—This new type of messianism is remotely related to the *idea of community*, which often grows out of Protestant soil and is also religious in character. Like the former, but for different reasons, the idea of community claims to be able to dispense with form in the human realm. According to this notion, the community strictly speaking is based neither on a definable notion, a received doctrine, nor even on a people's sense of belonging together, but rather on the "experience of community." This means that its continued existence depends on the positive inclination of those who freely will it, and thus it requires for its survival the continuously renewed spiritual exertion of its members. But once the community-affirming experience of the individual—where "individual" is understood in its contemporary, flawed sense—is made the primary foundation of the community, then the entirely logical consequence is, on principle, to condemn supraindividual forms saturated with meaning as the petrified product of pure experience and as unnecessary interventions between the I and the Thou.—In diametric opposition to this, the *believers in form* (such as one encounters, for example, in the George Circle)[2] worship holy law as the principle of community that holds everything together. Not only does it remove the element of chance from all relations to God and to other people, support those who are needy, and reflect a higher reality within the temporal; it also creates that hierarchical order, that stratification of circles, which the deep-seated differences among people make necessary. According to the judgment of these believers in form, integration into a firmly established association and devotion to the figure that embodies the absolute—an absolute which, however, becomes graspable at all only through this figure—liberate people from the lack of ties and set limits on the flawed striving for infinity.

These possibilities and realizations—which we will not honor with any further attention—differ in their orientation (although not necessarily in their essence) from the enterprises that aim to reawaken the old *humanist doctrines,* hoping to eliminate the vacuum, for instance, by joining up with established religions whose truth content must now be newly brought to the fore. Anyone approaching them from the zone of relativist contingency stumbles upon declarations of belief and cultural community, upon the force of the absolute which eliminates isolation and individuation, and upon a devout knowledge that frees one from undevout rambling. Those who today catch sight of the edifice of the various religions from the outside and with new eyes, with yearning eyes, have an experience similar to that of the wanderer who, after many odysseys, thinks he has spotted the sheltering homestead. These wondrous living constructs which have grown over time—both unconcerned with and defiant of it—encompass a world and a reality different from the one in which physical events and economic processes unfold in their chaotic diversity. They guarantee the faithful a unification of the I with God and with the Thou, and, thanks to the tradition in which they incorporate themselves and by means of which they endure, they transport the faithful out of the sphere of meaningless change into the sphere of an eternity saturated with meaning. The consequences of such insights and encounters are presently becoming apparent everywhere. Just as new life is pouring into Catholicism, there are also strong religious forces stirring within the Protestant community, forces that to some extent are already directed against the secular variant of Protestantism; and Judaism—above all, Zionist Judaism—is not far behind.

The fact that the smaller tributaries of the religions are also beginning to flow is evidenced by the turn toward mysticism and the establishment of various sects. The extensiveness of the scouting trips that religious neediness undertakes in search of fulfillment corresponds to the extent of the authentic (and perhaps at times also partly imagined) despair. It is thus hardly surprising that this religious neediness ultimately ends up with Eastern doctrines. In general, depending upon their particular needs, people seek at times unbridled authority and rigid development of the forms, and at other times more free and individual involvement in the domains of the religions: acceptance of already formulated tenets of faith alternates with attempts to relax the given strictures. One gladly makes allowances to the searchers for attaching, as they often do, too much importance to the security that makes it possible to repose within faith.

■ ■ ■

Returning now to those people who, conscious of their situation, linger in the void: How will they respond when faced with the various paths open to them? Two possibilities must be eliminated from the very start: first, that those facing the decision will turn to narcotics, fleeing into an unreal shadowy existence of distractions in order to avoid at all costs having to make any decisions; second, that they will find true faith without conflict, thereby attaining a higher plane of reality without going astray. If we exclude these from the start, we are left with three kinds of behavior that are by and large possible.

The first attitude is that of someone who is a *skeptic as a matter of principle,* a type perhaps best exemplified by Max Weber. This sort of person clearly grasps the uncanny seriousness of the situation but is at the same time convinced that he and those like him are unable to wrest themselves free of that situation. His intellectual conscience rebels against embarking on any of the paths toward supposed redemption that present themselves at every turn, since these appear to him as so many wrong tracks and illicit retreats into the sphere of arbitrary limitation. As a result, he decides out of inner truthfulness to turn his back on the absolute: his inability to believe becomes an unwillingness to believe. Hatred of the faith swindlers—a hatred in which an already forgotten and long-repressed yearning perhaps still resonates—drives him to fight for the "disenchantment of the world," and his existence runs its course in the bad infinity of empty space. This lonely existence, however, is no longer naïve in any sense; rather, it is born of an unequaled heroism. As such, it is closer to salvation in its self-imposed wretchedness than is the pampered existence of those who are merely just. Spirits/intellects of this sort willingly embrace a skepticism that can no longer be easily surpassed; they exhaust themselves demonstrating all imaginable determinations and relations, without ever prophetically touching upon meaning, and with only sporadic departures from the realm of value-free observation. Yet the insights they have attained in the domain of the humanities and anthropology—which are dubious and even superficial in certain respects precisely because they claim to be pure insights—are rooted in renunciation. Indeed, perhaps it is only the undertone of sacrifice reverberating through them that gives them ultimate significance and lends them the luster of depth.

The second attitude—which one encounters far more frequently and, for understandable reasons, especially often these days—is that of the *short-circuit people*. Whether one comes upon them in this camp or another (and one encounters them wherever there seems to be a ready solution in matters of faith), what they all have in common is a tendency to flee headlong from the dreariness and the world outside in order to slip quickly into a sheltering abode. Since from a distance they resemble true believers in more than merely superficial ways, and since their actions are governed at least partly by subjectively honest convictions, the dubiousness of their attitude, psychologically and objectively, is not readily apparent. Mind you, what is at stake here is not the verification of individuals' shifts of faith (Who would presume to be able to illuminate in others the spiritual depths one can hardly fathom in oneself?) but rather the demonstration of a typical transformation which, if this is as far as it goes, is precisely not the kind of transformation and shift in direction that really matters.

Considered as a type, the short-circuit people perhaps really do penetrate the religious sphere with part of their being, but their faith is not carried by the full breadth of the self and therefore does not quite invoke religious truth. It is more a will to faith than a lingering within faith, more a rash interpretation than an accomplished fact. Driven by true despair about the vacuum within and around them, these people stagger into one religious realm or another, happy to be relieved from their tiresome rambling and under the delusion that this homecoming terminates their wanderings on almost as happy a note as a novel that ends with a betrothal. Like the novel, however, their wanderings only appear to have ended, for besides the fact that now life once again starts from the beginning, they have fled their doubts much too quickly to have arrived at the first goal so early. But what exactly constitutes the short circuit which they produce and to which they fall victim? It consists in the fact that, recognizing the need for faith and consumed by an impatient yearning, they break into a realm of faith in which—since they lack the extensive prerequisites needed for its true conquest—they can maintain their ground only artificially and thanks to involuntary *self-deception.* In sum, the short circuit thus consists in their plucking a fruit which has not ripened for them and which they themselves have not ripened toward. Supposing they once have had something even faintly resembling a religious experience, they erect upon it without further ado (that is, on a very dubious foundation) an entire edifice meant to protect them against the tribulations they suffered in the empty space. But by trying to force their replete life into a position not completely adequate to it—more out of metaphysical cowardliness than out of a total conviction they have truly attained—they distort not only their own being but also that of the world of faith revealed from this position. In order to remain master of a situation that is by no means natural for them and that therefore awakens in them a secret mistrust of themselves, they must keep themselves in a continuous state of rapture. Everything they do becomes forced, and so they end up overemphasizing their faith—a fact that in itself is a sufficiently clear index of the fragility of that faith. The need to drown out opposing spiritual voices forces them into a fanaticism that falsifies the facts; uncertainty leads them to underscore their certainty and compels them to invest great energy advocating the doctrines they have accepted—much more energy than is expended, for example, by true believers, who have no need for such a continuously defensive stance directed both inward and outward. Indeed, despite (or perhaps because of) their profound certainty, such true believers may well be plagued by doubts. Fear of catastrophe, that is, fear of the collapse of the all too hastily erected edifice—whose construction actually blocks their access—drives the short-circuit people to exaggerate their declarations of loyalty more and more, such that they sound disturbingly hollow to sensitive ears. At least so far as sincerity is concerned, the intellectual desperado is far superior to these refugees from the vacuum in whom authenticity and inauthenticity combine in a very tricky and complicated way.

Of course, the intellectual desperado cannot be permitted to have the last word, since this would completely surrender the world to meaninglessness. But how is one to escape the terrible either-or of the two positions: that of the skeptic-as-a-matter-of-principle and that of the short-circuit people? Perhaps the only remaining attitude is one of *waiting*. By committing oneself to waiting, one neither blocks one's path toward faith (like those who defiantly affirm the void) nor besieges this faith (like those whose yearning is so strong, it makes them lose all restraint). One waits, and one's waiting is a *hesitant openness*, albeit of a sort that is difficult to explain. It can easily happen that someone who waits in this manner may find fulfillment in one way or another. Nevertheless, in this context one ought to think primarily of those people who have tarried and still do tarry in front of closed doors, and who thus, when they take it upon themselves to wait, are people who are waiting here and now. Let's assume that, based on the unalienable right of their natural being and their sense of reality, they reject the lust and fervor of messianic enthusiasts just as much as they refuse to be integrated into esoteric circles, that they recognize certain weaknesses in the modern idea of community, and that finally, in their attempt to immerse themselves in the tradition of established religions, they encounter insurmountable difficulties which are partly due to their definitive estrangement from the fabric of religious forms. In light of all this, what is the meaning of their waiting?

On the negative side, the *person who waits* and the intellectual desperado share, above all, a dauntlessness that manifests itself in the ability to hold on. It need hardly be emphasized that the skepticism of the person who waits does not degenerate into skepticism-as-a-matter-of-principle, since from the outset his entire being has been geared toward establishing a relationship with the absolute. The actual metaphysical meaning of his attitude rests upon the fact that the irruption of the absolute can occur only once an individual has committed himself with his entire being to this relationship. Those who wait will thus be as hard as possible on themselves, so as not to be taken in by religious need. They would much rather lose the salvation of their soul than succumb to the rapture of the moment and fling themselves into adventures of ecstasy and visions. Maintaining the furthest possible distance, they almost make it their ambition to be pedantic and somehow cool, as a means of protecting themselves against flying embers. Like the desperado, they do not attempt to make a virtue out of their necessity or become slanderers of their longing, any more than they carelessly entrust themselves to the flow of their longing, which might carry them to who knows what illusory fulfillment.

On the positive side, this waiting signifies an openness—one that naturally must not in any way be confused with a relaxation of the forces of the soul directed toward ultimate things; rather, quite the contrary, it consists of tense activity and engaged self-preparation. It is a long path—or, better, a leap requiring a lengthy approach—which leads to life in the religious sphere, to the religious word, and even to the closeness between men that is based on a communal belief. For anyone who dwells as cut off from the absolute as does the person in empty space, it is infinitely difficult to accomplish the turn he demands of himself. What exactly can the one-who-waits do, so that faith, while not magically attracted, is not excluded? This cannot be conveyed in the form of knowledge, since it must be lived and since the insight of the beholder anticipates that life and its lessons anyway. What can at best be said, in any case, is that what is at stake for the people under discussion here is an attempt to shift the focus from the theoretical self to the self of the entire human being, and to move out of the atomized unreal world of shapeless powers and figures devoid of meaning and into the world of *reality* and the domains it encompasses. The overburdening of theoretical thinking has led us, to a horrifying degree, to become distanced from reality—a reality that is filled with incarnate things and people and that therefore demands to be seen concretely. Anyone who tries to attune himself to this reality and to befriend it will not, of course, automatically come upon the meaning that constitutes this reality or upon an existence in faith. He may, however, discover one or another of the ties within that reality; it might become clear to him, for example, that life with his fellow man and, in general, the real world in all its breadth is subject to a multitude of determinations which can neither be gauged by theoretical-conceptual means nor explained as merely the fruit of subjective arbitrariness. This might lead him to change his position gradually and begin to grope upward in realms hitherto inaccessible to him.[3] Still, in these realms every indication is certainly anything but a pointer to the path. Must it be added that getting oneself ready is only a preparation for that which cannot be obtained by force, a preparation for transformation and for giving oneself over to it? Exactly when this transformation will come to pass and whether or not it will happen at all is not at issue here, and at any rate should not worry those who are exerting themselves.

CONSTRUCTIONS

Martin Munkasci, "Spectators at a Sports Event," from the *Crowd* series, ca. 1933

The Group as Bearer of Ideas

■ ■ ■

The social world is at all times filled with countless spiritual *[geistige]* forces or entities that one can simply call ideas. Political, social, and artistic movements embodying specific contents of some sort arise one day and run their course. What these ideas have in common is that they all want to penetrate the extant world; they all want to become reality themselves. They appear within human society as a concrete, material should-being *[Sollen]* and have an inborn drive to realize themselves. It is only once they cease being mere chimera without influence on reality and begin to have an effect on the social world, bringing it to a boil, that they take on sociological significance. All ideas that permeate the social world in this fashion in order to liberate it from its petrification undergo certain processes that can both be represented historically and characterized in formal sociological terms. A stone cast into a pool of water creates concentric waves whose shape and size are a function less of the stone's particular form and makeup than of the force and direction of the throw. Similarly, every idea which strikes the extant social world evokes in that world a response whose course is determined by general factors. In order to grasp these factors in their necessity, one will have to derive them through a phenomenological examination of the structure of spirit. Once one has "bracketed" all particularities, one arrives at a general formula for the course of all ideas from should-being to being—that is, one perceives the most general regularities that already constitute the foundation of all particular sociological investigations, though they are never explicitly articulated by them.

Whereas it is true that a socially effective idea is cast out into the world by individual personalities, its actual corporeality is produced by the *group*. The individual does generate and proclaim the idea, but it is the group that bears it and makes sure it is realized. Political parties advocate the achievement of certain goals, and clubs are formed for various purposes: there are groups of the most varied makeup. The very number of people united in a group transforms the essence and quality of that group, as Simmel has demonstrated convincingly.[1] The meaning and potential achievement of a group composed of two people cannot simply be transferred to a group entity consisting of an undetermined multitude of people. But here, where the point is to work out the laws that govern the movement of ideas, it is less important to order the groups according to their size than to be able to segregate the communities of life and fate from those groups that actually bear ideas. The designation "communities of life and fate" refers to all groups whose members live together in an indissoluble attachment rather than being welded together solely by ideas or various principles. The family and the nation, for example, are instances of the former sort. They envelop the person born into them just the way he is, from his birth through his death and even beyond his death, and are basically of the same unlimited duration as the life out of whose womb they arose. Given that their origins are just as irrational as their purposes, one cannot tie them to specific objectives; rather, they devote themselves over the course of their existence to an endless multiplicity of objectives, though they never find their definitive significance in any one of them. In contrast, groups whose accord is based on an idea arise and perish with this idea; their unity is not an immanent part of organic, growing life, but is fully encompassed by a specific concept that will come to life through them. It is obvious just which groups are actually at issue in this context—namely, those groups that must constitute themselves in order to realize an idea, if this idea is to move from the stage of proclamation to that of realization. Like the development of the idea itself, the development of all group individualities of this sort (groups that come into existence only by virtue of an idea) is subject to general regularities. Group and idea are intimately linked: the former represents the latter. Thus, one cannot grasp the course of an idea without determining the essence of the group individuality it creates.

In characterizing the essence of an idea-bearing group, there are two diametrically opposed approaches. According to one view, which could perhaps be called the *authoritative* type, the idea that establishes the group's unity is definitely placed above the individual members and is completely removed from their subjective will. The absolutely sovereign idea evolves in a sphere impervious to any individual impulses; the particular will (understood as the will of the autonomous individual) is irrelevant to it. According to the adherents of this doctrine, the particular person is an utterly accidental entity without an essential core; for them, only the idea has meaning and substantive content, an idea that demands submission from everyone. Individuals are ephemeral, whereas the idea, which is eternal, remains untouched by time. According to this theory, the state, for example, is an autonomous and transindividual entity which not only cannot be equated with the people currently embodying it, but ultimately has nothing more in common with them than this: these particular people are, as it were, only the material through which the idea of the state realizes itself, a passive material that must allow itself to be shaped and has no influence on the form of the idea itself. The commandments of the state are, accordingly, immune from all individual critique, no matter how justified it may be; the reigning law is a constitution which, once constituted, has its source in a beyond that is on the far side of all empirical deliberations and that therefore, even if at odds with contemporary legal sensibility, can in principle not be superseded. Thus, according to the authoritative doctrine, all groups that bear ideas or arise from them are indivisible entities whose ideal contents hover in the absolute as purposes unto themselves; they neither have been created nor are capable of being destroyed. There is no bridge that connects the realm of these eternally existing ideas with the constantly changing life of the group.

According to the other approach, which we might call *individualist*, every idea that seizes control of a group emanates from the spirit of all of the individuals that make up that group. Indeed, only individual people exist, and thus there is no reason to assume the existence of a group individuality which feels and thinks as a unit and is endowed with an essence of its own. The spirit of the group is simply the harmony of the spirits of all the group members; the group is but the sum of those that belong to it. The adherents of this atomizing tendency deny the qualitative unity and specificity of the group as a whole; instead, they accord reality and primary emphasis to the individuals rather than to the totality, to the temporally conditioned opinions of the multitude rather than to the supratemporal idea that governs the group. Their doctrine can be summed up in the practical political thesis that "the State (the law, and so on) exists for the people, and not the people for the state (the law, and so on)." As a result, the ideas to which the group professes its loyalty lose their substance, becoming an expression of the fickle volition of a multiplicity of individuals, maintaining their right to exist only so long as these individuals are inclined to accord it to them. If one embraces the first approach, the individual in the social world forfeits his significance to the existence of the group. The ideas detach themselves from him and, like stars, follow an orbit above his head. If one agrees with the second approach, the individual is the only reality in the social world, while the group individuality turns into a phantom. The ideas are relegated to the spirit of the individual people, outside which they do not exist.

Neither of these two approaches—whose roots in specific world views is obvious—corresponds exactly to the phenomenologically demonstrable facts. First of all, the authoritative doctrine clearly draws too sharp a line between, on the one hand, the ideas and the groups that embody them and, on the other, the people that always constitute these groups. Acting on the correct observation that the movements of groups and the destinies of the ideas borne by them behave de facto as if they were the movements and destinies of autonomous entities, it then stretches things too far, making the ideas that emanate from the group (or constitute it in the first place) into sovereign constructs which, as self-contained entities, no longer have the slightest relation to the existence of individual people. From the authoritative perspective, the historical genesis of ideas is just as inexplicable as their decline. When and where the ideas emerge is left open; it suffices that they are there, jutting into the hustle and bustle of the social world as entities outside time. According to this approach, the collective being of the group is wed to the eternal idea, while the individuals themselves tumble down into the realm of shadows without having created the idea or even been affected by it.

The other, individualist doctrine does justice to reality insofar as it establishes a direct relation between the socially effective spiritual entities and individual people. Here, ideas are not so unreachably distant that it is impossible for individuals to create or destroy them, nor are groups cast as ultimate, indissoluble entities that successfully resist all disintegration and decomposition into component parts. But despite all this, the individualist doctrine still fails to recognize that ideas, along with the groups that embody them, are much more than simply exponents of individual souls. It is neither able to account for the development of ideas in the social world (which experience teaches is often independent of individual volition), nor able to explain the powerful self-assertion of the individuality of the group over against its members. This second approach ties the ideas too closely to the single individual, whereas the first approach displaces them all too exclusively into the transindividual regions. In its desire to accord all power and grandeur to the individual soul, which it conceives as an end in itself, exaggerated individualism falls prey to the mistake (which one could almost call a logical error) of depreciating the greatest products of this individual soul—namely, the ideas—and thus robbing them of the significance and sovereignty that should already have been guaranteed them by their heritage. Equally inconsistent with the individualist position is the judgment that denies group entities any and all autonomy and selfhood, since, after all, they likewise emanated from individuals, and anyone who ascribes ultimate significance to such individuals surely cannot casually sacrifice the consistency and self-sufficiency of what is of their own making. If one concedes that all such creations (ideas, groups, and so on) lack any essence, then in the end the creator (the solitary self) also loses his substance; he is transformed into an eternal world-destroyer, yet could ultimately assert himself only by extending his self into effective works. The individualism being discussed here is an authentic product of the Enlightenment; overlooking differences in the world views of different peoples, it simply assumes the complete concordance of all rational beings and can therefore easily disregard the group as a special construct providing the transition from the idea to the individual. With the increasing differentiation of similarly oriented individuals into many cosmos-like personalities, the characteristic movements of ideas and of the group entities that correspond to them immediately surface on the horizon of consciousness. They then can no longer be reduced to spiritual effects of an endless multiplicity of heterogenous individual spirits.

The group is thus the mediator between individuals and the ideas that pervade the social world. Whenever an idea bursts out of the darkness and can be formulated, it produces a similar disposition of the soul in the people it encounters, and begins to be realized when these people join together to form a group that will struggle to make the idea a reality. The idea does not transcend the individuals, as is claimed by the authoritative doctrine, but instead works itself out in and through them. In the process, however, these individuals are transformed into bearers of the idea and are therefore no longer independent, individual selves with complete freedom of movement; they are now beings tied to and formed by the idea, their thinking and feeling both uniform and circumscribed. Because the idea shapes their inner element, they stand apart from the mass of people unaffected by the idea; they take a particular path whose direction is already designated by the idea. Suffice it to say, for the time being, that the group is only that union of people with the same spiritual constitution necessary for realizing ideas; it is not an association of arbitrary, spiritually irresolute individuals. It is a collective entity to the extent that the expressions of the consciousness of all its members arise from the same basis—namely, the ground of the idea—and therefore must also result a priori in uniform actions. The group and the idea that it embodies lead a special existence beyond the individuals only when compared with a multiplicity of arbitrarily acting individuals that has been assumed from the outset, but not when compared with individual souls of similar makeup. Only when the members of a group have detached themselves from the idea does it weigh upon them like an external obligation; only then does the group adhering to the idea seem to them an independent entity that oppresses them.

Having understood the group members in their capacity as bearers of ideas, there remains the further question of how such an idea (which stratifies their inner element) is received and processed. Every idea that amalgamates a group crystallizes into a form with sharp contours. It becomes a political program, a decidedly characteristic governing principle and dogma. In short, it makes its entrance as a should-being that has circumscribed contents and that demands realization. But this precisely specified should-being always points beyond itself; the formulation it is given by the group becomes merely a visible facet of a vast spiritual itinerary that the group traverses from beginning to end. There is absolutely no spiritual expression that is able to exist simply on its own, without being enmeshed in a large context of meaning. It always wells up from some ultimate convictions and always leads to other expressions, with which it combines to form a homogenous, meaningful whole. As a result, the socially effective idea always contains within itself the direction in which it is meant to be spun out. It is the abbreviated expression of some total perspective of which only one aspect is always emphasized: the aspect that proves necessary at a particular time and in specific social circumstances. Group members championing the content of a specific idea thus invariably experience and desire more than this one formulatable and formulated should-being. They are pursuing a path leading across the entire world, and the content to which they devote themselves is merely a wave hurled forth by the dammed-up stream of their consciousness; or, better, this content marks the spot where the flow of their thought happens to merge with a given situation. It is totally unimportant and at most of psychological interest whether the stream of consciousness in which the idea bobs up is already given, or whether it is the initially given content of the should-being that first compels one to start off on a far-reaching path. In any case, the group member always draws out all of the possibilities deposited in embryonic form in the idea, and develops the idea into the totality already implied within it. The programs of political parties have their foundations in world views, and all ideal demands leading to the formation of groups are the product of basic attitudes that affect everything around them and that thereby establish meaningful connections between these demands and other spiritual claims and valuations.

There is a big difference between people constituted as *individuals* and those constituted by the idea as *members of a group*, in the manner described above. Indeed, only through this difference can one gain insight into the specific nature of group individuality. Let us assume, to begin with, that some specific idea penetrates only the spirit of an individual. It will of course expand within this person and will want to open up a path that extends from one end of the world to the other. But the individual who exists for himself is (at least potentially) a microcosm in which diverse desires and spiritual forces are stirring; therefore, the context of meaning created through the idea occupies the entirety of consciousness only in the rarest cases. Thoughts and views that stem from other areas of the soul interfere with this context, loosening it up and traversing it. Even if one were to assume that the idea was able to develop itself fully within the individual, it would at most be able to achieve pure and unsullied supremacy over the individual spirit only if it were a sublime principle that stirred up the entire self. Thus, the subject does indeed experience ideas, giving them form and devoting himself to them, but is always more than merely the bearer of an idea; it is not so easy for the subject to break the chain of his unique fate in order to allow the idea to play itself out in the empty, unfulfilled space of his soul.

Matters are changed when this subject steps out of his isolation and becomes a member of a group. In the group, the individual counts only to the extent that he is a pure embodiment of the idea. His relationships to the other members serve exclusively and entirely to extend and realize the content of the should-being that constitutes the group; anything else that resides within this individual and wants to make itself known must exert an effect outside the group. Thus, in becoming a member of a group, a part of the individual's being—the part that is shaped by the idea—detaches itself from the overall plan of his being (a plan that, potentially, he is capable of realizing) and sets itself to work independently. Just as the tuning fork is tuned to only one pitch, the group is completely attuned only to the one idea it champions. The moment the group is constituted, everything unrelated to this idea is automatically excluded. The people united in the group are no longer full individuals, but only fragments of individuals whose very right to exist is exclusively a function of the group's goal. The subject as an individual-self linked to other individual-selves is a being whose resources must be conceived as endless and who, incapable of being completely ruled by the idea, still lives in realms located outside the idea's sphere of influence. The subject as a group member is a *partial-self* that is cut off from its full being and cannot stray from the path which the idea prescribes for it.

Having reached this point in the analysis, one can finally understand why there is something like a collective being, a group individuality that cannot be dissolved into a multiplicity of individuals but rather operates above their heads according to its own laws, often seemingly independent of the claims and (momentary) needs of its adherents. Thus, instead of being made up of fully developed individuals, the group contains only reduced selves, abstractions of people: it is a pure *tool of the idea* and nothing else. But is it surprising that people who are no longer fully in control of themselves act differently from people who are still in complete possession of their selves? There is a powerful necessity to the movement of ideas through the social world. The individual who spots it must ally himself with others in order to transform it from should-being into being. In that very moment, then, in which the group comes into being, a reduction of selves also occurs, and instead of many individuals striving to realize an idea there are now lots of creatures dependent on the idea and living through its grace. These creatures are compelled by the idea itself—but only by this idea—and would have to founder in insubstantiality were they to perceive themselves as something existing apart from it. The idea does not dawn on them but instead creates them. It is not they who realize the idea, but the other way around: it realizes and breathes life into them. There is good reason to speak of group individuality as if it were an independent being. For these partial-selves, these half-creations and quarter-creations, are born only in the course of preparations for collective actions (that is, in the group meetings); they do not reside within the separate individuals, but arise only out of the union of the individuals into spiritual entities that have detached themselves from these individuals and can exist only in the group.

The fact that the complete individual disappears within the group has a decisive effect on the character of the ideas that are represented and carried out by group individualities in the social world. So long as man comports himself as an individual entity, thousands of urges arise in him; desires, thoughts, and tender feelings are interwoven; and even the quietest, finest trace of the soul can be inserted into the fabric of the spiritual context. But if this subject unites with an indiscriminate multiplicity of people to form a group (determined by an idea), then the partial-self that detaches itself from that subject certainly no longer displays the endless manifold of traits proper to it as a single individual. And this for reasons essential to its nature. For when a number of people are welded together into a group, it is utterly impossible for them to enter into this relationship with the full range of their souls. The spiritual path on which the group's thought moves must be constructed in such a way that all of the group members can move along it. The subject's unique totality is thus banned from the newly emerging group-self, and only those traits common to all the various subjects belonging to the group can contribute to the construction of the group individuality. In other words, the instinctual, unconscious, organically swelling wealth of life of the solitary self is foreign to group individuality. In terms of features and aspirations, the latter is impoverished compared with the former, lacking the fruitful and creative spiritual foundation that emits a rationally incomprehensible abundance of contents. One searches the group individuality in vain for the smooth transitions, the nameless feelings, and the multiple layers of experience stored one on top of another that are found (at least potentially) in the individual. Incapable of extending itself into many dimensions, it actually moves only in one single direction, from which it cannot stray either to the right or to the left without disintegrating. Indeed, the *linearity* of its evolution is one of the fundamental characteristics of the nature of group individuality. But this one-dimensional character is also necessarily linked to a certain rigidity and crudity, which become features of the group-self because, as a matter of principle, it can never maintain the thoroughly homogeneous experiential mass characteristic of the individual-self. As a result, it loses some of its flexibility and tenderness, and many domains of reality and experience available to the individual remain forever inaccessible to it.

The character of any idea that engenders a group must naturally correspond to the character of group individuality that has been recognized as essential to its nature. For the single individual, by contrast, the idea can take any one of an endless number of forms, since he can handle both crude and subtly differentiated trains of thought. When he incorporates an idea, he spins countless threads that tie it in to the other contents of his consciousness, producing a web of relations in which the idea is so entwined that it can no longer extricate itself as an autonomous construct. But the group can constitute itself only for the sake of the sort of ideal contents that lack this intangible sparkle. And therein lies its very specificity—in this renunciation of the plenitude proper to the solitary self, and the retention of only a few primary colors from the latter's variegated spectrum of experience. Moreover, a being of this sort is able to digest ideational fare of only a relatively hearty sort, simply refusing to ingest contents for which it lacks the proper organ. Whenever an idea cultivated by an important figure embodies itself as a group, the unmistakable individuality tied to that figure gets lost in the transition, severing the connections between the idea and the manifold ranges of experience in which it was rooted while still controlled by the individual-self. Nothing indicates more clearly the change that the idea undergoes in this process than, for instance, Wagner's aversion to Wagnerians, or Marx's assurance that he was no Marxist. If one disregards the other grounds for such claims, they can also be explained by the very fact that the creators of the ideas no longer recognize their own ideas—and even want to repudiate them—once, in the course of their journey through the social world, they have given rise to a group and have begun to develop in another realm according to their own rules.

Ideas of this sort, however, are filled with an unbridled desire to develop themselves further: they want to be eternal. So long as it is still the solitary self entirely on its own that is committed to their realization, and so long as they are encircled by a radiating cluster of associations soaring toward infinity, they retain a certain flexibility, fitting in here and there and allowing themselves to be inflected in numerous ways. But once they are represented by groups, they lose this initial elasticity and turn into the much cruder constructs described above, which advance ponderously as if obeying an unrelenting compulsion. One may have one's doubts as to whether the single individual totally dominated by an idea will prove successful in one case or another, since the many sources of his being can never be entirely wrested free from their concealment. The group individuality, by contrast, has no sources other than the one idea that constitutes it, and thus bores into reality with relentless consistency. It is as if it were simply the thrust inherent in the idea that was driving it forward in the direction that it had taken, as if its path were the product of the developmental possibilities inherent in the idea and in the resistances that arise from case to case. Since the group individuality adopts none of the contents that otherwise fill up the social world, its actions are the purest expression that the idea can possibly be accorded in any given situation. Basically, the group individuality undertakes only those actions that would also be appropriate to the idea if it were to penetrate the manifold in an unembodied state and propelled only by its inborn primal power. One should add, however, that ideas that unfold in such a logical manner are always already somewhat schematic and cumbersome constructs; a coarsening of their nature is quite obviously the price they must pay for being able to make the long journey from should-being to being and not disappear without a trace in the process.

The group individuality is only valid so long as it fosters the realization of the idea to which it is subordinated. Just as the Golem is annihilated if one removes from his mouth the sheet on which the life-giving formula is written, so too the group will expire if one separates it from the idea to which it owes its existence.[2] Since the group-self, as split off from the full individual-self, exists only through the idea, it would fall apart immediately (or, as often happens, turn into an entirely new and differently constituted group entity) if the foundation on which it is built were pulled out from under it. In this respect, the group-self differs profoundly from the single individual. The latter is able to outlive every idea to which it has at one time devoted itself, yet still remains the same self. Whatever contents it may absorb over the course of time, the cohesion of its life is always restored, since whatever direction it takes, all paths ultimately lead back to the one inexhaustible fount of its life.

What separates the individual-self from the group-self, however, is above all the experience of the *radical shift*. A personality dedicated to a particular idea can forsake that idea and worship what it had previously denounced. Yet this individual's essential substance survives even after this shift; the old person is still present in the new, converted person, but as someone who has been transformed. The imbrication of experiences tolerates no break with what used to exist; in short, the individual being is not destroyed but is merely transported into another form of existence. This radical shift is impossible for the rigid individuality of the group. It can change (as remains to be shown), but cannot rebel against the idea in whose service it was created in the first place. Since it is no more than the living bearer and performer of the spiritual path established by the idea, it would have to destroy itself if it wished to eliminate this path. It is quite conceivable that the same people who have relinquished the material of a particular group may reappear in a new group whose orientation is the opposite of that of the previous one; but this is effectively the creation of a different group individuality, which is utterly foreign to, and contains no traces of, the one that preceded it.

The intimate connection between groups and ideas is, moreover, of some significance for the emergence of classes and social strata that consider themselves unified and accordingly isolate themselves from one another. There may be some truth to the view that the sharp class distinctions in modern states stem from the earlier usurpation of land by foreign conquerors who subsequently became the ruling class. Still, this does not suffice as an explanation, because, as the product of a historical and not a sociological perspective, it suppresses an important feature of the rise of classes and strata. Suppose there were a large community without any stratification whatever among its adherents, all of whom enjoyed more or less the same cultural and genuinely human sophistication. One can demonstrate with almost mathematical certainty that this situation cannot last for long, because it runs counter to certain basic qualities of human nature. Given the constitution of man as we have known it so far and since time immemorial, there is simply no way to avoid establishing a quite extensive division of labor in every large community, if all the needs of the civilization and culture of a mature *Volk* are to be satisfied. (Deliberately avoiding differentiation necessarily leads to a state of primitiveness.) Bureaucratic institutions take shape, the various commercial and intellectual professions rise above the farmers, and so on. So long as life remains in flux, myriad ideas that provide the occasion for creating groups will continue to spring up. The members of every profession invariably do develop among themselves a spiritual path appropriate to their social situation, which is to say that they transform themselves into socially typical individualities. Their shared manner of thinking and the many collegial relations between them usually also lead them to join together in concretely unified groups (guilds, vocational groups of all sorts), or at least to feel as if they were their own group. So in any case, the community presupposed here will give rise to a series of groups that is to some extent the product of the ideas circulating in the social world (if there were no such ideas, then should-being would turn entirely into being, marking the end of time) and to some extent the embodiment of the perspectival horizons that correspond to various social sites.

The group individuality is, however, always a uniform and to some extent primitive being which, as we have seen, develops according to its own laws and is in no sense synonymous with the sum of single individuals who constitute the group. Thus, within the community there arise individualities that cannot in any way be completely mastered by isolated human beings, since the former operate, as it were, above the latter's heads. But these stratum, class, and group spirits necessarily develop in different directions, since they are determined by the constant givens of different social sites (otherwise, there would be no division of labor, which contradicts our presupposition). The representatives of these spirits, the partial-selves that have been detached from the conceived full individuals, are, as such, rigid, stubborn, and unwilling to make any radical shifts, yet quite capable of being destroyed. The oft-observed egoism of the group can be explained by the very fact that the group individualities constituted by any idea are nothing but the embodiment of these would-be eternal beings; they must strive to assert themselves at all costs, since otherwise they cease to exist. Or, better, they must remain forever faithful to the context of meaning they represent, since they exist in the first place only for its sake and would cancel themselves out were they to aspire beyond it. In our ideal community, accordingly, group and stratum entities arise that conceive of themselves as units and, were they to be surrounded only by empty space, would certainly feel the need to extend themselves without limit. One group constitutes a resistance to the other, which each group deals with and overcomes by stressing only its own existence and by seeking to distinguish itself sharply from the other collective individualities that are also occupying the social space.

All this demonstrates that the formation of different classes, strata, and so on that set themselves apart from one another is an almost inevitable product of the gradual process of differentiation, except perhaps in a utopian community made up exclusively of people of the highest intensity. But this is not to imply either that the classes (especially the economic ones) must survive in the form they have had up to this point, or that they must fight each other as brutally as they do today. It should be noted in passing that a reduction of group egotism and of the contrasts between the group spirits, an eradication of excessive economic inequalities, and so on are things that can be achieved, whereas the complete elimination of hierarchically structured strata and of all differences in levels among groups cannot. Probably the most profound remarks that have ever been made on this subject are found in Thomist social philosophy. The idealist utopian may still imagine that, through education perhaps, one can really create a community of "the free and equal," a community whose individual members and groups gather without any friction in a perfect and, so to speak, prestabilized harmony. Such things can be beautifully imagined, and also serve an indispensable role as a regulative principle. Yet reality does not comply so readily with the demands of reason, and it is the task of ontology to disclose the terrible in-itself of this reality. The greatest obstacle to the realization of this ideal of reason is the fact that when people exert themselves fully in one direction (that is, develop themselves with great intensity), they can be receptive to other directions only when they are in a relaxed state. Once in the "sphere of relaxation," however, they do not bring to bear the accumulated power of their spirit, but lapse into numbness, allowing heavy and slothful matter to gain power over them. In other words, at some time and place, reality, the merely extant, is always insurmountable, and therefore the nature of group individuality cannot be suspended. It will always impress its characteristic hallmarks upon the community.

The life span of a group is determined primarily, though not entirely, by that of the goal in whose service the group constituted itself; it is in any case utterly independent of the life and death of the individuals who compose the group. Over the course of its life, the group individuality works out the immanent possibilities of the idea, or, more precisely, it seeks to assert the idea as the life that fills time glides by. The individual as an individual may think and feel how and what he will, but once he becomes a member of the group he must subordinate himself to the idea; he is then transformed into the extratemporal group individuality, and his particular self—which is rooted in the full breadth of his temporally bound existence—must give way to a self assigned exclusively to the idea. The papal nuncio Aeneas Sylvius was a free-thinker and looked quite favorably on reform plans; the moment he became pope, however, he considered himself strictly a champion of the church and its traditions, the spirit of the church having devoured his other, earlier self.[3]

The insights developed up to this point, belonging as they do to the domain of purely formal sociology, have a significance similar to that of the law of inertia in mechanics. The latter is valid only in Galilean space—that is, in a space that is empty, containing no masses. It is a limit case, a principle that expresses the movement of a body independent of surrounding reality. The moment one includes masses, the movement does not in fact proceed the way the principle stipulates it should. Nevertheless, the principle does retain its value, since, if one merely includes in the equation all the forces acting upon the body, one can derive from it the formula for the latter's real motion. In "Galilean space" the idea forms its group body, and a group-self arises which, in a pure fashion, independent of the particular life of the single individual, develops the forces and contents residing within the idea. If one now considers the same scenario but with the full range of reality factored in, it becomes clear that the formal determinations of the nature of the group are no longer necessarily valid in the material, sociological sphere, or at the very least cannot be unequivocally applied within it. The gravitational forces of extant reality distract the group-self from the straight course that, according to its general nature, it actually ought to take. These same forces also often interrupt the close contacts—which disclose themselves to pure phenomenological intuition—between the group-self and the idea borne by it. It is not our task here to pursue the manifold empirical destinies to which the ideas and the groups that embody them are subject in the real world. Anyone who tried to master this task—which is in principle unsolvable—would lose himself in a bad infinity and would eventually find himself making, among other things, psychological observations. Since, in the pursuit of his goal, he would have to get closer and closer to the utterly particular case, he would end up in subjectively conditioned descriptions of concretely existing reality, yet without being able to distill its regularities. Certain typical processes manifested by ideas or groups can, however, be rendered evident very well. These processes, which I have described elsewhere as the typical schemata of the highest sociological categories,[4] represent, as it were, the first station on the path from formal to material sociology; and even though they do make reference to individual events, they still retain almost the universal validity of the intuitions of essence undertaken in "Galilean space," intuitions from which they can be deduced as a thought experiment.

The phenomenon of *splitting* is especially typical of the idea-bearing group. In the course of its passage through the social world, the tactical question arises again and again as to how best to proceed in one situation or another so that the idea to which the group has dedicated itself can be realized. Let us assume that at the time of the group's founding the members set up a hard and fast program containing all the demands to be made of the current state of reality according to the idea that generated the group. While the group individuality then goes about intervening in reality according to the terms of this program, that reality itself changes (to some extent also as a result of the group's actions) and new situations arise that demand a different stance on the part of the group. Assuming that the idea is still viable, its program has to be changed in order to take account of the change in reality. (One might think, for example, of the positions that political parties take before and after a revolution, or of the changing stance of the church toward political powers.) But although the surrounding environment changes only gradually, shifts in the group's standpoint must always occur by fits and starts. Once certain guidelines for the behavior of the group-self have been established, the latter adheres to them with an imperturbable fidelity that allows nothing to derail it. Any change of orientation always first requires a new resolution. As individuals, the people belonging to the group can think whatever they want about the group movement, and may have long considered it inappropriate, as a result of, say, new circumstances that have arisen in the meantime. Despite this, the group continues to roll along the course it has already begun, so long as a fresh impulse does not direct it onto another course, on which it in turn remains without any change of direction until the advent of a new impulse. Irrespective of how this impulse arises—whether it is thanks to the initiative of a *Führer*, or by request of the group members themselves—the group needs it in order to shunt itself from one track onto another. The group's itinerary is thus hardly an unbroken curve, but rather a straight line with multiple kinks. To put it differently, if one thinks of reality as a curve, then one can visualize the movement of the group as the tangential polygon that encloses it. The kinks in the line, however, mark the points at which the group once again finds itself confronting a new beginning. The members must keep up with the outside world and accordingly make decisions regarding the group's actions; the point is that the group must determine its stance on a specific situation relative to the spirit of its idea. From any such kink-point, however, there is usually more than one route that can be taken. Even if the group members are all molded by the same idea, tactical considerations still can lead some to go one way and some another. The moment the group's individuality dissolves into the multiplicity of the group members, it splits, only to re-form immediately into newly ori-ented and unified group entities. But the split occurs not because some portion of the newly self-conscious group membership abandoned its fidelity to the idea, but because various opinions regarding the group's practical influence on reality had already developed secretly, while the old group still existed. The group entity breaks apart because of tactical considerations, but the members adhere steadfastly to the idea itself.

There is one type of splitting within groups that occurs regularly and therefore deserves particular explanation. Suppose that a group initially takes up an antagonistic stance toward the entire social reality. It attempts to confer reality on the idea for which it was created, and the steps it undertakes to this effect meet with some success. Initially sup-pressed, it rises bit by bit to an elevated position, expands and gains influence within the community. Increasing numbers of people get involved in the idea borne by the group, and thereby the idea, to a limited extent, moves from the realm of should-being to that of being. There then comes a point in the life of the group when many of its adherents begin to feel that the group has achieved its goal insofar as this is possible; in any case they no longer conceive of their interaction with reality as dominated exclusively by the idea. In other words, the more the group penetrates and simultaneously burrows into reality, the more it also experiences the power of that reality. True, it has trans-formed the extant, but extant reality is still there, without having been entirely overcome and transcended. The weightiness, ungainliness, and impenetrability of reality are revealed clearly and more distinctly to those who approach it from the vantage point of the idea. At the outset it seems shrouded in fog and easy to unsettle. It is only once people have begun to do battle with it that its craters become visible and everything that merely *is*—but also precisely *is* and therefore does not allow itself to be pushed aside—emerges with horrible clarity. And the fateful question, the tempting question, begins to spread among the group: Is there a point at which the group must abandon its struggle with reality and seek a reconciliation, a compromise? A point at which people say: this far but no further? Every group that seeks to realize an idea will be confronted with the need to respond to this question sometime during its development. Once individual devotees of the idea have realized that, besides the logic of the idea, there is something like a logic of reality, then the group's homogeneous individuality will eventually dissolve and the relationship to reality will become the subject of a discussion decisive for the reconstitution of the group entity.

From this kink-point onward, the group usually splits into *two* individualities that pursue different paths through the social world based on their respective understandings of the relation between idea and reality. To be more precise, from this point onward one part of the group reaches a sort of peace agreement with the merely extant. It does not cease to champion the idea; but, on the one hand, it feels that the entire prior development has already led to substantive gains, and, on the other, it is profoundly convinced that the extant will always stand its ground against the idea and that people must therefore reckon with it and make compromises. It is the "moderates," the "reformers," the "revisionists," and so on who hold this view. They form a group whose point of origin is no longer really the idea, but rather some sort of synthesis of idea and reality. The (zigzag) course they have chosen is the product of two components—namely, the will to achieve the group's original goal and the will to acknowledge existing realities. The other part of the group, by contrast, dedicates itself with even greater commitment to the initial idea in all its purity. It considers partial achievement to be no achievement at all. Any deference to indifferent reality is tantamount to desertion, and the incorporation of that reality into the group entity's horizon is deemed synonymous with submission to the Caudine Yoke.[5] Utterly intolerant of pacts with the extant, this "radical" group individuality wants to realize utopia in the precise way it envisioned it. The fact that every group probably splits up in this manner—or at least tends toward such a split—is in the final analysis only an expression of the metaphysical fact that the soul is an intermediate thing between idea and reality, unable either to condescend entirely to the latter or to rise up to the former. As the bearer of a movement from should-being to being, the group entity has to experience the conflict over whether it should accept reality and thereby transcend the idea, or whether it should carry out the idea to its utmost consequences and thereby skip over reality. It solves the problem by splitting up. The unfolding of the idea subsequently takes place on two paths, whose fork is nothing other than the fruit of man's paradoxical metaphysical situation.

As a rule, however, the group individualities that come into being through the division initially feud with each other intensely. Precisely because they are both the product of a single idea, one group must try to destroy the other (or, what is in effect the same thing, repeatedly try to woo the other), since each believes that it alone truly represents the idea and each therefore perceives the existence of the sibling group as a denial of its innermost essence. There is no hatred more dreadful and disturbing than the hatred of a spiritually related being that shares the same origins as we do and that one day breaks away from us in order to pursue its own path of salvation. Or rather, it is by no means only hatred that lies between such beings; it is also the fear of their terrible forsakenness that leads them constantly to seek each other. It is, moreover, love that binds them to each other—the love of two creatures that were born of the same womb and that, despite all alienation, have never lost their sense of being blood relations. Every idea encounters other ideas that are somehow at odds with it. The group individualities that embody such conflicting spiritual forces in the community will, however, never confront each other with the same fervor and consuming passion as will groups that were originally one and the same. The former case involves the settling of substantive differences, whereas the latter entails the idea's confronting itself—the punishment of the heretic or the redemption of a repentant sinner—and thus is always more than simply a dispute between antagonistic parties.

The behavior of the sibling groups differs, moreover, in a characteristic manner. The *radical* group, which scorns all compromise with reality, considers itself the actual bearer of the unadulterated idea and stigmatizes the moderate group as the disloyal member of the original group individuality. Since it rejects reconciliation with the extant, it can continue straight as an arrow along the path dictated by the idea, and, in the knowledge of its own purity, can with a semblance of justice brand as traitors those who have obviously strayed from this path. For its part the *(moderate)* group, imbued with the power of reality, in some respects has a harder time defending its standpoint against the radicals. It tends to slip into a defensive position and has to appeal to common sense, to *insight*, whereas the other group needs only to call upon a *belief* that soars above reality. It sees in this other, radical group almost something like its better self, which has been led astray and which it wants to convince and bring back from utopian daydreams to the attainment of what is possible. Its strength and good conscience are grounded in the knowledge that it is championing something within reach and that it is driving the wedge of the idea into reality. It renders the idea finite and in the process allows it to become partially stunted, whereas the utopian group wants to realize the idea to the full extent of its infinity and thus also deprives reality of its claim to the entire idea. Once the split in the mother group has taken place, both of the resulting sibling groups are in a very profound sense indispensable for the process in which the merely-extant becomes an idea; only together, and as a result of their bilateral friction, do they help the idea achieve the form of which it is capable.

Also typical of the fate of a group is its slow withdrawal from the idea as such, its progressive immersion in reality. So long as a group's existence is threatened, it naturally lives purely for the sake of the idea that breathed life into it. It would be pulverized by the community were it to forsake the idea that alone lends it coherence. Having split a certain number of times, a group individuality that still embodies the idea may finally rise to power and attain a position no longer threatened by anyone. Having reached this point in its development, however, the group entity begins to lose more and more of its energy and starts to fall prey to the forces of the merely-extant, either forever or for some period of time, depending on the circumstances. What is the cause of this type of degeneration, which one can observe in all group formations that have "made it"? The group is created by an idea that wants to become reality; it is thus a creature that as yet has no roots whatever in the world of the extant. For the group, the development of the idea is synonymous with its continued existence, since, after all, in view of the way it lives for the time being (disconnected from reality, hovering freely above everything that has existence and heaviness), it derives its entire existence from the idea that propelled it into the world. But in championing this idea and attaining reality for it bit by bit, the group itself gradually puts down roots in reality. It settles within the community and becomes more and more intimately entwined in its life, until in the end one can no longer imagine that reality without it. The organizations that it trains take on socially significant functions, and the institutions that it inspires become established and legally binding. Purely theoretically, there now exist two possibilities. Either the group dissolves as an autonomous entity because its purpose has on the whole been achieved, or it continues to exist because, for instance, it embodies one of those sublime religious ideas that require continuous representation.

De facto, however, it does not matter which of these two possibilities is given: in either case the group individuality will seek to assert itself without limits and will ward off all attempts to dismember it. It is like a body moving in "Galilean space"—a body that can be brought to rest only by means of another counterbalancing force. Its inertia can be adequately explained, however, by its origins and its nature. The single individual can change his direction (in principle) as often as he wants; he is capable of self-denial and utter reversal. The group self, by contrast, does not have a consciousness that extends beyond it; torn away from the individual souls, it is a self that can only always confirm but never limit and destroy itself. Even if its continued existence has already become meaningless and superfluous, it will still never dissolve itself on its own but will instead continue to hang on, empty, as it were, until some external influences put an end to it. Why does a group individuality tend somewhat to eschew the idea that it bears, once it has come to power and is thoroughly embedded in reality? The reason is that a collective entity of this sort now no longer depends for its existence solely on its exclusive dedication to serving the idea, since it is now securely and firmly anchored in the entire lived reality of the community itself. In other words, the group has put down roots in the region of being and can therefore dissolve its ties to the domain of should-being without fearing its own demise. Once situated within the extant and no longer facing resistance, it almost holds itself together on its own, thanks to the direction it was once given, and just by virtue of being a group. Because it no longer so urgently needs to develop the idea in order to continue to exist, the group also immediately relaxes and yearns only to assert itself in terms of power. During its period of struggle—indeed, during its entire nascent state—it was the group that borrowed its entire strength and glory from the idea, whereas now, in the period of attained power, it is the idea that must be thankful to the group for everything the group accords it. The group is careful, however, not to renounce the idea officially, so to speak, even if it has long since ceased being actively engaged in furthering its development. Instead, it forms a free alliance (an alliance made between two independent powers) that is to its own advantage, in order to use the idea as a protective cover behind which it can continue to exist with impunity.

Again and again one finds that the responsibility for such sociological phenomena lies in the fundamental fact that spirit, when it is not perpetually active, tends to sink back into matter. It is always in periods of highest intensity that the soul goes beyond the merely-extant, beyond what is rule-governed and necessary, and becomes part of the realm of freedom. But its wings cannot bear it aloft very long, and, exhausted, it tumbles down toward reality, a victim of the devil who is always on the lookout to snatch it away from God. As mentioned earlier, the group that has gained power certainly does not abandon the idea, even though it has in fact deserted the idea and is now just floating along in reality (one thinks, for example, of the church during the Renaissance). An infallible instinct teaches it that the idea is an excellent ally on whom it can always rely, if ever its right to exist were put in question. It therefore negotiates a daring tightrope of a dialectic in order to deduce all its undertakings in reality from the idea, so that naïve sensibilities can believe that the group is acting as its executor. But its relations to the contents of should-being that once constituted it are in truth now only

of a superficial sort, the idea having become pure decoration, an osten-
tatious façade for a partly rotten interior which represents, together with
this façade, a unity that is nothing short of a mockery of spirit. Yet spirit
does not tolerate being scoffed at, and the idea takes sublime revenge on
the now powerful group that has slipped from its grasp. Even though
the group has relegated it to one more means of self-preservation, to a
submissive tool that one can manipulate as one sees fit, it has by no
means forfeited its significance as a transcendent should-being. It has
simply been engulfed, raped, and abused by reality instead of transforming that reality according to its terms.

But, in the final analysis, is it really the idea itself that is destroyed
in this process? Once hurled into the world, it will never be lost to spirit,
and when a group that wants to use it to permeate the extant goes the
way of all flesh, it is only this one group, and not the idea in itself, that
fails in its journey through social reality. Immobile, it dwells on the
horizon, and a human world that did not demonically aspire to it again
and again would have to be a world forsaken by God; it would not be
our world. Thus, if a group entity cannot bear to live constantly under
the sign of the idea, then the latter, betrayed, begins once again to have
an effect on the spirit (whose demands go beyond what merely exists)
and to prove its attractiveness. The one attempt to make it a reality did
not succeed to a sufficient degree; other attempts will follow in its wake.
The manner in which the idea henceforth continues creatively to work
itself out within the material domain (by founding new groups and so
on) is, however, determined by too many individual factors for it still to
be considered typical. As a rule, it employs the following unspeakably
subtle ploy: it takes the group body from which it has been ousted and
erodes it from within, only to give birth to itself anew within it. For it
is, after all, the members of the group that most profoundly experience
the horror of the fall into hell and, by mounting an attack against the
antispirit governing the group, rouse the latter from its torpor and
rekindle it with the idea. In the process, it often happens that they end
up—either willfully or not—creating a collective entity that is useful to
the idea but that henceforth detaches itself from the mother group and
goes its own way (they are sect-creators, reformers). From the very

maelstrom of the extant into which the idea was dragged down, a longing for that same idea again gushes forth. It burns only in order to rise eternally, like a phoenix from the ashes.

Among the idea-bearing groups, there is one particular type of collective unit for which the idea serves from the outset as a mere pretext for the pursuit of what are in truth completely different goals. Like real buccaneers, these groups commandeer an idea that best suits their purposes and harness it, as it were, to whatever vehicle they are riding. Capitalist interest groups, for example, champion the culture of personality; state entities with a colonial appetite pretend to be patrons of "civilization"; political parties striving for power and influence randomly confiscate some currently circulating ideal, which, by virtue of that act, immediately turns into ideology. In all such cases, very real aspirations lie at the end of the road—aspirations that are costumed in an idea only out of shame for the nakedness of their reality. What holds the group together and directs all its movements is not its idea or, better, its ideology, but rather the real goal that conceals itself behind it. Since the group individuality is, in the end, scheming to realize its desired good and not the contents of should-being that it is dissimulating, one would expect theoretically that it would alter its costume depending on the circumstances and on the changing historical situation—in other words, that it would simply drop a worn-out ideology in order to replace it with another one better suited to the moment. In fact, however, the idea requisitioned for profiteering purposes can by no means be cast off so abruptly. For in the group that has perpetrated an idea-heist, the idea itself gradually fuses with the group's real unifying purpose, creating a unity that is hardly dissolvable, so that in the end the group-self regards both as equally essential and is no longer even capable of distinguishing between them. Even the *Führer*-figures that establish groups lack a clear consciousness of just exactly how the idea is stored within them, whether as the original impetus or as the exponent of some other contents. If initially the group leaders consciously enlist the idea as a stimulus, they do so after all for the purpose of attracting as many people as possible, so as to provide the group with the strength necessary to be effective. All the people flocking into the group profess their loyalty directly to the idea without realizing its real significance. But the very fact that a majority of the group members are sworn to the idea already distracts the group-self from its real aspiration and commits it to developing the contents of should-being that it introduced under false pretenses. The urges of this group individuality, whose greatest spiritual itinerary is essentially formed by the idea's point of origin, cannot be avoided, even by savvy *Führer* types. Ultimately they themselves have to do justice to the belief they delivered into the world, since once an inflexible group entity has been made to serve its purposes, it can no longer be easily changed, as if it were just any loose garment. "Those spirits I invoked—now I can no longer get rid of them," laments the sorcerer's apprentice, whose fate in this respect is often enough shared by the *Führer*.[6] There is a delicate balance in such groups between the idea and the practical goal. Should a divergence arise between these two (usually intimately intertwined) entities, it is always very questionable which one of them will impose itself on the other.

The movements of the group individuality take place in a realm whose constitution and whose relation to the individual person's realm of action can perhaps be clearly articulated only at this point. The itinerary of every group is symbolized by a multiply broken line, and the idea—the group's spirit—must display a simple and coarse form that corresponds to the primitiveness and rigidity of the group-self. Thus, whenever the manifold group spirits that are wandering through the social world cordially encounter each other or brutally collide with one another, it is always a matter of alliances and ruptures that are in a certain sense beyond the individual's influence. All this jostling of the group spirits is concentrated in a domain into which the subject as subject can no longer reach, and the eruptions are therefore catastrophes of incomparable horror. When the autonomous (solitary) self tears itself free from its involvement with the various groups and consciously observes their movements as an individual, it perceives thousands of solutions and possibilities that could never be achieved by the group itself. In the individual, ideas expand in many directions, but in the social world governed by the group they can develop only in one direction and must lose all flexibility. Whereas in the individual and in the dealings that people have with other people ideas encounter one another in their full scope (along all of their surfaces, so to speak), in the social world they touch each other only along one of their edges and otherwise have little contact with one another. Between the angular, schematic, and deformed group spirits there are lots of empty spaces; one idea-form is abruptly confronted with another. The solitary individual's attempt to fill these voids with substance and to create continuous transitions must founder because of the very constitution of the group individualities. For compared with the solitary self, they are ungainly giants against whom the dainty delicacy of the individual's limbs are no match. This is in no way contradicted by the fact that *Führer* personalities invariably try to interfere with the development of group movements or try to found new groups under the sign of a new idea. For in these circumstances they are not acting as fully distinct and complete individuals. Rather, their being has already been subjected to that peculiar reduction and confinement that alone renders it capable of creative action in the sphere of the group individuality.

Scene from *Ihr dunkler Punkt* (Johannes Guter, 1929), starring Lilian Harvey

The Hotel Lobby

...

The community of the higher realms that is fixated upon God is secure in the knowledge that as an oriented community—both in time and for all eternity—it lives within the law and beyond the law, occupying the perpetually untenable middle ground between the natural and the supernatural. It not only presents itself in this paradoxical situation but also experiences and names it as well. In spheres of lesser reality, consciousness of existence and of the authentic conditions dwindles away in the existential stream, and clouded sense becomes lost in the labyrinth of distorted events whose distortion it no longer perceives.

The *aesthetic* rendering of such a life bereft of reality, a life that has lost the power of self-observation, may be able to restore to it a sort of language; for even if the artist does not force all that has become mute and illusory directly up into reality, he does express his directed self by giving form to this life. The more life is submerged, the more it needs the artwork, which unseals its withdrawnness and puts its pieces back in place in such a way that these, which were lying strewn about, become organized in a meaningful way. The unity of the aesthetic construct, the manner in which it distributes the emphases and consolidates the event, gives a voice to the inexpressive world, gives meaning to the themes broached within it. Just what these themes mean, however, must still be brought out through translation and depends to no small extent on the level of reality evinced by their creator. Thus, while in the higher spheres the artist confirms a reality that grasps itself, in the lower regions his work becomes a harbinger of a manifold that utterly lacks any revelatory word. His tasks multiply in proportion to the world's loss of reality, and the cocoon-like spirit *[Geist]* that lacks access to reality ultimately imposes upon him the role of educator, of the observer who not only sees but also prophetically foresees and makes connections. Although this overloading of the aesthetic may well accord the artist a mistaken position, it is understandable, because the life that remains untouched by authentic things recognizes that it has been captured in the mirror of the artistic construct, and thereby gains consciousness, albeit negative, of its distance from reality and of its illusory status. For no matter how insignificant the existential power that gives rise to the artistic formation may be, it always infuses the muddled material with intentions that help it become transparent.

Without being an artwork, the *detective novel* still shows civilized society its own face in a purer way than society is usually accustomed to seeing it. In the detective novel, proponents of that society and their functions give an account of themselves and divulge their hidden significance. But the detective novel can coerce the self-shrouding world into revealing itself in this manner only because it is created by a consciousness that is not circumscribed by that world. Sustained by this consciousness, the detective novel really thinks through to the end the society dominated by autonomous *Ratio*—a society that exists only as a concept—and develops the initial moments it proposes in such a way that the idea is fully realized in actions and figures. Once the stylization of the one-dimensional unreality has been completed, the detective novel integrates the individual elements—now adequate to the constitutive presuppositions—into a self-contained coherence of meaning, an integration it effects through the power of its existentiality, the latter transformed not into critique and exigency but into principles of aesthetic composition. It is only this entwinement into a unity that really makes possible the interpretation of the presented findings. For, like the philosophical system, the aesthetic organism aims at a totality that remains veiled to the proponents of civilized society, a totality that in some way disfigures the entirety of experienced reality and thereby enables one to see it afresh. Thus, the true meaning of these findings can be found only in the way in which they combine into an aesthetic totality. This is the minimum achievement of the artistic entity: to construct a whole out of the blindly scattered elements of a disintegrated world—a whole that, even if it seems only to mirror this world, nevertheless does capture it in its wholeness and thereby allows for the projection of its elements onto real conditions. The fact that the structure of the life presented in the detective novel is so typical indicates that the consciousness producing it is not an individual, coincidental one; at the same time, it shows that what has been singled out are the seemingly metaphysical characteristics. Just as the detective discovers the secret that people have concealed, the detective novel discloses in the aesthetic medium the secret of a society bereft of reality, as well as the secret of its insubstantial marionettes. The composition of the detective novel transforms an ungraspable life into a translatable analogue of actual reality.

...

In the *house of God*, which presupposes an already extant community, the congregation accomplishes the task of making connections. Once the members of the congregation have abandoned the relation on which the place is founded, the house of God retains only a decorative significance. Even if it sinks into oblivion, civilized society at the height of its development still maintains privileged sites that testify to its own nonexistence, just as the house of God testifies to the existence of the community united in reality. Admittedly society is unaware of this, for it cannot see beyond its own sphere; only the aesthetic construct, whose form renders the manifold as a projection, makes it possible to demonstrate this correspondence. The typical characteristics of the *hotel lobby*, which appears repeatedly in detective novels, indicate that it is conceived as the inverted image of the house of God. It is a negative church, and can be transformed into a church so long as one observes the conditions that govern the different spheres.

In both places people appear there as *guests*. But whereas the house of God is dedicated to the service of the one whom people have gone there to encounter, the hotel lobby accommodates all who go there to meet no one. It is the setting for those who neither seek nor find the one who is always sought, and who are therefore guests in space as such—a space that encompasses them and has no function other than to encompass them. The impersonal nothing represented by the hotel manager here occupies the position of the unknown one in whose name the church congregation gathers. And whereas the congregation invokes the name and dedicates itself to the service in order to fulfill the relation, the people dispersed in the lobby accept their host's incognito without question. Lacking any and all relation, they drip down into the vacuum with the same necessity that compels those striving in and for reality to lift themselves out of the nowhere toward their destination.

The congregation, which gathers in the house of God for prayer and worship, outgrows the imperfection of communal life in order not to overcome it but to bear it in mind and to reinsert it constantly into the tension. Its gathering is a *collectedness* and a unification of this directed life of the community, which belongs to two realms: the realm covered by law and the realm beyond law. At the site of the church—but of course not only here—these separate currents encounter each other; the law is broached here without being breached, and the paradoxical split is accorded legitimacy by the sporadic suspension of its languid continuity. Through the edification of the congregation, the community is always reconstructing itself, and this elevation above the everyday prevents the everyday itself from going under. The fact that such a returning of the community to its point of origin must submit to spatial and temporal limitations, that it steers away from worldly community, and that it is brought about through special celebrations—this is only a sign of man's dubious position between above and below, one that constantly forces him to establish on his own what is given or what has been conquered in the tension.

Since the determining characteristic of the lower region is its lack of tension, the togetherness in the hotel lobby has no meaning. While here, too, people certainly do become detached from everyday life, this detachment does not lead the community to assure itself of its existence as a congregation. Instead it merely displaces people from the unreality of the daily hustle and bustle to a place where they would encounter the void only if they were more than just reference points. The lobby,[1] in which people find themselves *vis-à-vis de rien*,[2] is a mere gap that does not even serve a purpose dictated by *Ratio* (like the conference room of a corporation), a purpose which at the very least could mask the directive that had been perceived in the relation. But if a sojourn in a hotel offers neither a perspective on nor an escape from the everyday, it does provide a groundless distance from it which can be exploited, if at all, *aesthetically*—the aesthetic being understood here as a category of the nonexistent type of person, the residue of that positive aesthetic which makes it possible to put this nonexistence into relief in the detective novel. The person sitting around idly is overcome by a disinterested satisfaction in the contemplation of a world creating itself, whose purposiveness is felt without being associated with any representation of a purpose. The Kantian definition of the beautiful is instantiated here in a way that takes seriously its isolation of the aesthetic and its lack of content. For in the emptied-out individuals of the detective novel—who, as rationally constructed complexes, are comparable to the transcendental subject—the aesthetic faculty is indeed detached from the existential stream of the total person. It is reduced to an unreal, purely formal relation that manifests the same indifference to the self as it does to matter. Kant himself was able to overlook this horrible last-minute sprint of the transcendental subject, since he still believed there was a seamless transition from the transcendental to the preformed subject-object world. The fact that he does not completely give up the total person even in the aesthetic realm is confirmed by his definition of the "sublime," which takes the ethical into account and thereby attempts to reassemble the remaining pieces of the fractured whole. In the hotel lobby, admittedly, the aesthetic—lacking all qualities of sublimity—is presented without any regard for these upward-striving intentions, and the formula "purposiveness without purpose"[3] also exhausts its content. Just as the lobby is the space that does not refer beyond itself, the aesthetic condition corresponding to it constitutes itself as its own limit. It is forbidden to go beyond this limit, so long as the tension that would propel the breakthrough is repressed and the marionettes of *Ratio*—who are not human beings—isolate themselves from their bustling activity. But the aesthetic that has become an end in itself pulls up its own roots; it obscures the higher level toward which it should refer and signifies only its own emptiness, which, according to the literal meaning of the

Kantian definition, is a mere relation of faculties. It rises above a meaningless formal harmony only when it is in the service of something,
when instead of making claims to autonomy it inserts itself into the
tension that does not concern it in particular. If human beings orient
themselves beyond the form, then a kind of beauty may also mature that
is a fulfilled beauty, because it is the consequence and not the aim—but
where beauty is chosen as an aim without further consequences, all that
remains is its empty shell. Both the hotel lobby and the house of God
respond to the aesthetic sense that articulates its legitimate demands in
them. But whereas in the latter the beautiful employs a language with
which it also testifies against itself, in the former it is involuted in its
muteness, incapable of finding the other. In tasteful lounge chairs a
civilization intent on rationalization comes to an end, whereas the decorations of the church pews are born from the tension that accords them
a revelatory meaning. As a result, the chorales that are the expression of
the divine service turn into medleys whose strains encourage pure triviality, and devotion congeals into erotic desire that roams about without
an object.

   The *equality* of those who pray is likewise reflected in distorted
form in the hotel lobby. When a congregation forms, the differences
between people disappear, because these beings all have one and the
same destiny, and because, in the encounter with the spirit that determines this destiny, anything that does not determine that spirit simply
ceases to exist—namely, the limit of necessity, posited by man, and the
separation, which is the work of nature. The provisional status of communal life is experienced as such in the house of God, and so the sinner
enters into the "we" in the same way as does the upright person whose
assurance is here disturbed. This—the fact that everything human is
oriented toward its own contingency—is what creates the equality of the
contingent. The great pales next to the small, and good and evil remain
suspended when the congregation relates itself to that which no scale
can measure. Such a relativization of qualities does not lead to their
confusion but instead elevates them to the status of reality, since the
relation to the last things demands that the penultimate things be con-
vulsed without being destroyed. This equality is positive and essential,

not a reduction and foreground; it is the fulfillment of what has been differentiated, which must renounce its independent singular existence in order to save what is most singular. This singularity is awaited and sought in the house of God. Relegated to the shadows so long as merely human limits are imposed, it throws its own shadow over those distinctions when man approaches the absolute limit.

In the hotel lobby, equality is based not on a relation to God but on a relation to the nothing. Here, in the space of unrelatedness, the change of environments does not leave purposive activity behind, but brackets it for the sake of a freedom that can refer only to itself and therefore sinks into relaxation and indifference. In the house of God, human differences diminish in the face of their provisionality, exposed by a seriousness that dissipates the certainty of all that is definitive. By contrast, an aimless lounging, to which no call is addressed, leads to the mere play that elevates the unserious everyday to the level of the serious. Simmel's definition of society as a "play form of sociation"[4] is entirely legitimate, but does not get beyond mere description. What is presented in the hotel lobby is the formal similarity of the figures, an equivalence that signifies not fulfillment but evacuation. Removed from the hustle and bustle, one does gain some distance from the distinctions of "actual" life, but without being subjected to a new determination that would circumscribe from above the sphere of validity for these determinations. And it is in this way that a person can vanish into an undetermined void, helplessly reduced to a "member of society as such" who stands superfluously off to the side and, when playing, intoxicates himself. This invalidation of togetherness, itself already unreal, thus does not lead up toward reality but is more of a sliding down into the doubly unreal mixture of the undifferentiated atoms from which the world of appearance is constructed. Whereas in the house of God a creature emerges which sees itself as a supporter of the community, in the hotel lobby what emerges is the inessential foundation at the basis of rational socialization. It approaches the nothing and takes shape by analogy with the abstract and formal *universal concepts* through which thinking that has escaped from the tension believes it can grasp the world. These abstractions are inverted images of the universal concepts conceived within the relation; they rob the ungraspable given of its possible content, instead of raising it to the level of reality by relating it to the higher determinations. They are irrelevant to the oriented and total person who, the world in hand, meets them halfway; rather, they are posited by the transcendental subject, which allows them to become part of the powerlessness into which that transcendental subject degenerates as a result of its claim to be creator of the world. Even if free-floating *Ratio*—dimly aware of its limitation—does acknowledge the concepts of God, freedom, and immortality, what it discovers are not the homonymic existential concepts, and the categorical imperative is surely no substitute for a commandment that arises out of an ethical resolution. Nevertheless, the weaving of these concepts into a system confirms that people do not want to abandon the reality that has been lost; yet, of course, they will not get hold of it precisely because they are seeking it by means of a kind of thinking which has repudiated all attachment to that reality. The desolation of *Ratio* is complete only when it removes its mask and hurls itself into the void of random abstractions that no longer mimic higher determinations, and when it renounces seductive consonances and desires itself even as a concept. The only immediacy it then retains is the now openly acknowledged nothing, in which, grasping upward from below, it tries to ground the reality to which it no longer has access. Just as God becomes, for the person situated in the tension, the beginning and end of all creation, so too does the intellect that has become totally self-absorbed create the appearance of a plenitude of figures from zero. It thinks it can wrench the world from this meaningless universal, which is situated closest to that zero and distinguishes itself from it only to the extent necessary in order to deduct a something. But the world is world only when it is interpreted by a universal that has been really experienced. The intellect reduces the relations that permeate the manifold to the common denominator of the concept of energy, which is separated merely by a thin layer from the zero. Or it robs historical events of their paradoxical nature and, having leveled them out, grasps them as progress in one-dimensional time. Or, seemingly betraying itself, it elevates irrational "life" to the dignified status of an entity in order to recover itself, in its delimitation, from the now liberated residue of the totality of human being, and in order to traverse the realms across their entire expanse. If one takes as one's basis these extreme reductions of the real, then (as Simmel's philosophy of life confirms) one can obtain a distorted image of the discoveries made in the upper spheres—an image that is no less comprehensive than the one provided by the insistence of the words "God" and "spirit." But even less ambiguously than the abusive employment of categories that have become incomprehensible, it is the deployment of empty abstractions that announces the actual position of a thinking that has slipped out of the tension. The visitors in the hotel lobby, who allow the individual to disappear behind the peripheral equality of social masks, correspond to the exhausted terms that coerce differences out of the uniformity of the zero. Here, the visitors suspend the undetermined special being— which, in the house of God, gives way to that invisible equality of beings standing before God (out of which it both renews and determines itself)—by devolving into tuxedos. And the triviality of their conversation, haphazardly aimed at utterly insignificant objects so that one might encounter oneself in their exteriority, is only the obverse of prayer, directing downward what they idly circumvent.

The observance of *silence,* no less obligatory in the hotel lobby than in the house of God, indicates that in both places people consider themselves essentially as equals. In "Death in Venice" Thomas Mann formulates this as follows: "A solemn stillness reigned in the room, of the sort that is the pride of all large hotels. The attentive waiters moved about on noiseless feet. A rattling of the tea service, a half-whispered word was all that one could hear."[5] The contentless solemnity of this conventionally imposed silence does not arise out of mutual courtesy, of the sort one encounters everywhere, but rather serves to eliminate differences. It is a silence that abstracts from the differentiating word and compels one downward into the equality of the encounter with the nothing, an equality that a voice resounding through space would disturb. In the house of God, by contrast, silence signifies the individual collecting himself as firmly directed self, and the word addressed to human beings is effaced solely in order to release another word, which, whether uttered or not, sits in judgment over human beings.

Since what counts here is not the dialogue of those who speak, the members of the congregation are anonymous. They outgrow their names because the very empirical being which these names designate disappears in prayer; thus, they do not know one another as particular beings whose multiply determined existences enmesh them in the world. If the proper name reveals its bearer, it also separates him from those whose names have been called; it simultaneously discloses and obscures, and it is with good reason that lovers want to destroy it, as if it were the final wall separating them. It is only the relinquishing of the name—which abolishes the semisolidarity of the intermediate spheres—that allows for the extensive solidarity of those who step out of the bright obscurity of reciprocal contact and into the night and the light of the higher mystery. Now that they do not know who the person closest to them is, their neighbor becomes the closest, for out of his disintegrating appearance arises a creation whose traits are also theirs. It is true that only those who stand before God are sufficiently estranged from one another to discover they are brothers; only they are exposed to such an extent that they can love one another without knowing one another and without using names. At the limit of the human they rid themselves of their naming, so that the word might be bestowed upon them—a word that strikes them more directly than any human law. And in the seclusion to which such a relativization of form generally pushes them, they inquire about their form. Having been initiated into the mystery that provides the name, and having become transparent to one another in their relation to God, they enter into the "we" signifying a commonality of creatures that suspends and grounds all those distinctions and associations adhering to the proper name.

This limit case "we" of those who have dispossessed themselves of themselves—a "we" that is realized vicariously in the house of God due to human limitations—is transformed in the hotel lobby into the isolation of anonymous atoms. Here profession is detached from the person and the name gets lost in the space, since only the still unnamed crowd can serve *Ratio* as a point of attack. It reduces to the level of the nothing—out of which it wants to produce the world—even those pseudo-individuals it has deprived of individuality, since their anonymity no longer serves any purpose other than meaningless movement along the paths of convention. But if the meaning of this anonymity becomes nothing more than the representation of the insignificance of this beginning, the depiction of formal regularities, then it does not foster the solidarity of those liberated from the constraints of the name; instead, it deprives those encountering one another of the possibility of association that the name could have offered them. Remnants of individuals slip into the nirvana of relaxation, faces disappear behind newspapers, and the artificial continuous light illuminates nothing but mannequins. It is the coming and going of unfamiliar people who have become empty forms because they have lost their password, and who now file by as ungraspable flat ghosts. If they possessed an interior, it would have no windows at all, and they would perish aware of their endless abandonment, instead of knowing of their homeland as the congregation does. But as pure exterior, they escape themselves and express their nonbeing through the false aesthetic affirmation of the estrangement that has been installed between them. The presentation of the surface strikes them as an attraction; the tinge of exoticism gives them a pleasurable shudder. Indeed, in order to confirm the distance whose definitive character attracts them, they allow themselves to be bounced off a proximity that they themselves have conjured up: their monological fantasy attaches designations to the masks, designations that use the person facing them as a toy. And the fleeting exchange of glances which creates the possibility of exchange is acknowledged only because the illusion of that possibility confirms the reality of the distance. Just as in the house of God, here too namelessness unveils the meaning of naming; but whereas in the house of God it is an awaiting within the tension that reveals the preliminariness of names, in the hotel lobby it is a retreat into the unquestioned groundlessness that the intellect transforms into the names' site of origin. But where the call that unifies into the "we" is not heard, those that have fled the form are irrevocably isolated.

In the congregation the entire community comes into being, for the immediate relation to the supralegal *mystery* inaugurates the paradox of the law that can be suspended in the actuality of the relation to God.

That law is a penultimate term that withdraws when the connection occurs that humbles the self-assured and comforts those in danger. The tensionless people in the hotel lobby also represent the entire society, but not because transcendence here raises them up to its level; rather, this is because the hustle and bustle of immanence is still hidden. Instead of guiding people beyond themselves, the mystery slips between the masks; instead of penetrating the shells of the human, it is the veil that surrounds everything human; instead of confronting man with the question of the provisional, it paralyzes the questioning that gives access to the realm of provisionality. In his all-too contemplative detective novel *Der Tod kehrt im Hotel ein* (Death Enters the Hotel), Sven Elvestad writes: "Once again it is confirmed that a large hotel is a world unto itself and that this world is like the rest of the large world. The guests here roam about in their light-hearted, careless summer existence without suspecting anything of the strange mysteries circulating among them."[6] "Strange mysteries": the phrase is ironically ambiguous. On the one hand, it refers quite generally to the disguised quality of lived existence as such; on the other, it refers to the higher mystery that finds distorted expression in the illegal activities that threaten safety. The clandestine character of all legal and illegal activities—to which the expression initially and immediately refers—indicates that in the hotel lobby the pseudo-life that is unfolding in pure immanence is being pushed back toward its undifferentiated origin. Were the mystery to come out of its shell, mere possibility would disappear in the fact: by detaching the illegal from the nothing, the Something would have appeared. The hotel management therefore thoughtfully conceals from its guests the real events which could put an end to the false aesthetic situation shrouding that nothing. Just as the formerly experienced higher mystery pushes those oriented toward it across the midpoint, whose limit is defined by the law, so does the mystery—which is the distortion of the higher ground and as such the utmost abstraction of the dangers that disrupt immanent life—relegate one to the lapsed neutrality of the meaningless beginning from which the pseudo-middle arises. It hinders the outbreak of differentiations in the service of emancipated *Ratio*, which strengthens its victory over the Something in the hotel lobby by helping the conventions take the upper hand. These are so worn out that the activity taking place in their name is at the same time an activity of dissimulation—an activity that serves as protection for legal life just as much as for illegal life, because as the empty form of all possible societies it is not oriented toward any particular thing but remains content with itself in its insignificance.

PERSPECTIVES

Herbert Schürmann, "Lattice between Panes of Glass," 1933

The Bible in German

ON THE TRANSLATION BY MARTIN BUBER AND FRANZ ROSENZWEIG

■ ■ ■

Das Buch Im Anfang (The Book in the Beginning)[1] has just been published, the first part of a translation of the Old Testament which will eventually encompass twenty volumes. Martin Buber and Franz Rosenzweig are the germanizers. The project marks a stage in their development, but this development is not theirs alone.

In his major philosophical work *The Star of Redemption,*[2] Franz Rosenzweig—whose insight is more profound than Buber's and thus more difficult to penetrate—attempted fundamentally to renounce the declining idealist philosophy. As an exemplary expression of a period rushing toward its completion, the book—a systematic study rich in sound interpretations—is a historical document of high rank. In accordance with this renunciation it is entirely consistent that Rosenzweig was captivated by the reality of religiously committed Jewish life. The founding of the *Freies jüdisches Lehrhaus* (Free Jewish House of Learning) in Frankfurt[3] and his translations of writers such as Yehuda Halevi[4] are external proof of his shift from theory to praxis.—Buber, the leader of part of the younger Jewish generation (particularly those who are more Zionist in orientation), joins Rosenzweig in this shift. Buber is known in the German public sphere less for his translations of Eastern literature[5] than for his efforts over many decades to make Hasidism accessible. The result of these efforts is the series of collections of Hasidic tales that he edited and that have become a significant addition to the western European cultural tradition.[6] The attitude toward life and knowledge that is manifested today by both Buber and Rosenzweig can be called "religious" only with some qualification. The term may be used only if it does not serve, as it usually does, to demarcate a special domain unto itself—in this case a religious one. Rather, it must be understood here as designating a form of existence whose intention is to situate the entire person in reality. "Religious" here means a *practice of life* that flourishes on the basis of a real connection to essential truth contents—in this case, those conveyed by the documents of Jewish scripture—and not a theoretical orientation of consciousness or a purely internal religious undertaking like that of the liturgical movement.

The new germanization of the Bible may well have arisen out of the will to strengthen this sort of life. One should understand the translation not as an autonomous literary product but as the testimony and outgrowth of a religious circle—irrespective of whether it in fact already exists or is only hoped for. The expectation of the fulfillment of this hope determines the translation's form. Its *lack of commentary* can have resulted only from the intention to address immediately the whole person or even the entire community. The elimination of the critical textual apparatus presupposes as well the conviction that the written word retains its staying power. The authors aspire to literal translation and rhythmic fidelity according to the principles that Rosenzweig developed in his translation of Yehuda Halevi.[7] The Hebrew language is not to be germanized; rather, German should extend into the Hebrew so that it can move those who turn to it with the force of an exact likeness.

The first volume poses numerous philological challenges: comparison of the text with the original, examination of the rhythm, discussion of the deviations from the masoretic version (that is, from the version which Jewish tradition considers standard).[8] Still, no matter how essential these philological issues may be, they are not the most urgent ones. Even more pressing is the obligation to inspect the self-contained *form of the German language* in the translation itself, a narrowing of focus that can be undertaken without hesitation because the authors did in fact proceed in a competent and conscientious way. Through an analysis of the language, one can also characterize the stance to which the work subscribes; its linguistic expression indirectly renders the meaning of this stance transparent. It is the stance of the religious circle that may be the most immediate audience for this rendition into German. Under the sign of "religious renewal,"[9] groups have also formed within Catholic and Protestant circles which concur formally with those that have coalesced around Buber and Rosenzweig in their common attempt to reestablish people's relationships to the truths revealed in religion. What one can say about the ideal community of readers for this version of the Bible will also have to be relevant to them. Language is like the spot between Siegfried's shoulder blades on which the linden leaf fell: it is the only place on the body of the powerful realities that is not protected by the magic of the dragon's blood.[10]

■ ■ ■

Translations of the Bible are unlike translations of other texts in that they do not, as the latter do, take predominantly aesthetic criteria as their norm. In contrast to works that exist in time and change along with it, the Bible demands to be accorded the status of truth at all times. The insistence that the Bible have immediate relevance for the present (an insistence legitimated by the Bible's claim to truth) subordinates the purely aesthetic offering to the translator's *obligations to knowledge:* prior to anything else, the translator must discover the point at which the truth captured by the word can penetrate the time to which it, as truth, must refer. The content of this knowledge determines the feasibility of the translation and its form; it can preclude an attitude toward the original that, from an immanently aesthetic perspective, might be appropriate toward other texts. Borchardt's translation of the *Divine Comedy* into the German of Dante's time[11]—a legitimate achievement in the realm of the merely aesthetic—is based on a principle that is inappropriate for the text of the Bible, if only because it would give it an aesthetic distance which would rob its truth of its meaning. Bringing this truth into the present is not, however, synonymous with assimilating it facilely to that present. In a period alienated from the biblical word, the Bible's contents are not well served either by a translation that gains access to everyday language only by sacrificing what was originally meant. The correct *actualization* of Scripture that is called for here resists the compromise that destroys the very word it thinks it is conveying. Such an actualization must by nature be infused with a revolutionary spirit, because truth does not unfold within the extant. The ur-text returns to its untranslatable remoteness when the revolutionary language of a historical epoch—the language that now, no matter how transformed and incomplete it may be, alone captures the truth—has dissociated itself from the formulations of that ur-text.

The *Luther Bible* is actual in this sense. Thanks to the historical constellation at the time of its composition, the revolutionary protest against church abuses (which were also socioeconomic abuses) found precise expression in the return to the word of Scripture. Its translation was a weapon that was meant to impede the "papist" employment of the vulgate. Here the truth of the Bible proves itself through its actualization; as in Moses Mendelssohn's later translation of the Pentateuch,[12] the religious encroaches on the *political*, which it cannot deny if it is ever to cause the untruth in the world to wither away. But the suitability of the Luther text as a revolutionary instrument is due not least to the fact that, at the time of its production, secular thinking had hardly begun to emancipate itself from theological thought. It is only the intimate relation between the two that makes it possible to expand "ordinary" German language into the language of the Bible, enabling the latter to invade the former. The conservative church powers are dispossessed of their carefully guarded property, which is disseminated among the lower classes in order to help prepare anew a true order of things. In exemplary fashion (even though it can no longer be imitated), Luther thus takes Scripture out of the inaccessible spheres and inserts it into the life of the people, drags it down to the humblest of places, to which truth is attracted because this is the locus of the flaw in the construction of man's framework. "Anything but castle and court words," he writes to Spalatin. "This book can be explained only in a simple and ordinary way."[13]

. . .

The *profane* has long since outgrown the theological categories that were still able to contain it (more or less) at the time of the Reformation, or that at least functioned as its fitting superstructure. Out of the shell of these theological categories have emerged interests that are now entirely secular in character: the communities of the extant religions are confronted with a society that has come into its own, as an entity with its own concepts and objectives. It is in this society, and not in the extant religions, that the actuality of the present resides. This actuality is always located precisely at the point where the communal life of people in truth is decisively threatened. One sees, however, that the economic and social power relations which determine the intellectual/spiritual structure of today's society in all its ramifications are the factual impediment to proper coexistence. In the course of the historical process, these power relations have come to light more and more openly; the most self-confident cultures were doomed to decline because they were based on the rotten foundation of these power relations. It is for the sake of truth—which announces itself in the historical process as a logical compulsion—that the secular realm of economic facts has gained such decisive actuality. For if the self-determined authority of the material factors has ruined the cultural products linked to them, a new order can be achieved only by changing these factors. This, in turn, cannot happen until these factors emerge stripped of all the veils that shelter and obscure them. At present, therefore, the locus of truth itself is in the midst of "common" public life—not because the economic and social aspects are significant in and of themselves, but because they are the determining factors. Admittedly they cannot fully account for the realm of religious and spiritual/intellectual experiences. On the one hand, the contents of these experiences lack a real basis, because social relations have been shattered. On the other hand, lingering in this religious and spiritual/intellectual realm distracts people from the task of rearranging the social order. Most of today's literary products that remain naïvely in purely spiritual/intellectual spheres—to which corresponds a private individual that no longer exists—are either intentional or involuntary attempts at stabilizing the ruling societal situation. Their status as manifestations of repression robs them of their weight. In these realms, truth can no longer be encountered directly.

Along with truth, *language* has departed as well. Luther could still trust in his ability to fuse the language of the Bible with that of the people; classicism, romanticism, and idealism were able to use a language that could legitimately claim to be both determined by spirit/intellect and carried by a self vacillating between transcendental subjectivity and personality, because the partial dependence of their beliefs and ideas on the external structure of profane society was still hidden. Once the decisive role of the material forces becomes apparent, however, these linguistic constructs lose their exacting power. They have not disappeared completely. They are preserved by a historicist stance and, marked by sorrow, now reside in the aesthetic realm. The lengths of their sentences and their configurations still speak of a self-evident harmony with an object world that has long since taken flight. It is not in these linguistic forms that reality is to be found, even if beauty still lingers in their midst. Rather, following the course taken by truth, reality has sought refuge in a language whose form and categorial material expresses the awareness that the essential events today are playing themselves out on profane ground. No matter how reticent and negative this language may be, it alone has necessity on its side, for it alone constitutes itself at the point where suffering can be reversed. In contrast, it is entirely consistent that linguistic constructs demonstrating their disregard for the current situation in their carefree appropriation of extant and now dubious meanings lose their claimed ontological power and are surrendered to subjective arbitrariness. The vulgarization of concepts taken from the domain of inner and exalted existence is as unaccidental and unalterable an event as the rapid loss of substance in every language, which currently pretends to be sacred and esoteric (like the prose of the George Circle, for example). To enter into these abandoned linguistic spheres is to renounce reality.

...

Buber and Rosenzweig's translation claims to renew the reality of Scripture in its purity. Indeed, one feels their desire (and this desire should be acknowledged and respected) to restore to the text the power that truth bestowed upon it. In coinages such as the one describing Abraham's dying "at a good old age" *[in gutem Greisentum]*, one hears an attempt to resurrect the rhythm of the Hebrew within the foreign idiom. The trust in the German word here is unlimited in a way matched only by Luther's. Does it carry the translators over to Scripture?

Under the pressure of their work—which they took upon themselves of their own free will—they have run aground on a form of language that is certainly not of today. But these tones do not resonate forth from the biblical era either, even though that is the locus to which the authors want to transfer the scene. Just exactly where between present and antiquity this scene has been set up can be determined by a few samples. The definitive Luther formulation "and the spirit of God hovered above the water" [*und der Geist Gottes schwebte auf dem Wasser*], which takes on a thin but clean and real form in the Zunz edition of Scripture[14] ("and the spirit of God hovering over the surface of the water" [*und der Geist Gottes schwebend über die Fläche der Wasser*]), is transformed by our translators into the resounding formulation "God's surging that brooded everywhere above the waters" [*Braus Gottes brütend allüber den Wassern*]. The question as to which Zeitgeist brooded this surging becomes clear from the fact that they lift up high-gifts, becloud cloud, and slaughter slaughter-animals, whereas Luther lets Noah sacrifice burnt offerings, has clouds travel over the earth, and, to put it simply, slaughters. It is also evident from the fact that they take the Luther text "and the LORD smelled the lovely scent" and elevate it to the lofty German formulation "Thus HE scented the scent of assentment" [*Da roch ER den Ruch der Befriedigung*]. The stench of these alliterations stems not from the Bible but from runes of a Wagnerian sort. The highest Germanist standards of the Ring of the Nibelungen would be satisfied by the following rhythmic question:

> Want to be king, you a king among us,
> Or be ruler, you a ruler over us?
> *[König wärst wohl gern, bei uns du König?*
> *Oder Walter du, über uns Walter?]*

Similarly, the use of restorative expressions such as "cultmaiden" [*Weihbuhle*] (as opposed to Luther's "whore" and Zunz's police-like "concubine" [*Beischläferin*]) and "markplace" [*Malstatt*] (where Luther simply writes "mark" [*Mal*]) corresponds to the way in which gods and warriors speak in musical dramas. This is equally true of the exhortation "May thy seed occupy the *high gate* of its haters!" *[Besetze dein Same das Hochtor seiner Hasser!]* (compared with Luther's "and your seed shall possess the gates of its enemies"). A well-trodden path leads from Wagner's heroic upper realms down to the nearby flatlands of Felix Dahn and Gustav Freytag,[15] to which one is quickly transported by words such as "beyond measure" *[ohnemaß]* and "forsooth" *[fürwahr]* or the excitedly punctuated stained-glass salutation "By your leave, my lord!" *[Mit Verlaub, mein Herr!]*.

Enough said: the language is to a great extent *archaizing*. As a result of considerations that fail to take account of their effects, the translation uses precisely those now utterly delegitimated "castle and court words" that Luther deliberately rejected. Their origin is obvious: they stem from the mythological busy-ness and antiquarianizing neo-Romanticism of the waning nineteenth century, which were maintained by a cultivated middle class in need of spiritual/intellectual backing, and which at the time may have been able to lay claim to a certain reality because of their appropriateness to the social situation. That this language has in the meantime decayed into ruins becomes clear through a comparison with the German of Luther that has survived.

The linguistic hinterland that these misplaced words demarcate is cultivated to the fullest extent by the translators—a practice that is all the more burdensome since both mean for language to be treated with respect, and Wilhelm Michel can remark that Buber belongs "among the foremost contemporary German voices."[16] Their belief in the atemporal ontological power of the German they have created lures them out of the domesticated realm of the word "altar" *[Altar]* and toward the wild "slaughterplace" *[Schlachtstatt]*; it prompts them to replace Luther's idiomatic "all the world" *[alle Welt]* or "all the lands" *[alle Lande]* with the expression "folk of the earth" *[Erdvolk]*, which smacks of pseudo-native soil. But instead of bringing the fixed distance of Scripture into the present, these ur-German expressions drag Scripture into an ur-German that is only a few decades old. It is language's act of vengeance against the impertinence of presenting it as a reality where it no longer is one. Language's current lack of consistency (particularly in the spheres that point beyond the mundane), just like its inability to name many essentialities (which can be explained as due to the functionalization of the object world), is overlooked to such an extent that one resolutely gives new shadings to concepts which have been handed down for centuries. (It is good, at least, that what is meant to be ontological occasionally reveals itself involuntarily as a flat functionalization—as in the transformation of Luther's "lineage" *[Geschlecht]* into "progeny" *[Zeugungen].*) According to the publisher's brochure, the books of Chronicles will become the books of "Incidents" *[Begebenheiten],* and the Prophets will become *harbingers [Künder]*—a coinage that seems to be taken less from the Old Testament than from Stefan George's *Stern des Bundes.*[17] As such it is an idiom whose entry into common usage can hardly be harbingered, since it already belongs to the past, albeit a bourgeois one. In a time that is essentially historicist in orientation, it is unlikely that the "tendency to become a reality," which Wilhelm Michel attributes to Buber, will be substantiated by these and other germanizations that ignore their own historical position. If it were, the reality achieved would reveal itself as disturbingly close to that planned by *national romanticism [Völkischer Romantik].* Nor is this necessarily contradicted by the fact that, contrary to the ultra-Lutheran tendency to germanize everything, proper names are inserted in Hebrew: *Eszaw* (Esau), *Ribka* (Rebekah), and *Jirmejahu* (Jeremiah) *the harbinger.* Perhaps here national concerns claim their folk-of-the-earth *[erdvölkisches]* rights.

If the reality of these names is not what is intended, then one can only surmise that an *aesthetic* interest has caused the exotic vegetation of Hebrew nomenclature to be transplanted in the purely German environment. Such an aesthetic interest would, of course, be at odds with an interest in reality. Still, regardless of whether or not the work is motivated by this aesthetic interest, its disposition and language do seem determined by it in the end. As questionable as the translation's aesthetic effect may be, it indirectly confirms that its reality is only an aesthetic one. But at the very point where it wants most decisively to have a real effect, it sinks back into the impotence of the aesthetic. The decision not to include a commentary—supposedly in order to present the truth of Scripture without any intervention—gives the impression of having been made for the sake of artistic purity. The linguistic progenies, created as a means of reawakening the substance of Scripture, do not come across as very essential in the empathetically recreated rhythm (Borchardt would be better at this) but rather are forced into it with great effort and deliberately emphasize their own beauty, no matter how faded it is. Here art is not basing itself on reality; instead, reality vanishes into the artistic.

This germanization of Scripture does not stir up the present. In contrast to Luther's version, which erupted into its time as a revolutionary accomplishment, this translation lacks topical relevance. The remoteness of the language betrays that of its substance; truth is not conveyed by the unavailable words of an only recently past epoch whose sociological structure would not have been hard to see through. The translators ought to have recognized which domains today need to be blasted apart by truth. Whereas the Luther Bible attacked at precisely the decisive point, Buber and Rosenzweig's German rendering veers away from the public sphere of our social existence and into the *private*. In their translation, the text of the Bible, which is meant to tear open the quotidian, is removed from the realm of the quotidian and made into the foundation for an imaginary stage-consecration-festival play.[18] It is only as such that this German might have once had limited validity; it was never an expression of real oppression or a means to knowledge.

The anachronistic quality of the translation gives the stance underlying it a *reactionary* meaning. By avoiding profane language, it represses the profane; by taking flight from the realm of the ordinary public sphere, it abandons the pressing needs that have truth on their side. Admittedly this realm is the realm of externality, but the elevation of the interior is tied to the transformation of the exterior. The vocabulary of the German rendering of Scripture proves that this rendering is meant to speak in binding terms to individuals whose social relations have not been taken into account. It misappropriates the focus of significance away from externality and thereby becomes an instrument directed against the survival of truth. The private self that it addresses must, because of the false elevation of that self, obstruct its own access to the public sphere. Its unreality is exposed by the romantic gesture of the translation whose aesthetic effect marks it as a symptom of flight and marks the private realm as its refuge. The potential consequences (including the political ones) of such a retreat emerge from the nationalist intonation of some of the neobiblical manifestations.

A fundamental critique of the translation is necessary because it is sustained by a firm concept of *reality*. Buber develops this concept in his book on the philosophy of religion, titled *I and Thou*,[19] which was published a few years ago. Here he differentiates the "Thou-World" (in which the *I* and the *Thou* stand as complete individuals in a nonobjectified relation to each other) from the "It-World" (in which people objectify the other and thereby enter into an abstract relation with these objects, from which they have separated themselves). Whereas in the former all beings achieve reality through their inner connectedness, in the latter, he claims, everything that could testify to real life petrifies into declarations of an inauthentic sort. It is man's fate to sink into this "It-World," and our duty to turn our backs on it. Thus, for Buber, truth can manifest itself only where man grasps it with his entire being; yet it also resists every theoretical contemplation that thinks it possesses truth in abstract form as an object. For one part of the intellectual/ spiritual leadership, this interpretation, which plays out the real against the unreal and the concrete against the nonconcrete, has become an *ideology* that is all the more welcome since in formal terms it is entirely correct. In light of social conditions, the educated classes depend upon precisely those attitudes (which in themselves are innocuous) as a life vest for their conscience. Buber's concept of reality immediately takes on an ideological character when, for instance, a reality that no longer exists in substance wants to claim superiority over a theory that despite (or, more correctly, because of) its abstraction is the locus of actuality today. Buber and Rosenzweig's germanization of Scripture is convincing evidence of such a practice; the character of its reality is denounced by its language, whose poeticizing tendency is more foreign to reality than a good deal of everyday prose. Buber forgets—and many forget along with him—that truth itself wanders from point to point, from sphere to sphere, and that at a given time it can very well be compelled to attack in the profane realms in which a social critique (no matter how abstract) is more at home than a contemplation of reality that skips over it. These profane realms are currently the essential site where truth breaks through. Buber sacrifices them when he withdraws into his "Thou-World," where, to use his own terminology, he can hope to encounter merely an "it."

But if reality can be reached only by means of a path that leads through the "unreality" of the profane, then today Scripture can *no longer* be translated. The very intention of this germanization already leads away from the truth to the extent that it presumes to convey the Word directly, with all of its original force. Luther's situation is not ours; the time is past when the German language—or any language, for that matter—was capable of legitimately harboring the truth of Scripture. For us this truth must remain preserved in Luther's translation, or else it no longer exists. For it is through Luther's version and only through his version that Scripture entered reality at a specific point in our history. Furthermore, the tradition that may still be able to maintain Scripture in that reality, once the profane has separated itself from the theological spheres, is also based on Luther's translation. The only thing that might live up to the profane would be a *critical textual edition* which, for instance, would bring Kautzsch[20] up to the current state of modern Jewish scriptural research and, as one is wont to say, would satisfy all the legitimate claims of science. Between philological exegesis on the one hand and Luther's translation on the other, there is no room for a third undertaking. There is not the slightest doubt that an annotated edition born of today's historicist way of thinking and whose aim was merely to clarify and preserve the ur-text would, over time, convey the spirit of Scripture—which such a work would deliberately render mute—more faithfully than the romantic and arbitrary attempt by Buber and Rosenzweig, which wants to force it to speak in an untimely fashion.

■ ■ ■

The problem raised by the translation is that of *religious renewal* in general. Spellbound by the word of such renewal, movements, circles, and groups have arisen and, out of a sometimes tenuous, sometimes closer contact with extant faiths, have endeavored to proclaim a shift in Being. The rendering of Scripture into German, which cannot be separated from the current state of this religious renewal, provides an indication of the dangers to which such movements are subject. It could be that in their "move into reality"[21] those groups might in fact miss what is real in the visible external world. It could be that they think they are entering that reality with their lives, whereas in fact they are leaving public reality to take care of itself in order to save their own private existence. It could be that they believe they are serving the truth, whereas in fact they have no idea how to find truth in all its actuality. For today access to truth is by way of the profane.[22]

Georg Muche, "Photo Composition," 1921

Catholicism and Relativism

ON MAX SCHELER'S ON THE ETERNAL IN MAN

∎ ∎ ∎

The recently published first volume of *On the Eternal in Man,* the latest work by the Cologne philosopher Max Scheler,[1] contains a series of essays either previously published or given as lectures during the war. The collection—which, as its subtitle indicates,[2] is meant to foster religious renewal—contains only one newly written text, the lengthy study titled "Problems of Religion."[3] Since the book is effectively an anthology, a form that permits the juxtaposition of differently oriented trains of thought, it is somewhat difficult to see through to the common intellectual/spiritual foundation shared by the purely philosophical observations on the one hand, and by the more cultural-political studies on the other. For authors of Scheler's stature, however, examinations of underlying principle bear the most fruit. Thus, it isn't as important to examine the contents of the widely divergent essays themselves as it is to extract the conceptual kernel that gives rise to the book's essential findings.

In the preface, Scheler characterizes the task that he has set for himself in the book's central section on the philosophy of religion. He wants to lay bare "the underlying foundations for the systematic construction of a *natural theology*"[4] and to provide, by means of this presentation, a platform on which the adherents of different religions can encounter one another and, transcending the specific incompatibilities of their respective faiths, be reconciled. The natural knowledge of God, Scheler goes on to say, will accomplish this task only "once it has liberated the kernel of Augustinism from its historical husks and has employed the conceptual resources of *phenomenological* philosophy to provide it with a fresh and more deeply rooted foundation."[5] It is clear that the author has set two goals for himself—one philosophical, the other pedagogical. To get to the point right away, his attempt to extract the "natural" acts and contents of faith ultimately proves to be a failure. Although such criticism is certainly justified, one will nevertheless also always have to acknowledge the grandeur of this attempt and recognize the intuitive power with which Scheler immerses himself in the world of religious phenomena. Scheler's mistakes are the product of his general approach to the question, an approach that in turn itself arises with a certain necessity from our current spiritual/intellectual situation.

To begin with, a few conceptual definitions are essential for the remarks that follow! Scheler distinguishes between extant and "natural" religion, the latter understood as the naïve knowledge of God that every person endowed with reason can obtain at any time by means of a religious act. Natural religion gains possession of its objects of faith through *natural revelation,* which, in contrast to spontaneous knowledge, is the self-disclosure of essential facts that the individual can experience in the natural religious act. As such it is not tied to the being and *doctrine* of specific people, as in the revelation of extant religions.

The calamitous ambiguities that pervade the entire book are already evident in the discussion of the concept of natural religion. At some points one gets the impression that Scheler presupposes a natural religion common to all people, whereas at other points he explains that the "natural religion in all religions" depends on the specific natural-historical form of a particular world view. The latter implies, however, that in the end natural religion has a different character within different cultural spheres, in which case, obviously, one can no longer speak of a universally valid natural religion.

Even if one ignores this disconcerting vacillation for the moment, one still must confront the question of how the natural knowledge of God relates to insights gained by *metaphysical* means. In his systematic investigations, which are in themselves highly commendable, Scheler criticizes the various decisions about the relationship between philosophy and religion that have been reached in the course of the history of Western thought. In the process, he himself ends up drawing a sharp distinction between metaphysical rational knowledge and religious knowledge that can be gained through the actions of natural religion (a distinction that seems quite dubious, however, for reasons that cannot be articulated here). According to Scheler, philosophy and religion represent two entirely independent and equally valid realms of action, neither of which can in any way be derived from the other. The task of weaving into a higher unity the knowledge that flows from these two separate spheres is assigned to "natural theology," which thereby finally comes into play.

With the help of "phenomenological philosophy," Scheler wants to work out objectively, among other things, the specific essence of the natural religious act, as well as the essence of the object sphere assigned to it. At the same time, he tries to develop laws for what is right and wrong in the religious domain. If *phenomenology* is to accomplish everything that Scheler demands of it, then it must have truly miraculous powers and one will be eager to know just what is so special about it. To put it concisely (as the present context requires), phenomenology strives to intuit spiritual "essences" and therefore is not concerned with the presentation and explanation of existing reality. It is much more interested in exposing the incomparable "whatness"—that is, the *essence*—of all possible given things. According to Scheler, grasping such essences requires the philosopher to cultivate a love for absolute value and being, to humble his natural ego, and to practice self-discipline. Scheler does not reveal, however, whether satisfying all these prerequisites (which are psychological, despite his claims to the contrary) would indeed be a sufficient guarantee that one would actually get at the essence of things. Attaining the "moral uplift" that Scheler calls for does not, in any case, constitute in itself a sufficient criterion for the truth of the knowledge gained in this way.

The effort to work out a natural religion (or for that matter a natural theology) can surely be termed successful only if the results produced through the "intuition of essences" that Scheler performs in the domains of metaphysics and natural religion are absolutely unimpeachable. But, as a few test samples have already shown, these results contradict one another in part and are rather dubious as a whole. At one point, for example, Scheler shows that the groups of essential intuitions that arise among different subjects (peoples, races, and so on) differ in character, leading him to the thoroughly relativistic view that all these different insights into, and ideas about, the spirit of God could all be true. A bit later, however, he remarks that the doctrine of the creation of the world by God's will (a claim generated out of the context of essences) definitely refutes other famous metaphysical doctrines concerning God and the world; at another point, he even speaks of Calvin's "terrible mistakes." Where do these standards of value and these truth criteria suddenly come from?

One asks in vain—or rather one can already anticipate the answer. Before giving it, however, it would be advisable to examine more closely a few intuitions of essence regarding natural religion, as well as the relation of man to religion in general. Using the contents of these intuitions, one will then be able to reveal their true origin with the desirable clarity and will be able to judge their supposed self-evident character and their objectivity. According to Scheler, for example, a proper metaphysics of value must firmly adopt the doctrine that all misfortune in the world is rooted in a concentrated power of evil and that, furthermore, since "evil" can only be an attribute of the essence of a person, it is rooted in the power of an evil *person*. Similarly, Scheler holds as an essential fact (worthy of consideration) that Theism implies a belief in the Fall, that the appearance of the heretic and religious singularism[6] is absurd (!), and so on. With the help of phenomenology, Scheler is also able to demonstrate with great ease that for us contemporary people a new religion (which means, to be honest, any religion other than Catholicism) would be impossible. For example, one comes upon passages which claim that the goal of all great *homines religiosi* is the restoration of an originary religion (in the process of which, of course, something like a new religion can perhaps arise after all); that the saint is the "highest conceivable form of being" whose very idea renders it necessarily "unique" (a conclusion that in itself surely does not exclude the advent of new saints); that mankind as a species is aging and that therefore today's older mankind has an obligation to cling faithfully to what a younger mankind once experienced as transcendent realities; and so on. You'd better join the church (this is more or less the tone of these arguments), since any other action is "essentially impossible," or rather "absurd."

But enough examples—the secret of Schelerian phenomenology is as clear as day. Concisely put, it consists in the fact that at one moment, *renouncing his own valuation*, Scheler tries to capture the essence of a particular thing more or less in empty space; in the next moment, however, he's once again describing things as they would be perceived by a beholder from a very *specific point of view* that naturally entails a particular valuation. Depending on what he needs, he's sometimes a *relativist* and other times—*Catholic*. If only he would at least openly admit his Catholicism throughout! But this is just what he does not do. Most of the time it is precisely the moment he has thrown relativism overboard—when he claims, for example, that the absence of an infallible "church authority" in matters of salvation is absurd in a world created and guided by an all-benevolent and true God—that he maintains a preconceived Catholic viewpoint, passes off insights gained through its perspective as essential necessities, and then uses these as a basis for Catholicism.

A Münchhausen who pulls himself out of the water by his own hair![7] As a relativist *malgré lui*, he grants all peoples their own way of knowing God, pays homage to pluralism, and so forth. As a Catholic, he acknowledges no form of knowing God except Catholicism—which of course can't be called by its proper name but is instead a pure essential necessity. One has to admire the dexterity with which this pilot, so thoroughly familiar with all channels of phenomenology, maneuvers around countless dangerous obstacles. Still, this admiration does not dispel the uneasiness that overcomes one during such an erratic itinerary of critical spirit—a zigzag course, incidentally, that is already manifest in Scheler's very style.

One need hardly waste any further words on the arbitrariness of a great many of the so-called intuitions of essences. Scheler surreptitiously transforms subjectively determined opinions into objective truths that are supposedly grounded in the being of the given things themselves. It makes little difference if his insight is at some points deeper and elsewhere more superficial than that of other writers, since in every case it is the essence of things that always ends up doing the work. Moreover, this arbitrariness often degenerates into empty Scholasticism when Scheler occasionally designates statements that are neither necessarily valid nor verifiable in their generality (such as, for example, the statement that knowledge is always grounded in love, or that every finite spirit believes either in God or in an idol) as "essential axioms" and subsequently uses these to derive other statements, which one can then either believe or not, depending upon one's disposition.

And how do things stand with the phenomenology of natural religion? If Scheler the relativist is speaking, then there is a multiplicity of natural religions. But if it is Scheler the Catholic speaking, then natural religion is nothing more than bashful Catholicism, or rather a Theism that can at any time easily emerge as Catholicism. By creating this hermaphrodite of natural religion, Scheler has now really fallen between two stools. On the one hand he offends Catholics, because it relativizes Catholic views and provides the sort of phenomenological basis for the church's concrete truths of salvation that de facto destroys their dogmatic significance.[8] Admittedly, natural religion is church doctrine; but precisely because it is, its contents cannot be perceived free of presuppositions in empty space. On the other hand, however, Scheler also offends non-Catholics, because they very quickly detect the disguised Catholic behind the intuitions of essence and become suspicious of insights whose source is so deliberately kept hidden. Scheler would have done better either to have clearly revealed his point of view or to have really carried out his impartial project. Those who, like him, try to please everyone end up pleasing no one.

So long as the philosophical issue remains unresolved, the *pedagogical* goal cannot be achieved either. In view of what has been said above, one can hardly expect that devotees of different faiths will meet, much less be reconciled, on the bridge of natural religion that Scheler has constructed. It also seems questionable (as Catholics themselves will be the first to point out) whether one can arrive at Catholicism through the gate of phenomenology—that is, whether the intuition of essences can in fact have a missionary effect. Phenomenology is—as demonstrated not least by Scheler's example—a factotum, as it were, that can be used by Buddhists just as well as by Protestants or Catholics. By employing and surely also misusing phenomenology as a lead-in to a Catholic world view, Scheler proves himself a real *eclectic*, for only an eclectic in religious matters would try to enlist the aid of phenomenological observation to force together metaphysical insights and religious truths of salvation in this way.

This is a practice that results in the loss of both naïve devoutness and philosophical unselfconsciousness, leaving only an artificial product that at best satisfies the educated latecomer. Who among us doesn't know such a person—a contemporary intellectual who, unable to stand it any longer in the vacuum of nonbelief, seeks shelter anywhere based on a romantic act of will. For this sort of person, perhaps, Scheler has smoothed out the path leading over to Catholicism. But people of this type, who make use of such back alleys of weakness (even if it is a very understandable weakness) are certainly not the best, since they prematurely desire fulfillment of their short-winded longing instead of bravely holding out in the vacuum and . . . waiting.—As for the rest, one should give a thoroughly positive rating to the fact that Scheler also attempts, in his most recent book, to spread and strengthen the contemplative spiritual/intellectual attitude specific to the essence of Catholicism. For this attitude functions as an imperative counterbalance both to vacuous industriousness and to an activism that considers movement as such an end in itself.

The untenability of Scheler's basic philosophical position does not in any way lessen the significance of his philosophical achievements in the other domains of thought he investigates. This intellect, endowed with the most brilliant gifts, displays a *psychological* insight whose depth is virtually unmatched among today's thinkers. For example, his essay "Repentance and Rebirth"[9] (included in the new book) is, despite a number of highly disputable passages, a masterpiece of the largely psychological analysis of intellectual/spiritual essentialities—a type of analysis that is one of the most wonderful flowers ever to have blossomed from the Christian ethos. By unpacking the specificities of certain intellectual/spiritual constructs from a Catholic perspective, Scheler really clarifies many issues and, incidentally, probably infuses Catholic life with more energy than he does through his constructs in the domain of natural religion. Furthermore, his ability to encompass and dissect intellectual/spiritual manifolds provides him with an outstanding capacity to discover hidden sociological connections. It is thus hardly surprising that among the book's most valuable findings are the numerous statements concerning the sociologically necessary reciprocal relations between, on the one hand, religious denominations considered as a series of historical philosophical systems, and, on the other, societal conditions. In general, one can approve of Scheler's critical disparagement of the systems of formal idealism and of Schleiermacher's philosophy of religion[10] (which stem from Scheler's effort to grasp the material being of things)—even if they are not all consistently grounded and sufficiently basic, because of the flaws in his core conceptions.

The *figure* of Scheler that shines forth from this work with all its weaknesses and merits is in many respects characteristic of our time. These days, despair over the alienation from God joins a religious impoverishment that is vastly greater than any known in earlier times. People today are striving to find an entrance to religious belief, but in general are able to achieve this goal only through a mindset that manifests more a *will to believe* than belief itself. Rootless as we still are, we can hardly escape relativism and thus roam restlessly from one manifestation to another and from one culture to another, submerging ourselves—for want of our own being—in the being of any phenomenon whatsoever. Scheler, too, is such a roamer. He is animated by a limitless inclination toward the essence of all beings, and if he is unable to grasp the being-in-itself of this essence it is not his fault alone; it's also the fault of an epoch that lacks absolute meaning. This, too, is what makes him look beyond the extant faiths for a natural religion that, for someone approaching it from the position of pure knowledge, can exist in the end only as an idea that is unrealizable within the material realm. All in all,

Scheler's phenomenology thus remains an emanation of a relativist spirituality *[Geistigkeit]*, a method that enables him to constantly break away from the Catholic principle unnoticed and slip out into infinite distances, only to flee those frightening expanses and beat an equally unnoticed hasty retreat into the security of Catholicism. Let there be no misunderstanding: Scheler's lack of principles is ultimately due to the spiritual condition of an era that is only just beginning to realize all it is lacking and that now—in what is actually more of an end than a beginning—is glittering in the thousand refracted colors of the transition.

Sasha Stone, Photographic telescope at the Einstein Tower, 1928

The Crisis of Science

ON THE FOUNDATIONAL WRITINGS OF MAX WEBER AND
ERNST TROELTSCH

■ ■ ■

1

The crisis of the sciences—which is by now a topic of commonplace discussion—is most visible in the empirical sciences such as history and sociology, which are dedicated to the investigation of intellectual/spiritual contexts and to the explanation of meaningful human action.[1] Over the last century, as these sciences have become ever broader in scope, it has become evident that realizing the claim to universal validity (which, as sciences, such disciplines must assert for their findings) poses seemingly insurmountable difficulties. If, for example, they attempt to maintain their objectivity by limiting themselves exclusively to establishing value-free knowledge, they end up either in a conceptual formalism devoid of content or in the boundless infinity of interminable fact gathering, and ultimately find themselves tangled up in valuation after all. But if they approach their material in valuational terms from the outset, they succumb from the very start to a manner of observing things which contemporary science calls "subjective," since these values cannot themselves be accounted for scientifically and "objectively." The consequences of this dilemma have become quite palpable: senseless *amassing of material* on the one hand and unavoidable *relativism* on the other.

These alone suffice to explain the "hatred of science" rampant among the best of today's academic youth. The members of this younger generation demand concepts that are true to life, a comprehensive overall view of the constructs of intellect/spirit, and above all a response to the "what for" question free of any and all skepticism. They are disappointed that the very sciences concerned with intellectual/spiritual being and activities are unable to satisfy their demands. As a result, the rebellion against the specialization being imposed upon them and against the compulsion of relativistic thinking not infrequently escalates into a passionate protest against these very sciences as such. In the process, however, these young people all too often forget that science simply may not be able to satisfy their demands, and that furthermore the sciences themselves are after all only a partial expression of the total intellectual/spiritual situation in which we find ourselves today.

■ ■ ■

Max Weber and Ernst Troeltsch, both affected by the moral distress of the younger generation, have tried to come to terms with this menacing crisis, raising anew the question of the tasks and *raison d'être* of their science, which finds itself in the position of the indicted. In the recently published first volume of his new work *Historism and Its Problems*,[2] Troeltsch, who will be the focus of the first part of our discussion, undertakes something akin to a redemption of the honor of historical thought and of the philosophy of history. That is, he attempts both to eliminate the dubious character of historicism's world view (according to which all institutions and values are to be deduced from historical development—however this may be conceived) and to protect this historicist world view from the suspicions of a younger generation that has become ahistorical. To this end, he develops his own theory of the meaning and essence of the philosophy of history, which in his eyes appears immune to any further attacks. To clarify his position, Troeltsch appends to his theory a comprehensive presentation of the systems of the philosophy of history, from Hegel and Ranke up through Croce and Bergson. This first critical overview of the history of historicism itself is marked by a strong sense of direction, and testifies to Troeltsch's oft-noted masterly ability to organize massive amounts of material. Throughout, it also confirms his art of distilling what is essential (his treatise on the Marxist dialectic is but one example). Troeltsch conceived of the entire wide-ranging book as a preparation and foundation for a material philosophy of history, which he hoped to complete in a few years.

Though it would be extremely useful to give an appreciation of Troeltsch's entire corpus—particularly his historical analyses, which can hardly be overestimated—we must limit our discussion here to his attempt to solve the core problem of historical thinking and thus to his principal stance on the crisis of science. A detailed examination of the fundamental categories of the historical object and historical development—categories constitutive of every historical observation—leads Troeltsch to make the assertion (which he adduces in a thoroughly unobjectionable manner) that historical life defies assimilation to the categories of natural science. He then goes on to disarm the arguments that insist on the necessary imbrication of historicism and relativism. It must be acknowledged that Troeltsch really advances the problem to a decisive point. He demonstrates strikingly that the universal historical process—which one must understand before one can even begin to be able to interpret an individual historical event—cannot be grasped in its absolute state through pure contemplation. Instead, the understanding of this process—like that of any context of meaning whatsoever—is based as a matter of principle on firmly held values, which in turn are a function of the particular position of the observer. Since, after all, the universal historical process extends up to the present and beyond it into the future, its construction always presupposes the value decisions of a person located in the present and oriented toward the future. The makeup of this process is, to use Troeltsch's expression, necessarily tied to the "contemporary *cultural synthesis*."[3] But where should one look to establish the standards of value that constitute this "cultural synthesis"? Troeltsch, who is simply unable to conceive of them as atemporal absolutes, objects strongly to the "fantastic mysticism" of a younger generation which would love nothing more than to escape history by taking shelter in "absolute dogmas" and "religious authorities." Troeltsch finds himself forced into the circular conclusion that the "cultural synthesis" of the observation must stem from the same historical process that it is supposed to help explain. A "scientific-historical self-reflection" alone, however, does not get one very far. To really discover the sought-after standards, there must also be an "intuition" supported by this self-reflection—an intuition that erupts from the depths of a person who is prepared to make decisions and that enables such a person to establish contemporary objectives in the first place. The creation of the "cultural synthesis" thus requires the "risk" of intuition, a risk that Troeltsch repeatedly attempts to justify by calling upon *Kierkegaard*. For, according to Troeltsch, Kierkegaard's doctrine of the "leap" implies precisely that everything depends on a decisive leap "in which we move from the past into the future through our own decision and responsibility."[4] He does not fail to add, however, that the product of intuition has "inner objective necessity" only when the person making the leap leaps off the platform of secure historical knowledge. According to Troeltsch, wherever this occurs the standards gained in the process assume—despite their temporal determination—a metaphysical significance that frees them from the clutches of relativistic thought. "The creation of such standards is distinguished from mere subjectivism . . . by its deep and living empathy with the historical totality out of which these standards arise and by the certainty that through such empathy one can grasp an internal trait of their development, a movement in the inner life of the universe or of God."[5] To substantiate this theory, Troeltsch assumes (with recourse to Leibniz and Malebranche) that, as a monad, finite spirit partakes of the infinite and is thereby capable of discovering in every moment a sense of universal history, which each time would have to be understood as an expression of world reason. Thus, in the final analysis, the way Troeltsch attempts to solve our problem is by relinquishing the general validity of the "contemporary cultural synthesis" while nevertheless still trying, with the help of metaphysical interpretation, to accord it an elevated status beyond the merely relative.—One should just briefly mention that in pursuing his investigations Troeltsch also manages to delimit the historical material in a manner consistent with his basic convictions. Since, according to him, history must be considered only to the extent that it manifests coherent meaning that is significant for the present, the subject matter of universal history is almost automatically limited to the development of *Mediterranean-European* culture. In order to jettison even more material ballast, Troeltsch also advocates that one cultivate above all a history of those fundamental *intellectual/spiritual* powers that continue to be active in the present, since to understand the political, economic, and legal conditions of the present situation it is not necessary to derive them from the past.

These few observations already show that Troeltsch has seen through a series of errors to which the formal logic of history and the philosophy of history have fallen victim often enough. They also testify adequately to Troeltsch's secure knowledge of the antinomies of historical thought. The only question is whether Troeltsch's alleged overcoming of relativism can actually withstand closer scrutiny. If so, then the crisis of science would be over and the younger generation's "hatred of science" would have become groundless. Troeltsch teaches us that the way to escape relativism is by seizing, in the leap of intuition, the standards necessary for the construction of the historical process; such a leap places the one who undertakes it into the heart of the "creative vitality of divine will."[6] This view certainly does confer a bit of metaphysical luster on one's own value decisions. But considered purely scientifically and objectively, as is appropriate here, it in no way precludes the simultaneous existence of other standards of value that have also been gained intuitively through historical experience and that can therefore all equally claim to have the same suprarelative significance. One can see that the relativism which necessarily accompanies history [Historie] has not been changed one iota, despite Troeltsch's attempt to eliminate it through his interpretation. Rather, everything remains just the way it was before.

But why? Because Troeltsch—and this is the crucial point—never truly makes the leap. Kierkegaard, his star witness, really does leap; but unlike Troeltsch, he does not want to secure the "inner objective necessity" of his intuition through "scientific-historical self-reflection." Instead, Kierkegaard decides (precisely because it is absurd) to accept the paradox that the eternal has at some point entered into time, and thus actually jumps straight into the absolute. In doing so, however, he has found the Archimedean point outside the historical process, and nothing could ever lead him to do what Troeltsch did—that is, to reinsert the newly grasped absolute back into history in order to relativize it anew. How fundamentally Troeltsch misunderstands Kierkegaard in this respect! It is with an air of supercilious regret that he remarks, "If Kierkegaard . . . by making this leap plunged into an . . . ascetic Christianity, then, in addition to everything else, there is clearly still an instinctive need here for absolute authorities."[7] An instinctive need! As if Kierkegaard had risked the leap out of instinctive need and not out of desperation, as if what he was up to were just a little leaping in order to then resume—with the help of value standards happily gained through this leaping—the very same historical-philosophical speculation he had just tried to escape by making the leap in the first place. But Troeltsch wants both: to jump out of relativism and at the same time as a scientist to remain in the contingent and do history. He does not see that once one enters into a relationship with the absolute, historicism immediately becomes impossible; and that, conversely, where historicism reigns, access to the absolute is unavoidably cut off. Too distressed by the younger generation's indictments of science to admit unhesitatingly that historical thought on its own will never again be able to force the absolute into its sphere of influence, Troeltsch nevertheless tries to reconcile the irreconcilable. In the process, he becomes caught up in an illusory circle whose illusory dissolution understandably must lead him to an unpleasant compromise. For it is a compromise to take value standards and cultural syntheses that are removed from history and embedded in history and touch them up after the fact with the cosmetics of an absolute meaning, just for the sake of a more dignified appearance. Troeltsch's metaphysical interpretations demonstrate only one thing: that the observer of history as such cannot elude relativism and must take great care not to confuse the leap of intuition with the leap into the absolute. The natural consequence of the relativism of Troeltsch's cultural synthesis is the relativism of his choice of subject matter.

2

Max Weber—whom Troeltsch aptly characterizes as "one of the most powerful German figures, and one of the most comprehensive and at the same time most methodologically rigorous intellectuals of the period"[8]—flatly refused to make compromises of the sort that Troeltsch did. His essays on the theory of science have finally become available in a collection entitled *Gesammelte Aufsätze zur Wissenschaftslehre* (Collected Essays on the Theory of Science);[9] the volume includes the Munich lecture "Science as a Vocation," which unleashed the so-called "Dispute over Science."[10] These texts expose Weber's negative religious attitude in all its demonic character. Weber has experienced as intensely as anyone the suffering of the younger generation due to the "disenchantment of the world" brought about by science. But he also knows that the younger generation's yearning for the absolute cannot be satisfied by science itself. According to Weber's judgment—which in this respect is more profound than Troeltsch's because it is more radical—the leap into the absolute is a leap over the abyss into the realm of faith, and is thus a leap that leads definitively out of the realm of science. Weber—a Kierkegaard with completely reversed premises—explains point-blank that "the tension between the value sphere of 'science' and that of religious salvation is unbridgeable."[11] If, however, from the perspective of science, all the value decisions and objectives of our actions are necessarily relative, then, according to Weber, in order for science to live up to its ideal of objectivity it must *eliminate all valuation* and limit itself strictly to demonstrating connections between states of affairs and facts, revealing the internal structural relationships of cultural goods, and so on. For him, this is the stuff of "intellectual uprightness," and it compels him to dismiss every scientifically spruced-up "podium prophecy" that pretends to deliver in the lecture halls what "only a prophet or a savior" is able to proclaim.

The procedure that Weber follows in order to achieve an objective and value-free understanding of meaningful events can only be roughly sketched here, its difficulties merely touched upon. From the start, he assumes that the pervasive causal interconnectedness of the infinite

sequence of events within the intellectual/spiritual world (an interconnectedness, by the way, whose self-evident character Troeltsch doubts
for good reasons) can never be elucidated entirely. One therefore must
limit oneself to a comprehending grasp of only certain selected parts of
the inexhaustible context of experience. To this end, Weber simplifies
and schematizes whatever intricate context he is examining (for
example, "Christianity" or "capitalism") to the point where, through a
one-sided emphasis on certain more or less random details, he is able to
obtain some sort of internally noncontradictory, unreal conceptual
image—the so-called *ideal type* (such as the "ideal type" of "capitalism"). This ideal type, because it is so unambiguous and completely
graspable, can then serve as the point of departure for an understanding
of reality. The number of ideal-type constructs is just as limitless as the
number of values in terms of which the reality to be examined can be
considered. Usually these ideal-type constructs take on a form which is
"purposively rational"—in other words, they express how an action
would occur *if* it pursued a specific purpose (such as economic advantage) free of affective influence, purely rationally. But even where this
is not the case, ideal-type constructs always rely on such an "if," since
to present any ideal-type state of affairs they must of necessity first
impose certain conditions on the experiential manifold. Now just how
does the explanation of reality itself proceed by means of these ideal
constructs? According to Weber, one reaches an objective understanding
by comparing the particular context of experience with the ideal-type
construct that has been abstracted from it, and then determining to what
extent the two correspond to or differ from each other. In this way, by
constantly using the unambiguous ideal-type concepts, one gradually
disentangles the particular context more and more—an unraveling that
is, however, never anything more than an approximation. A direct consequence of Weber's basic position is that his treatment of material
tends to be primarily sociological; such an approach, Troeltsch observes,
"lacks any model of a philosophy of history and any interpretation of the
meaning of this process."[12] This ethically founded renunciation of large-
scale historical syntheses, which arises from Weber's insight into their
value-ladenness, naturally does not prevent him from constructing cer-

tain historical developments as ideal types (see his 1901 study *The Protestant Ethic and the Spirit of Capitalism*).[13] Yet Weber never ceases to warn against confusing these ideal types with reality. Finally, so far as the meaning of science is concerned, Weber assigns it a thoroughly menial role. Its task is to facilitate the technological domination of life, to identify the best strategies for the pursuit of various goals, and above all to trace back every personal value decision to the world view from which it arose, in order thereby to force the person engaged in this valuation to account for his actions. One can easily see that such a positioning of science in the totality of life also results in a certain delimitation of the material infinity.

As with Troeltsch, one must also ask whether Weber succeeds in mastering relativism and fulfilling science's claim to objectivity. One can certainly grant him that, according to his own intentions, he refrains from starting out with personal value judgments and that he selects experiential material and ideal types solely in relation to values. Yet not only are the ideal types themselves very questionable constructs, in view of their largely empirical character, but when they are employed to investigate the contexts of experience in the manner described above, it becomes apparent sooner or later that Weber is de facto unable to realize the sought-after objectivity. Because the quintessence of all the inter-connections that constitute a given reality is virtually inexhaustible, in order to grasp that quintessence objectively Weber would have to sup-plement endlessly, with one constructive determination after another, the ideal-type case that discloses reality. It is clear that the full realiza-tion of this process of determination is in principle impossible, since it will inevitably have to break off at some point. The point at which it comes to a standstill, however (the point where the ghostly "if" of the ideal-type constructs collides with the "is" of an expression of reality), depends entirely on the way the experiential context under examination is understood and judged. In other words, despite all precautions, the perpetually deferred valuations ultimately do slip back in; it is impos-sible forever to elude them and, concomitantly, subjectively determined points of view. Thus, Weber's method resembles an endless chase in the netherworld of the empirical, a chase in which he is both the pursued

and the pursuer; he is attacked from behind by valuations he denies
when looking at them face to face. In the meantime, the objectivity he
is trying to get hold of flees into infinity before his very eyes; and flee
it must, since, were he ever to capture it, it would become for him—
even if only in its mirror image, in its empty form, as it were—the
absolute itself. Such expeditions, undertaken with unparalleled frenzy,
are a doubly tragic drama—not only because in their futile flight and
futile search they lead astray beyond all bounds, but also because in their
refusal to give meaning to events, their own meaning ultimately becomes
problematic as well. Weber does in fact place the sciences explicitly in
the service of the deliberating person, who, with their help, should be
able to understand the origin and the consequences of his actions. The
question, however, is whether this very limitless desire to understand
(which ultimately makes the delimitation of the material an arbitrary
matter) precludes the possibility of making a decision. This would be
merely the secret revenge of the valuations for having been heroically
sacrificed in favor of the phantom of objectivity, which in the end
cannot be hunted down anyway.

■ ■ ■

In contrast to Weber, Troeltsch is right to link the construction of
contexts of meaning to valuations. Contrary to what he believes, however, within the framework of scientific discovery such valuations may
not be allowed to cross the line from the relative into the absolute.
Weber, though, rightly insists (against Troeltsch) on the relativity of all
value decisions from the perspective of science; he is mistaken only in
his belief that he can dispense with such decisions. The result is that the
sciences, to the extent that they aspire to understand the world of
intellectual/spiritual experience, necessarily succumb to relativism.
Incidentally, the insurmountable difficulties that the scientific project
encounters (to touch briefly upon this aspect as well) can be explained
by the inadequacy of the specifically scientific categories for the material
of intellectual/spiritual being and activities. But so long as the sciences
that are concerned with this material constitute themselves as pure
sciences, they cannot be anything else but what they currently are. It
would be an entirely misguided effort to try to limit them from within.

The "crisis of science" that has been provoked by the awakening con-science of the younger generation will not be solved by science itself or with the help of philosophical speculation. Overcoming this crisis calls instead for a real withdrawal from the entire intellectual/spiritual sit-uation in which sciences like those under discussion here are even possible in such magnitude. Eliminating relativistic thought, cutting off the perspective onto boundless infinities—all these are tied to a *real transformation of our entire essence*, and perhaps not even to this alone. After the entrance into the absolute that such a transformation might bring about, one wonders what intellectual/spiritual activity would look like and what limits would be placed on the "sciences" dedicated to its understanding. But to establish answers to such questions would lead far beyond the intentions and scope of this essay.

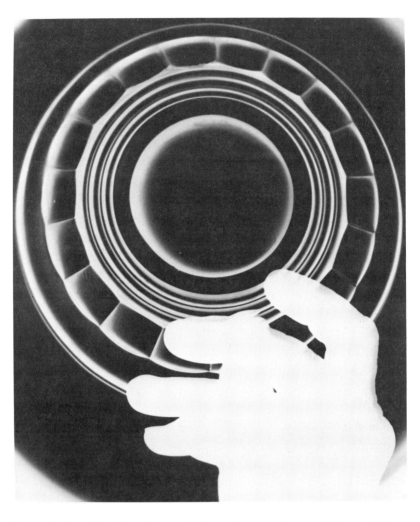

August Sander, Advertising photograph for a glass manufacturer, Cologne, 1932

Georg Simmel

...

Simmel has often been described as a philosopher of culture. One could just as well call him a philosopher of the soul, of individualism, or of society. All of these labels, however, are imprecise and one-sided and do not even begin to encompass the scope of his work. So what exactly is the actual subject matter of his thought?

From the outset, one must exclude a number of tasks and basic problems from the sphere of Simmel's observations, since the philosopher never made any attempt to tackle them. With the exception of the work from his late period, he seldom interpreted the world through the prism of a sublime metaphysical idea, in the tradition of Spinoza, the German idealists, or Schopenhauer. He never discovered the magic word for the macrocosm that underlies all forms of existence, and he still owes us a far-reaching, all-encompassing notion of the world. He likewise lacks a grand style of grasping history: the interpretation of historical events is foreign to him, and he takes little account of the historical situation in which people find themselves at any given moment. He has almost no relationship to the natural sciences: his thoughts do not grow out of an engagement with biological problems (as Bergson's do, for example), nor does he ever make use of the research methods of experimental psychology. Simmel by no means covers the full range of the domain of pure spiritual/intellectual *[geistigen]* phenomena. He refuses, for instance, to pay any attention to the general structural makeup of consciousness—that is, to thought processes, emotions, acts of imagination, love and hate, and so on. Even though he often touches on these elements in his writings (where one does encounter various discussions that refer to them), he nonetheless never makes them the object of separate theoretical investigation. Such a rejection of phenomenology in the narrow sense does not, however, lead Simmel to join the camp of those empirical psychologists who, modeling themselves on the great French essayists (such as La Rochefoucauld and Chamfort), take pleasure in depicting typical characters, lovingly work out individual qualities of the soul, and seek to dissect the various moral properties. Wherever one does encounter these sorts of descriptions and analyses in Simmel's work, they have no inherent value in themselves, despite their indispensability for the train of thought as a whole. The philosopher's itinerary does not conclude with them but rather leads over and beyond them toward other ends.

To begin with, I will attempt to give a rough sketch of the world in which Simmel is at home. The raw material of his thinking is made up of the inexhaustible multiplicity of spiritual/intellectual states, the events and modes of being of the soul that are significant both within communal life and within the intimate sphere of personal life. In fact, in countless cases the objects that engage the philosopher's reflections stem from the realm of experiences and encounters of the highly differentiated individual. It is always man—considered as bearer of culture and as a mature spiritual/intellectual being, acting and evaluating in full control of the powers of his soul and linked to his fellow man in collective action and feeling—who stands at the center of Simmel's field of vision. This world has an upper and lower limit. It is bounded above by the realm of the cosmic, from which it has been cut away and which therefore surrounds it; put differently, it is the counterpart to a terrestrial and not to an astronomical philosophy. It is bounded below by the realm of elementary, nonspiritual/nonintellectual activity, that of human drives: anything that is merely nature and not the emanation of a developed soul is exiled.

A more precise inspection soon enables one to distinguish the different material realms in which Simmel operates. The greatest demands on his attention seem—at least at first glance—to have come from societal conditions and formations, as well as from the human behavior that takes place within them. His sociological investigations extend over nearly his entire career; only late in his life does he turn his attention increasingly to new objects of study. His very first book, *Über sociale Differenzierung* (On Social Differentiation),[1] already deals with certain regularities of communal life. In two of his major works, the *Philosophy of Money* and above all his *Soziologie* (Sociology),[2] he continues these investigations, motivated by the desire to render fully visible the fabric of societal relations. He probes the structure of all sorts of human relations, depicts the specific makeup of smaller and larger social bodies, and reveals the influence of one group on another and the necessary links between the greatest variety of societal mechanisms. A number of Simmel's studies are devoted to understanding individual social phenomena: for example, he explores the essence of fashion, flirtation, sociability, and so on.[3] He pays particularly thorough attention to the process of the division of labor, which is of such great significance today. He pursues its implications for the community at all levels of societal existence, and shows (among other things) how this process, which controls the external relationship of individuals to each other in the age of capitalism, also influences and decisively shapes their inner life.[4]

The second realm of material that Simmel traverses encompasses everything relating to the life of the individual as such. As a thinker, he is fascinated by matters of soul *[das Seelische]* in all forms; his writings are a veritable treasure trove for the psychologist. Equipped with unusually discriminating powers of observation and unparalleled sensitivity, he immerses himself in the depths of human existence and sheds light on the processes that take place within us, often below the surface of consciousness. With gentle fingers he carefully probes the soul, laying bare what was previously hidden, exposing the most secret impulses, and untangling the tightly knit weave of our feelings, yearnings, and desires. The conclusions that Simmel develops from this context concern man in general, as well as specific, isolated individuals. At times the philosopher elucidates general psychological conditions which are sufficiently typical such that if the appropriate preconditions for their manifestation are present, they are realized in the soul of any person. For example, he dissects the essence of femininity and depicts the inner makeup of certain types such as the miser and the adventurer.[5] At other times he explores the spiritual/intellectual world of a few important figures, illuminating their being and their creative output for reasons that are significant to his own development (and that will be articulated below). What is at stake for him is always the exploration of the rule-governed developmental process, be it that of the soul of mankind in general or that of the individual; his gaze is always focused on the necessary interrelationships of our inner forces; he never considers it his task—as the mere empiricist does—to merely describe the accidental concurrence of individual essential traits.

Finally, Simmel's third realm of conceptual material, which cannot be very sharply distinguished from the one just mentioned, encompasses the domains of objective values and people's achievements within these domains. Almost all of the philosopher's works are shot through with epistemological investigations; these are the primary focus of his texts *Kant* and *The Problems of the Philosophy of History*.[6] Simmel introduces both his *Über sociale Differenzierung* and his *Soziologie* with an epistemological/critical justification of his sociological research method. Indeed, this is typical of his general tendency to shift the focus away from the contents of his thought to the process of thinking itself, since an understanding of the latter makes it possible to explain how contents of this or that sort are acquired in the first place. The relationship between the knowing subject and the object known is one of this philosopher's most central problems, and it is highly instructive to observe how, over the course of his development, his observations on this subject become increasingly abundant and to some extent correct one another. He also strives again and again to find a concept of truth that could provide a foundation for his relativism. His engagement with these questions often takes the form of incidental remarks: typically, Simmel will interrupt his sojourn in the foregrounds of existence, turn away from the particular phenomenon upon which he was just dwelling, and dive down to a theoretical speculation on the conditions of knowing.

Simmel entered the field of ethics early on, and never left it entirely. In his early work *Einleitung in die Moralwissenschaft* (Introduction to Moral Science)[7] he dissects the fundamental concepts of ethics, and in one of his last studies, "Das individuelle Gesetz" (The Individual Law),[8] he attempts to demonstrate that the contents of the ethical demands to which the individual must always submit are a fruit of the individual's life process. These two texts frame the thinker's creative activity and mark the beginning and the end of the course he traveled. One might already mention provisionally that Simmel never revealed his own ethos in any unmediated fashion. He did, however, bring to light the ethical convictions of a number of great figures, such as Kant, Schopenhauer, Nietzsche, and Goethe,[9] and rarely passed up an opportunity to work out the ethical significance of the cultural trends and conditions of the soul that he portrayed. His innate ethical viewpoint often shines forth quite unmistakably, as if from a mirror.

Simmel's engagement with aesthetic problems does not begin to take on its full dimensions until the second half of his corpus, yet it never solidifies into a theory of art. In the aesthetic domain—in contrast to his aims in his epistemological/critical investigations—he is less interested in investigating the conditions of possibility of aesthetic sensation and creation. Instead, he focuses more on the reconstruction of experiences that give rise to certain typical and individual artistic achievements. He exposes the spiritual foundations *[Seelengründe]* in which the creations of Michelangelo, Rodin, and Rembrandt have their roots, and in the process reveals the essence and meaning of the art of each of these masters.[10] His aim is always to pull back the veil from the core insight that underlies the creativity of the artist he is treating—or even of an entire period, such as the Renaissance. On occasion, he reads a deeper symbolic meaning into certain things we appreciate aesthetically (such as a handle or an architectural ruin),[11] a meaning that explains all at once the impact these objects have on our feelings. Simmel enters into the spirit of artistic creations with utmost ingenuity and then struggles to establish formulas capable of conveying the specific content of the phenomena in question.

Simmel ploughed the wide-ranging field of religious questions and experiences only to a limited extent. This may be due to the general makeup of his being, which doubtless never had any basic religious instincts or needs. Yet even here—where, more than anywhere else, he approaches his object from the outside—this thinker still demonstrates an incomparable empathetic power. He returns time and again to the sociological role played by religious feeling, showing, for example, which forms of sociation are sustained by a religious drive to live one's life to the fullest.[12] Bright spotlights are also directed (as in *Rembrandt*) onto the nature of pure faith, whose wellsprings are located so deep within the soul that it no longer depends on any dogma or extant religion. It is just this piety, which requires no particular garments and is a characteristic of our being, that Simmel has read into some of Rembrandt's figures.

Having surveyed the diverse worlds in which this philosopher has manifested his creativity, one must now look at the way in which he structures his matter. How does Simmel process the given raw material? What route does he take between the various manifestations accessible to him? And into what kinds of unities do the multiplicity of phenomena coalesce for him? There are two different ways to gauge the substance of a person's achievements. Either one concentrates primarily on how these achievements differ from one another, emphasizing the transformations and shifts in perspective in order to reach an understanding of the spiritual/intellectual development of their creator as it manifests itself through them. Or one can emphasize the common elements in these achievements and try to discover the leitmotif that resonates in all of them. The latter method is advisable in cases where it is important first of all to penetrate a thinker's spiritual/intellectual world and get a preliminary picture of its particular makeup. If one assumes that every soul forms a living unity that manifests some sort of invariable determinations throughout (even if its development consists of a series of violent overturnings), then the expressions of this soul must also be held together, despite extensive internal contradictions, by a tie that links them all and gives objective expression to this unity. A person's essence objectifies itself, for example, in an idea that runs through its work like a red thread; alternatively, that essence is mirrored in some other peculiarity that is constantly being crystallized anew out of that person's creations. It may often be difficult to discover the characteristic trait that marks the actions and opinions of certain individuals as the emanations of a single personality. There are artists, for example, who are so variable that their late work always seems to arise out of a spiritual constitution that is entirely different from that of their early work. Yet even such self-fleeing types cannot escape from themselves; their penchant for transformation and even their self-betrayal still reveals that self. In the end, the substance of what they have accomplished is somehow marked by a unified essential trait. The philosopher, in contrast, as one who seeks the ultimate and who must therefore, in order to reach it, be firmly rooted in the center of his essence, is sure of the truth only to the extent that he is sure of himself. He is the exact opposite of the artist-type, and as such is surely the least susceptible to transformations of the soul. Whatever type of truth he eventually attains must forever remain one and the same, yet it is simultaneously also the counterpart to his spiritual being, which, more than in other types of people, plays itself out in him in the form of conscious principles, maxims, and so on. He who lives in yearning for the absolute exhibits precisely those enduring elements within him that remain the same amid all changes.

Anyone who has become even slightly familiar with the world of Simmel's thought will soon find himself in the grip of a characteristic spiritual/intellectual atmosphere that envelops him with an almost physical tangibility. One is struck by the essential unity of all of the thinker's works, and becomes aware that he solves the most numerous and varied problems in the same manner. The experience is similar to that of the traveler visiting foreign lands who comes upon a type of people with which he is unfamiliar. Initially unable to perceive the differences among the individual inhabitants, his attention is captured solely by the common features, which, in their totality, are unfamiliar. One conquers new spiritual/intellectual territory only by first embracing it as a whole. Only once one has made out its silhouette can one clearly perceive the pieces out of which it is composed and grasp the relationships that are developing between them one by one. The extent to which Simmel's work in particular displays a profound unity is itself a function of the entire nature of his philosophy (a point that we shall take up below). It is by no means necessary, however, that the source of this unity be a principle that can be precisely articulated in conceptual terms. The more unsystematic the spirit/intellect—and Simmel definitely belongs to the camp of unsystematic thinkers—the less his accomplishments are rooted in convictions that tolerate the full light of conceptual clarity. While the living unity of the work he has produced can be empathetically reexperienced, it can never be deduced from a fundamental principle that is rigid and alienated from life. Still, insofar as Simmel *was* a philosopher, one can venture ahead in his work until one comes upon a core idea that is located in a conceptual sphere and serves as the anchor for most of his works. This would simultaneously provide a *cross section* of his philosophy which, however, would admittedly not reveal all aspects of his conceptual edifice. In exactly analogous fashion, it is only in the rarest cases that the architectural cross section of a building reveals the structure of the entire house, the disposition of all the interior rooms. Some elements of the structure usually remain invisible; in order to discover them, one requires a longitudinal section or additional cross sections. Yet one of these sections always does take precedence over the others, since it renders visible the layout of the structure's main volumes. The core principle of Simmel's thought (which I will develop below) should be understood as such a privileged cross section, which introduces us to the essence of Simmel's philosophy without, however, fully underpinning it. The principle in question might be formulated something like this: *All expressions of spiritual/intellectual life are interrelated in countless ways. No single one can be extricated from this web of relations, since each is enmeshed in the web with all other such expressions.* This view reflects one of Simmel's fundamental experiences; his understanding of the world is based on it. Using it as a guide, one can find one's way through the labyrinth of the philosopher's thought and its far-reaching bifurcations, albeit leaving untouched certain side passages and parallel trajectories (such as the epistemological studies of the relationship between subject and object).[13]

There are two types of relations between things, both of which Simmel articulates again and again. First, there are relationships of *essential congruence [Wesenszusammengehörigkeit]* between the most disparate phenomena. There is no individual being or individual event that can be extracted from the totality of spiritual life such that it can then be explained by itself and observed in itself. Still, if we regularly detach parts from the manifold context in which they are entwined and consider them as sharply defined entities, we do so sometimes out of quite understandable practical needs and other times because the relatively self-contained nature of many of these parts and groups of parts (such as a historical epoch or a group of spiritual characteristics) justifies our doing so. Most of the time, however, people do not keep in mind the intimate reciprocal relations among the pieces that have been split off from the living totality. Instead, these pieces are considered to be independent and eventually congeal into rigid entities, whose meanings are irrevocably attached to features singled out more or less arbitrarily from their semantic totality rather than developing out of a consideration of that totality itself. Thus, for example, people make feelings or character traits into constructs with hard contours, into things which are sharply isolated from one another and which can be so cut to size and made presentable that their concepts no longer in any way refer to the manifold of being, which is, after all, simultaneously presented along with them. One of Simmel's fundamental aims is to rid every spiritual/ intellectual phenomenon of its false being–unto–itself and show how it is embedded in the larger contexts of life. In this way, his manner of thinking functions both to connect and to dissolve: the former in that he reveals connections everywhere between seemingly separate things; the latter insofar as he makes us aware of the complexity of many supposedly simple objects and problems. One encounters instances of such linkings of phenomena everywhere one turns in the philosopher's writings. They occur quite frequently in his sociological investigations, whose primary concern, after all, is to discover the necessary relationships among countless social manifestations. Simmel demonstrates, for example, how a highly developed money economy also determines the conduct of individuals in domains other than the economic, indeed the entire lifestyle of an epoch.[14] He thus examines how the occurrence of a particular social event can bring about a specific condition in the total social manifold. Or else, as in his essays on sociability, flirtation, and so on, Simmel liberates a series of phenomena from their isolation by exposing the meaning or the originary ground that they all have in common and from which their individual meanings can be explained. In this manner he ties together what is separated, collects into large bundles what is scattered, and draws aside the veil that, like the billowing fog in the high mountains, usually obscures the linkages of things so densely that only the peaks of isolated things existing on their own can tower above it. Simmel also pays regular attention to relationships located entirely within the soul. When, for example, he asks himself whether virtue and happiness in any way determine each other (a question which, by the way, he answers in the negative),[15] this is only one of many instances where he seeks certainty about the relations linking man's feelings, acts of will, valuations, and so on. On occasion he describes an unusually characteristic spiritual totality that arises out of the meshing of certain essential traits: he draws a portrait of the miser, the blasé person, and various other common human types.[16]

The relations of *essential congruence* are opposed to the relations of *analogy [Analogie]*. Just as shallow, everyday understanding obliterates all fluid transitions between phenomena, rips apart the texture of appearance, and incarcerates its henceforth isolated parts, each on its own within a concept, it also narrows down another dimension of our consciousness of the world's manifold. Having entrusted excerpts of reality to various concepts, it renders visible only their most imperative aspects, attaching, as it were, a label to each concept—a label that displays only what common practical necessity deems noteworthy. In their rigid conceptual housings, things become univocal; only one of their facets is ever facing us, and we grasp them in whatever way they are useful to us. No wonder they are lying about next to each other, unreconciled! Their commonalities fade, and of their many meanings only the one that indicates their intended use has survived; they have become narrow and short-winded. The more reality opens itself up to man, the more foreign to him the average world with its distorted conceptual petrifications becomes. He recognizes that a boundless plenitude of qualities inhabits each phenomenon, and that each is subject to widely differing laws. But the more he becomes aware of the many-sidedness of things, the more it becomes possible for him to relate them to each other. Among the many determinations of some phenomenon that are unveiled to him, one of them can also be attributed to another phenomenon: everywhere he looks, relations between phenomena impose themselves upon him.

Simmel is indefatigable when it comes to establishing analogies. He
never misses a chance to show that some of the essential characteristics
of an object (be they formal or structural) are realized not only by the
very object in which they were discovered, but also by an entire series
of objects. He points out, for example, the resemblance between the
structural relations in the artwork and those in certain societal organizations. Or he explains how certain processes in the life of society and
within the soul operate according to one and the same schema. He
compares the structure of the economy to the structure of the law, and
brings out analogies between art and play, between adventure and love.
Often Simmel must first completely pick to pieces the familiar, commonplace image of whatever object he is examining, so that the aspect
it shares with other objects can come to the fore. What is always at stake
for the thinker in this process is the liberation of the thing from its
isolation. He turns it this way and that way, until we recognize in it the
fulfillment of a lawfulness that is simultaneously embodied in many
other places, and we can thereby weave it into an extensive net of
relations. But such a highly developed sensitivity to the formal similar-
ities of phenomena is, by nature, linked to an equally unerring sensitivity to differences. Thus, Simmel also appears as someone who breaks
apart the surface resemblances that exist everywhere between things,
demonstrating in the process the fallaciousness of various doctrines
based on the silent acceptance of such resemblances.

At this point we should say a few words about the difference
between *analogy [Analogie]* and *metaphor [Gleichnis]*. The former brings
together two phenomena that in some way manifest the same behavior;
the latter tries, by means of an image, to give sensuous expression to the
meaning that a certain phenomenon has for us. When, for example, one
compares the way of life in late antiquity with that in western Europe, or
when one draws a parallel between the reflection of light and that of
sound, one is dealing with analogy. In both cases relations between phenomena are established by virtue of their corresponding course of action.
In a metaphor, on the other hand (such as Goethe's line "Poems are
painted windowpanes"),[17] the essence of the lyrical poem is illustrated
not immediately and in so many words, but by taking a detour via

a phenomenon that allows the poem's meaning to shine through more or less veiled. If two objects, A and B, stand in a relation of analogy to each other, this means that both A and B are subject to the same general rule, the same general law. Analogy never refers to that specific being of a thing (its value, its makeup) which is available only through experience. Instead, analogy considers things only to the extent that they fulfill a function, embody a type, take on a form—in short, to the extent that they are a particular case of something general, the understanding of which is the prerequisite for the construction of the analogy. The value of an analogy depends exclusively on its objective validity, since the only processes it compares are those that really operate according to one and the same schema. When you have an authentic analogy, the parallelism of events that it claims must actually exist. Their synonymy is free of all subjective arbitrariness; we discover it, but we do not constitute it. Along these same lines, one can draw conclusions about the behavior of a phenomenon on the basis of analogies only to a limited extent, since after all the phenomenon enters into the analogous relation only as the realization of a general lawfulness governing its unfolding. Whereas analogy is content to establish that processes of some sort are occurring in a similar manner, the metaphor offers an explanation of a phenomenon. To put it better, a metaphor outlines our impression, our conception of the phenomenon; it mirrors its meaning or its content in an image. Analogous processes have equal status, whereas the elements of a metaphor are of entirely different value, such that one element gives sensuous expression to the essence of the other. What takes on form in the metaphor is precisely the incomparability of an object, its internal makeup. The more profound our experience of things is, the less it can be subsumed to its full extent under abstract concepts. Initially clothed in the image, it shines forth brightly; we shroud it in order to possess it nude. What is most secret needs the veil of a metaphor so that it can be completely exposed. Analogy is either true or false, whereas metaphor is either beautiful or ugly. In other words, no matter how ingenious and surprising the analogy may be, it stands and falls with its factual verification. We recognize it; it is a feature of the phenomena themselves. The metaphor, however, is a creation of fantasy, of the imaginative power of the psyche; we evaluate it aesthetically and furthermore require that it be striking and illuminating—that it render visible, in a complete and unadulterated way, everything we have projected intellectually or emotionally onto the object. It is not a type of knowledge like the analogy, but is rather a receptacle for our thoughts about things, an expression of our interior, a mirroring of the self in the world of appearances. The analogy: a relationship between objects. The metaphor: a representation of the relationships between subject and object. In the metaphor the base phenomenon and that which articulates its meaning counterbalance each other wonderfully. Of course the latter likewise has an abundance of meanings, but, placed in relation to the former, it radiates with the very meaning capable of illuminating the obscurity of the base phenomenon. Of the two phenomena that have been woven into a unity of meaning in the metaphor, the one casts its light onto the other, and onto it alone. Both yearn to fuse with each other in the metaphor, the one because it hopes for clarification of its murkiness, and the other because it wants to become the vehicle of illumination. Each thing can be a torch; each has its own torch. Since language is always a faithful guide for those who delve into essentialities, it also helps one get on the right track in distinguishing analogy from metaphor. The little word "like," which may be absent in the latter, is compulsory in the linkage of analogous processes. One can say that poems *are* painted windowpanes because here (as everywhere) the image takes the place of the predicate. The "like" in analogy, on the other hand, functions to designate similarly structured actions and thus cannot be eliminated. Any metaphor can be transformed into an analogy (at least a formal one). This is what leads to the quite frequent confusion of the two modes of relation. One need only change the intention, and the same material that was previously a metaphor changes into an analogy. The phrase "life is like a stream" makes sense as a metaphor if the word "stream" has the meaning of an image; it becomes an analogy when "life" and "stream" are grasped as parallel phenomena, as processes that unfold according to the same general rule.

The core of mankind's essence is accessible through even the smallest side door. From the entire preceding reflection, one can draw a far-reaching conclusion about the essence of thinkers who live either primarily in analogies or predominantly in metaphors. Assuming the philosopher has the discoverer's gaze needed to understand the former and the imagination and creative gifts necessary to envision the latter, he will turn to analogies when it is simply a matter of working out the relations between things and will prefer metaphors when he wants to present his insight into the core content of things. The analogy person never gives an explanation of the world, since he is not driven by a preconceived idea; he is content to identify the laws of the event and, by observing the many facets of the event itself, to pair together those things that have the same form. He restrains his self at all times. The metaphor person has a much less objective attitude. He allows the world to affect him; it has a meaning for him that he wants to convey. His soul is filled with the absolute, toward which his self yearns to emanate. The large number of analogies—relative to the limited number of meta-phors—in Simmel's work thus already indicates (I here anticipate a claim which will be elaborated below) that Simmel refrains from inter-preting the world, that his self does not possess the metaphysical depth that alone would enable him to encounter phenomena in terms of value judgments. How different from Schopenhauer, who is a metaphor man through and through! Schopenhauer has been given a password by means of which he can decipher the phenomenal world, in order to convey it to us in an image.—[18]

Laying bare the filiations that wind about the phenomena is only one (infinite) task that arises for Simmel out of his fundamental con-victions. His other task must be to grasp the manifold as a totality and to somehow master this totality, experience its essence, and express it. The unity of the world follows directly from the principle that every-thing is related to everything else. Every individual relationship points to it, being only a fragment of the larger universe that one must already have grasped and encompassed if one is to bring to light more than merely fragmentary and incomplete complexes. It is just this alleged thorough interrelatedness of phenomena that requires one to contem-plate their totality, since, if one does not take this totality into consid-eration, one can achieve at best only an understanding of partial unities that refer beyond themselves on all sides. This does not, however, satisfy the essentially philosophical drive to master the totality. It remains incumbent upon me to show how Simmel is constantly trying to free himself from the individual object, so as to embrace the world in its totality. He starts out on two paths—one epistemological, the other metaphysical—in order to realize his goal. The former leads him to a truly relativistic denial of the absolute, to a renunciation of any grasping of the totality on one's own, and to the presentation of numerous typical pictures of the world. The latter leads him to a metaphysics of life, to a far-ranging attempt to understand the phenomenal by means of an absolute principle. A short preview of the philosophy of life [Lebensphilosophie] which is expressed only during the very last period of Simmel's work might indicate to what extent the world actually entered his consciousness as a unity. All objective constructs, all ideas and spiritual/intellectual forces, all hard and fast structures of existence originally emerged from the stream of life that endlessly, indefatigably flows by. This "life," which also sweeps through individuals, is the foundation of the world, or, to be more precise (and this must not be forgotten), of Simmel's world, which means the totality of those states of affairs and processes that directly affect humans as spiritual/intellectual beings. As a result, for this thinker the totality splits into a polar opposition: on the one hand, objective regularities, meaning the rigid forms that govern us, and, on the other hand, the relentless violation of the just recently rigidified forms, the constant transformation of our cultural and spiritual condition. He can consider the world as understood when he can show that it is the movement of life that mediates between these two poles of the totality, that it is the life process itself that creates the opposition which splits the manifold and that this opposition therefore does not extend to the very depths of the world. Yet how is it possible that not only everything transient but also everything enduring wells up out of life? According to Simmel, everything that gushes forth from life tends to solidify, to become a self-sufficient construct, and to subjugate the very life from which it initially arose, imposing its own form on that life. Life is after all always more than life; it wrenches itself free of itself and encounters itself as a sharply defined form. It is simultaneously the stream and the firm shore; it yields to the creations that have come from its own womb, and in turn liberates itself from their power. Simmel's conception of life is so broad that even the truths and ideas which govern the course of life fall under its purview; nothing is henceforth excluded from this concept's sphere of influence. By means of the concept of life, the totality is traced back to a single originary principle. Although the formula for the world that Simmel ultimately arrives at testifies to his effort to encompass the coherence of the manifold, one must at least mention at this point that this does not seem a satisfying fulfillment of his desire for unity. Certainly no one was more profoundly convinced than Simmel himself that only a person of absolute values and certainties would be able to frame the manifold, to capture the totality. But his own venture into the realm of the absolute met with failure, and indeed, given the entire makeup of his being, had to have met with failure.

Since Simmel is not allowed to envelop the world completely, he attempts to conquer it by spreading out in all directions from the individual phenomenon. After all, his own core principle demands that he master the totality. There are really only two ways to get hold of it: either one formulates a concept of its entirety and incorporates all particulars into it, or one begins with the particulars and advances from them into increasingly remote regions of the manifold, gradually forcing the entirety into the field of view. So just what are the entities from which Simmel radiates out into the world? What are the foci around which he draws his circles? If one wanders through the world of appearances, one encounters an endless number of phenomena, each of which possesses its own peculiar essence and is intimately related to other phenomena. Simmel's subject matter encompasses, as I have shown, the extensive regions of sociological phenomena, people's value experiences, countless individual traits of the soul, and so on. From out of the midst of these phenomena arise the individuals who are clearly different from the mass of remaining essentialities, in that they are organically grown unities, totalities of a specific makeup. Depending on the position from which one surveys the manifold, these individuals either also belong to the world (as its members) or find themselves facing the world (as

worlds unto themselves): either they are parts or they are wholes. Whenever Simmel contemplates individual figures, he splits them off from
the macrocosm and extricates them from their entwinement with the
phenomena. He considers them as independent unities and refuses to
incorporate the individual microcosm into the greater totality. If one
wanted to describe Simmel's widening forays into the world, one would
have to ignore from the outset his appreciations of major spiritual/
intellectual figures, since for him the individual person is after all not
part of the world but is a well-rounded and sovereign construct that can
be grasped only in and through itself. In what follows, the terms
"world" and "totality" designate the manifold as understood by the
subject, but excluding individualities.

As the basis for his worldwide scouting trips, Simmel chooses certain general concepts that enable him to reveal the law-governed coherence of phenomena. In order to demonstrate this coherence, the concrete
individual event must not be experienced as something unique and
incomparable but must be grasped as the fulfillment of some general
essentiality that resides in wide expanses of various worlds—an essentiality to which the laws tend to adhere exclusively (precisely because of
its generality). In order to meet the challenge posed by the knowledge-
goal he has set himself, Simmel first tries to move up to concepts that,
while still describing a phenomenon that exists in reality, nevertheless do
not express its purely individual content. Some of his sociological investigations that belong in this context include, for example, his studies
"The Poor," "The Stranger," and "The Secret and the Secret Society."[19] Even more frequently, the philosopher Simmel takes one abstract
moment of such general concepts as the point of departure for his observations. In the abstraction, what we have recognized as the nonindepen-
dent, decisive element of an object's essence is detached from it and
elevated to the status of a category which groups together a multiplicity
of objects. Among the abstract moments of the artwork, for example, one
may include the reciprocal dependence of its parts, its unity, and its self-
sufficient perfection; furthermore, the artwork is an expression of the
soul, a mirror of its time, and so on. Such abstractions constitute the
crystallizing core of many of Simmel's studies, including "Über Kollek-

tivverantwortlichkeit" (On Collective Responsibility), "Group Expansion and the Development of Individuality," "Das soziale Niveau" (The Social Level), "The Web of Group Affiliations," "Quantitative Aspects of the Group," and "Superordination and Subordination."[20] Every phenomenon embodies a wealth of concepts; each is more precisely determined by a series of abstract moments that is in principle interminable. The question of which generalities one turns to is not only a function of the investigator's essential makeup but also depends on the aims of his contemplation. Simmel delves into a layer of generalities that occupies more or less the middle ground between the highest abstractions and strictly individual concepts; that is, he robs objects of only so much of their full substance as is necessary in order to discover any rule-governed connections between them. Since it is his fundamental desire to take account of the individuality of the phenomena as far as possible, he is naturally not content to subsume them under forms that are so broad they obscure the particular singularity of the objects. In this regard he sets himself apart from thinkers rooted in transcendental idealism who try to capture the material manifold of the world by means of a few wide-meshed general concepts, with the result that the existential plenitude of these phenomena floats right through their nets and escapes them. Simmel snuggles much closer to his objects, although he pays for this proximity to life by renouncing comprehensive principles. He submerges himself in multifariousness, and in the process sacrifices an overarching unity. Starting out from the general concepts that serve as his foci, Simmel subordinates the material of the world to his ends. His procedure looks something like this. He presents us with every conceivable condition, behavior, and so forth in which the core concept that he is currently examining plays a decisive role; this enables him to discover the law-governed development of the phenomena subsumed under this concept. He is like the chemist who combines a substance unknown to him with all other substances, in order to get a picture of the essence and the properties of the body in question by means of its reactions to all of the remaining chemical substances. It is in such a manner that Simmel undertakes experiments on the concept, submits it to the widest range of situations, and poses one question after another. Wherever the concept is accorded any meaning whatever—at every site and at every level of the totality—he examines and observes its behavior from the most varied perspectives. In the short study "The Social and the Individual Level,"[21] which ought to be mentioned as an example in the context of these remarks, Simmel first notes how primitive the goals of a mass of people are. He then spells out the consequences of the fact that the volition of such a mass is determined solely by the most general basic drives. He further examines just what aspects of the individual's fully laden being remain in effect when the individual becomes part of a mass. Elementary instincts blend into the collective spirit/intellect *[Gesamtgeist]*; the more subtle spiritual *[seelischen]* qualities of the individual must be abandoned when it descends to the social level. How is one to evaluate the primitiveness of the collective and the differentiatedness characteristic of the private self? Depending on the circumstances, they should both be valued equally highly. The former is considered venerable, is sacred by virtue of its age, its pervasiveness, and its incontrovertibility; the latter is respected because it bespeaks a higher spirituality, is rare, provokes us to action, and so on. Simmel follows this with a more detailed presentation of the painful changes in their being that individuals undergo when they become part of a mass. The intellect becomes significantly restrained, while the capacity for feeling, sensitivity, and passion often increases. The mass does not lie, but it lacks a sense of responsibility: it lets itself be guided by its immediate impressions, without any self-criticism; its moral inhibitions are suspended. The status of the social level relative to the individual level is expressed by the following formula: "What is common to all can only be what is owned by those who possess the least."[22] It always lies far below the theoretical average level, but never drops all the way down to the level of the lowest member of the community. Finally, Simmel calls attention to a frequently encountered exception to this formula. There are some people, namely, who refuse to capitulate to the collective spirit, who are unwilling to participate in this lowering of the level because they live completely in the continuous accomplishment of their most valuable powers and, as personalities, are much too highly developed ever to be able to sacrifice the higher portion of their being for the sake of the lower portion.

Simmel thus uses the concept of the social level in order to convey many of the manifold's essential determinations; wherever the concept is realized within the totality, he explores the manner of its realization and thereby extends himself from one point out into the world. By subjecting his object—in our example, the "social level"—to continually varying conditions, he is constantly discovering new characteristics for which, once he has established them in very general terms, he then seeks confirmation within experience. In this way he is able to discover the laws and forms of actions that superficially often seem to have nothing in common with one another. His exploration of the makeup of the social level leads him to expose numerous relations of essential congruence. He discloses, for example, the fact that individuals united in a mass are robbed of their highest spiritual/intellectual properties; or he shows that a desire for differentiation leads initially unified groups to split apart into separate bodies; and so on. Every such aspect of the social level is embodied in a series of highly varied phenomena that stand in a relation of analogy to each other, since they are subject to one and the same lawfulness, form, or structure.

Most of the time, however, Simmel is not content merely to pursue the various realizations of a general concept within the phenomenal world; he also seeks to find out why things relate to one another the way they do. He wants not only to establish but also to explain the connectedness of phenomena, and in the process to trace the relations between them back to a general formula that will account for the full range of the now-unveiled regularities. In order to achieve this goal, Simmel often buttresses a multiplicity of events, conditions, and so on with a common meaning that serves him as a base from which to radiate out into the totality. Once this thinker renounces such an all-pervading meaning, he can then spread out into the world from any general concept or abstract moment. All he must do is lay bare all the facts that are designated in any way by the relevant focal concept. It is not his task to do more than this, and indeed he is forbidden from doing so at every point where the unity of the concept (under which all the uncovered facts are subsumed) is not simultaneously a unity of meaning. In a series of sociological investigations, Simmel limits himself to wandering along the exterior of the phenomena; the concept that serves him as a guiding thread in each case cannot sustain any profound interpretation. As a result, the phenomena that can be disclosed through the concept lack a shared background of meaning. This state of affairs changes immediately when the concept is not an artificial construct, an arbitrary abstraction, but instead designates realities that are characteristic essentialities in and of themselves. Compare, for instance, the topic of "The Web of Group Affiliations" to the focus of another essay such as "The Adventure."[23] In the former, Simmel employs a basic concept that arises strictly out of his epistemological interests, and he directs attention to a manifold that does not constitute a natural unity. The basic concept employed in the latter essay, in contrast, designates a reality whose unity can be experienced, and it is only to this sort of reality that a meaning can be ascribed; only this sort of a reality can be sustained by a meaning-giving interpretation. In his study of "society," for example, Simmel interprets society as a *play form of sociation*[24] and in the process arrives at an explanation of the essence of all manifestations of sociability. Or, to take another example, it strikes him that the meaning of the handle resides in the handle's symbolizing the encounter of the world of the artwork with the world of practical life.[25] What is always at stake for Simmel in examples such as these is the conceptual expression of the unity of meaning that he has experienced in a group of phenomena—that is, the expression of this unity in a formula that is a perfect reflection in the conceptual sphere of what he experienced. For example, he sees the multiplicity of interhuman relations, spiritual/intellectual processes, and so on—all that is encompassed by the word "sociability"—as constituting just as much a self-contained totality of meaning as the individual does.[26] Although unable to reduce the plenitude of the world to the common denominator of a single meaning, he does perceive complexes of the manifold all over the world into which he can project himself. He extracts the essential core of such a complex with great clarity, and makes its concept into the explanatory principle of the phenomena belonging to the complex in question. Yet since within the greater totality no groups are sharply differentiated from each other, but instead every phenomenon stands in relation to all others, Simmel ultimately radiates out from every principle—which is initially only the focus of meaning of a quite circumscribed group of phenomena—further and further into the entire world.

I will illustrate his passage through the world by means of a carefully chosen example. According to Simmel, the essence of *fashion* resides in its capacity to satisfy people's need to imitate others, as well as people's need to differentiate themselves from others. It is the unified manifestation of both of these fundamental social drives, which it combines into a single activity. With respect to this determination of its essence, an analogy immediately arises between fashion and social honor, since both phenomena apparently have a common genesis as products of class-based distinctions and therefore serve "to constitute a circle of people, and at the same time to cut that circle off from others."[27] From the formulation of fashion's essence, it immediately follows that the creations of fashion are never based on any factual necessities but are instead the product of social and formal psychological needs. This discovery allows the thinker to draw a parallel between fashion and duty: both phenomena share a "foreignness to reality" in their disregard for the "what"—in other words, for the material through which they are realized. Simmel's method is clearly recognizable here. He shows that each of the newly discovered characteristics and modes of behavior of his object are also embodied in other objects, and in this manner he spreads a net of analogies across the world. It is easy to explain why domains like religion and science, which involve purely matter of fact decisions, are freed from the rule of fashion, or why, at least within such realms, its rule has no existential justification. Fashion befits only the upper classes, among which the need to set oneself apart is most highly developed. The claim that one must understand fashion as a result of both of the abovementioned fundamental drives is confirmed by the invariability of mourning clothes (to take just one example), whose meaning consists in making visible the mental state of mourning and which Simmel therefore calls a "manifestation of fashion in negation."[28] Once a fashion has become successful, it is soon imitated everywhere and the entire world tries to get hold of it. But the moment it is appropriated by the masses, it is no longer fashion—that is, it no longer provides the upper class with a formal means of proclaiming itself. Fashion "thus belongs to the type of phenomenon that aspires to increasingly unlimited expansion, to an always greater realization—but that, having reached this absolute goal, falls into self-contradiction and destruction."[29] One can observe analogous behavior, for instance, in moral endeavors or in economic work. Simmel's insights into the essence of fashion help one understand why it has gained such prevalence in the age of civilization—that is, in the era that Simmel still knew as the present. According to his explanation, we lack the deeply rooted convictions that anchor our entire life in a metaphysical ground. Since we lack the resoluteness that arises from within, fashion can take control of most of the domains of our existence and can direct various activities and expressions according to its own wishes. Moreover, we have become touchy; we love change, possibly because we want to flee the emptiness of our soul. But it is just such qualities and tendencies that foster the emergence of fashion, which, in order to maintain its power, depends not least on our capacity to change readily and on our desire for the new. Which group within society will become the primary supporter of fashion? The middle classes. The lower classes are immobilized by the weight of their economic burden; the highest classes, by their conservative attitude. The need to stand out grows in proportion to the density of cohabitation; that is why fashion is a metropolitan phenomenon. Simmel then proceeds to scrutinize the various typical attitudes toward fashion on the part of the individual. The person who obeys the dictates of fashion distinguishes himself from others not as an individual but as a member of a particular group. This explains the response he receives: "One envies the fashionable person as an individual but approves of him as a member of a set or group."[30] Having brought to light the spiritual qualities of the fashion hero, Simmel then calls attention to the fact that the person who is deliberately out of date endorses fashion just as much as someone who openly professes his loyalty to it. The behavior of the former type also grows out of the need to be different from—and the need to be identical to—others; he is a fashion hero with a reversed polarity. In a similar way, atheism not infrequently springs from a religious impulse: indeed, fundamental spiritual drives often find expression through utterly opposed forms. The fact that women yield to fashion more than men can be explained by the innate lack of objectivity of the female sex and by its dependence on the social environment. It is thus entirely logical that the emancipated woman who wants to participate in male endeavors must also rebel against fashion's claim to power. Since fashion always affects only a person's surface, in many cases it serves more substantively oriented people as a mask. They use it to disguise themselves; for them, submitting to fashion signifies a "triumph of the soul over the actual circumstances of existence."[31] A fashion can be almost shameless yet still not offend the sense of shame, which, according to Simmel's (admittedly quite inadequate) definition, is essentially based on the *individual's* efforts to stand out. That is why low-cut evening gowns immediately strike one as embarrassing when they are worn at unceremonious occasions, for which they were not intended. Like law, fashion is one of those forms of community life that govern people's external behavior. The more willingly people acknowledge these forms, the greater the inner freedom they gain. The individual no doubt also develops a "personal fashion" in order to satisfy the need to unify the impulses of the soul, as well as the need to emphasize one or another of his essential traits that strikes him as important at the time and that he therefore feels should be expressed. He adopts a specific style, favors certain idiomatic expressions now and then, lets one or another of his traits stand out with particular emphasis. Every fashion behaves as if it had been granted eternal life, even though it is in the end inevitably ephemeral. According to Simmel, this behavior stems from the fact that immortality actually suits fashion as a general concept because fashion provides a form which embodies basic human drives. Fashions change, but fashion remains, and it is from this superiority over time that each of fashion's fleeting moments apparently derives its claim to last forever . . .

Simmel does not always employ the types of unities just discussed—conceptual unities and unities of meaning—as starting points for his advances into the totality. Indeed, he also dissects *inauthentic unities,* which encompass a manifold that de facto does not belong together at all. Most of the concepts of everyday life are not, after all, born out of the immediate observation of the given; instead, the material on which they are based is brought into consciousness only in an indefinite and unclear form. These quotidian concepts are not experiences; they are common currency. For example, in his early work *Einleitung in die Moralwissenschaft* (Introduction to Moral Science), Simmel strives to disperse the fog of hazy ideas that has gathered around certain fundamental moral concepts (such as egotism and altruism) by exposing the myriad ethical facts that underlie these concepts. Instead of accepting the concepts in question sight unseen and making them the core of one or another ethical doctrine, he descends to their foundations and, by shedding light on reality itself, destroys a series of theories that arise out of the misty realm of concepts which imposes itself between the knowing subject and reality. Incidentally, Simmel's procedure in this case is the same as the one described above, except that here it is more a question of dissolving a world constructed from illusory concepts than of elucidating the relations of meaning that exist in the world.

The most outstanding example of this manner of conquering the totality is provided by Simmel's *Philosophy of Money*. In the foreword to this work, he notes: "In this problem-complex, money is simply a means, a material, or an example for the presentation of the relations that operate between the most superficial, the most realistic, and the most coincidental phenomena and the most idealized powers of existence, the most profound currents of individual life and history."[32] And in fact the thinker here traverses all of the material spheres that are in any way accessible to him, exhibiting the countless relations that develop within these realms among the equally countless phenomena. Simmel cuts one cross section after another through the social and individual life of people in the age of a highly developed money economy. His observations, however, do not stem from the perspective of either national economy or history; instead, they arise from the purely philosophical aim of bringing to consciousness the interwovenness of all the pieces of the world manifold. Nowhere else does Simmel develop such a comprehensive image of the interlocking and entwining of phenomena. He clearly elaborates the essence of these phenomena, only to dissolve it immediately in a multitude of relations; he shows how they determine one another and uncovers the many inherent meanings they have in common. Among the phenomena examined are, for instance, exchange, property, miserliness, waste, cynicism, individual freedom, lifestyle, culture, and the value of personality. At some points Simmel's analysis begins with the concept of money itself, from which he radiates out into the manifold in all possible directions (that is, he acknowledges the constitution of money, its relations to objects, its functional character, its position in the ranks of purposes). At other points he begins his analysis with certain phenomena that strike him as essential and then, having made them into new foci, allows the focus to wander from them back to money. For example, he exposes the significance of the capitalist type of economy in the formation of individuality, in the structuring of our internal and external lives. The inexhaustible mass of interspersed analogies points repeatedly to the unified core idea of the entire work, which can also be briefly formulated as follows: every point in the totality is accessible from every other point; one phenomenon carries and supports another; there is nothing absolute that exists outside any links to the remaining phenomena and that has validity in and for itself. This relativism, which Simmel not only practically employs but also theoretically justifies in the *Philosophy of Money*, will be presented more thoroughly below.

Now, as regards the manner in which Simmel penetrates the world in general, it is obvious from the outset that the unraveling of the totality must take on a form that is all the more exhaustive the wider apart the phenomena (each of whose interconnections are supposed to be illustrated) seem to lie. It is very indicative that in his journey through the world he always strives to bring together the things that are furthest apart. One gets the distinct impression that Simmel always wants to arouse in us a sense of the unified connectedness of the manifold, that he wants to convey its totality (which is actually never available to him in its entirety), at least by approximation. And so he tends to prefer exploring the relations between objects that are entirely foreign to each other on the surface and that stem from radically different material realms. He especially enjoys leaping from one or another layer of being into the experiential realm of the intimate personality. He glides quickly over abysses from one pole to the other, connecting a delicate, purely individual impulse with an expression of societal life and in turn building a bridge from the latter to the thought-motif of a world view. His spirit/intellect moves with agility and confidence to and fro among these numerous spheres, and flashes of affinity and similarity abound everywhere.

Given the aims of this type of thinking (indeed, one can almost deduce this a priori from its essence), it does not matter to the philosopher Simmel which problems he chooses to study, so long as they belong in some way to the material domains accessible to him. Any individual phenomenon can serve as the target for his philosophical examination, since all phenomena afford equally good entry points from which to delve into the interconnections of the life totality that surrounds them all. Whatever his object of contemplation is at the time, it becomes a focus of inquiry only to the extent that it consists of a more or less finite group of relationships that points beyond itself on all sides to the plenitude of relations in the universe that surrounds it. This is why Simmel quite often reduces his objects of study to the status of mere examples. From this perspective one can understand why, despite the variety of the subject matters he treats (indeed, scarcely any other thinker has marked out so wide a circle of objects of reflection), his works consistently manifest such a strongly developed uniform quality. This is due to the fact that most of the phenomena make their appearance in their capacity as complexes of connections. In many cases they are no more than nodal points and passageways for his investigation of the structure of the total manifold, out of whose weave they have been removed in order subsequently to be woven back in.

The procedure Simmel employs to spread himself across the totality produces results that are peculiarly impalpable. This wandering from relation to relation, this sprawling out both far and near, this crisscrossing—all these prevent the spirit/intellect that wants to embrace an entirety from taking a rest, and it gets lost in the infinite. Since the only significance of the threads spun between the phenomena is to make the hidden connections visible, their paths are quite irregular and arbitrary; they are almost systematically unsystematic. It is utterly insignificant where one ends up when casting them out and fastening them together, so long as one ends up somewhere. This web is not constructed according to a plan, like a firmly established system of thought; instead, it has no other purpose than to be there and to testify through its very existence to the interconnectedness of all things. Loose and light, it extends itself far and wide and gives the impression of a world that emits a curious shimmer, like a sunny landscape in which the hard contours of objects have been dissolved and which is now only a single undulation of trembling light veiling individual things. This shimmering is generated in particular by the fact that Simmel continually interrupts his train of thought so that he can present analogies (taken from the most varied spheres) to whatever behavior he happens to be examining. The fruit we reap from this sort of scouting is a growing sensitivity to the intertwinement of the elements of the manifold. We feel it: every phenomenon reflects every other phenomenon, varying a basic melody that also sounds in many other places.

Even though, as I have shown, Simmel ties the phenomena together in a variety of ways, almost all of the paths he maps out among the countless points of the manifold do share a specific orientation. In the preface to his *Rembrandt*, Simmel writes that he considers it an essential task of philosophy to "drop a plumb line from the immediate particular, from what is simply given, down to the stratum of the ultimate spiritual/intellectual meanings."[33] It is conceivable, after all, that in his meanderings through the totality Simmel either could have spent all his time in the realm of individual objects (carefully establishing their reciprocal relations) or could have remained in the sphere of ideas without ever considering the objects to which those ideas refer. The former situation is that of the empiricist who is content to discover connections between facts and balks at attributing a meaning to them. The latter situation is that of the pure metaphysician who does disclose an absolute meaning of the world but is unable to find his way back from this meaning to the plenitude of reality. Indeed, such a metaphysician is perhaps able to experience world-encompassing thoughts only because he denies himself the experience of a wide range of individual phenomena. In contrast, Simmel is a born mediator between phenomena and ideas; using a net of relations of analogy and of essential homogeneity, he advances from the surface of things to their spiritual/intellectual substrata everywhere he looks. In the process, he demonstrates that this surface is symbolic in character and that it is the manifestation and result of these spiritual/intellectual powers and essentialities. The most trivial event leads down into the shafts of the soul; from some perspective, there is a significant meaning to be obtained from every action. Thus, in Simmel's work a light from within makes the phenomena glow like the cloth and jewels in certain paintings by Rembrandt. All dullness and shabbiness disappear from the world's external surface, as if it had suddenly become as transparent as glass, enabling one to look in and through it into otherwise hidden layers of being which it reveals and simultaneously covers up.

The unity of meaning that Simmel denies to the world he accords instead to individuals. He wrests individuals from the context of the manifold and juxtaposes them with the latter as self-contained totalities that develop and pass away according to their own laws. In his investigation of the microcosm of the individual person, he uses a procedure that is precisely the opposite of the one he uses to master the macrocosm. With the latter he radiates outward, whereas with the former he encloses by means of a formula of essence. Apart from this, however, the way in which Simmel accounts for spiritual/intellectual individuality is completely identical to the way in which he discloses the inner connections of any clusters of the manifold that constitute a unity of meaning. So, for instance, he tries to convey the common explanatory basis for the many phenomena and types of behavior that fall under the conceptual rubric of fashion. For Simmel, sociological phenomena and man as a spiritual/intellectual totality are both individualities whose essence one must understand if one is to grasp the shared meaning that is equally manifest in all their expressions. Except that Simmel completely removes human individuality from the universe, whereas he considers every other individual complex in terms of its interwovenness with this whole. Simmel thus also applies his core principle—that everything is related to everything else—to the individual person. A person's actions, feelings, and thoughts are fused inseparably, and, if one is to gain insight into the "why" of their connectedness, it seems necessary to work out the essence of which they are all an expression. As mentioned earlier, a number of Simmel's works—such as *Kant, Schopenhauer and Nietzsche, Goethe,* and *Rembrandt*—all focus on major figures. Understandably, in these studies Simmel provides neither a biography of these men nor primarily a factual or critical appreciation of their achievements. Instead, he is driven to formulate the intuitive experience of the spiritual/intellectual significance of the figures in question and then to show how the observed significance is embodied, indeed must be embodied, in the various expressions of these personalities. He wants to unveil the innermost being of individuality, to bring to light the essential core which the individual himself (for reasons that must remain unarticulated here) cannot perceive.

The extent to which the phenomenal appearance of a person solidifies into an image and is experienced as a unity depends upon both the person's makeup and the standpoint one adopts toward him. One can focus one's attention primarily on his works; or one can just extract from them the characteristic contents of his world view; or one can try to figure out the significance of his fully lived life; and so on. Just which features strike us as constituting the individuality of a person depends primarily on the person himself. There are two types of creative personalities, and these react differently to the disclosure of its spiritual/intellectual essence. For some, this essence is contained entirely in their work. Even if one knew nothing about the real life of such figures, one could still extrapolate the meaning of their existence solely from their achievements, which, cut off from the lived reality of their producers, continue to exist as independent entities. Here, the spiritually/intellectually significant dimensions of such persons are entirely objectified, having detached themselves from these individuals in order to pass over into the creative work, where they are preserved as if under glass. The genius of the other type of person, by contrast, not only expresses itself through the works but also manifests itself through this personality's entire course of development, is embodied in the totality of their concrete existence. The significance of this type of person is by no means limited to their achievements; rather, one can seek and understand it only by scrutinizing all the manifestations of their lives. Just which essential traits and which effects of a person coalesce in each case into an individual unity naturally depends just as much on the spiritual/ intellectual attitude of the one who is trying to understand the person in question. Depending on the basic experiences of the investigator, he or she will direct special attention to this or that part of the individual manifold under examination: certain aspects of the object will force their way to the foreground, while others will appear only in abbreviated form, will overlap, or may even disappear. In an era alienated from meaning, after all, every phenomenon—be it a thing or an individual—is endlessly polyvalent, and the understanding one gains of it is the product of both its own essence and that of the observer.

Simmel treats almost all of the figures he studied over the course of his intellectual development as *individualities of works* [*Werkindividual-itäten*]. Whether the subject is Kant, Schopenhauer, Nietzsche, Rembrandt, or one of the types of thinkers he discusses in his book *Hauptprobleme der Philosophie*,[34] Simmel considers only what these spirits/intellects achieved, without in any way pursuing the details of their lives. Since it is his goal to unearth the relations of essential homogeneity among the individual creations of this sort of personality, his first priority must be to lay bare the unifying central idea of the works being considered (or whatever else strikes him as their core). This, in turn, allows him to demonstrate how the entirety of the creative output, including its most far-flung repercussions and ramifications, is a function of the makeup of that core and is necessarily rooted in precisely that ideational ground and no other. Guided by the aforementioned aspiration, Simmel completely dissolves the tightly knit coherence of the work and then reconstructs it by drawing numerous structural lines from the ideational center to the visible surface.[35] The connections that he establishes in the process in no way correspond to the ones that become clearly visible in the work itself and that were clearly evoked by the author. Rather, they are read into the work and lead like radii from the most varied parts of the embodied achievement to one and the same middle point—namely, to the fundamental idea that is expressed in this achievement and that is also intuitively recognized by the observer. All interconnections among the elements of the body of work are approached via the detour through the center. The ultimate point of the presentation is never a mere description of the factual contents of the work. Specific details of the manifold content are emphasized only when a path leading from the central idea happens to run into them—which is to say, when it is meaningful to describe the relationship between the detail and the idea that illuminates the entire work. Otherwise the method that Simmel employs in the investigation of individuals is identical to the procedure described above with regard to fashion. The only difference is, perhaps, that since Simmel conceives of the spiritual/intellectual figure as an autonomous multiplicity of relations with a unified meaning, he is less concerned to discover analogies by means of which he can traverse the world in all of its breadth. Simmel sees the essence of Rembrandt's art, for instance, in the way in which it masters life. Rembrandt strikes him as someone who has grasped the absolute continuity of life; in his work it seems as if "the depicted moment contains the entire impetus of a life lived up to that moment; it recounts the story of this stream of life."[36] Simmel then makes his way from the fundamental essence of Rembrandt's creativity to the master's various artistic revelations, including his series of self-portraits, his religious works, his freehand drawings, and so on. Simmel grasps all of these works—both in their willful particularity and in the context of their relatedness to one another—in terms of that idea of the artist which is given along with the artist's life, an idea which these works both express and symbolize.

Only once did Simmel try to get at the root of the *individuality of a life*—namely, in his book on Goethe. According to Simmel, the secret of Goethe's greatness lies, among other things, in the fact that the poet, "in fully obeying his own law, was also corresponding through this very process to the law of things,"[37] and that all of his experiences, including everything that confronted him from without, merged in a wonderful and fateful way into the stream of his entire personality and, fused with it, found creative expression. The unique reality of Goethe's existence is itself the ur-phenomenon; it has an experienceable meaning that can be captured in formulas. The development of his soul, relation to the natural and social environment, type of feelings, degree of devotion and self-preservation, and so on—everything about Goethe's life is essential and has symbolic character, that is, must be interpreted in terms of the spirit/intellect with which it is saturated.

As a concluding supplement to this cross section of Simmel's philosophy, I will give a quick preview of the way in which he consistently masters his material. He observes it with an inner eye and describes what he sees. As remains to be explained in greater detail,[38] it goes against his grain to deduce individual facts from abstract general concepts in a systematic and conceptually rigorous manner. All of his conceptual articulations cling to an immediately experienced (but admittedly not universally accessible) lived reality, and even the most abstract presentations have no other source than the observation that fills them to the brim. Simmel never engages in acts of thought that are not supported by a perceptual experience of some sort and that cannot accordingly be realized through such an experience. He always describes what he has seen; the entirety of his thought is basically only a grasping of objects by looking at them.

Once one has become aware of the core principle of Simmel's thought, one also gains access to the deeper reasons that account for the entire formal appearance of his philosophy. Critics have, after all, reproached Simmel often enough for the affectation of his style and his occasionally sophistic subtlety—as if all this were only incidental trimming and could just as well be eliminated without significant consequences for the core of the thought! If from time to time he conveys seemingly trivial events in quite complicated formulations, one can explain this as the philosopher Simmel's attempt to understand even the simplest phenomenon as a symbol, as something that refers to many other circumstances and events. He has no interest in grasping a phenomenon in terms of its obvious meaning, but instead wants to allow the entire plenitude of the world to pour into it. This is why the far-fetched analogies that soar over numerous spheres throughout Simmel's work must not be seen as the fruit of baroque arbitrariness. Anything but witticizing deviations from the goal of the particular investigation, they are to a large extent themselves this goal.

Umbo (Otto Umbehr), "The Uncanny Street, No. 1," 1928

On the Writings of
Walter Benjamin

■■■

Ernst Rowohlt Verlag[1] has recently published two works by Walter Benjamin: *The Origin of the German Tragic Drama* and *One Way Street.*[2] The former is a presentation and interpretation of the essential elements embodied in the reality of the Baroque tragic drama (it contains much more as well). The latter is a collection of aphorisms which, through a network of little-known streets, branch off from or lead into the phenomena of contemporary life.

Despite their thematic differences, the two works belong together as expressions of a type of thinking that is foreign to current thought. Such thinking is more akin to talmudic writings and medieval tractates, for, like these, its manner of presentation *[Darstellungsform]* is interpretation. Its intentions are of a theological sort.

■■■

Benjamin himself calls his procedure monadological. It is the antithesis of the philosophical system, which wants to secure its grasp of the world by means of universal concepts, and the antithesis of abstract generalization as a whole. Whereas abstraction links phenomena with one another in order to arrange them in a more or less systematic context of formal concepts, Benjamin avails himself of Scholasticism and the Platonic doctrine of ideas in order to assert the discontinuous multiplicity not so much of phenomena but of *ideas.* These manifest themselves in the murky medium of history. The tragic drama, for instance, is an idea.

It is decisive for such thinking that its ideas do not arise out of immediate contact with living phenomena. The observer who maintains an immediate relation to the phenomena may experience their form or may grasp them as the realization of some abstraction. But it makes no difference how he perceives them, since, according to Benjamin, the way in which a phenomenon manifests itself in an immediate encounter reveals virtually nothing of the essentialities it contains. Its living form is transitory and the concepts gleaned from it trifling. In short, he who faces the world in its immediacy is presented with a figure that he must smash in order to reach the essentialities.

In his study of the tragic drama, Benjamin, in exemplary fashion, breaks down the "Baroque tragic drama" complex into its significant elements, a dissection necessary for the presentation *[Darstellung]* of the idea. One of these elements is *allegory*. Using primary sources, Benjamin retraces the intentional origin of allegory, that is, he follows it back to the point in its history at which its true meaning reveals itself. A rare intuitive capacity enables him to penetrate the ancestral world of essentialities and to discover what is theirs from the beginning. His interpretation of allegory is worthy of admiration. Using the original texts, this interpretation is the first to demonstrate how nature that has succumbed to death (and for the Baroque, history—as the story of the world's suffering—is nature) turns into allegory under the gaze of the melancholic. Once all the elements are charged with the extremes of their significance, Benjamin points out the *dialectical* movement into which they are drawn within the structure of the Baroque tragic drama. It is thoroughly logical that he can never allow essentialities to be subsumed under an abstract general concept but instead insists only upon a dialectical synthesis which preserves their full concreteness. Where meanings come together under the sign of an idea, they jump to one another like electric sparks rather than being "sublated" into a formal concept. In the course of history, they eventually also undergo dialectical separation, and each acquires a subsequent history of its own, on its own.

The difference between traditional abstract thinking and Benjamin's manner of thinking is thus as follows: whereas the former drains objects of their concrete plenitude, the latter burrows into the material thicket in order to unfold the dialectic of the essentialities. It accepts no generalities whatsoever, pursuing instead the progression of specific ideas through history. But since, for Benjamin, every idea is a *monad*, the world seems to him to proffer itself in every presentation of such an idea. "The being that enters into it [the idea] with its previous and subsequent history brings—concealed in its own figure—an abbreviated and darkened figure of the rest of the world of ideas."[3]

■■■

Scholars of history, literature, and art—not to mention philosophers— will all find material of interest in Benjamin's work on the tragic drama. It combines an extraordinary knowledge of meanings and ideas with the profound erudition of a researcher who finds himself driven by his philosophical insights particularly toward unknown and marginal sources. The book proposes a new theory of ancient tragedy and, in addition to its interpretation of allegory, discloses important essential- ities such as fate, honor, and melancholy in the material contents *[Sachgehalte]* of the Baroque scene. The book elucidates the signifi- cance of the characters involved in the tragic drama and of all its elements, also taking into account the classical drama of fate and its Romantic descendants. Never before has anyone shown so strikingly that essentialities begin with history, though they do not stem from it. As a result of Benjamin's work, one will have to view the Baroque—and not only the Baroque—with different eyes.

Especially important here, where methodology is so critical, is the fact that the book on tragic drama contains not merely the history of the different meanings of a materially embodied idea, but also an observation of the timeless *order* of the world of ideas. The same intuitive capacity that leads Benjamin to the origin of essentialities provides him with the knowledge of their proper place, a knowledge that one is fully justified in calling theological. For Benjamin, the world is *obscured and obstructed*, in the way that it always has been from a theological perspective. This is also precisely the basis for Benjamin's belief that it is not necessary to respect the immediate—that the façade must be torn down, and form cut to pieces. It is entirely consistent with his approach that Benjamin hardly ever tackles constructs and phenomena when they are in their prime, pre ferring instead to seek them out once they have entered the realm of the past. For him, living constructs and phenomena seem jumbled like a dream, whereas once they are in a state of disintegration they become clearer. Benjamin gathers his harvest from works and states of affairs that have died off, that are removed from the contemporary context. Since the most pressing life has left them, they become transparent, allowing the order of the essentialities to shine through them.

Empowered by his insights into this order, Benjamin wishes to carry out the act of *redemption* appropriate to theological contemplation. His particular concern is always to demonstrate that big matters are small and small matters big. The divining rod of his intuition hits upon the realm of the inconspicuous, upon the realm of the generally deprecated, upon the realm that history has passed over, and it is precisely here that it discovers the greatest significance. There are good reasons for the fact that Benjamin expatiates on the wasteland of the Baroque tragic drama and accords allegory an importance which, compared to the symbol, it does not possess in traditional accounts. Symptomatically, in Benjamin's presentation allegory redeems the ancient gods, enabling them to survive in the hostile world of medieval Christendom. The other motif of his contemplation is the uncovering of those hidden moments and nodal points in the course of history where *salvation* is intended or appears in the image. "Yea, when the Highest comes to bring in the harvest from the graveyard, so will I, a death's-head, become an angel's countenance": these words, uttered by a speaking skull in Lohenstein's *Hyacinthen*,[4] serve as the epigraph to the last chapter of the book on tragic drama, a chapter that deals with the sudden shift of melancholy into the world of God and that interprets the image of apotheosis as a sign of salvation. Perhaps Benjamin's actual aim in his meditation is to pursue here and there the process that takes place, between heaven and hell, behind the backs of things and that at times visibly breaks into the world of our dreams. Benjamin can call himself a secret agent, in the sense that Kierkegaard described himself as a "secret agent of Christianity."[5]

■ ■ ■

That Benjamin wants to wake the world from its dream is proved by some radical aphorisms in *One Way Street,* a number of which were previously published in our feuilleton section.[6] This small book, whose presentation is a bit too coy, combines thoughts from the most diverse realms of personal and public life. To take a few random examples: curious accounts of dreams, childhood scenes, and numerous cameos devoted to exemplary sites of improvisation (such as fairs and harbors), whose delicate contours are reminiscent of bas-reliefs; statements about love, art, books, and politics, some of them recording astounding troves of meditation. The rest of the observations are uneven. In addition to notes that perhaps still await further elaboration, there are expressions of bare *esprit*[7] and now and then (for example, in the "Imperial Panorama" section, which attempts to characterize the German inflation)[8] private impressions that are quite arbitrarily monumentalized. It is as if in this book Benjamin purposely opened up the many perspectives available to him, in order to corroborate the discontinuous structure of the world from this side as well. As for the overall position of *One Way Street*, the sum of the aphorisms consciously announces the end of the individualistic, naïvely bourgeois era. Benjamin's method of dissociating immediately experienced unities—which he uses in his book on the Baroque—must take on a meaning which, if not revolutionary, is nonetheless explosive when applied to the present. Indeed, the collection is full of detonations. But what emerges from behind the heap of rubble is not so much pure essentialities but rather small material particles that point to essentialities (Benjamin discusses the meaning of morning sobriety, of washing, and so on). In general, the book distinguishes itself from the earlier work by its particular *materialism*. The clearing away and enlightenment that Benjamin practices here on sites which normally go unnoticed correspond entirely with his procedure. As he puts it in his very first aphorism, "Opinions are to the vast apparatus of social existence what oil is to [the] machines. One does not go up to a turbine and pour machine oil over it; one applies a little to hidden spindles and joints that one has to know."[9]

■ ■ ■

Yet Benjamin hardly takes into account the very life he intends to stir up. It is certainly no coincidence that the interpretations wrested from the present in *One Way Street* are not nearly as forceful as those elicited from the material of the Baroque tragic drama. This can be explained as a function of Benjamin's conviction that anything whose existence is immediate lacks all substance; such things strike him as muddled. He turns away from immediacy to such an extent that he does not even really come to terms with it. He neither records the impressions of any form of that immediacy nor ever gets involved with the dominant abstract thinking. His proper material is what has been: for Benjamin, knowledge arises out of ruins. Thus, there is no attempt here to redeem the living world; instead, the meditator redeems fragments of the past. It is not without good reason that, from the perspective of the world in its immediacy, the dialectic of essentialities—which takes place behind the back of this world of immediacy and must be demonstrated in disintegrating works—takes on an *aesthetic* appearance. Benjamin would break through to reality in its fullness only if he were to unravel the real dialectic between the elements of things and their figures, between concretions and the abstract, between the meaning of form and form itself.[10]

■ ■ ■

The kind of thinking that Benjamin today embodies, one-sidedly and in however extreme a fashion, has fallen into oblivion since the advent of idealism. He consciously restores such thinking within our philosophy's sphere of influence, thanks to the capacity he ascribed to Karl Kraus (the ability to perceive "a murmur from the chthonic depths of language")[11] in combination with the capacity that enables him to taste essentialities. It is not without good reason that Benjamin translated sections of Proust, an author with whom he has close affinities.[12] In Benjamin, philosophy regains the determinateness of its content; the philosopher is placed in the "elevated position midway between researcher and artist."[13] Even if he does not reside within the "realm of the living,"[14] he retrieves from the storehouses of lived life the meanings that were deposited there and that are now awaiting a recipient.

Willy Otto Zielke, Pyramid, 1929

Franz Kafka

ON HIS POSTHUMOUS WORKS

■ ■ ■

A collection of unpublished prose works from the literary estate of Franz Kafka has recently appeared under the title *The Great Wall of China*,[1] a volume put together by Max Brod, friend of the deceased writer and guardian of his estate, in collaboration with Hans Joachim Schoeps. According to the afterword by the two editors (whose interpretations are not entirely adequate), all of the narrative fragments and aphorisms presented in the collection are late works that Kafka produced during the last period before his death in 1924. They were written during the years of the war, the revolution, and the inflation. Although not a single word in the entire volume makes immediate reference to these events, they figure among its presuppositions. Perhaps it was only the intrusion of these events that enabled Kafka to discern and elaborate the confusion in the world. "There can be knowledge of the diabolical," runs one of the aphorisms, "but not belief in it, since more of the diabolical than there already is does not exist."[2]

■ ■ ■

The image of building reappears often in the texts; its primary aim is to designate the efforts of distracted and confused people. In "Investigations of a Dog," the narrator, an animal of rare philosophical gifts with whom Kafka identifies for extended stretches, wonders, "Can I contemplate the foundations of our existence, divine its profundity, watch the laborers at the construction, at their sinister work, and still expect that all this will be brought to an end, destroyed, abandoned, just because of my questions?"[3] Indeed, the building that one generation after another constructs is sinister, because this structure is to guarantee a security that men cannot attain. The more systematically they plan it, the less they are able to breathe in it; the more seamlessly they try to erect it, the more inevitably it becomes a dungeon. It rears up like a nightmare in the story "The Burrow,"[4] where an unnamed animal, which is perhaps a mole or a hamster, tells of the cave-like construction it has built out of fear of an invasion by all conceivable forces. Since this fear also wants to eliminate those insecurities, inherent to creaturely existence, the burrow is a work of self-deception. It is no accident that its labyrinthine passageways and squares extend through subterranean night. Kafka's presentation of the burrow, which has the clarity of a daydream, takes particular care to point out the reciprocal relation between the hopeless fear and the ingenious intricacy of the architectural system. If the latter is a product of an anxiety arising from a reprehensible attempt at self-assertion, it, too, in turn creates anxiety—an increasingly threatening entanglement that eventually obliterates the animal's freedom of action. Thousands of precautionary measures must be taken before the animal dares to venture out of the cave, and its return from its daily promenade is transformed into a most unusual undertaking. Moreover, the futility of the burrow becomes apparent in the end, for no matter how well it protects against the trivial things that dig about in the earth, it cannot withstand the real enemy and may in fact even attract it. The measures provoked by existential fear are themselves a threat to existence.

Kafka also undeniably conceives of science—at least to the extent that it crosses certain boundaries—as a building, but a building that is a product less of fear than of confusion. In the prose piece "The Village Schoolmaster [The Giant Mole],"[5] he brings the dark, boundless, and all-embracing edifice of science into confrontation with a trivial discovery by a village schoolmaster. While the latter has meaning under all circumstances because and so long as it is inseparably tied to the person who discovered it, the former, towering dizzyingly upward, abandons mankind. "Every discovery," we read in the story of the giant mole, "is introduced at once into the sum total of knowledge, and with that ceases in a sense to be a discovery; it dissolves into the whole and disappears, and one must have a schooled scientific eye even to recognize it after that. For it is immediately related to fundamental axioms of whose existence we don't yet even know, and in the debates of science it is raised on these axioms into the clouds. How are we to grasp such things?"[6] Similarly, in the "Investigations of a Dog," it is remarked that the science of nutrition "in its prodigious compass is not only beyond the power of comprehension of any single scholar, but beyond that of all our scholars put together . . ."[7] Just as animal fear ends up in the self-constructed labyrinth, spirit/intellect gets lost in the excesses of science.

Laborers building: Kafka sees them everywhere. They hammer and pound, and their masonry is so thick that no sound can get through to us. Foolish to expect that someone could still slip out! The doors lack keys, and the few holes that do appear are immediately walled up again. "Leopards break into the temple and guzzle the sacrificial chalices dry. This is repeated time and again. Finally it can be reckoned upon beforehand and becomes part of the ceremony."[8]

■ ■ ■

At one point the philosophical dog admits that if he were tested by a scholar he would have trouble passing even the easiest of scientific tests. This is not because he lacks intelligence but because he possesses a certain instinct whose orientation is characterized as follows: "It was this very instinct that made me—perhaps for the sake of science itself, but a different science from that practiced today, an ultimate science— prize freedom above everything else."[9] This explanation amplifies the earlier ones, since it implies there is an ultimate science that might possibly be attained in freedom. Our world is thus a locus of unfreedom, and we are slaving away at a building that is obstructing our view. Conceivably, in his description of the mole's cave, Kafka had in mind those human organizations whose triumphs consist in trenches, barbed-wire barriers, and wide-ranging finance projects. His awareness of finding himself imprisoned is deepened by premonitions of a state of freedom in which the lessons of the ultimate science can come to the fore. Almost the opposite of a believer in progress, he transposes this state of freedom, or rather the possibility of partaking in it, into the past.

Earlier generations, remarks the narrator of the "Investigations of a Dog," were younger. "Their memory was not so overburdened as ours today; it was easier to get them to speak out, and even if nobody actually succeeded in doing that, the possibility of it was greater . . . The true word could still have intervened, planning or replanning the structure, changing it at will, transforming it into its opposite; and the word was there, was very near at least, on the tip of everybody's tongue—anyone might have hit upon it."[10] All of Kafka's work circles around this one insight: that we are cut off from the true word, which even Kafka himself is unable to perceive. Moreover, it is this insight that provides sufficient justification for the parable of the sinister building. How is it that its walls, which used to be so much thinner, have now become so impermeable? The answer proves that it is not a romantic intention that motivates Kafka's backward glance: "No, whatever objection I may have to my age," the investigating dog assures us, "former generations were no better than recent ones; indeed, in a certain sense they were far worse, far weaker."[11] The attitude manifested by this statement divests the subsequent tale about our ancestors' misdeeds of any semblance of longing for the past. "When our first forefathers [Urväter] strayed, they certainly did not think that theirs was to be an endless wandering; after all, they could still literally see the crossroads. It seemed an easy matter to turn back whenever they pleased, and if they hesitated to turn back it was merely because they wanted to enjoy a dog's life for a little while longer."[12] The reproach of indolence raised here—Kafka considers it one of the cardinal sins—also appears in the short story "The City Coat of Arms."[13] Here it is directed against the builders of the Tower of Babel, who, trusting in the progress of their successors, did not push themselves to the limit of their energies. Nevertheless—and this is quite important—Kafka puts less weight on the allusion to the presence of a past failure than on the memory of the loss of the true word. The latter is a leitmotif that recurs constantly, as in the fable of the dying emperor who has sent you, and you alone, a message that never arrives;[14] in the tractatus "The Issue of the Laws," where one reads that by their very nature laws must remain a secret;[15] and in the image of the monumental group to which Kafka once belonged.[16] By invoking that which has been lost, Kafka simultaneously shifts it into an unreal distance, as if to show that even the dream can hardly offer refuge to it. The emperor's messenger attempts in vain to leave even the innermost palace chambers, and the populace does not know whether the laws, which have been kept secret and which they are trying to guess, even exist. And in the strange account "The Knock at the Manor Gate,"[17] the knock—which probably did not even take place—does cause the court gate to open wide, but nothing emerges except a troop of horsemen that has dashed in only to turn back again immediately afterward.

■ ■ ■

The hallmark of the philosophical dog is his incessant inquiring about the unascertainable. The answer of the fellow dogs is—silence. This resolute silence about the "crucial things,"[18] which is constantly erecting itself anew in front of him like a bulwark, is one of the bitter fundamental experiences that the small group of authentic questioners have always had to endure. It is as if the dog were speaking in their name when he complains, "We are those who are oppressed by silence, who long to break through it, literally in order to breathe."[19] If the questioner is condemned to loneliness, then the others are silent allies who find happiness in "the warmth of togetherness"[20]—if they do not isolate themselves by choice, like the cave animal, who loves the silence. Indeed, the silence that reigns or is supposed to reign in the interior of his utterly dark burrow is really the only drastic cure for the true word. Since it is impossible for an entire group of creatures to fall silent simultaneously, the silence of the dogs takes a different form. Sometimes they avoid the required response; at other times they try to repress their particular way of life by spouting intolerable babble, like the aerial dogs.[21] How can the behavior of the canine community be explained? For there are doubtless good grounds for it. The investigating dog surmises "that those who remain silent are in the right as the preservers of life."[22] This is why he does not want to despair after all but instead unceasingly implores his allies to join him in opening the "roof of this low life,"[23] in order to ascend to freedom. But just as he is about to lift off the roof and thus eliminate the decisive obstacle, he encounters a new resistance which he is completely unable to overcome. He hears music, which forces him to give up. For Kafka, music is the highest form of silence. It paralyzes the dog twice. The first time is during his encounter with seven musical dogs who are producing marvelous sounds. The still youthful questioner wants them to explain what drives them to such activity: "But they—incredible! incredible!—they never replied, behaved as if I were not there."[24] The second time, music disturbs a hunger experiment which the dog, who has grown older in the meantime, undertakes as part of his daring investigations. As a trial that gambles with existence, its relationship to the much more noncommittal achievements of science is similar to that of the discovery of the village schoolmaster in "The Village Schoolmaster [The Giant Mole]." No sooner is the experiment—which is meant to be explosive—really in process when a foreign dog approaches the fasting one and, after trying in vain to persuade him, finally chases him away from the hunger site by means of magical song. The conversation that precedes the forced abandonment is enlightening. In the course of the conversation, the dog who has prepared himself for fasting and who does not want to allow himself to be chased away remarks that the unknown dog has gotten himself entangled in contradictions. The latter, however, refrains from correcting them and merely asks, "Don't you understand that which is self-evident?"[25] The self-evident: this is the last pretext for those who want to maintain this low life, the last bulwark behind which the guardians of silence can dig themselves in.

■ ■ ■

The treatment that the silent dogs accord the investigator leads him to raise the following suspicious question: "Did they want to lull me to sleep, to divert me, without violence, almost lovingly, from a false path, yet a path whose falseness was not so completely beyond all doubt that it would have permitted the use of violence?"[26] Like the dog who is constantly being distracted—this is how Kafka feels. He looks at the world as someone who has been pushed back into it, as someone who must turn back from the pursuit of those places where the emperor lives and where the unknown laws are housed. It is not as if he would have ever found his way to them; rather, his experience is more like that of someone who has only partially awakened, whose thinking—still half caught up in sleep—remains occupied with the dream that has just barely dissolved and in which the solution of all riddles was present. Even as he still believes that he can grasp and, yes, even taste the key word, the incomparably clear image into which the world has congealed under the sign of the revealed secret begins to melt. Tortuously he attempts to gather its disintegrated parts, which, to make things worse, begin to reassemble themselves in a fundamentally wrong arrangement. The less he is able to succeed in reconstructing the magnificent image that has now disappeared, the more desperately he dashes about among the scattered fragments in order to preserve them and, where possible, put them in order. This chase conditions Kafka's artistic process. As he reports in an aphorism, in earlier years he found himself wishing "to attain a view of life . . . in which life, while still retaining its natural rise and fall, would simultaneously be recognized no less clearly as a nothing, a dream, a hovering."[27] And a few lines later: "But he could not wish in this fashion, for his wish was not a wish at all, but only a defense, a bourgeois version of nothingness, a wisp of gaiety which he wanted to lend to nothingness."[28] In fact, Kafka hardly ever complies with his former wish, but instead verifies for himself that the confused world that he traverses from one end to the other is a nothing. In order to unveil the world's presumption that it is a something, he shows that the relation of things to people is completely skewed. The anecdote "A Common Confusion,"[29] for instance, recounts how A wishes to conclude an important business deal with B from H. They plan to meet, but despite their best intentions to keep the appointment they miss each other. One could term Kafka's portrayals reversed adventure novels, since here, instead of the hero conquering the world, the world becomes completely unhinged in the course of his wanderings. According to Kafka, Don Quixote was actually Sancho Panza's devil, who knew, however, how to render this devil harmless by distracting him from himself. Thus, the devil incessantly performed the craziest deeds, and Sancho Panza, who followed him out of a certain sense of responsibility, "derived from them a great and useful entertainment to the end of his days."[30] In just the same way, Kafka wards off the reasonableness that is impotent despite its logical power, and accompanies it through the thicket of human conditions. Thanks to the continual intervention of reasonableness, the world's defectiveness is exposed once and for all. Even if stupidity were to reign in the world, the expectation that intelligence might be able to change things would still be justified. But this very expectation is disappointed by the actual uselessness of the intervention of reasonable reflection.

Countless rational and realistic insights, doubts, and reservations pervade Kafka's poetic writing for the sole purpose of ultimately fizzling out in the void. How carefully, for example, the cave animal ponders whether it should post a confidant as a watchman at ground level, to increase its security. But: "If there is someone whom I can trust when I can see him eye to eye, can I still trust him as fully when I can't see him and the moss covering separates us? It is comparatively easy to trust someone if you are supervising him or at least can supervise him; perhaps it is possible even to trust someone at a distance. But completely to trust someone outside the burrow when you are inside the burrow—that is, in a different world—seems to me impossible. But such doubts are not even necessary; it suffices to simply imagine that during or after my descent any one of the countless accidents of existence might prevent my confidant from fulfilling his duty . . ."[31] Although generally there is method to madness, here the methodological reflections—which are meant to be entirely realistic—are the hallmark of the world's madness, and the fact that they do not work out unmasks their irreality completely. This irreality is not a dream; on the contrary, it is real. It is not a something, however, and is all the more negligible the more coherent it pretends to be. In this, its form of existence, it releases beings from within itself that, while invisible to the average viewer, reveal themselves to those returning with the rumor of the true word resonating in their ears: mythical beings correlated to the jumbled murmuring of life and its reasoning. Among them belong the unnamed burrow animal, which defies observation, and the freezing "scuttle rider,"[32] who gallops on his scuttle to the coal store but is unable to attract the attention of the coal dealer's wife. They are neither spirits *[Geister]* nor ghosts but corporeal embodiments of the current state of the world, in which instead of kings there now exist only couriers. "They were given the choice of becoming kings or the couriers of kings. Like children, they all wanted to be couriers. This is why there are so many couriers scurrying about the world, shouting messages to each other which—since there are no kings—have become meaningless."[33] The world in which these couriers scurry to and fro is like a pattern sheet depicting parts that do not match. Kafka often takes pleasure in singling out one of the misleading lines, pursuing it, and then in a sense playfully developing it further. The investigating dog, for instance, not content with having grasped the insignificance of scientific results, makes the following observation: "In this regard the essence of all knowledge is enough for me, the simple rule with which the mother weans her young ones from her breast and sends them out into the world: 'Wet everything as much as you can.' "[34] It is the abstruseness of things that every now and then demands a touch of gaiety.

■ ■ ■

In "The Great Wall of China,"[35] a study that Kafka himself describes as historical, he depicts the ancestral world, the one in which "the social structure of the dog world . . . was still a loose one."[36] His depiction of its structure is less an attempt to raise this former mode of existence to the level of a realized utopia than it is an effort to characterize the impenetrability of today's situation. At least, what is most important for him is to play off the dense structure of the present against the looseness of the earlier moment. The entire investigation is, if you will, a grand experiment meant to examine what a world that granted entrance to the "old, yet actually simplistic stories"[37] might have looked like. It is with this intention that Kafka discusses extensively the "system of piecemeal construction"[38] supposedly employed in the construction of the Chinese wall. On orders from the leadership—"where it was and who sat there no one whom I have asked knew then or knows now"[39]—gaps were left everywhere. "This is the way it was done: gangs of some twenty workers were formed who had to accomplish a length of, say, five hundred yards of wall, while a neighboring gang erected another stretch of the same length to meet the first. But after the junction had been made the construction of the wall was not carried on from the point, let us say, where this thousand yards ended; instead the two groups of workers were transferred to begin building again in quite different areas."[40] To emphasize further the fundamental importance of such a working method, the narrator continues: "In fact it is said that there are gaps which have never been filled in at all, an assertion, however, which is probably merely one of the many legends surrounding the building of the wall."[41] The reproach of inexpediency could be made against the piecemeal construction system as described above, since according to what one hears the wall was after all meant to serve as a protection against the races from the north. But Kafka refutes the objection that he himself has raised: if the gap-riddled construction is inexpedient, then it follows that the leadership wanted something inexpedient. He then closes with the curious supposition that the decision to build the wall probably existed since the beginning of time and thus was not directed against the races from the north at all. This information rounds out the picture of a past life that the story of the Chinese wall tries to capture. It is both an invocation and an entreaty.[42] It is the former in that it invokes and transfigures a lost form of existence in which the properly integrated human creature does not plug up the gaps out of a fear of life and a false need for protection—gaps that apparently permitted this creature to hear the echo of the true word. It is an entreaty to the extent that it contains the admonition to become aware of the state of suspension. The light of olden times streams from it into the present era, not in order to direct us back to its shimmer, but rather in order to illuminate our utter darkness just enough so that we can take the next step.

■ ■ ■

Are we even capable of taking this step? In the "Investigations of a Dog" one reads that "our generation may be lost."[43] This weak "may be" leaves a trace of hope. When he gets more specific on the subject of this hope, Kafka betrays an uncertainty that corresponds precisely to the immeasurable distance from the true word. This uncertainty is juxtaposed to the certainty with which the reflections of diabolical reason appear and lose their footing. Just as Kafka neither acknowledges nor entirely rejects progress, he links together the far and the near in a similarly ambiguous fashion. "The true way goes over a rope which is stretched out not at any great height but just above the ground. It seems designed more to make people stumble than to be walked upon."[44] The view that the sought-after solution is unattainable, yet at the same time attainable here and now, is touched on briefly in the aphorism that grasps the Last Judgment as martial law. It is contained in the octavo notebooks of 1917–1919, which, to the best of my knowledge, also contain Kafka's only reference to the events of the [October] revolution: "The decisive moment in human development is everlasting. For this reason the revolutionary movements of intellect/spirit that declare everything before them to be null and void are in the right, for nothing has yet happened."[45] Estranged from the world, this thought barges in upon the world, much too close to the language of the world not to be subject to confusion. The decisiveness with which this thought approves the radicality of intellectual/spiritual movements derives its justification from its inkling of the true path. Perhaps due to the just-mentioned insecurity, Kafka avoids attributing revolution to this true path out-right. But instead, he does clarify his inkling at various points. According to him, only the community possesses the explosive power capable of lifting the roof off the low life. The investigating dog rec-ognizes that what he shares with his fellow dogs is not only blood but also knowledge, and not only knowledge but also the key to knowledge. "Bones hard as iron, containing the richest marrow, can be gotten at only by a united crunching of all the teeth of all dogs."[46] The related lesson of the text "On the Issue of the Laws" reads: "That which is so gloomy for the present is lightened only by the belief that a time will eventually come when the tradition and our research into it will jointly reach their conclusion, and, with a sigh of relief, everything will have become clear, the law will belong to the people alone, and nobility will vanish."[47] Here and there, the individual who is lost together with the community is advised to save himself along with that community, but without any guarantee of redemption. There is no safeguard, and the fact that alongside the belief in a redemption to come in this world there is another belief that the confusion of the world is ineradicable—this in itself is not really confusing. In one aphorism is a formulation that reads:

"One develops in one's own manner only after death, only when one is alone. Death is to the individual like Saturday night to the chimney sweep: both wash the soot from the body."[48] Or could it be that the breakthrough does not occur only after death? The tale "The City Coat of Arms" ends with the lines: "All the legends and songs that originated in this city are filled with longing for a prophesied day when the city would be destroyed by five successive blows of a gigantic fist. This is why the city has a fist on its coat of arms."[49] It is not certain whether the legends and songs that herald the destruction of the dwelling are accurate, and what perspective will then open up for us. "I have never been in this place," Kafka says at one point. "Breathing is different, and a star adjacent to the sun shines even more brightly than the sun itself."[50] It is here that we remain, with the unconfirmed longing for the place of freedom.

The Movies

Aerial view of the UFA studios in Neubabelsberg, ca. 1930

Calico-World

THE UFA CITY IN NEUBABELSBERG

■ ■ ■

In the middle of the Grunewald[1] is a fenced-in area that one can enter only after going through various checkpoints. It is a desert within an oasis. The natural things outside—trees made out of wood, lakes with water, villas that are inhabitable—have no place within its confines. But the world does reappear there—indeed, the entire macrocosm seems to be gathered in this new version of Noah's ark. But the things that rendezvous here do not belong to reality. They are copies and distortions that have been ripped out of time and jumbled together. They stand motionless, full of meaning from the front, while from the rear they are just empty nothingness. A bad dream about objects that has been forced into the corporeal realm.

We find ourselves in the film city of the UFA studios in Neubabelsberg,[2] whose 350,000 square meters house a world made of papier-mâché. Everything guaranteed unnatural and everything exactly like nature.

■ ■ ■

In order for the world to flicker by on film, it is first cut to pieces in the film city. Its interconnections are suspended, its dimensions change at will, and its mythological powers are turned into amusement. This world is like a child's toy that is put into a cardboard box. The dismantling of the world's contents is radical; and even if it is undertaken only for the sake of illusion, the illusion is by no means insignificant. The heroes of antiquity have already made their way into the schoolbooks.

The ruins of the universe are stored in warehouses for sets, representative samples of all periods, peoples, and styles. Near Japanese cherry trees, which shine through the corridors of dark scenery, arches the monstrous dragon from the *Nibelungen,* devoid of the diluvial terror it exudes on the screen.[3] Next to the mockup of a commercial building, which needs only to be cranked by the camera in order to outdo any skyscraper, are layers of coffins which themselves have died because they do not contain any dead. When, in the midst of all this, one stumbles upon Empire furniture in its natural size, one is hard pressed to believe it is authentic. The old and the new, copies and originals, are piled up in a disorganized heap like bones in catacombs. Only the property man knows where everything is.

On the meadows and hills the inventory organizes itself into patterns. Architectural constructions jut upward as if meant to be inhabited. But they represent only the external aspects of the prototypes, much the way language maintains façades of words whose original meaning has vanished. A Frisian village church, which beckons to simple piety from afar, turns out upon closer inspection to be a hut on a painted slope. And the cathedral a few hundred meters further contains no church choirs, since its roof adorned with gargoyles sits separately off to the side, for filming purposes. Together with the façades of a pleasure resort and a billionaire's club, it is part of the film *Metropolis* (1925–1926), which Fritz Lang is making. On some nights elegant extras live it up between the spiritual *[geistlich]* and worldly imitations. The underground city with its grottoes and tunnels—in which the film's narrative houses the thousands of workers—is already gone, blown up, flooded. The water was not really as high as it appeared in the film, but the burning elevators actually did come crashing down in their full, original size. Meticulously filed cracks in the furnaces still testify to those elemental events. Near the center of the catastrophe are stretches of decaying wall—a fortress with bowers, ramparts, and moats. It stymies the archaeologists in the well-known film *Die Chronik von Gries-*

hus.[4] When mounted soldiers occupied it recently, in the Middle Ages, the director brought in croaking frogs, from ponds, to keep the troops in the right mood. When it comes to deception, the heart and soul appreciate authenticity. In the meantime the fortress has fallen apart; the materials of its construction are peeking through. It cannot deteriorate into a ruin, because ruins have to be made to order. Here all objects are only what they are supposed to represent at the moment: they know no development over time.

■■■

The masters of this world display a gratifying lack of any sense of history; their want of piety knows no restraint—they intervene everywhere. They build cultures and then destroy them as they see fit. They sit in judgment over entire cities and let fire and brimstone rain down upon them if the film calls for it. For them, nothing is meant to last; the most grandiose creation is built with an eye to its demolition.

Destruction catches up with some things when they've scarcely had a chance to enjoy their place in the sun. The racetrack tribune in front of which sensational sports events took place has been toppled, and the Vienna woods that rustled in *Ein Walzertraum*[5] have been cut down. Other things change unpredictably. The remains of modern houses have been integrated into an old-fashioned alley, an anachronism that does not seem to disturb anyone. Political interests play no role in such reorganizations, no matter how violent the latter may be. A Bolshevist guardroom turns into a peaceful Swedish train station, which is subsequently transformed into a riding school and today is used to store lamps. It is impossible to tell what it will become next. The laws of these metamorphoses are unfathomable. No matter what may happen to the objects, however, in the end their plaster of paris shines through and they are junked.

■■■

The regime of arbitrariness does not limit itself to the world as it is. The real world is only one of the many possibilities that can be moved back and forth; the game would remain incomplete if one were to accept reality as a finished product. That is why its objects are stretched and shortened, make-believe objects are sprinkled among the existing ones, and miraculous apparitions are created without hesitation. The magic acts of yesteryear were a faint prelude to *cinematic special effects,* which give short shrift to nature. For them, the cosmos is a little ball to be batted around at will.

At times, the things projected onto the screen take on such a quotidian appearance that they seem as if one could encounter them on the street. Their creation, however, was marked by abnormal circumstances. Lampposts whose steel and cement existence seems tangible are made of wood and are broken off halfway up; the fragment suffices for the section framed by the image. An impressive skyscraper does not tower nearly as dizzyingly as it does in its screen appearance: only the bottom half is actually constructed, while the upper section is generated from a small model using a mirror technique. In this way, such structures refute the colossi: while their feet are made of clay, their upper parts are an insubstantial illusion of an illusion, which is tacked on.

The evocative powers of special effects lend themselves particularly well to the domain of the supernatural. The upcoming blockbuster film version of *Faust* being directed by W. Murnau uses them extensively. In a hall previously employed by pirates for their life of thievery, the planet Earth now expands *en miniature.* Faust will fly through the air from one backdrop to another. A wooden roller coaster that curves down to the valley describes his aerial itinerary. The camera glides down the chute and, thanks to expert guidance, spews forth images of the journey. Fog made of water vapor produced by a steam engine envelops the range of appropriately sculpted mountain peaks from which Faust emerges. For the horrible crash of the foaming deluge, some water is sprayed through a side canyon. The wild urges subside when the wheat covering the fields and meadows beneath the jagged, pine-covered summits rustles in the wind of the propeller. Cloud upon cloud wafts eastward, masses of spun glass in dense succession. Upon Faust's landing, huts surrounded by greenery will most likely shimmer in the blazing, high-wattage glow of the evening sun. Things are also rather Faustian in the Tempelhof UFA studios,[6] where Karl Grune is directing *Die Brüder Schellenberg.* Here apocalyptic riders sweep across the glass studio on horses suspended in midair from the ceiling by wires. Among them is a menacingly huge set of black wings with which Jannings,[7] as the head devil, casts shadows over cities, while the archangel Michael soars on a pair of white wings.

···

Nature, in body and soul, has been put out to pasture. Its landscapes are surpassed by those that are freely conceived and whose painterly appeal is no longer subject to chance. Nature's suns likewise leave much to be desired. Since they do not function nearly as reliably as floodlights, they are simply locked out of the newest American film studios. Let them go on strike if they want to.

Still, some remnants of the natural are put into storage on the side. Exotic fauna, the by-product of a few film expeditions, thrive along with representatives of the local animal world on the margins of the studio grounds. Some of the creatures captured in Brazil were transferred to the zoological gardens, where they can be a purpose unto themselves and enrich science. Those that have been kept function like a specialty act that travels with its own impresario. Each type of animal has its act in the program. In a sculptured garden, gold and silver pheasants can illustrate the luxury of American billionaires; the rare black hawk evokes the thrill of the exotic; cats in close-up shots lounge in salons. The doves from Berger's beautiful Cinderella film[8] are still flying around. The wild boar that appears in hunting films and a swarm of live crocodiles number among the prominent beasts. They play a major role in the film *Die drei Kuckucksuhren*, directed by Lothar Mendes. The baby crocodile is a prop that one can hold in one's hands, but even the fully grown monstrosities are not as dangerous as their lifeless counterparts, which the monkeys fear. Greenhouses complete the collection: their vegetation forms the appropriate background for scenes of jealousy in the tropics.

The occupants of the wildlife preserve are lovingly cared for by the zoologist of the expedition. He calls them by name, grooms them, and gives them acting lessons. Despite their inherent imperfections as creations of nature, they are the most spoiled objects of the enterprise. The fact that they leap or fly without being moved by a mechanism elicits delight, and their ability to propagate without the help of obvious special effects seems miraculous. One would never have thought these primitive creatures capable of this, so much do they seem almost like cinematic illusions.

■ ■ ■

The world's elements are produced on the spot in immense laboratories. The process is rapid: the pieces are prepared individually and delivered to their locations, where they remain patiently until they are torn down. They are not organisms that can develop on their own. Woodworking shops, glassmaking shops, and sculpture studios provide what is necessary. There is nothing false about the materials: wood, metal, glass, clay. One could also make real things out of them, but as objects in front of the lens *[Objektiv]* the deceptive ones work just as well. After all, the lens is objective *[objectiv]*.[9]

Certain preparatory measures are necessary in order to integrate things and people. If both remained in their traditional state, they would stand apart like rare museum pieces and their spectators. Light—whose source is the huge electric power plant providing the energy for the entire undertaking—melts them together. The actors are groomed in the makeup room. This is not a workroom like any other but a studio full of skilled artistry. The physiognomies formed here from the raw materials of the human face reveal their secrets only under the beams of the spotlights. The masters of their discipline preside over makeup tables filled with cosmetics of every shade. A chart shows the degree of luminosity that the colors attain when photographed; but when subsequently forced into the black-and-white scale, their color values vanish. This makes the preparatory stage all the more seductive—the degenerate garishness of the wigs in glass cases. Portrait-like masks hang on the walls, fireproof creations that are custom-made for the main actors of whatever film is currently being produced. In certain scenes, these make it unnecessary for the actor to appear in person: other actors transform themselves into the stars by wearing their masks. These disguised figures are stiff and move about like the dead. In the adjoining screening room, one can test the effect of a make-up job on film.

Both films and people are enveloped by this self-sufficiency; every available resource is used to ensure that they flourish. The means of technical reproduction—such as color film stock—are checked and improved in an experimental laboratory. Comparable energies are expended to train a new generation, which will know how to use the various techniques. A real fire department is standing by to put out real fires, and doctors and medics are on call at all times. Luckily accidents, as popular as they are, seldom occur. During the shooting of *Metropolis*, hundreds of children had to rescue themselves from the flood—a horrible sight in the film. The actual event was so harmless that the offstage nurses were left with nothing to do. One of the primary hubs is the canteen, where people in full costume sit among white-collar workers, technicians, and chauffeurs, looking like leftovers from a carnival. They wait.

■ ■ ■

They wait endlessly for their scene. There are many such scenes, pieced together like the little stones of a mosaic. Instead of leaving the world in its fragmented state, one reconstitutes a world out of these pieces. The objects that have been liberated from the larger context are now reinserted into it, their isolation effaced and their grimace smoothed over. Out of graves not meant to be taken seriously, these objects wake to an illusion of life.

Life is constructed in a pointillist manner. It is a speckling of images that stem from numerous locations and initially remain unconnected. Their sequence does not follow the order of the represented events. A person's fate may already have been filmed even before the events leading up to it are determined; a reconciliation may be filmed earlier than the conflict it resolves. The meaning of the plot emerges only in the finished film; during the gestation, it remains unfathomable.

The cells must be formed one after the other. Here and there, pieces of inventory come together to shape a light-drenched environment where things human unfold. The movements suffused in light are pursued by the cranking boxes. These perch in every spot where people can possibly be ensconced: on the floor, on scaffolding—no point of view is safe from them. Sometimes they pursue their victims. The smallest fragment is born only following terrible labor pains; assistants and assistant assistants are involved, and, amid much gesticulation, it slips out.

The director is the foreman. It is also his difficult task to organize the visual material—which is as beautifully unorganized as life itself—into the unity that life owes to art. He locks himself and the strips of film into his private screening room and has them projected over and over. They are sifted, spliced, cut up, and labeled until finally from the huge chaos emerges a little whole: a social drama, a historical event, a woman's fate. Most of the time the result is good: glass clouds brew and then scatter. One believes in the fourth wall. Everything guaranteed nature.

August Sander, Cinema staff, 1929

The Little Shopgirls Go to the Movies

...

Films are the mirror of the prevailing society. They are financed by corporations, which must pinpoint the tastes of the audience at all costs in order to make a profit. Since this audience is composed largely of workers and ordinary people who gripe about the conditions in the upper circles, business considerations require the producer to satisfy the need for social critique among the consumers. A producer, however, will never allow himself to be driven to present material that in any way attacks the foundations of society, for to do so would destroy his own existence as a capitalist entrepreneur. Indeed, the films made for the lower classes are even more bourgeois than those aimed at the finer audiences, precisely because they hint at subversive points of view without exploring them. Instead, they smuggle in a respectable way of thinking. The fact that films as a whole reaffirm the ruling system was demonstrated by the excitement over *Potemkin.*[1] It was perceived to be different and was aesthetically endorsed, but only for its meaning to be repressed. In comparison with that film, the differences among the various types of films produced in Germany or the United States evaporated, providing conclusive evidence that the cinematic productions of the latter countries are the homogeneous expression of one and the same society. The attempts by some directors and authors to distance themselves from this homogeneity are doomed from the start. Either such rebels are simply tools of society, unwittingly manipulated yet all the while believing they are voices of protest, or they are forced to make compromises in their drive to survive.

(Even Chaplin ends up as a millionaire in *The Gold Rush,* without having achieved any real goals.) Society is much too powerful for it to tolerate any movies except those with which it is comfortable. Film must reflect society whether it wants to or not.

But is it really society that manifests itself in sensationalist film hits? The breathtaking rescues, the impossible noblemindedness, the smooth young gents, the monstrous swindlers, the criminals and heroes, the moral nights of passion and the immoral marriages—do they really exist? They really do exist: one need only read the *Generalanzeiger* newspapers.[2] There is no kitsch one could invent that life itself could not outdo. Servant girls do not imitate professional love-letter writers; rather, the opposite is true—the latter model their letters on those of servant girls. Virgins still drown themselves if they believe their bride-grooms have been unfaithful. Sensational film hits and life usually correspond to each other because the Little Miss Typists model themselves after the examples they see on the screen. It may be, however, that the most hypocritical instances are stolen from life.

Still, this is not to deny that, in the majority of contemporary films, things are pretty unrealistic. They give the blackest settings a pink tinge, and smear reds liberally everywhere. But the films do not therefore cease to reflect society. On the contrary: the more incorrectly they present the surface of things, the more correct they become and the more clearly they mirror the secret mechanism of society. In reality it may not often happen that a scullery maid marries the owner of a Rolls Royce. But doesn't every Rolls Royce owner dream that scullery maids dream of rising to his stature? Stupid and unreal film fantasies are the *daydreams of society,* in which its actual reality comes to the fore and its otherwise repressed wishes take on form. (The fact that major issues do get expressed—albeit in a distorted way—in both sensational film hits and in literary bestsellers does not detract from this claim.) Members of the higher and next-to-highest classes may not recognize their portraits in these films, but this does not mean there is no photographic resemblance. They have good reasons not to know what they themselves look like, and if they describe something as untrue, then it is all the more true.

Today's world can be recognized even in those films that are set in the *past*. It cannot examine itself all the time, because it may not examine itself from all sides; the possibilities for inoffensive self-portraits are limited, whereas the demand for material is insatiable. The numerous historical films that merely illustrate the past (rather than showing the present in historical guise, as in *Potemkin*) are attempts at deception according to their own terms. Since one always runs the danger, when picturing current events, of turning easily excitable masses against powerful institutions that are in fact often not appealing, one prefers to direct the camera toward a Middle Ages that the audience will find harmlessly edifying. The further back the story is situated historically, the more audacious filmmakers become. They will risk depicting a successful revolution in historical costumes in order to induce people to forget modern revolutions, and they are happy to satisfy the theoretical sense of justice by filming struggles for freedom that are long past. Douglas Fairbanks, the gallant champion of the oppressed, goes to battle in a previous century against a despotic power whose survival is of no consequence to any American today.[3] The courage of these films declines in direct proportion to their proximity to the present. The most popular scenes from World War I are not a flight to the far reaches of history but the immediate expression of society's will.

The reason this expression of societal will is reflected more directly in films than in theatrical works can already be explained simply by the greater number of elements that intervene between the dramatist and capital. It may seem to both the dramatist and the theater director as if they were independent of capital and thus able to produce timeless and classless works of art. Of course, this is impossible, but nevertheless shows are staged whose social determinants are harder to perceive than those in films, where the head of the corporation stands guard in person. This is particularly true of the social determinants of comedies, tragic dramas, high-class revues, and products of directorial artistry produced for the intellectual (Berlin) bourgeoisie—determinants that remain only partly unrefracted in society. In the end, the audiences for such works read a radical magazine and pursue their bourgeois profession with a bad conscience, in order to have a good conscience. The artistic qualities of a theater piece may also shift it outside the social sphere. Writers are often stupid, however, and if they renounce one aspect of traditional society, they are all the more taken in by another. (In the *Literarische Welt*, Bert Brecht called bourgeois lyricism suspicious and devoted himself instead to sports.[4] Sports as a nonbourgeois phenomenon: Samson-Körner's biographer is not to be envied for making this discovery.)[5] Apart from such exceptions, which consciously extricate themselves from some of the constraints, the majority of the remaining second-rate works for the stage are a precise response to the feelings of the theater crowds. They're just as indebted to the existing order of things as films, only they're more boring.

In order to investigate today's society, one must listen to the confessions of the products of its film industries. They are all blabbing a rude secret, without really wanting to. In the endless sequence of films, a limited number of typical themes recur again and again; they reveal how society wants to see itself. The quintessence of these film themes is at the same time the sum of the society's ideologies, whose spell is broken by means of the interpretation of the themes. The series "The Little Shopgirls Go to the Movies" is conceived as a small collection of samples whose textbook cases are subjected to moral casuistry.

Clear Road

A prison inmate who has seen better days is released and lands in a Zille-type milieu[6] full of little shopowners, whores, proletarians, and shady characters.[7] He had been wrongly convicted. In vain the fallen man looks for respectable work; only a whore takes pity on him. One day, he rescues a woman in a carriage whose horses have gone out of control in the Tiergarten park; she's the sister of a manufacturer, who expresses his thanks by giving the former inmate a job in his business. Now the road is clear for the diligent man: his achievements are recognized, his innocence considered proven. Following the timely death of the whore, who succumbs to consumption, the fellow—now dressed in a business suit—becomes engaged to the woman he rescued. A typical situation on screen, which attests to the social mentality of today's world. Using true-to-nature studio images of back-alley interiors, it depicts the impoverished conditions that give rise to transgressions which are not the real social crimes. It wanders without prejudice among the underprivileged classes, which provide gripping material for the film. The themes, however, have been carefully screened. All mention of class difference is avoided, since society is far too convinced of its first-class status to want to become conscious of the real conditions of its classes. Also avoided is any mention of the working class, which is attempting through political means to escape from the misery that the directors present so movingly. In films based on real-life situations, the workers are respectable lower-level railroad functionaries and patriarchal foremen; or, if they are supposed to be discontented, they have suffered a personal tragedy, so that the public misfortune can be all the more easily forgotten. One prefers the *Lumpenproletariat* as emotionally moving subject matter, because it is politically helpless and contains dubious elements who seem to deserve their fate. Society disguises the sites of misery in romantic garb so as to perpetuate them, and lavishes pity on them because here it doesn't cost a cent. It is full of pity, this society, and wants to express its emotional excess so as to soothe its conscience—assuming, of course, that everything can remain the way it is. Out of pity, it extends a hand to one or two of the foundering people and rescues them by pulling them back up to its level, which it really considers to be quite a height. This is how it assures itself moral support, while at the same time maintaining the underling as underling and society as society. On the contrary: saving individual people is a convenient way to prevent the rescue of the entire class; one proletarian who has been promoted to the drawing room ensures the perpetuation of many a beer joint. The manufacturer's sister will later go with her husband to visit his beer joint. Maybe these two will once again save another person. One need not fear that this is why the proletarians are dying out. The little shopgirls gain unexpected insights into the misery of mankind and the goodness from above.

Sex and Character[8]

A young and pretty girl has made up her mind to win the heart of her cousin, who owns the adjacent property.[9] She puts on pants, gets him to hire her as his domestic servant, and from then on appears as an ambiguous figure in the most unambiguous situations. The word "gay" is also ambiguous, its meaning depending on the context of its utterance.[10] In order to establish the boy's true identity, the owner of the estate breaks into the servant's room. The half-undressed girl—from the waist up in livery, below the waist in lace panties—has crawled under the covers. The thorough master grabs her by the feet and, slowly and systematically, pulls her out. All out of love. The outcome: an engagement. The owner of the estate is rich. Before his domestic servant's hips began to arouse his suspicion, he had had an affair that began in a dance club. Dance clubs are no less numerous and no less important today than churches were in previous centuries. No film without a dance club; no tuxedo without money. Otherwise women would not put on and take off their pants. The business is called eroticism, and the preoccupation with it is called life. Life is an invention of the haves, which the have-nots try to imitate to the best of their inability. Since it is in the interest of the propertied classes to maintain society as it is, they must prevent others from thinking about that society. With the help of their money, they are able in their free time to forget the existence for which they slave during the day. They live. They buy themselves an amusement which allows the brain to take time off because it keeps the other organs so completely busy. If the dance clubs were not already fun in themselves, the state would have to subsidize them. Girls who disguise themselves as domestic servants and gentlemen whose ultimate goal can be grasped under bedcovers do not have evil thoughts—that are good thoughts. They might stumble upon such thoughts out of boredom. In order to alleviate the boredom that leads to the amusement that produces the boredom, the amusement is supplemented with love. Why did the girl do it? Because she loves the owner of the estate. Any objections to love are destroyed by the judgment of a society that has lost love. Out of the earthly realm of the club, society allows oaths of fidelity to blossom between lives that do not exist, and out of the revue environment it conjures up engagement apotheoses whose luster should not be dismissed as trivial. The light such apotheoses radiate is so festive that people no longer wish for society to conceive of things in a different light. Particularly if love is financially secure. In the dark movie theaters, the poor little shopgirls grope for their date's hand and think of the coming Sunday.

Nation in Arms

An impoverished hotel in eastern Austria during World War I has just been occupied by the Russians.[11] Here, a servant lass hides an Austrian officer who has stayed behind. The Russian general who has taken up residence in the hotel harasses the patriotic lass with lascivious propositions. She resists, out of patriotism. Shortly thereafter the Austrians march back in and the officer and the woman who rescued him are honored by the entire company, to the tune of the Radetzky March. (A wartime wedding is in the offing.)—On another occasion, an intrepid East Prussian woman rescues her son (likewise an officer) during an enemy occupation.[12] He wins his hardy cousin as his wife. The battle scenes are edited more decently than the uniformed acts of heroism.— These military and war films, which resemble each other down to the last detail, are a striking refutation of the claim that today's world is fundamentally materialistic. At the very least they prove that certain influential circles are very interested in having others adopt a heroic attitude instead of the materialism which these influential circles themselves support. In fact, those circles can achieve their aims—which may lead to new wars—only when the masses, which are still slightly contaminated by the revolution, have once again been morally purified; when the pleasure provided by war in the form of decorations and virgins replaces the memory of its horrors; when, once again, a new generation grows up which does not want to know what it is battling for, so that it can triumph and perish with all the more honor. The moral intent of these films is confirmed by the fact that they also acknowledge the humanity of the enemy. The Russian general who is after the patriotic lass is an honest man. Respect for the opponent makes war into an absurdity. This is precisely the aim of its producers, since, as such, war must be accepted as an inexplicable necessity. Only when the populace considers a heroic death a senseless fate can it endure it ethically. Military films serve to educate the populace. This is particularly true of the Fridericus Rex movies, in which—always according to the wishes of the same influential circles—the audience is once again treated to a king that inspires more enthusiasm than its real leaders, who, in turn, profit from this enthusiasm.[13] When good old Sombart called the Germans "heroes" and the English "merchants" in a war pamphlet, he erred as profoundly as only a professor can.[14] The film heroes of all countries unite as the propaganda bosses of their nation's businessmen. It is hard for the little shopgirls to resist the appeal of the marches and the uniforms.

The World Travelers

The daughter of an airplane engine manufacturer takes off on an air race around the world—a flight that is supposed to demonstrate the quality of daddy's motors.[15] A competitor she has previously turned down tries to delay her all along the voyage. A young man whom she will assuredly not turn down helps her all along the voyage. Against the backdrop of India, China, the calm ocean, and America, a love affair develops with great speed, and great speed develops with this affair. The woman aviator always appears in the traditional garb of each respective country. In the end, triumph and an engagement. In other films, the characters get engaged on the shores of northern Italian lakes or in Spain (the choice of country depends on the whims of fashion). Each engagement is linked with the continuous use of one's own car.—I have traveled around the entire world in order to find myself, Count Keyserling affirms in his philosopher's travelogue.[16] Society likewise never finds itself through its voyages; but unlike the count, it travels precisely in order not to find itself. Whether at home or in some modern means of transportation, society's actions remain everywhere the same. Changes in the landscape, however, distract attention from the hypocrisy of societal events, whose monotony is forgotten in the adventure of the voyage. The woman aviator who overcomes danger in India pretends to be a modest damsel in distress; nobody recalls the capitalist transaction in Berlin that prompted her to take the trip in the first place. Travel is one of the best means for a society to maintain a permanent state of absentmindedness, which prevents that society from coming to terms with itself. It assists fantasy along mistaken paths; it occludes one's perspective with impressions; it adds to the wonder of the world, so that the world's ugliness goes unnoticed. (The concomitant increase in knowledge about the world serves to transfigure the existing system in which it is gained.) Some important social figures who can afford to spend their vacations in St. Moritz truly feel like human beings when they're there; they go to St. Moritz only to repress the fact that they really aren't human beings. Even the lower social classes, which have to stay at home, are sent away. The illustrated newspapers disseminate images among them from every country; and anyway, whom does the woman aviator fly for, if not for them? For the more they travel, the less they understand anything. When all geographic hideouts have been photographed, society will have been completely blinded. The little shopgirls want so badly to get engaged on the Riviera.

The Golden Heart

A young Berlin wholesaler, an industrious manager of a first-rate company, visits a business friend of his father's in Vienna; the paternal friend's firm is going to pieces because of the disorder in Austria.[17] The guest would leave, if it were not for the business friend's daughter, a sweet Viennese gal who makes it clear to him that there are other things besides management: the waves of the Danube and the wine gardens specializing in new vintages. With delight, the young man from Berlin discovers his dormant feelings. He cleans up the company, which will soon be turning a profit again, and gets the gal for home use.—Even without close-ups, this course of events would be believable. Whether in the city of waltz dreams or on the beautiful beaches of the Neckar— someplace, but not here in the present, the rich are falling in love and discovering in the process that they have hearts. It is not true that they are heartless: films refute what life would make one believe. Outside business—which admittedly would not be the right place for heart—their hearts are always in the wrong place. They are brimming with feeling in situations where it is of little consequence and are often unable to do as they like, only because they waste their feelings so uneconomically in private affairs that their supply is continually running out. One needs to have experienced the tenderness and gentleness the young man from Berlin expresses to the Viennese girl under the Stephansturm in order to understand once and for all that his brutal behavior on the telephone does not indicate a lack of sentiment. The camera reveals this. What he really loves is operettas, and what he really longs for is an idyllic retreat in which, undisturbed, he can open his poor heart, which he has had to close off in all other situations. If there were no Viennese woman in the house to keep his heart from interfering in economic matters, it could, in a pinch, be well accommodated by the record player. Through films, one can prove on a case-by-case basis that with rising prosperity the number of emotional nature preserves is constantly growing. The little shopgirls learn to understand that their brilliant boss is made of gold on the inside as well; they await the day when they can revive a young Berliner with their silly little hearts.

The Modern Haroun al Raschid[18]

A billionaire's daughter appears incognito as a poor girl, because she wants to be loved purely for who she is as a human being.[19] Her wish is fulfilled by a rather plain young man who is actually an impoverished lord. Before he has even confessed his affection he learns, by chance, of the billions. He withdraws from his courtship in order to avoid any misunderstandings. Now, more than ever, the two come together, and since money loves to come into money, in the end the lord inherits an immense fortune.—In another film a young billionaire roams the world as a vagabond, because he wants to be loved purely for who he is as a person and so on.[20] Incognito revealed, the girl hesitates, and a honeymoon on a comfortable yacht ensues.—As in the

Thousand and One Nights, today's fairy tale prince also chooses dis-
cretion; but here the opulence of the ending stems from his billions,
which outshine every social opulence. A huge fortune can be kept
secret for instrumental reasons. The rich pauper and the tramp who
isn't one do not appear incognito for any purpose other than perhaps
wanting to be taken purely for who they are as human beings and so
forth. Why don't they just throw the money away if they want to be
loved as human beings? Why don't they demonstrate that they are
something worth loving by doing something decent with their money?
They don't throw it away, and they don't do anything decent with it.
Instead, the feigned poverty serves to shine a bright spotlight on the
luckiness of wealth, and the desire to be loved disinterestedly is a
sentimentality that serves to obscure the lack of true love. For true
love has interests; it is of great interest to it that its object be a worthy
one. It might get uncomfortable for the billionaire's daughter if a
suitor desired her out of real interest. So she hushes up the billions
with which she has been provided and procures for herself, at the
giveaway price of the open market, a husband whose unselfishness
consists in the fact that he stumbles across a girl without billions who
is nothing without her billions. But (so preach the moralists among
the rich) what is important is the girl, not the wealth. According to
the cinematic testimony, a human being is a girl who can dance the
Charleston well and a boy who knows just as little. The love between
one person and another—that is, between two private bagatelles—is
therefore not superfluous but serves to justify property ownership.
This ownership, in turn, is not nearly so aggravating to those without
property if those who own property can show through so-called love
that they can own it as human beings. The fairy tales have remained,
while the theme of the incognito has been inverted. The authentic
Haroun al Raschid traveled among the people anonymously in order
to get to know them independently of property, and in the end
revealed himself as their judge. The modern Haroun al Raschid presents himself independently of his wealth in order to be recognized as
something special in this anonymity, and in the end reveals the only
thing he really is: his wealth. If the little shopgirls were approached

tonight by an unknown gentleman, they would take him to be one of the famous millionaires from the illustrated magazines.

Silent Tragedies

A banker goes bankrupt as a result of such immense incompetence that he commits suicide out of propriety.[21] The insolvent estate includes a daughter. The first lieutenant who loves her must abandon his dreams of escorting her down the aisle; her lack of means and his career make this impossible. She goes on to earn her living as a dancer under an artistic pseudonym. The first lieutenant, who has long regretted his refusal of the relationship, meets her again after years of futile searching, and wants to be united with her at last. The only thing needed for a happy ending is his letter of resignation, which he has been planning to hand in. But the selfless dancer poisons herself in order, through her death, to force her lover to think only of his career. The officer, dressed in civilian clothes, stands wistfully beside the stretcher.—The young man need not be a first lieutenant; in other professions as well, an individual's career depends on marrying wealth. This leads to such tragedies, which really aren't tragedies. But for society's sake, it's imperative that they appear to be tragedies. If a woman kills herself so that a man can reach great heights, this guarantees the irrevocability of social structures. They are raised to the level of eternal laws, since, for their sake, people are willing to suffer a death reminiscent of a five-act tragic drama. The film companies know (or perhaps do not know) why they peddle such morbid fare. The death that confirms the power of the ruling institutions prevents a death in the course of a struggle against these institutions. In order to make the latter impossible, the former is glorified. The film producers glorify it, however, by passing off as tragic what is really lack of knowledge or, at best, a misfortune. The noble-mindedness that the dancer wants to prove by voluntarily killing herself is a squandering of feeling, which is cultivated by the better classes because it weakens the feeling of injustice. There are many people who sacrifice themselves noblemindedly because they are too lazy to rebel; many tears are shed which flow only because crying is sometimes easier than contemplation. Today's tragedies are private affairs with a bad outcome which society has metaphysically dressed up in order to preserve the status quo. The stronger the power positions of society, the more tragically weakness and stupidity will behave. And with every new international agreement that heavy industry reaches, the number of suicidal dancers will certainly rise. The audience is so touched by the signs of the poisoning by which these dancers take their leave that it no longer wants to get rid of the poison. Thus, only the attempts to detoxify society can be called tragic. Furtively, the little shopgirls wipe their eyes and quickly powder their noses before the lights go up.

Close to the Edge

At times, films go mad. They have terrifying visions and spew images that expose society's true countenance. Luckily, they are healthy at root. The schizophrenic outbursts are only momentary; the curtain is lowered once again, and everything returns to normal. A girl from the provinces, for example, comes to Berlin with her admirer, a clumsy young fellow.[22] Since she is a beauty, a board chairman makes her into a revue star and gives the youth a job. He would be a bad businessman if he did not want to cash in on his investment. The girl, however, refuses his advances, packs up her young man, and turns her back on dirty favoritism. (The film's scriptwriter is a man of letters.) An unmasking of social practices? The film producer deserves to go broke, since nothing is more demoralizing for an audience than the revelation of immoral activities that are officially sanctioned so long as they take place in secret. The danger is avoided at the last minute, when the board chairman regrets his actions and catches up with the innocent couple, who, following his renunciation, happily allow him to drive them back to town. There have to be such board chairmen in order to whitewash favoritism. (The author is a man of letters.) The following case is even more drastic. The king of a tiny impoverished southern country has brought home a lover from Paris that an American billionaire wants to include among his possessions.[23] In order to win her, the billionaire buys the cooperation of the discontented masses and bribes the king's general. A patriotic insurrection is quickly staged. Machine guns open fire, producing a picturesque distribution of corpses in the streets and squares. The general informs the billionaire that, thanks to the incarceration of the king, the girl is now free; his attitude toward his new patron is that of an obsequious servant. Is this how coups d'état and bloodbaths are staged by big capital? The film is insane. It portrays events as they actually happen, instead of maintaining the dignity usually accorded them such that they can continue to take place. Thank God the film recovers its rosy-cheeked smile immediately. The American is really a good person who deserves his billions. Upon learning that the Parisian woman is loyal to her lover, he frees the ex-king from prison and sends the happy pair on their honeymoon. Love is stronger than money when money is supposed to win sympathy. The little shopgirls were worried; now they can breathe easy again.

Willy Otto Zielke, Agfa, early 1930s

Film 1928

■ ■ ■

Film production has become as stabilized as the audience itself. Its output invariably features typical, always recurrent motifs and tendencies, and even films that differ from the average fare no longer offer many surprises. This rigidification extends to both film narrative and the technological process. The number of outsiders—films such as *Die freudlose Gasse, Manege, Die Hose, Primanerliebe,* and *Thérèse Raquin*—can be counted on one's fingers.

It is high time to settle accounts with this type of film production, which is stupid, false, and often mean. It should not be allowed to develop further along these lines.

Its liquidation is all the more imperative now, due to the dramatic increase in the popularity of film during the last few years. Countless new movie theaters (which call themselves "palaces") have sprung up, and the circle of film's sworn enemies is dying out. Today all segments of the population stream to the movies, from the workers in suburban movie theaters to the haute bourgeoisie in the cinema palaces. The single largest segment of these new audiences, presumably, is composed of low-level white-collar workers, whose number has increased not only in absolute but also in relative terms since the rationalization of our economy. But although film has found its way to the masses, one should not make the producers alone responsible for their commodity. In order to survive they must try to satisfy the needs of the consumers, and even Hugenberg[1] can control the market only to a certain degree. The critique of current film production is thus by no means directed exclusively against the industry, but focuses just as much on the public sphere which allows this industry to flourish. Lie together, die together: this saying holds here in the strictest sense.

One hopes it is unnecessary to reaffirm explicitly that the indictment of contemporary film cannot and should not serve as an implicit justification of today's theater. Nor should the fact that this indictment is based on an investigation of conditions in *Germany* be taken to imply that foreign (that is, non-Russian) production is being privileged over our own. Indeed, more than any others, the American products that have made their way to us recently—with the exception of a few astonishingly fine achievements—would have done better never to have left. But the wretchedness of film production in Germany is of more immediate concern to us than that in other countries.

■ ■ ■

It is not the employment of genre clichés that is so reprehensible in these films. On the contrary: the variation of specific patterns is in fact preferable to indiscriminate experimentation, and, besides, even the biggest firms cannot deliver new and original models week after week. What is so reprehensible about these films is their *attitude.* In all of the genres that have emerged lately, our social reality is evaporated, petrified, and distorted in a manner that is sometimes idiotically harmless and sometimes pernicious. The very things that should be projected onto the screen have been wiped away, and its surface has been filled with images that cheat us out of the image of our existence. Need one give examples? A survey of our *run-of-the-mill film productions* will suffice.

In order to avoid showing the present at all costs, fiction films stage the most daring *escape attempts.* Instead of positioning itself on a streetcorner, the camera remains in the studio, racing through faraway times and places that are completely irrelevant to us. It is not even necessary to enlist a schoolbook Luther, an Otto Gebühr, the young Queen Louise,[2] or indeed any historical hero whatever in order to distract attention from the more essential heroism of nameless people; the most recent past is already so distant from us that it can once again be brought closer. Material from lost musical comedies of that recent past is just right for modern films, so long as their humor stems less from *Simpli-*

cissimus than from the *Fliegende Blätter*.[3] But if there is one subject that has appealed to screenwriters above all others, it is the long-since abolished feudal courts. The film companies are convinced that these courts comprise just what republican audiences yearn to see: an illustrious circle of princes and barons, gallantry as a way to pass time, splendid costumes, and freshly polished parquet floors. This glitter reappears in countless movies, and if success depended on nothing more than smiling in a dragoon's uniform, Harry Liedtke would already have won the masses' support for the old regime long ago.[4] He is the man of Marlitt's dreams[5] and the hero of many operettas. The more passé the operettas are, the more they seem to lend themselves to being filmed. *Der Bettelstudent, Der Orlow, Die Geliebte seiner Hoheit*—these films inundate spectators with their frivolous but lovable princes, fairy tale castles, and insipid couplets. The rubbish that appeared to have been reduced to dust after the revolution acts as if it were full of life. The presentation of such trash usually provides a good opportunity to evoke Vienna, a city that Berlin film producers have taken to heart because it is among the most reliable of opiates: the Vienna, that is, of the "K and K" period which knows nothing of the seventh of October.[6] This Vienna is dreamy and full of music; it has no housing problems and consists entirely of cafés in Biedermeier style. Strauss is played here to this day, and as for the girls, "Just go and kiss a stylish Viennese gal."[7] There is also good kissing, by the way, in current war films such as *Opfer* and *Leichte Kavallerie* (both watered-down remakes of *Hotel Stadt Lemburg*), in which occasional scenes of trenches are supposed to heighten the desires of private affairs.

When the *present* finally does get depicted, it really disappears from sight. "Blessed are the poor, for the Kingdom of Heaven shall be theirs"—a large number of the films that deal with our time operate according to this dictum from the Sermon on the Mount. They value predestination more than unions, or at any rate they choose from among the laborers and white-collar workers (which they consistently picture as unorganized) only some isolated poor person who is then allowed to become blessed. This is the basic strategy of the Zille films,[8] which combine the comfortable with the useful by depicting the proletarian

environment as horrible and simultaneously rescuing one person from
this hell. The film lords work in mysterious ways. Even telephone
operators, shopgirls, and executive secretaries can hope, without having
to call upon their professional unions. After all, Lotte—a simple man-
icurist—wasn't the only one who had a lucky day;[9] so did lots of other
fellow workers, who never dreamed that such things could happen to
them. Admittedly, you have to be pretty. The heavenly realm into
which these carefully screened people are transported is *society*. This
society glows as brightly in mainstream cinema as Paradise does in
medieval paintings. Its members chauffeur themselves, live in Berlin, in
Paris, and on the Riviera, dress almost exclusively in sports clothes or
full evening attire, and fall on hard times only once (at most) in order
to marry into money immediately afterward. For them, things are getting better and better day by day. At night they go dancing in clubs, sit
at gaming tables, or almost commit adultery; that is, they get undressed
only out of pure frivolity and then something interrupts them—in this
case because of the morality that must be maintained, since otherwise
belief in society might begin to falter. Films sometimes ensure the
steadfastness of that society merely by demonstrating that the hit song
from the latest revue is the music that belongs to this sphere. Yes, the
Lotte who marries into this society has really had a lucky day.

Not all films practice such theology. Some of the more enlightened
ones try to appeal to the tastes of a more intellectual audience. They begin
in a more or less radical fashion, but their radicality is always directed
solely against now-deposed great men of days past. If tyrants are being
fought, they are the early capitalist despots of *Die Weber*. Popular targets
of scorn are the kaiser's underlings (as in *Biberpelz*), whose positions are
currently occupied by the lackeys of financial power. These modern
underlings, however, are themselves spared any disturbance. Or one
snickers at the backwardness of the provinces (as in the film *Sechs Mädchen suchen ein Nachtquartier*) with an arrogance that is typical of the
Reich's capital and that is itself provincial. Representative of this entire
genre is the despair of the Domela film,[10] in which the Saxo-Borussians[11]
come off in a way that runs counter to the official line, and in which satire
gives way to mockery that pets instead of punching.

Unlike most fiction films, *documentary* films have to deal not with artistically constructed scenes but with a reality they are supposed to understand. One might think they would aspire to present the world as it is, but just the opposite is the case. They cut us off from the very life that is our only concern, inundating the audience with such a profusion of irrelevant observations that it becomes indifferent to the important ones. Someday this audience will go completely blind. The *newsreels* spliced together by various well-known companies—shots of ship christenings, destructive fires, sports events, parades, and idyllic scenes of children and animals—may well contain items of current news, but certainly not events worth watching a hundred times. One need hardly mention that the various motorcycle races look so similar it's enough to drive you to despair. The monotony of this hodgepodge is the just revenge for its inconsequentiality, which is heightened by the thoughtless way the individual sequences are combined into a mosaic. This was drastically exposed by the "People's Association for Film Art," which in its day put together decidedly polemical weekly news shows out of materials from the image archives.[12] The run-of-the-mill *cultural films* are also terribly careful not to put any pressure on our culture, preferring instead to roam abroad: African tribes, the customs and rituals of the Eskimos, snakes, bugs, palm trees. The fact that some of these films are well made is less astounding than the fact that, as if by some prior arrangement, almost all of them avoid the most urgent human concerns, dragging the exotic into daily life rather than searching for the exotic within the quotidian. Furthermore, most of them are badly made, quite nonsensical productions that, without having been asked to do so, give an educational lesson that any encyclopedia could better provide. From horse breeding to carpet weaving, no out-of-the-way subject is safe from the clutches of the popular pedagogy of cultural films. They are at their worst when they ingratiate themselves by means of poetic titles abounding in adjectives. Pseudo-poetry celebrates its definitive triumph in the UFA culture film *Natur und Liebe*, in which it does not limit itself to words but enhances its poetry-potency with visions of creation and the rise of mankind.[13] Not satisfied with explaining sexual life, UFA also insists on dreaming and portending like a sibyl.

For now, one can make the following observation: all narratives of run-of-the-mill film productions are conscious or unconscious avoidance maneuvers. Some of them simply withdraw from our reality into a remote zone of indifference, while others, for the sake of a stabilized society, construct *ideologies* that obstruct the view for one of the principal groups of movie spectators—namely, the lower white-collar workers. These on-screen ideologies are much more outdated than some of the three-dimensional ideologies currently circulating in the rest of Germany. Neither a clever salesgirl nor a progressive employer would be swayed by them. It is, at the very least, high time for UFA to learn of the existence of AFA.[14] But it is precisely ignorance that characterizes the general failure of the film producers in their confrontation with reality—a failure that encompasses but is not reducible to *political backwardness*. This failure is manifest not only in the previously mentioned wares, but also in the countless compromise films that try to appeal to both enemies and friends of the Republic, to both pacifists and warlords—but at the price of their plausibility. It is also evident in the moneymaker film series that rework a popular topic—the circus, the crisis of puberty, the problem of sex—not in order to make any true statements but in order to make money. None of the abovementioned film types attempt to give shape to life; their aim instead is to exploit it. The result is confusion. One would be hard pressed to find anything quite as muddled as the way in which they manipulate emotional stereotypes—one need only recall films such as *Charlott etwas verrückt* or *Heut tanzt Mariett'*. The fact that these films are also tasteless can be amply demonstrated. For example, in what is supposedly an attempt to be funny, fashionable young ladies are always linked in close-up shots with stuffed dolls, which are conceived as counterparts to their mistresses. Or, to take a different example, one regularly encounters depictions of the bad table manners of common people, which the common people in the audience inevitably find hilarious because they do not eat like that.

■ ■ ■

Corresponding to the inadequacy at the level of the material, there is, as there must be, an inadequacy at the level of the aesthetic. Parallel with the consolidation of various narrative genres, a *ready-made manufac-*

turing technique has become established; screenwriters, more or less experienced directors, and their assistants use it unhesitatingly. It is obvious from a distance that these works have not been custom made. Although business demands tend to impose a certain systematization, they do not justify the low standard of such operational procedures.

In most cases, these films display nothing that could properly be called a *filmic construction*. The subjects that are chosen—apparently indiscriminately—are not at all visually conceived; Schnitzler, Zuckmayer, and Sudermann are the victims.[15] There are, of course, motifs and sections in many novels and plays that could serve as the basis for an authentic film, but the producers make no effort to disassemble the literary originals into their cinematically usable elements in order to then build something new out of them. Instead they translate the original work scene for scene, changing only the story line (if they change anything at all) to please the audience. The resulting film is thus the uninterrupted *illustration* of a text foreign to it, whereas the film itself ought to be the text that is read. The story does not develop according to a law determined by the sequence of images; instead the film's scenes are organized in a sequence dictated by a story that progresses independently from them. The average historical films are likewise mere illustrations; what is more, they portray episodes that are usually badly told—history lessons in images, instead of history emerging out of the images. Indeed, almost all of the films based on scripts that were written from the start especially for the screen share the same fate as films based on preexisting stories. Their compositional structure is anticinematic: the narrative is not produced through the film but is tacked on, giving the impression that it could be detached from the screen. Such films are translations of novels even when the novels do not exist.

This sort of procedure inevitably robs many *details* of their significance—details that should be the supporting framework of a film, since, when the progression of a film is tied to a narrative external to it, the visual elements that present that narrative become merely incidental. In order for the individual visual unit to attain its proper function, it must be an essential component of a completely visually conceived narrative. This is the case, for example, at various moments in the film *Thérèse Raquin*, in which the petit bourgeois apartment plays an important role of its own. It is true that established film techniques make extensive use of cars, show the pistons of the express-train engine every time the hero goes on a trip, depict legs walking and car wheels rolling, and are not afraid to stage expensive catastrophes. But all these fragments are of only *ornamental* significance and could easily be eliminated without in any way diminishing the film's intelligibility. This contrasts starkly with a real film, which becomes immediately unintelligible or at least suffers a noticeable loss in perfection when a single image-atom is removed.

If only the detail that has sunk to the level of an embellishment were treated with a bit of care! Yet most of the time it remains as unmastered as the extra-cinematic reality itself. The work is slovenly. Streets are constructed in such a way that it is obvious they lead nowhere. Filmmakers are satisfied with the most superficial correspondence between a close-up and a full shot of the same object; for example, an architectural environment depicted in its full expanse may not at all match the studio fragment of this landscape that is supposed to serve as the set for the actual story. Whenever images of architectural models are followed by shots of real houses, the two are usually so different that the model can immediately be recognized as such. The backdrops and the environments in these films are all too often imprecise. Producers tend to be particularly fraudulent when it comes to depicting the interiors of elegant hotels. This is either because they assume—perhaps not incorrectly—that the audience is unfamiliar with such interior spaces, or because they do not know these spaces themselves. The carelessness with which they treat the details of social situations is hardly worth mentioning. Sometimes even third-class train compartments (which, after all, everyone knows well) are reproduced incorrectly. The lack of fidelity in such observations is all the more noticeable because the *photography* is generally on such a high level. It almost seems as if, with the increasing perfection of photographic technique, the object that this medium is meant to convey disappears.

When the visual material is bad and, even worse, when the composition of the film has to follow an uncinematic plot, *montage* can be no more than a flourish. Directors have learned how to manipulate the apparatuses; they shift quite adroitly between close-ups, foreground, and master shots, employ dissolves, and attempt to link the various scenes through visual transitions. These artifices, which ought to express the meaning of the narrative and thus would have to change along with that narrative, have in fact petrified into mere trimmings. Over the course of time, certain montage sequences have become enshrined and are imposed on all films, regardless of whether or not they are appropriate. If the scene is a dance club, there are usually glimpses of saxophones and the swaying bodies of musicians mixed in among shots of hysterical pairs of dancers—most often a crudely cut and established visual formula for representing the pseudo-high of amusement. Someone experienced it this way once, and now everyone else does the same. The dreams of the inebriated or the nostalgic are also completely *mechanized.* One particular means of transition has recently become popular and is employed on every possible occasion. Two scenes that follow each other but that are not directly related need to be fused. For example, in the first scene there might be an elegant gentleman and in the second scene a tattered woman. How are they to be linked? The viewer's gaze is led from the full view of the gentleman to his oxford shoes, which imperceptibly transform themselves into dirty boots, out of which the woman emerges. In certain instances this sort of modulation can be quite meaningful. But when it does not express anything substantive it becomes an aesthetic fraud, since it simulates a relationship that does not really exist. What is at issue here is the connection of *contents* in the visual medium, and not just a purely *formal,* visual combination of disconnected elements. For some time now, *war montage* has also taken on a definite form that is supremely offensive. Whenever the war serves as even the most modest background to a more important cinematic event, one is served small doses of marching military columns, barbed wire, and grenade attacks. Out of such battle mixtures they concoct panaceas.

∎ ∎ ∎

Films proclaiming themselves much better than average are scarcely in short supply. They consciously make *artistic* claims and are often shot at great expense. When a great sum has been invested in them and the amount of money they are meant to generate is even greater, then they are called "great" films.[16]

The majority of these elite creations are just as hopelessly ossified as the general cinematic output on which they are piled. They can all be subsumed under the category of *high-class feature films.* The fundamental lack they share with other feature films is that they do not capture reality—a failure which is doubly disappointing in these high-class feature films because they are doubly committed to reality. They are distinguished from average films by numerous misdemeanors, which arise from the fact that certain essential contents appear at this higher level, providing new objects against which one can now also sin.

As a rule, the producers of films feel that they have satisfied the artistic requirements by simply elevating *colportage* to the level of a peak performance. As if colportage needed to be rescued like a fallen girl! But this is just what film companies believe when they undertake such attempts at improvement—attempts that, as is so often the case in life, only reduce the value of the supposedly improved object. Colportage is the projection of major issues onto the level of triviality. The clash of good and evil, the marvelous, reconciliation—many important themes are presented in however a distorted manner by colportage. This is what justifies Harry Piel's sensational films, which do have some excellently crafted moments;[17] indeed, there is certainly nothing objectionable about nice confidence-men pieces like *Casanovas Erbe.* Unfortunately, these are all too rare. For in the drive toward higher and higher products, the film industry inflates narratives of this sort to the point where they become cinematic pageants that cannot live up to their own standards. The results are elaborate and horrific creations, like Lang's *Spione* or *Die Jacht der sieben Sünden.* In these films the sensational elements are not just tossed off but are elaborated with unacceptable refinements: ridiculous psychological explanations sneak in between events that need only be soberly juxtaposed, and the illusion of improvisation is offset by means of a décor that would be too pompous and permanent for a gala opera. Characteristic of the film manufacturers' lack of instinct is their desire to transform into a quality product the subject matter of colportage, which is foreign to such quality by its very nature. Things that breathe in pamphlet form suffocate in polished leather bindings. (This is literally true: on *Spione*'s opening night, critics were handed a volume that was a marvel of the art of bookbinding and that contained nothing more than Thea von Harbou's novel.)[18] And the same upper-class revisions are also shamefully imposed on material that is not even colportage, as well as on texts that were originally more than colportage but that were reduced to dust, apparently so as to render them suitable for film (see, for example, *Die Liebe der Jeanne Ney*).

Since *tragedy* is at home in the upper artistic regions, the number of films with somber conclusions is on the rise; producers believe they can come off as tragic merely by sacrificing the usual "happy end."[19] What is tragic according to their jargon?—An arbitrary misfortune. They provide it, and in this way do business with art. In the Henny Porten film *Zuflucht*, a young man who runs away from his family during the revolution finally makes his way back to them, only to die just when everything seems to have been resolved. There is no reason for his death, since even his poor bride has been graciously accepted by the forgiving family. But the movie manufacturer remains implacable: the audience demands art, and so there has to be some dying. Since one can also read the *malheur*[20] as a punishment for the youth's revolutionary attitude, two birds are killed with one stone.—In order to achieve a high standard, the manufacturers also seize on works whose contents are so tied to their *language* that they resist all attempts at cinematic rendition. In the recently made film *Heimkehr*, based on a novella by Leonhard Frank,[21] the main scene shatters the barriers imposed on the cinematic medium. A man who has returned from the war is given shelter by his friend's young wife. He and the woman desire each other; the friend is still absent. We see at length how the woman tosses and turns in her bed, and how the man, separated from her by only a thin wall, is equally tormented as he lies on his cot. Both are so excited that they cannot sleep. Nothing happens. But what does take place is incomparably obscene in the silent language of film. Only words are capable of evoking such scenes, because they can express what is not conveyed through the terrible corporeality of the image.—Some of the more elevated films even get bogged down in *arts and crafts*. They are stuffed with furnishings—yet these furnishings do not suffuse the film but only veil what is in fact uncinematic pretense. In *Doña Juana*, Czinner has the fountains of Granada cascading behind his Bergner[22] and takes her on itineraries that Don Quixote might have followed. He builds an entire nature and art salon around her, yet there is not a single scene in which the drapery is more than just drapery.

There has hardly been any artistic experimentation of the sort that pushes film into new territory. The abstract films cultivated primarily in Paris are an eccentric breed that is not at issue here. Ruttmann's interesting film symphony *Berlin* is worth mentioning as the only significant attempt to break away from the common production fare. A film without a real plot, it attempts to allow the metropolis to arise out of a sequence of microscopic individual traits. But does it convey the reality of Berlin? No: it is just as blind to reality as any other feature film, and this is due to its lack of a political stance. Instead of penetrating its enormous object in a way that would betray a true understanding of its social, economic, and political structure, and instead of observing it with human concern or even tackling it from a particular vantage point in order to resolutely take it apart, Ruttmann leaves the thousands of details unconnected, one next to the other, inserting at most some arbitrarily conceived transitions that are meaningless. At best, the film is based on the idea that Berlin is the city of speed and of work—a formal idea that in no way leads to any content and that perhaps for this reason intoxicates the German petit bourgeois when it appears in society and literature. There is nothing to see in this symphony, because it has not exposed a single meaningful relationship. In his book *Film Technique*, Pudovkin reproaches the film for its lack of internal organization. In what is obviously a jab at Ruttmann, he writes: "Quite a number of film technicians maintain that montage should be the only organizing process of film. They hold that the pieces can be shot in any way and anywhere, just so long as the images are interesting; afterward, by simply joining them according to their form and kind, a way will be found to assemble them into a film."[23]

...

In their essential details, the "art" film products are no better than the average wares. They are neither less politically biased nor a millimeter closer to reality. They convey nothing of the sphere that they presume to capture. They have no content. *Lack of substance is the decisive trait of the totality of established film production.*

The desperate state of affairs is so widespread that it absorbs even the forces that are attempting to counter it. There is a whole series of excellent directors—Lang, Grune, Murnau, Reichmann, Boese, and so on. But how can their insights be fruitful when wasted on material that slips through one's fingers like water? Their talents are squandered and even weakened through such misuse. Using famous actors is also no help. No matter how many stars there are in the sky, they will not be able to overcome the Egyptian gloom of these productions. It is much more likely that the stars will simply burn out. In *Alraune*, Wegener is a fat, demonic mask.[24]

The decline is too apparent to have gone unnoticed. Recently the first signs of *criticism* have begun to appear in the German public sphere. Admittedly, critics generally tend to reprimand only individual films and to point out symptoms such as the profit mentality and the star system. A few courageous assailants have gone a bit further and have at least mentioned the relationship, articulated above, between the inter- ests of the industry and the ideology of its films. But no one has yet undertaken an analysis of the entire current state of affairs. The pro- ducers themselves try to justify their actions by referring lamely to the tastes of an international audience.

All these explanations and arguments are simply inadequate, because they in no way explain the downright monstrous fact that our cinematic production might well exceed even the American cinema in lack of substance. If the emptiness of our films and the way in which they strangle every decent tendency are not the result of a decrease in substance, then they can only be the result of *obstinacy*—the peculiar obstinacy that has reigned in Germany since the end of the inflation and that has influenced many public forms of expression. It is as if during the time of the social upheavals and the rationalization of the factories, German life was severely paralyzed. One could almost say that it became diseased. The state of film production—as mentioned at the outset—is after all only a symptom of the general state of the established nonculture. In one large provincial city, *Thérèse Raquin* had to be withdrawn after a few days whereas *Die Heilige und ihr Narr* ran for three weeks to sold-out houses. Something is very wrong here. At any rate, the current degree of emotional confusion and irreality cannot be fully accounted for by even the worst industrialism. The extent of the bewilderment becomes apparent in those films that seek to profit from the success of Russian films, cinematic documents whose significance rests only to a small degree on their propagandistic intentions. What is more essential is that Eisenstein and Pudovkin—in contrast to a mere caricaturist such as George Grosz—are informed about human affairs. Both they and their actors have really experienced poverty, hunger, injustice, and happiness, and are able to asses the full range of the consequences of these experiences. For this and only this reason, they are able to find the framings and perspectives that give streets, courtyards, city squares, and pillared buildings the power of speech. The few German directors who have learned their lessons from the Russians were bad students. They adopted the tricks of the trade without paying attention to their meanings. In the previously mentioned film *Zuflucht*, images of the proletarian sections of the city are incorporated according to the Russian style; the images are superb, but they lack any internal relationship to the plot. The way in which Russian cinema presents the environment reveals the kernel of the story. Here, in the German film, the surroundings are the more or less superfluous decoration of a petit bourgeois plot. This is the limited extent to which the obstinate are aware of the world.

Should a course of action be prescribed? Is a recipe expected? There is no recipe. Uprightness, the gift of observation, humaneness—such things cannot be taught. Let it suffice that the situation has been brought out in the open.[25]

Titania Palace Cinema, Berlin, 1928

Cult of Distraction

ON BERLIN'S PICTURE PALACES

■ ■ ■

The large picture houses in Berlin are palaces of distraction; to call them *movie theaters [Kinos]* would be disrespectful. The latter are still abundant only in Old Berlin and in the suburbs, where they serve neighborhood audiences, and even there they are declining in number. Much more than such movie houses or even the ordinary theaters, it is the picture palaces, those optical fairylands, that are shaping the face of Berlin. The *UFA palaces* (above all, the one at the Zoo), the *Capitol* built by Poelzig, the *Marmorhaus,* and whatever their names may be, enjoy sellouts day after day. The newly built *Gloria-Palast* proves that the style these palaces have initiated is still developing in the same direction.[1]

Elegant *surface splendor* is the hallmark of these mass theaters. Like hotel lobbies, they are shrines to the cultivation of pleasure; their glamor aims at edification. But while the architecture does perhaps bombard the patrons in its attempt to create an atmosphere, it in no way relapses into the barbaric pomposity of Wilhelminian secular churches—like the Rhinegold, for example, which seeks to give the impression that it harbors the Wagnerian Nibelungen treasure. Instead, the architecture of the film palaces has evolved into a form that avoids stylistic excesses. Taste has presided over the dimensions and, in conjunction with a refined artisanal fantasy, has spawned the costly interior furnishings. The *Gloria-Palast* presents itself as a baroque theater. The community of worshipers, numbering in the thousands, can be content, for its gathering places are a worthy abode.

The programs, too, display a well-wrought grandiosity. Gone are the days when films were allowed to run one after another, each with a corresponding musical accompaniment. The major theaters, at least, have adopted the American style of a self-contained show, which integrates the film into a larger whole. Like the program sheets which have expanded into fan magazines, the shows have grown into a structured profusion of production numbers and presentations. A glittering, revue-like creature has crawled out of the movies: *the total artwork [Gesamt-kunstwerk] of effects.*

This total artwork of effects assaults all the senses using every possible means. Spotlights shower their beams into the auditorium, sprinkling across festive drapes or rippling through colorful, organic-looking glass fixtures. The orchestra asserts itself as an independent power, its acoustic production buttressed by the responsory of the lighting. Every emotion is accorded its own acoustic expression and its color value in the spectrum—a visual and acoustic kaleidoscope that provides the setting for the physical activity on stage: pantomime and ballet. Until finally the white surface descends and the events of the three-dimensional stage blend imperceptibly into two-dimensional illusions.

Alongside the legitimate revues, such shows are the leading attraction in Berlin today. They raise distraction to the level of culture; they are aimed at the *masses.*

...

The masses also gather in the *provinces,* but there they are subjected to a pressure that does not allow them the spiritual and cultural *[geistig]* fulfillment appropriate to their number and real social significance. In the industrial centers where they appear in great numbers, they are so overburdened as workers that they are unable to realize their own way of life. They are handed down the rubbish and outdated entertainment of the upper class, which, despite its repeated claims to social superiority, has only limited cultural ambitions. In contrast, in the larger provincial towns not dominated primarily by industry, the traditional forces are so powerful that the masses are unable to shape the cultural and spiritual *[geistig]* structure on their own. The bourgeois middle classes remain segregated from them, as if the growth of this human reservoir meant nothing, and thus they maintain the illusory claim that they are still the guardians of culture and education. Their arrogance, which creates sham oases for itself, weighs down upon the masses and denigrates their amusements.

It cannot be overlooked that there are *four million* people in Berlin. The sheer necessity of their circulation transforms the life of the street into the ineluctable street of life, giving rise to configurations that invade even domestic space. The more people perceive themselves as a mass, however, the sooner the masses will also develop productive powers in the spiritual and cultural domain that are worth financing. The masses are no longer left to their own devices; rather, they prevail in their very abandonment. Refusing to be thrown scraps, they demand instead to be served at laid-out tables. There is little room left for the so-called educated classes, who must either join in the repast or maintain their snobbish aloofness. Their provincial isolation is, in any case, at an end. They are being absorbed by the masses, a process that creates the *homogeneous cosmopolitan audience* in which everyone has the *same* responses, from the bank director to the sales clerk, from the diva to the stenographer. Self-pitying complaints about this turn toward mass taste are belated; the cultural heritage that the masses refuse to accept has become to some extent merely a historical property, since the economic and social reality to which it corresponded has changed.

■ ■ ■

Critics chide Berliners for being *addicted to distraction,* but this is a petit bourgeois reproach. Certainly, the addiction to distraction is greater in Berlin than in the provinces, but the tension to which the working masses are subjected is also greater and more tangible; it is an essentially formal tension, which fills their day fully without making it fulfilling. Such a lack demands to be compensated, but this need can be articulated only in terms of the same surface sphere that imposed the lack in the first place. The form of free-time busy-ness necessarily corresponds to the form of business.[2]

A correct instinct will see to it that the need for entertainment is satisfied. The interior design of movie theaters serves one sole purpose:

to rivet the viewers' attention to the peripheral, so that they will not sink into the abyss. The stimulations of the senses succeed one another with such rapidity that there is no room left between them for even the slightest contemplation. Like *life buoys*, the refractions of the spotlights and the musical accompaniment keep the spectator above water. The penchant for distraction demands and finds an answer in the display of pure externality; hence the irrefutable tendency, particularly in Berlin, to turn all forms of entertainment into revues and, parallel with this tendency, the increasing number of illustrations in the daily press and in periodical publications.

This emphasis on the external has the advantage of being *sincere*. It is not externality that poses a threat to truth. Truth is threatened only by the naïve affirmation of cultural values that have become unreal and by the careless misuse of concepts such as personality, inwardness, tragedy, and so on—terms that in themselves certainly refer to lofty ideas but that have lost much of their scope along with their supporting foundations, due to social changes. Furthermore, many of these concepts have acquired a bad aftertaste today, because they unjustifiably deflect an inordinate amount of attention from the external damages of society onto the private individual. Instances of such repression are common enough in the fields of literature, drama, and music. They claim the status of high art while actually rehearsing anachronistic forms that evade the pressing needs of our time—a fact that is indirectly confirmed by the artistically derivative quality of the respective works. In a profound sense, Berlin audiences act truthfully when they increasingly shun these art events (which, for good reason, remain caught in mere pretense), preferring instead the surface glamor of the stars, films, revues, and spectacular shows. Here, in pure externality, the audience encounters itself; its own reality is revealed in the fragmented sequence of splendid sense impressions. Were this reality to remain hidden from the viewers, they could neither attack nor change it; its disclosure in distraction is therefore of *moral* significance.

But this is the case only if distraction is not an end in itself. Indeed, the very fact that the shows aiming at distraction are composed of the same mixture of externalities as the world of the urban masses; the fact that these shows lack any authentic and materially motivated coherence, except possibly the glue of sentimentality, which covers up this lack but only in order to make it all the more visible; the fact that these shows convey precisely and openly to thousands of eyes and ears the *disorder* of society—this is precisely what would enable them to evoke and maintain the tension that must precede the inevitable and radical change. In the streets of Berlin, one is often struck by the momentary insight that someday all this will suddenly burst apart. The entertainment to which the general public throngs ought to produce the same effect.

■ ■ ■

Most of the time it does not, as is demonstrated in exemplary fashion by the programs of the large movie theaters. For even as they summon to distraction, they immediately rob distraction of its meaning by amalgamating the wide range of effects—which by their nature demand to be isolated from one another—into an "artistic" unity. These shows strive to coerce the motley sequence of externalities into an organic whole. To begin with, the architectural setting tends to emphasize a dignity that used to inhabit the institutions of high culture. It favors the lofty and the *sacred* as if designed to accommodate works of eternal significance— just one step short of burning votive candles. The show itself aspires to the same exalted level, claiming to be a finely tuned organism, an aesthetic totality as only an artwork can be. The film alone would be too paltry an offering, not primarily because one would want to increase the sheer quantity of distractions but because the show has pretensions to artistic form. The cinema has secured a standing independent of the theatrical stage, yet the leading movie theaters are once again longing to return to that stage.

This thespian objective of the movie theaters—an objective that may be considered symptomatic of Berlin social life as well—displays *reactionary* tendencies. The laws and forms of the idealist culture that haunts us today only as a specter may have lost their legitimacy in these movie theaters; nonetheless, out of the very elements of externality into which they have happily advanced, they are attempting to create a new idealist culture. Distraction—which is meaningful only as improvisation, as a reflection of the uncontrolled anarchy of our world—is festooned with drapery and forced back into a unity that no longer exists. Rather than acknowledging the actual state of disintegration that such shows ought to represent, the movie theaters glue the pieces back together after the fact and present them as organic creations.

This practice takes its revenge in purely artistic terms: the integration of film into a self-contained program deprives it of any effect it might have had. It no longer stands on its own, but appears as the crowning event of a type of revue that does not take into account its particular conditions of existence. The *two-dimensionality* of film produces the illusion of the physical world without any need for supplementation. But if scenes of real physicality are nevertheless displayed alongside the movie, the latter recedes into the flat surface and the deception is exposed. The proximity of action that has spatial depth destroys the spatiality of what is shown on the screen. By its very existence, film demands that the world it reflects be the only one; it should be wrested from every three-dimensional surrounding, or it will fail as an illusion. A painting, too, loses its power when it appears alongside living images. Nor should one fail to mention that the artistic ambitions behind the move to incorporate film into the pseudo-totality of a program are inappropriate, and hence remain unsuccessful. The result is at best *applied art [Kunstgewerbe]*.

But the movie theaters are faced with more urgent tasks than refining applied art. They will not fulfill their vocation—which is an aesthetic vocation only to the extent that it is in tune with its social vocation—until they cease to flirt with the theater and renounce their anxious efforts to restore a bygone culture. Rather, they should rid their offerings of all trappings that deprive film of its rights and must aim radically toward a kind of distraction that exposes disintegration instead of masking it. It could be done in Berlin, home of the masses—who so easily allow themselves to be stupefied only because they are so close to the truth.

FADEAWAY
TOWARD THE VANISHING POINT

Werner David Feist, "Alarm Clock," ca. 1929

Boredom

...

People today who still have time for boredom and yet are not bored are
certainly just as boring as those who never get around to being bored.
For their self has vanished—the self whose presence, particularly in this
so bustling world, would necessarily compel them to tarry[1] for a while
without a goal, neither here nor there.

Most people, of course, do not have much leisure time. They
pursue a livelihood on which they expend all their energies, simply to
earn enough for the bare necessities. To make this tiresome obligation
more tolerable, they have invented a work ethic that provides a moral
veil for their occupation and at least affords them a certain moral[2]
satisfaction. It would be exaggerated to claim that the pride in considering oneself an ethical being dispels every type of boredom. Yet the
vulgar boredom of daily drudgery is not actually what is at issue here,
since it neither kills people nor awakens them to new life, but merely
expresses a dissatisfaction that would immediately disappear if an occupation more pleasant than the morally sanctioned one became available.
Nevertheless, people whose duties occasionally make them yawn may be
less boring than those who do their business by inclination. The latter,
unhappy types, are pushed deeper and deeper into the hustle and bustle
until eventually they no longer know where their head is, and the
extraordinary, radical boredom that might be able to reunite them with
their heads remains eternally distant for them.

There is no one, however, who has no leisure time at all. The office
is not a permanent sanctuary, and Sundays are an institution. Thus, in
principle, during those beautiful hours of free time everyone would have

the opportunity to rouse himself into real boredom. But although one wants to do nothing, things are done to one: the world makes sure that one does not find oneself. And even if one perhaps isn't interested in it, the world itself is much too interested for one to find the peace and quiet necessary to be as thoroughly bored with the world as it ultimately deserves.

■■■

In the evening one saunters through the streets, replete with an unfulfillment from which a fullness could sprout. Illuminated words glide by on the rooftops, and already one is banished from one's own emptiness into the alien *advertisement*. One's body takes root in the asphalt, and, together with the enlightening revelations of the illuminations, one's spirit—which is no longer one's own—roams ceaselessly out of the night and into the night. If only it were allowed to disappear! But, like Pegasus prancing on a carousel, this spirit must run in circles and may never tire of praising to high heaven the glory of a liqueur and the merits of the best five-cent cigarette. Some sort of magic spurs that spirit relentlessly amid the thousand electric bulbs, out of which it constitutes and reconstitutes itself into glittering sentences.

Should the spirit by chance return at some point, it soon takes its leave in order to allow itself to be cranked away in various guises in a *movie theater*. It squats as a fake Chinaman in a fake opium den, transforms itself into a trained dog that performs ludicrously clever tricks to please a film diva, gathers up into a storm amid towering mountain peaks, and turns into both a circus artist and a lion at the same time. How could it resist these metamorphoses? The posters swoop into the empty space that the spirit itself would not mind pervading; they drag it in front of the silver screen, which is as barren as an emptied-out palazzo. And once the images begin to emerge one after another, there is nothing left in the world besides their evanescence. One forgets oneself in the process of gawking, and the huge dark hole is animated with the illusion of a life that belongs to no one and exhausts everyone.

Radio likewise vaporizes beings, even before they have intercepted a single spark.[3] Since many people feel compelled to broadcast, one finds oneself in a state of permanent receptivity,[4] constantly pregnant with London, the Eiffel Tower, and Berlin. Who would want to resist the invitation of those dainty headphones? They gleam in living rooms and entwine themselves around heads all by themselves; and instead of fostering cultivated conversation (which certainly can be a bore), one becomes a playground for worldwide noises that, regardless of their own potentially objective boredom, do not even grant one's modest right to personal boredom. Silent and lifeless, people sit side by side as if their souls were wandering about far away. But these souls are not wandering according to their own preference; they are badgered by the news hounds, and soon no one can tell anymore who is the hunter and who is the hunted. Even in the café, where one wants to roll up into a ball like a porcupine and become aware of one's insignificance, an imposing loudspeaker effaces every trace of private existence. The announcements it blares forth dominate the space of the concert intermissions, and the waiters (who are listening to it themselves) indignantly refuse the unreasonable requests to get rid of this gramophonic mimicry.

As one is enduring this species of antennal fate, the five *continents* are drawing ever closer. In truth, it is not we who extend ourselves out toward them; rather, it is their cultures that appropriate us in their boundless imperialism. It is as if one were having one of those dreams provoked by an empty stomach: a tiny ball rolls toward you from very far away, expands into a close-up, and finally roars right over you. You can neither stop it nor escape it, but lie there chained, a helpless little doll swept away by the giant colossus in whose ambit it expires. Flight is impossible. Should the Chinese imbroglio be tactfully disembroiled, one is sure to be harried by an American boxing match: the Occident remains omnipresent, whether one acknowledges it or not. All the world-historical events on this planet—not only the current ones but also past events, whose love of life knows no shame—have only one desire: to set up a rendezvous wherever they suppose us to be present. But the masters are not to be found in their quarters. They've gone on a trip and cannot be located, having long since ceded the empty chambers to the "surprise party"[5] that occupies the rooms, pretending to be the masters.

■ ■ ■

But what if one refuses to allow oneself to be chased away? Then boredom becomes the only proper occupation, since it provides a kind of guarantee that one is, so to speak, still in control of one's own existence. If one were never bored, one would presumably not really be present at all and would thus be merely one more object of boredom, as was claimed at the outset. One would light up on the rooftops or spool by as a filmstrip. But if indeed one is present, one would have no choice but to be bored by the ubiquitous abstract racket that does not allow one to exist, and, at the same time, to find oneself boring for existing in it.

On a sunny afternoon when everyone is outside, one would do best to hang about in the train station or, better yet, stay at home, draw the curtains, and surrender oneself to one's boredom on the sofa. Shrouded in *tristezza,* one flirts with ideas that even become quite respectable in the process, and one considers various projects that, for no reason, pretend to be serious. Eventually one becomes content to do nothing more than be with oneself, without knowing what one actually should be doing—sympathetically touched by the mere glass grasshopper on the tabletop that cannot jump because it is made of glass and by the silliness of a little cactus plant that thinks nothing of its own whimsicality. Frivolous, like these decorative creations, one harbors only an inner restlessness without a goal, a longing that is pushed aside, and a weariness with that which exists without really being.

If, however, one has the patience, the sort of patience specific to legitimate boredom, then one experiences a kind of bliss that is almost unearthly. A landscape appears in which colorful peacocks strut about, and images of people suffused with soul come into view. And look— your own soul is likewise swelling, and in ecstasy you name what you have always lacked: the great *passion.* Were this passion—which shimmers like a comet—to descend, were it to envelop you, the others, and the world—oh, then boredom would come to an end, and everything that exists would be . . .

Yet people remain distant images, and the great passion fizzles out on the horizon. And in the boredom that refuses to abate, one hatches bagatelles that are as boring as this one.

Linden Aracade, Berlin, 1930

Farewell to the
Linden Arcade

■ ■ ■

The *Lindenpassage* (Linden Arcade) has ceased to exist.[1] That is, it remains a means of passage *[Passage]* between Friedrichstraße and Linden Avenue in terms of its form, but it is no longer an arcade *[Passage]*.[2] When I recently strolled through it once again, as I so often did during my student years before the war, the work of destruction was already almost complete. Cold, smooth marble plates covered the pillars between the shops, and arching above them already was a modern glass roof of the sort one finds by the dozen nowadays. Fortunately, the old Renaissance architecture—that horribly beautiful imitation of style from the time of our fathers and grandfathers—still peeked through here and there. A gap in the skeleton of the new glass roof allowed one to see through to the upper stories and the endless succession of corbels beneath the primary cornice, the linked round windows, the columns, the balustrades, the medallions—all the faded bombast that now no passerby will ever again be able to appreciate. And one pillar, which apparently was to be saved till the end, still brazenly displayed its brick relief work: a composition of dolphins and vine-scroll decoration, with a mask in the middle cartouche. All this is now sinking into a mass grave of cool marble.

I still recall the shivers that the word "passageway" *[Durchgang]* aroused in me when I was a boy. In the books I was devouring at the time, the dark passageway was usually the site of murderous assaults subsequently testified to by a pool of blood. At the very least it was the proper environment for the dubious characters who gathered there to discuss their shady plans. Even if such boyhood fantasies tended to be a bit excessive, something of the significance they attributed to the passageway clung to the former Linden Arcade. This was true not only of the Linden Arcade but of all authentically bourgeois arcades. There are good reasons *Thérèse Raquin* is set in the rear section of Paris' Passage des Panoramas,[3] which has in the meantime likewise been destroyed—crushed by the concrete weight of luxurious new buildings. The time of the arcades has run out.

The peculiar feature of the arcades was that they were passageways, ways that passed through the bourgeois life that resided in front of and on top of their entrances. Everything excluded from this bourgeois life because it was not presentable or even because it ran counter to the official world view settled in the arcades. They housed the cast off and the disavowed, the sum total of everything unfit for the adornment of the façade. Here, in the arcades, these transient objects attained a kind of right of residence, like gypsies who are allowed to camp only along the highway and not in town. One passed by them as if one were underground, between this street and the next. Even now the Linden Arcade is still filled with shops whose displayed wares are just such passages *[Passagen]* in the composition of bourgeois life. That is, they satisfy primarily bodily needs and the craving for images of the sort that appear in daydreams. Both of these, the very near and the very far, elude the bourgeois public sphere—which does not tolerate them—and like to withdraw into the furtive half-light of the passageway, in which they flourish as in a swamp. It is precisely as a passage that the passageway is also the place where, more than almost anywhere else, the voyage which is the journey from the near to the far and the linkage of body and image can manifest itself.

Among the exhibitions in the Linden Arcade that are dedicated to corporeality, the place of honor is occupied by the Anatomical Museum.[4] It is an arcade sovereign that has established its rightful kingdom among the cartouches, vine-scrolls, and dolphins. Since all the objects that have been driven behind the façade must nevertheless maintain a bourgeois appearance, the inscriptions that encourage people to enter are sanctimonious. One of them reads: "The *Mankind* Exhibition is devoted to the Improvement of Health." Just what sort of revelations await the spectator inside are betrayed by a picture in the display window which shows a doctor in a frock coat, accompanied by numerous gentlemen whose dress is just as old-fashioned as his, performing a stomach operation on a naked woman. This person was once a lady. Yes, the focus here is on the stomach, the intestines, everything having to do solely with the body. Inside the exhibit, tumors and monstrosities are scrupulously examined, and for adults only there is also an extra display room seething with every possible venereal disease. These are the result of reckless sensuality, whose flames are fanned in a nearby bookstore. Once, during the infla- tion, a communist bookstore was housed in the arcade of a major German metropolis; it did not last long, however, despite the fact that the arcade had its origin in prewar modernity and, with its cast-iron sunflowers, reminded one more of a decorated underpass. Its tenuous relation to the arcade was already sufficient, however, to force the propaganda literature out, since illegality seeks to break through to daylight whereas pornog- raphy is at home in the twilight. The bookstore in the Linden Arcade knows how indebted it is to its surroundings. Paperbacks whose titles arouse desires that their contents could hardly fulfill sprout in an inten- tionally harmless undergrowth of books. Sometimes the permitted joins the prohibited in curious combinations, as in a book about sexual perverts written by a police chief. In the vicinity of the bodily drives, knickknacks flourish—the countless small objects which we carry around and with which we surround ourselves, partly because we use them and partly because they are so useless. The arcade bazaar is teeming with them: nail clippers, scissors, powder boxes, cigarette lighters, hand-stitched Hun- garian doilies. Like vermin, the odds and ends appear in swarms and terrify us with their claim to keep us perpetual company. As if wanting to devour us, they crawl through the worm-eaten building in which we live, and if someday the rafters come crashing down, they will even darken the sky. Stores from the street with wares that satisfy our better corporeal needs are also moving into the arcade, to pay their respects to the Anatomical Museum. Pipes made of amber and meerschaum glisten; shirts dazzle like an entire evening party; shotguns aim their barrels upward. And at the end of the passageway, a beauty parlor beckons with its fragrance. In the semidarkness it reveals its kinship with the café located under the cupola.[5] The café patrons wander, even if only through the illustrated newspapers, floating away with the murmuring, following for a bit the train of images that undulates behind the cigarette haze. The motto is: Away!

It is a meaningful coincidence that two travel agencies flank the entrance to the arcade on Linden Avenue. But the trips to which one is tempted by their model ships and poster hymns no longer have anything in common with the journeys one used to undertake in the arcade; the modern luggage store likewise barely belongs inside the passageway. Ever since the earth began shrinking noticeably, bourgeois existence has incorporated travel just as it has appropriated the Bohemian lifestyle; it maintains itself by appropriating these sorts of dissipation for its own purposes and devaluing them into distractions. How much more distant and familiar the foreign was during the age of souvenirs! One of the stores in the arcade is stuffed full of them. "Souvenir de Berlin" is written on plates and mugs, and the flute concert at Sanssouci[6] is often requested as a little something to bring home. These memory aids that can be fondled, these authentic copies of locally resident originals, are part of the very body of Berlin and doubtless are more qualified to convey to their buyers the energies of the city they have devoured than the photographs which the photograph store invites one to have personally made. The photos claim to bring the traveled lands home; the World Panorama, in contrast, provides the illusion of places one longs for, and distances the familiar ones all the more.[7] The World Panorama is enthroned in the arcade like the Anatomy Museum; indeed, it is only a tiny leap from the graspable body to the ungraspable distance. As a child, whenever I visited the World Panorama—which in those days was likewise hidden in an arcade—I felt myself transported to a faraway place that was utterly unreal, just as I did when looking at picture books. It could hardly have been otherwise, for behind the peepholes, which are as close as window frames, cities and mountains glide by in the artificial light, more like faces than destinations: Mexico and the Tyrol, which itself turns into another Mexico in the Panorama.

These landscapes are already almost homeless images, illustrations of passing impulses that gleam here and there through the cracks in the wooden fence that surrounds us. It is images such as these that one would see with the help of magic glasses, and one wonders why the optician in the arcade does not offer such spectacles for sale. The glass foliage that, hard and round, climbs up the sides of the optician's display window at least seems to present things correctly, according to the concepts valid in the passageway. The disintegration of all illusory permanence, a disintegration required by the arcade, is achieved by the stamp shop, in which heads, buildings, heraldic animals, and exotic places are stuck tightly together with numbers and names. (It is no accident that my friend Walter Benjamin, whose work has been focused for years on the arcades of Paris, discovers this image of the stamp shop in his book *One Way Street*.)[8] Here in the arcade the world is rattled and shaken until it can serve the daily needs of the passerby. Anyone who passes through it might also try the lottery store to see whether Lady Luck, his companion, is well disposed toward him, or he might put her to a test in a card game. And if he wants to confront his glossy paper dreams in person, he can go to the postcard shop, where he will discover them realized in a variety of colorful versions. Flower arrangements greet him with their ingenious language; little dogs run up to him full of trust; student life is marvelously and drunkenly resplendent; and the nakedness of rosy women's bodies immerses him in desire. Next door, imitation bracelets nestle around the neck and arms of a shapely beauty almost on their own, and an outdated hit tune emanating from the music shop lends wings to the arcade wanderer amid the illusions he has discovered.

What united the objects in the Linden Arcade and gave them all the same function was their withdrawal from the bourgeois façade. Desires, geographic debaucheries, and many images that caused sleepless nights were not allowed to be seen among the high goings-on in the cathedrals and universities, in ceremonial speeches and parades. Wherever possible, they were executed, and if they could not be completely destroyed they were driven out and banished to the inner Siberia of the arcade. Here, however, they took revenge on the bourgeois idealism that oppressed them by playing off their own defiled existence against the arrogated existence of the bourgeoisie. Degraded as they were, they were able to congregate in the half-light of the passageway and to organize an effective protest against the façade culture outside. They exposed idealism for what it was and revealed its products to be kitsch. The arched windows, cornices, and balustrades—the Renaissance splendor that deemed itself so superior—was examined and rejected in the arcade. Even while traversing it—that is, effecting the movement appropriate to us alone—we could already see through this splendor, and its pretentiousness was unveiled in the light of the arcade. The reputations of the higher and highest ladies and gentlemen, whose portraits with their guarantees of fidelity stood and hung in the display windows of the court painter Fischer, fared no better. The ladies of the kaiser's court smiled so graciously that this grace tasted as rancid as its oil portraits.[9] And the highly touted inwardness wreaking havoc behind the Renaissance façades was given the lie by lighting fixtures in the form of red and yellow roses, which illuminated the interior in a horrible fashion. In this way the passageway through the bourgeois world articulated a critique of this world which every true passerby understood. (That passerby, who roams like a vagabond, will someday be united with the person of the changed society.)

By disavowing a form of existence to which it still belonged, the Linden Arcade gained the power to bear witness to transience. It was the product of an era that, in creating it, simultaneously created a harbinger of its own end. In the arcades, and precisely because they were arcades, the most recently created things separated themselves from living beings earlier than elsewhere, and died still warm (that is why Castan's panopticon[10] was located in the arcade). What we had inherited and unhesitatingly called our own lay in the passageway as if in a morgue, exposing its extinguished grimace. In this arcade, we ourselves encountered ourselves as deceased. But we also wrested from it what belongs to us today and forever, that which glimmered there unrecognized and distorted.

Now, under a new glass roof and adorned in marble, the former arcade looks like the vestibule of a department store. The shops are still there, but its postcards are mass-produced commodities, its World Panorama has been superseded by a cinema, and its Anatomical Museum has long ceased to cause a sensation. All the objects have been struck dumb. They huddle timidly behind the empty architecture, which, for the time being, acts completely neutral but may later spawn who knows what—perhaps fascism, or perhaps nothing at all. What would be the point of an arcade *[Passage]* in a society that is itself only a passageway?

Notes

Bibliographic Information

Credits

Index

Notes

■ ■ ■

Introduction

1. See Kracauer's review of Benjamin's *Einbahnstraße* and *Ursprung des deutschen Trauerspiels*, titled "On the Writings of Walter Benjamin," in this volume. See also Benjamin's 1930 review of Kracauer's *Die Angestellten*, titled "Ein Außenseiter macht sich bemerkbar," in Benjamin, *Gesammelte Schriften*, ed. Rolf Tiedemann and Hermann Schweppenhäuser, vol. 3 (Frankfurt: Suhrkamp Verlag, 1972), 219–228. A partial portrait of their complex friendship emerges from their correspondence, published as Walter Benjamin, *Briefe an Siegfried Kracauer*, ed. Theodor W. Adorno Archiv (Marbach: Deutsches Literaturarchiv, 1987); see also Klaus Michael, "Vor dem Café: Walter Benjamin und Siegfried Kracauer in Marseille," in Michael Opitz and Erdmut Wizisla, eds., *"Aber ein Sturm weht vom Paradiese her": Texte zu Walter Benjamin* (Leipzig: Reclam, 1992), 203–221. For a comparison of their respective readings of Paris, where both spent years together in exile, see Remo Bodei, "L'Expérience et les formes: Le Paris de Walter Benjamin et de Siegfried Kracauer," trans. Jacqueline Liechtenstein, in Heinz Wismann, ed., *Walter Benjamin et Paris* (Paris: Editions du Cerf, 1986), 33–47.

2. An overview of Kracauer's publications in the United States, which include both the ground-breaking pamphlet "Propaganda and the Nazi War Film" (written, as the preface explains, for "the purposes of psychological warfare") and the book-length study written with Paul L. Berkman titled *Satellite Mentality: Political Attitudes and Propaganda Susceptibilities of Non-Communists in Hungary, Poland and Czechoslovakia* (New York: Praeger, 1956), can be found in Thomas Y. Levin, "Siegfried Kracauer in English: A Bibliography," *New German Critique* 41 (Spring–Summer 1987): 140–150.

3. *Jacques Offenbach und das Paris seiner Zeit* (Amsterdam: Allert de Lange, 1937), translated by Gwenda David and Eric Mosbacher as *Orpheus in Paris: Offenbach and the Paris of His Time* (London: Constable, 1937; New York: Knopf, 1938). On Kracauer's difficult period of exile in France, see "Archäologie des Exils: Siegfried Kracauers Briefe an Daniel Halévy," in Michael Kessler and Thomas Y. Levin, eds., *Siegfried Kracauer: Neue Interpretationen* (Tübingen: Staufenburg Verlag, 1990), 345–417, a collection of the papers from the international Kracauer conference held on the centennial of his birth in 1989.

4. A comprehensive overview of Kracauer's work is provided in *Siegfried Kracauer: Eine Bibliographie seiner Schriften*, ed. and introd. Thomas Y. Levin (Marbach: Deutsche Schillergesellschaft, 1989). For a survey of the response to Kracauer's writings in the Anglo-American world, see Thomas Y. Levin, "The English-Language Reception of Kracauer's Work: A Bibliography," *New German Critique* 54 (Fall 1991): 183–189. Much of the important recent Kracauer scholarship in English can be found in "Special Issue on Siegfried Kracauer," *New German Critique* 54 (Fall 1991). For an illuminating discussion of the disregard for Kracauer's early writings (as well as some of his later works) in the former Eastern Bloc—remarkably similar to the reception in the Anglo-American sphere, albeit with very different stakes—see Jörg Schweinitz, "Schwierigkeiten mit Kracauer: Zu Edition und Rezeption der Filmschriften Siegfried Kracauers in Osteuropa," *Soziographie: Blätter des Forschungskomitees "Soziographie" der Schweizerischen Gesellschaft für Soziologie* 8/9 (1994).

5. Letter to Wolfgang Weyrauch (June 4, 1962), cited in the chronology of Kracauer's life and work edited by Ingrid Belke and Irina Renz, *Siegfried Kracauer 1889–1966, Marbacher Magazin* 47 (Marbach: Deutsche Schillergesellschaft, 1989), 118. For a biographical portrait in English, see Martin Jay, "The Extraterritorial Life of Siegfried Kracauer," *Salmagundi* 31–32 (Fall 1975–Winter 1976): 49–106, reprinted in Jay, *Permanent Exiles: Essays in the Intellectual Migration from Germany to America* (New York: Columbia University Press, 1986), 152–197. Unless otherwise noted, all translations are my own.

6. Kracauer, *Die Angestellten: Aus dem neuesten Deutschland* (Frankfurt: Frankfurter Societäts-Druckerei, 1930); reprinted in Siegfried Kracauer, *Schriften*, ed. Karsten Witte, vol. 1 (Frankfurt: Suhrkamp Verlag, 1971), 205–304.

7. Theodor W. Adorno, "Der wunderliche Realist: Über Siegfried Kracauer" (1964); in English as "The Curious Realist: On Siegfried Kracauer," trans. Shierry Weber Nicholsen, *New German Critique* 54 (Fall 1991): 160; reprinted in Adorno, *Notes to Literature*, vol. 2, trans. Shierry Weber Nicholsen (New York: Columbia University Press, 1992), 58–75. On the vital and altogether underexplored Weimar period in the history of the *Frankfurter Zeitung* feuilleton, see Almut Todorow, " 'Wollten die Eintagsfliegen in den Rang höherer Insekten aufsteigen?': Die Feuilletonkonzeption der *Frankfurter Zeitung* während der Weimarer Republik im redaktionellen Selbstverständnis," *Deutsche Vierteljahresschrift für Literaturwissenschaft und Geistesgeschichte* 62, no. 4 (December 1988): 697–740; and idem, *Das Feuilleton der Frankfurter Zeitung während der Weimarer Republik: Zur Rhetorik einer publizistischen Institution* (Tübingen: Max Niemeyer Verlag, 1995).

8. Kracauer, *Die Angestellten*, in *Schriften*, vol. 1, 252.

9. With the exception of a central chapter included in *The Mass Ornament*, "Georg

Simmel: Ein Beitrag zur Deutung des geistigen Lebens unserer Zeit" (written 1919–1920) remains unpublished to this day. There are, however, plans to include it in a final volume of the *Schriften*, which will be devoted to early writings from the Kracauer papers. For a discussion of Kracauer in the context of German sociology in general, and Simmel in particular, see David Frisby, *Fragments of Modernity: Theories of Modernity in the Work of Simmel, Kracauer and Benjamin* (Cambridge, Mass.: MIT Press, 1986), esp. 109–186. On Kracauer's book reviews, see Karsten Witte, " 'Light Sorrow': Siegfried Kracauer as Literary Critic," *New German Critique* 54 (Fall 1991): 77–94.

10. On Kracauer's paratactic method, see Hans Heinz Holz, "Philosophie als Fragment: Siegfried Kracauer und das Denken der zwanziger Jahre," *National-Zeitung* (Basel), March 26, 1972: 3. On the *Denkbild*, see Heinz Schlaffer, "Denkbilder: Eine kleine Prosaform zwischen Dichtung und Gesellschafts-theorie," in Wolfgang Kuttenkeuler, ed., *Poesie und Politik: Zur Situation der Literatur in Deutschland* (Stuttgart: Kohlhammer Verlag, 1973), 137–154. On the history of the word, see Eberhard Wilhelm Schulz, "Zum Wort 'Denk-bild,' " in Schulz, *Wort und Zeit* (Neumünster: Wachholtz, 1968), 218–252.

11. Kracauer, *Soziologie als Wissenschaft: Eine erkenntnistheoretische Untersuchung* (1922); reprinted in *Schriften*, vol. 1, 7–101.

12. Having remained a family undertaking well into the 1920s, the paper's dire financial situation was resolved in the spring of 1929 by the sale of 48 percent of its stock to the holding company "Imprimatur GmbH," which was a cover for I. G. Farben, as reported in the Berlin newspapers at the time and officially denied by the *Frankfurter Zeitung* in a front-page editorial on April 29, 1929. Given its historical origins as a financial and business newspaper, the *Frankfurter Zeitung* had always been vulnerable to accusations of being indebted to corporate interests and thus was especially concerned to suppress the details of this sale at all costs. In May 1934, Imprimatur GmbH took over the remaining stock of the paper's printer, the Frankfurter Societäts-Druckerei, which was still in the possession of the Simon family; Imprimatur thus gained control of 97.92 percent of the *Frankfurter Zeitung*'s parent company, thereby accomplishing what the Nazis had demanded in order for the paper to have a future: the elimination of its Jewish owners. By 1939 it was controlled by Eher Konzern, the publishing operation of the NSDAP. (See Werner Wirthle, *"Frankfurter Zeitung" und Frankfurter Societäts-Druckerei GmbH: Die wirtschaftlichen Verhältnisse, 1927–1939* [Frankfurt: Societäts-Verlag, 1977], esp. 11–15.) Though ultimately banned by the Nazis in 1943, the paper did more than just cooperate with the NSDAP for many years, a fact curiously at odds with its contemporary mythologization as the unsullied foundation of post–World War II journalism in Germany. Perhaps the most dramatic example of this revi-

sionist historiography is the massive account of the *Frankfurter Zeitung* during the Third Reich compiled by the editor of the paper; see Günther Gillessen, *Auf verlorenem Posten: Die "Frankfurter Zeitung" im Dritten Reich* (Berlin: Siedler Verlag, 1987). For a devastating exposé of this work's tendentious slant, see Uwe Pralle, "Eine Titanic bürgerlichen Geistes: Ansichten der *Frankfurter Zeitung*," *Frankfurter Rundschau*, January 20, 1990: ZB 3.

13. Completed in Paris in 1933, Kracauer's second novel remained unpublished during his lifetime. It appeared posthumously in Kracauer, *Schriften*, vol. 7 (Frankfurt: Suhrkamp Verlag, 1973), together with his first novel, *Ginster*.

14. Kracauer, "Über den Schriftsteller" (1931), reprinted in *Schriften*, vol. 5, pt. 2 (Frankfurt: Suhrkamp Verlag, 1990), 344; translated as "On the Writer," in Anton Kaes, Martin Jay, and Edward Dimendberg, eds., *The Weimar Republic Sourcebook* (Berkeley: University of California Press, 1994), 307–308.

15. Compare, for example, Hans Speier's contrast between the writer and the poet in his essay "Zur Soziologie der bürgerlichen Intelligenz in Deutschland" (*Die Gesellschaft* 6, no. 2 [1929]: 68–69) with Bernard Shaw's analogously polemical pro-journalist position published as "Shaw über den Journalismus" (*Frankfurter Zeitung* 72, no. 168 [1928]: Feuilleton 1).

16. This is true whether the relation is one of more or less unbroken continuity, as Kracauer himself claims in *History* ("At long last all my main efforts, so incoherent on the surface, fall into line. They have all served, and continue to serve, a single purpose: the rehabilitation of objectives and modes of being which still lack a name and hence are overlooked or misjudged"; 4), or whether, as Miriam Hansen has recently argued with regard to *Theory of Film*, this relation is much more highly mediated and ultimately repressed. See Hansen, " 'With Skin and Hair': Kracauer's Theory of Film, Marseille 1940," *Critical Inquiry* 19 (Spring 1993): 437–469. For a reading of *History* sensitive to its film-theoretical resonances, see David Rodowick, "On Kracauer's *History*," *New German Critique* 41 (Winter 1987): 109–139.

17. Kracauer, "On the Writer," 307.

18. Kracauer, "Der Fachmann" (1931), reprinted in *Schriften*, vol. 5, pt. 2, 404.

19. Kracauer, Letter to Adorno (Berlin: July 22, 1930); Kracauer Papers, Deutsches Literaturarchiv, Marbach am Neckar (hereafter abbreviated as DLA). Cited in Levin, "Der enthüllte Kracauer: Eine Einleitung," in *Siegfried Kracauer: Eine Bibliographie seiner Schriften*, 12.

20. Kracauer, Letter to Adorno (Berlin: Aug. 1, 1930); cited in Levin, "Der enthüllte Kracauer," 32, n. 9.

21. The three headings under which Kracauer grouped his texts for the initial *Straßenbuch* project (according to a typewritten table of contents preserved among his papers at the DLA) reappear with some modifications in *Straßen in*

Berlin und anderswo (Frankfurt: Suhrkamp Verlag, 1964) as "Straßen" (Streets), "Lokale" (Locales), "Dinge" (Things), and "Leute" (People).

22. Kracauer, Letter to Adorno (Berlin: August 1, 1930), cited in Levin, "Der enthüllte Kracauer," 32, n. 9.

23. Letter to Adorno (October 1, 1950), cited in *Marbacher Magazin,* 110.

24. Letter to Leo Löwenthal (October 28, 1956), cited in *Marbacher Magazin,* 113.

25. *Von Caligari bis Hitler: Ein Beitrag zur Geschichte des deutschen Films,* trans. Friedrich Walter (Hamburg: Rowohlt's Deutsche Enzyklopädie, 1958). The political disfiguration of Kracauer's text by a senior editor at Rowohlt named Hintermeyer, a former Nazi who had been responsible for "Aryanizing" Jewish bookstores in Silesia, was exposed in print as early as 1958 in an East German film journal; see Werner W. Wallroth, "Der entschärfte Kracauer," *Deutsche Filmkunst* 7 (1958): 206–207, 211. A reliable and full-length German edition did not become available until the translation by Ruth Baumgarten and Karsten Witte, published as volume 2 of *Schriften* (Frankfurt: Suhrkamp Verlag, 1979). The German translation of *Theory of Film* which Rowohlt planned to publish in the early 1960s was so poor that Kracauer had to spend months reworking it line by line; then, in 1962, Rowohlt changed the terms of the contract and the deal fell through. The book appeared in German only in 1964, under the Suhrkamp imprint.

26. The publication history of these two books reveals a curious disregard for Kracauer's careful editorial selection and arrangement of his own essays. Despite its title, the Italian volume *La massa come ornamento* (trans. Maria Giovanna Amirante Pappalardo and Francesco Maione [Naples: Prismi Editrice, 1982]) is in fact a selection of texts taken from both collections. In the compilation of Kracauer's essays edited by Inka Mülder-Bach (vol. 5 [1990] of the eight-volume edition begun in 1971 under the editorship of Karsten Witte), the ornamental logic of the texts in *Das Ornament der Masse* has been replaced by a strictly chronological arrangement according to the year of their production. For a list of Kracauer texts *not* included in the three parts of *Schriften,* vol. 5, see Andreas Volk, "Siegfried Kracauer in der *Frankfurter Zeitung:* Ein Forschungsbericht," *Soziographie* 4 (June 1991): 43–69.

27. A chronological listing of the respective contents of these collections can be found in Volk, "Siegfried Kracauer in der *Frankfurter Zeitung,*" 65–66.

28. Kracauer, "Autorität und Individualismus" (1921), reprinted in *Schriften,* vol. 5, pt. 1, 81; and "Deutscher Geist und deutsche Wirklichkeit" (1922), reprinted in *Schriften,* vol. 5, pt. 1, 153.

29. On Kracauer's early works, see Inka Mülder-Bach's important book-length study, *Siegfried Kracauer—Grenzgänger zwischen Theorie und Literatur: Seine frühen Schriften, 1913–1933* (Stuttgart: J. B. Metzler, 1985). See also Michael

Schröter, "Weltzerfall und Rekonstruktion: Zur Physiognomik Siegfried Kracauers," *Text und Kritik* 68 (October 1980): 18–41.

30. Kracauer, *Der Detektiv-Roman: Ein philosophischer Traktat*, first published in its entirety only posthumously in *Schriften*, vol. 1, 103–204. While unavailable in English, except for the chapter "The Hotel Lobby," which Kracauer included in *Das Ornament der Masse*, it has been translated into French by Geneviève and Rainer Rochlitz as *Le Roman Policier: Un Traité Philosophique* (Paris: Payot, 1981).

31. Kracauer, *Der Detektiv-Roman*, 116.

32. Kracauer, "Theorie des Romans," *Die Weltbühne* 17, no. 35 (September 1, 1921): 229–230. Idem, "Georg von Lukács' Romantheorie" (1921), reprinted in *Schriften*, vol. 5, pt. 1, 117–123.

33. Kracauer, *Der Detektiv-Roman*, 115.

34. On the proto-semiotics of Morelli and Freud, see Carlo Ginzburg, "Morelli, Freud and Sherlock Holmes: Clues and Scientific Method," trans. Anna Davin, *History Workshop* 9 (1980): 5–36.

35. Heide Schlüpmann insists that despite the lack of references to his work in Alexander Kluge and Oskar Negt's canonical *Öffentlichkeit und Erfahrung* (1972)—translated as *The Public Sphere and Experience* (Minneapolis: University of Minnesota Press, 1993)—Kracauer nevertheless remains "possibly the most competent among the critical theorists" as a reader of the relation of mass media to the public sphere. See Heide Schlüpmann, "Der Gang ins Kino—Ein 'Ausgang aus selbstverschuldeter Unmündigkeit': Zum Begriff des Publikums in Kracauers Essayistik der Zwanziger Jahre," in Kessler and Levin, *Siegfried Kracauer: Neue Interpretationen*, 276.

36. Theodor W. Adorno and Max Horkheimer, *Dialektik der Aufklärung* [1947], reprinted in Adorno, *Gesammelte Schriften*, vol. 3, ed. Rolf Tiedemann (Frankfurt: Suhrkamp Verlag, 1981); translated by John Cumming as *The Dialectic of Enlightenment* (New York: Seabury Press, 1972).

37. Letter to Kracauer (Jan. 12, 1933), cited in Inka Mülder-Bach, "Der Umschlag der Negativität: Zur Verschränkung von Phänomenologie, Geschichtsphilosophie und Filmästhetik in Siegfried Kracauers Metaphorik der 'Oberfläche,' " *Deutsche Vierteljahresschrift* 61, no. 2 (1987): 366. Besides this important essay, to which I am indebted, see also Martin Jay's insightful study "Adorno and Kracauer: Notes on a Troubled Friendship," *Salmagundi* 40 (Winter 1978): 42–66; reprinted in Martin Jay, *Permanent Exiles*, 217–236.

38. See Herbert Schnädelbach, "Die Aktualität der *Dialektik der Aufklärung*," in Harry Kunneman and Hente de Vries, eds., *Die Aktualität der Dialektik der Aufklärung: Zwischen Moderne und Postmoderne* (Frankfurt: Campus Verlag, 1989), 15–35.

39. Schlüpmann, "Der Gang ins Kino," 269.
40. Kracauer, "Der Künstler in dieser Zeit" (1925), reprinted in *Schriften*, vol. 5, pt. 1, 305. When thinking through the ramifications of this image, one should recall Martin Heidegger's observation that "Americanism is something European." See Heidegger, "Die Zeit des Weltbildes," in *Holzwege* (Frankfurt: Klostermann, 1950); in English as "The Age of the World Picture," trans. William Lovitt, in Heidegger, *The Question Concerning Technology* (San Francisco: Harper and Row, 1977), 115–154, addendum 12.
41. Kracauer, "Der Künstler in dieser Zeit," 305. In a recent essay, Miriam Hansen insists there is an even earlier epistemological overdetermination for Kracauer's materialism: modern, secular Jewish messianism. Despite Kracauer's explicit polemics against it, Hansen argues that his theologically inflected philosophy of history and the specific type of materialism that it entails is informed by a version of secular Jewish messianism similar to that which had an important effect on Bloch and Benjamin. Although Kracauer was much more committed to a discourse of enlightenment and was in fact a vociferous critic of the renaissance of messianism, according to Hansen a messianic sensibility is subtly manifest at both the thematic and figural levels in his writing. It is this messianism that accounts for the apocalyptic perspective informing his texts, his notion that historical change is not a gradual process but a radical rupture, and the resulting double imperative of an anticipation (of that rupture) and the labor of redemption (understood as the task of inventorying, storing, and preparing everything previously and presently extant for that yet-to-come moment). See Miriam Hansen, "Decentric Perspectives: Kracauer's Early Writings on Film and Mass Culture," *New German Critique* 54 (Fall 1991): 47–76.
42. See, for example, J. Dudley Andrew, *The Major Film Theories: An Introduction* (New York: Oxford University Press, 1976), ch. 5; and idem, *Concepts in Film Theory* (New York: Oxford University Press, 1984), 19. For contrast, one could consult the following readings of Kracauer's notion of cinematic and photographic "realism," which are among those thoroughly informed by a familiarity with his early works: Heide Schlüpmann, "Phenomenology of Film: On Kracauer's Writings of the 1920's," trans. Thomas Y. Levin, *New German Critique* 40 (Winter 1987): 97–114; and, more recently, Miriam Hansen, "Decentric Perspectives: Kracauer's Early Writings on Film and Mass Culture."
43. This notion is first elaborated in Benjamin, "Eine kleine Geschichte der Photographie" (1931), in Benjamin, *Schriften*, vol. 2, pt. 1, 371; in English as "A Small History of Photography," trans. Kingsley Shorter, in *One Way Street and Other Writings* (London: NLB, 1979), 240–257, citation on 243; and later in Benjamin, "Das Kunstwerk im Zeitalter seiner technischen Reproduzierbarkeit" (1935–1936), in *Schriften*, vol. 1, pt. 2 (1974), 431–469 (= version 1),

vol. 7, pt. 1 (1989), 350–384 (= version 2), and vol. 1, pt. 2 (1974), 471–508 (= version 3). In Harry Zohn's translation of this last version, "The Work of Art in the Age of Mechanical Reproduction," in *Illuminations*, ed. Hannah Arendt (New York: Schocken, 1969), the discussion of the "optical unconscious" is on 236ff.

44. Kracauer, "Zwei Arten der Mitteilung" (1929), reprinted in *Schriften*, vol. 5, pt. 2, 166.

45. Kracauer, "Die Filmwochenschau" (1931), reprinted in Kracauer, *Kino: Essays, Studien, Glossen zum Film*, ed. Karsten Witte (Frankfurt: Suhrkamp Verlag, 1974), 11–12.

46. "Über die Aufgabe des Filmkritikers" (1932), reprinted in *Kino*, 11; translated as "On the Task of the Film Critic," in Kaes, Jay, and Dimendberg, eds., *The Weimar Republic Sourcebook*, 634–635.

47. Kracauer, *Die Angestellten*, in *Schriften*, vol. 1, 216. Hansen, "Decentric Perspectives," 64–65.

48. See, for example, Rudolf Harms, *Philosophie des Films: Seine ästhetischen und metaphysischen Grundlagen* (Leipzig: Felix Meiner, 1926; facsimile rpt. Zurich: Hans Rohr, 1970); Béla Balázs, *Der sichtbare Mensch oder die Kultur des Films* (1924) and *Der Geist des Films* (1930), reprinted in Balázs, *Schriften zum Film*, 2 vols. (Berlin: Hanser, 1982–1984); or Rudolf Arnheim, *Film als Kunst* (1932), partly translated together with later essays as *Film as Art* (Berkeley: University of California Press, 1957). For a concise overview of the theoretical stakes in the discourse surrounding Weimar cinema, see Anton Kaes, "The Debate about Cinema: Charting a Controversy, 1909–1929," trans. David J. Levin, *New German Critique* 40 (Winter 1987): 7–33.

49. See, for example, Thomas Elsaesser, "Cinema: The Irresponsible Signifier," and idem, "The Gamble with History: Film Theory or Cinema Theory," *New German Critique* 40 (Winter 1987): 65–89.

50. The limited discussion of cinema in *Die Angestellten*, where it is mentioned only as one of the types of "pleasure barracks" frequented by the employee class after work, can be found in "Shelter for the Homeless," one of the few sections of this unfortunately still untranslated text currently available in English; scc Kaes, Jay, and Dimendberg, eds., *The Weimar Republic Sourcebook*, 181–191.

51. One of the rare readings of Benjamin's essay that is aware of its debt to Kracauer can be found in Miriam Hansen, "Benjamin, Cinema and Experience: 'The Blue Flower in the Land of Technology,'" *New German Critique* 40 (Winter 1987): 179–224, esp. 208ff. For a more extended treatment of the historicity of attention, see Jonathan Crary, *Techniques of the Observer: On Vision and Modernity in the Nineteenth Century* (Cambridge, Mass.: MIT Press, 1990).

52. Benjamin reads shock—and especially its manifestation in the cinema—both as

a signature of the cultural moment and as a strategy for learning to cope with its new demands. In the 1939 essay "On Some Motifs in Baudelaire," for example, Benjamin writes: "Technology subjected the human sensorium to a training of a highly complex sort . . . There came the day when film corresponded to a new and urgent need for stimulation. This shock-like perception comes into play as a formal principle in film" ("Über einige Motive bei Baudelaire," *Schriften*, vol. 1, pt. 2, 631; "On Some Motifs in Baudelaire," *Illuminations*, 630). The productive aspect of the experience of shock—which acclimates the spectator to the new tempo and quality of experience in late capitalist urbanism—is evident in the following italicized passage from the "second," untranslated version of the "Artwork" essay: *"Film serves to train people in those sorts of perceptions and reactions which are necessary for any interaction with apparatuses—apparatuses whose roles in the lives of such people are increasing almost daily"* (*Schriften*, vol. 7, pt. 1, 359–360).

53. Adorno, "The Curious Realist: On Siegfried Kracauer," 162.

54. See, for example, Lars Kleberg and Hakan Lövgren, eds., *Eisenstein Revisited: A Collection of Essays* (Stockholm, 1987); and the special "André Bazin" issue of *Wide Angle* (no. 9, 1987), edited by Dudley Andrew.

55. The importance of situating Kracauer's later books in relation to his earlier writings is apparent in two new editions of his most well known works forthcoming from Princeton University Press: *From Caligari to Hitler*, which will be reissued with an appendix containing nearly 100 pages of translations of Kracauer's Weimar film criticism; and *Theory of Film*, which will be republished with excerpts from the draft manuscript of the 1940 "Marseille Film Theory." On the complex relationship between the latter two texts, see Hansen, " 'With Skin and Hair.' " For an example of the rearticulation of the Weimar writings in the postwar *Caligari* book, compare the latter's treatment of the mass-ornament topos (*Caligari*, 93–95).

56. As an instance of this, see Patrice Petro, "Kracauer's Epistemological Shift," *New German Critique* 54 (Fall 1991): 127–138.

57. A recent example of such a revisionist historiography is Miriam Hansen, "Mass Culture as Hieroglyphic Writing: Adorno, Derrida, Kracauer," *New German Critique* 56 (Spring–Summer 1992): 43–73.

58. Kracauer, "Tessenow baut das Berliner Ehrenmal" (1930), reprinted in *Die Tageszeitung* (Berlin), November 13, 1993: 22; and in *Schriften*, vol. 5, pt. 2, 211–214. On the current debate, see *Streit um die neue Wache: Zur Gestaltung einer zentralen Gedenkstätte* (Berlin: Akademie der Künste, 1993).

59. Kracauer, "Über Arbeitsnachweise: Konstruktion eines Raumes" (1930), reprinted in *Die Tageszeitung* (Berlin), April 30, 1994: 37; and in *Schriften*, vol. 5, pt. 2, 185–192.

Two Planes

1. In letters to Kracauer, Walter Benjamin recounts how, in Marseille, the two of them discovered this uncanny square, which Kracauer christened the "Place de l'Observance." See Walter Benjamin, *Briefe an Siegfried Kracauer*, ed. Theodor W. Adorno Archiv (Marbach: Deutsche Schillergesellschaft, 1987), 33, 44.

Photography

1. A group of dancing girls, trained in military fashion, that was named after the Manchester choreographer John Tiller. Introduced in the late nineteenth century, the troupe was hired in Germany by Eric Charell, who from 1924 to 1931 was the director of Berlin's Großes Schauspielhaus theater and whose revues and operetta productions were the forerunners of today's musicals. See Derek Parker and Julia Parker, *The Natural History of the Chorus Girl* (London: Newton Abbot, 1975).

2. In the autobiographical novel *Georg*, which Kracauer completed in 1934 during his exile in Paris, the main character at one point recalls his childhood delight at "the glass battlefields of former times" filled with tin soldiers. "His grandmother," we learn, "had occasionally set [the soldiers] up on a glass plate and then tapped on the surface from underneath with her finger, in order to bring the ranks into disorder." Kracauer, *Georg*, in *Schriften*, vol. 7 (Frankfurt: Suhrkamp Verlag, 1973), 251.

3. A fashionable woman's jacket from the 1860s, modeled after the uniform of the Zouave, a French colonial troop composed of Berber tribes and Europeans and recruited in Algiers in 1830–1831.

4. When this essay was first published in the *Frankfurter Zeitung* in 1927, Kracauer here explicitly named Wilhelm Dilthey as an exemplary advocate of such historicist thinking.

5. Kracauer refers to this passage in the introduction to *History: The Last Things before the Last* (New York: Oxford University Press, 1969), when describing his surprising realization of the continuity between the work he had done on film and his present concern with history: "I realized in a flash the many existing parallels between history and the photographic media, historical reality and camera-reality. Lately I came across my piece on 'Photography' and was completely amazed at noticing that I had compared historicism with photography already in this article of the twenties" (3–4).

6. The German mythological hero, faithful protector, and counselor Eckart warns the Nibelungen at the border of the Rüdegers Mark of the threatening Hunns. Kracauer here plays on the association of Eckart and fidelity as manifest in

Ludwig Tieck's fable "Tannenhäuser and the Faithful Eckart" (1799) and Goethe's text "The Faithful Eckart" (1811).

7. Johann Peter Eckermann (1792–1854), Goethe's private secretary, in a discussion with Goethe on April 18, 1827, reported in *Gespräche mit Goethe in den letzten Jahren seines Lebens* (Wiesbaden: Insel Verlag, 1955), 578; translated by John Oxenford as *Conversations of Goethe with Eckermann and Soret* (London: George Bell, 1874), 248. Compare also the translation by Gisela C. O'Brien, *Conversations with Goethe* (New York: Ungar, 1964).

8. Wilhelm Trübner (1851–1917), a German "naturalist" painter best known for his early, sober, Courbet-inspired "realist" portraits. Following a period in the 1870s during which Trübner produced large historical and mythological scenes, he became a member of the Munich Secession in the 1890s and adopted an Impressionist idiom in which he painted a large corpus of landscapes. For his views on photography, rendered in Bavarian dialect in the original German quotation, compare for example the sections "Die photographische Darstellung" and "Die Grenzen zwischen productiver und reproductiver Thätigkeit," in Wilhelm Trübner, *Die Verwirrung der Kunstbegriffe* (Frankfurt: Literarische Anstalt Rütten und Loening, 1900), 44–46.

9. Ludwig von Zumbusch (1861–1927) was a German painter of naïve canvases, portraits, and pastel landscapes.

10. Ewald André Dupont, *Wie ein Film geschrieben wird und wie man ihn verwertet* (Berlin: Reinhold Kühn, 1919), cited in Rudolf Harms, *Philosophie des Films* (Leipzig: Felix Meiner, 1926; facsimile rpt. Zurich: Hans Rohr, 1970), 142. Shortly after its publication, Kracauer reviewed Harms's study in the book review section of the *Frankfurter Zeitung* on July 10, 1927 (vol. 60, no. 28): 5.

11. Aristide Briand (1862–1932), foreign minister of France (1925–1932), and Gustav Stresemann (1878–1929), foreign minister of Germany (1923–1929), shared the 1926 Nobel Peace Prize and were instrumental in gaining acceptance of the Kellogg-Briand Pact.

12. Johann Jakob Bachofen (1815–1887), "Oknos der Seilflechter" (1923), in *Versuch über die Gräbersymbolik der Alten*, in *Gesammelte Werke*, vol. 4 (Basel: Benno Schwabe, 1954), 359; translated as "Ocnus the Rope Plaiter" in *Myth, Religion, and Mother Right: Selected Writings of J. J. Bachofen*, tr. Ralph Manheim (Princeton: Princeton University Press, 1967), 54–55. Known for his punishment in Hades, the mythical Ocnos was condemned to twist a straw rope that would be devoured incessantly by an ass.

13. Karl Marx and Friedrich Engels, *Die Deutsche Ideologie* (1845–1846), in *Marx/Engels Werke*, vol. 3 (Berlin: Dietz, 1958), 31; translated as *The German Ideology*, in *Marx/Engels Collected Works*, vol. 5 (London: Lawrence and Wishart, 1976), 44.

14. Georg Friedrich Creuzer (1771–1858), *Symbolik und Mythologie der alten Völker, besonders der Griechen,* vol. 4 (Leipzig: Carl Wilhelm Leske, 1836–1843; rpt. Hildesheim: G. Olms, 1973), 540.

Travel and Dance

1. Johann Wolfgang Goethe, *Italienische Reise, Gedenkausgabe der Werke, Briefe und Gespräche,* ed. Ernst Beutler, vol. 11 (Zurich: Artemis, 1950), 7–613; *Italian Journey,* ed. Thomas P. Saine and Jeffrey L. Sammons, trans. Robert R. Heitner (New York: Suhrkamp, 1989).
2. English in original.
3. Reference to "Ein Waltzertraum," an operetta in three acts by Felix Doermann and Leopold Jacobson with music by Oskar Straus (1870–1954). The premiere of what would become Straus's most successful operetta took place in Vienna in 1907.
4. Kracauer here introduces two sets of terminological pairs which map onto each other: *Diesseits* ("this side," or, in my translation, "this life here") and *Jenseits* ("that side," "the far side," or, as I have translated it, "the Beyond"); and *das Hier* ("the Here") and *das Dort* ("the There"). These, in turn, correspond to the realms of the *Bedingtes* (the "limited" or the "contingent") and the *Unbedingtes* (the "unconditioned" or the "absolute").
5. Vladimir Sergeyech Solovyov, *Opravdanie Dobra: Nravstvennaia Filosofia* (Moscow: Tipo-litografiia D.A. Bonch-Bruevich, 1899); translated by Natalie A. Duddington as *The Justification of the Good: An Essay on Moral Philosophy* (New York: MacMillan, 1918), 164. Besides this volume, which is Solovyov's general system of ethics originally published in 1895–1896, a further selection of the work of this late nineteenth-century Russian poet and philosopher of Christian inspiration is available in English as *A Solovyov Anthology,* ed. S. L. Frank, trans. Natalie Duddington (London: SCM Press, 1950).

The Mass Ornament

1. A group of militarily trained dancing girls named after the Manchester choreographer John Tiller. Introduced in the late nineteenth century, the troupe was hired in Germany by Eric Charell, who from 1924 to 1931 was the director of Berlin's Großes Schauspielhaus theater and whose revues and operetta productions were the forerunners of today's musicals. See Derek Parker and Julia Parker, *The Natural History of the Chorus Girl* (London: Newton Abbot, 1975); and Fritz Giese, *Girl-kultur* (Munich: Delphin Verlag, 1925).
2. Walther von Stolzing, a young knight in Richard Wagner's *Die Meistersinger*

von Nürnberg (1867), who in Act Three sings the "prize song" which wins him his beloved Eva.

On Bestsellers and Their Audience

1. Siegfried Kracauer, "Richard Voß: *Zwei Menschen,*" *Frankfurter Zeitung* 75, no. 161 (March 1, 1931), Literaturblatt 7–8, reprinted in *Schriften* 5, pt. 2, 287–294; Friedrich Burschell, "Stefan Zweig's Novellen," *Frankfurter Zeitung* 75, no. 192 (March 15, 1931), Literaturblatt 6; Ephraim Frisch, "Erich Maria Remarque: *Im Westen nichts Neues,*" *Frankfurter Zeitung* 75, no. 254 (April 5, 1931), Literaturblatt 7–8; Erich Franzen, "Jack London," *Frankfurter Zeitung* 75, no. 270 (April 12, 1931), Literaturblatt 6; and Siegfried Kracauer, "Bemerkungen zu Frank Thieß," *Frankfurter Zeitung* 75, no. 327 (May 3, 1931), Literaturblatt 22, reprinted in *Schriften* 5, pt. 2, 312–318. All of these texts were republished, together with Kracauer's analysis in the present essay, as an advertising supplement to the *Literaturblatt* in 1931. Combined with facsimiles of sample pages from the book review, letters from book publishers confirming the positive value of advertising in the book review, and an anonymous publisher's defense of the value of paperback editions ("Für das broschierte Buch: Ein Verleger Spricht"), this sixteen-page leaflet was distributed to potential advertisers in the book industry.
2. See Kracauer's essay "The Biography as an Art Form of the New Bourgeoisie," in this volume.
3. Kracauer here plays on the words *Wünschelrute* ("divining rod") and *Wünsche* ("wishes").
4. A reference to the Berlin publisher Ullstein Verlag, which brought out Remarque's novel *Im Westen nichts Neues* in 1929. The book was translated into English the same year by A. W. Wheen as *All Quiet on the Western Front* (Boston: Little, Brown). See Kracauer's review of Lewis Milestone's very popular 1930 film based on the book, " 'Im Westen nichts Neues': Zum Remarque-Tonfilm," reprinted in *Schriften* 2, 456–459.
5. Siegfried Kracauer, *Die Angestellten: Aus dem neuesten Deutschland,* first published in serial form in the *Frankfurter Zeitung* in 1929 and subsequently as a book (Frankfurt: Frankfurter Societäts-Druckerei, 1930); reprinted in *Schriften* 1, 205–304.
6. Kracauer here uses the term *abbauen*—literally, "to deconstruct"—which has a variety of semantic registers: to reduce in number, to discharge to lay off (fire someone from a job), and so on.
7. Kracauer, "Bemerkungen zu Frank Thieß," in *Schriften* 5, pt. 2, 312. Just over one year later Kracauer also reviewed a volume of Thieß essays and lectures

titled *Die Zeit ist reif* (Berlin: Paul Zsolnay, 1932); see Kracauer, "Zwischen Blut und Geist" (1932), reprinted in *Schriften* 5, pt. 3, 93–96.

8. Kracauer, "Richard Voß: 'Zwei Menschen,' " 291.
9. Burschell, "Stefan Zweigs Novellen," 6.
10. Ibid.
11. Frisch, "Erich Maria Remarque: *Im Westen nichts Neues*," 8.
12. Kracauer, "Bemerkungen zu Frank Thieß," 317.
13. A play on the title of Zweig's novella *Amok* (Leipzig: Insel Verlag, 1922), translated under the same title by Eden Paul and Ceder Paul (New York: Viking, 1931).
14. Burschell, "Stefan Zweigs Novellen," 6.
15. Franzen, "Jack London," 6.
16. Frisch, "Erich Maria Remarque: *Im Westen nichts Neues*," 8.
17. This final paragraph of the article, which Kracauer omitted from the 1963 edition of *Das Ornament der Masse,* was subsequently reinserted by Karsten Witte in his 1977 posthumous reedition of the book.

The Biography as an Art Form of the New Bourgeoisie

1. Emil Ludwig (1881–1948), German author known above all for his numerous biographies including *Napoleon* (Berlin: Rowohlt, 1926), translated under the same title by Eden Paul and Ceder Paul (New York: Bonie Liveright, 1926); *Lincoln* (Berlin: Rowohlt, 1930), translated by Eden Paul and Ceder Paul (Boston: Little, Brown, 1930); and *Goethe* (Stuttgart: Cotta, 1920), translated by Ethel Colburn Mayne as *Goethe: The History of a Man, 1749–1832* (New York: Putnam's, 1928).
2. Kracauer here plays with the relation between *Flucht* ("escape") and *Ausflucht* ("evasion").
3. Leon Trotsky, *Moia Zhizn: Opyt Autobiografii* (Berlin: Izdvo Granit, 1930); anonymously translated as *My Life: An Attempt at an Autobiography* (New York: Scribner's, 1930); reprinted, with an introduction by Joseph Hansen (New York: Penguin, 1975).

Revolt of the Middle Classes

1. A monthly philosophical and religious journal founded in 1909 and published by Eugen Diederichs Verlag starting in 1912. Under the direction of Hans Zehrer, who took over the editorship in 1929, the publication became the organ of the *Tat* Circle, a group of writers who, as disciples of the writings of Carl Schmitt, advocated an anti-parliamentarian state doctrine. In its arguments for

an authoritarian synthesis of nationalism and socialism, *Die Tat* (Act, Fact, Action, Deed) was central to the conservative revolution and paved an ideological path for the nascent National Socialism. It reached its height as a thoroughly political publication in 1931–1932, with a circulation of nearly 30,000. From 1933 to 1939, under the direction of G. Wirsing, it openly adopted a radically Fascist stance and continued from 1939 to 1944 under the title *Das zwanzigste Jahrhundert* (The Twentieth Century). See Hans Hecker, *Die Tat und ihr Osteuropa-Bild, 1909–1933* (Cologne: Wissenschaft und Politik, 1974).

2. Unsigned [Hans Zehrer], "Wohin treiben wir?" *Die Tat* 23, no. 5 (August 1931): 354.

3. Ferdinand Fried was the pseudonym of Ferdinand Friedrich Zimmermann (1898–1967), a German journalist and professor of state economy. From 1923 to 1932 he was the economics editor of the *Vossische Zeitung* and of the *Berliner Morgenpost;* from 1931 to 1933 he was on the staff of *Die Tat* and a member of the *Tat* Circle. In 1933 he succeeded Hans Zehrer as the editor-in-chief of the *Tägliche Rundschau*, in 1934 he became a member of the SS, and in 1953 he took the position of economics editor of *Die Welt.* Fried's economic analyses in *Die Tat* in 1931, to which Kracauer here refers, include the following: "Kapital und Masse," 22, no. 10 (January): 768–798; "Wende der Wirtschaft," 22, no. 11 (February): 848–868; "Der Umbau der Welt," 23, no. 2 (May): 81–126; "Der Weg der Reichsfinanzen," 23, no. 3 (June): 161–180; "Wo stehen wir?" 23, no. 5 (August): 354–385; "Die Auflösung," 23, no. 8 (November): 601–632.

4. In the first publication of this essay in the *Frankfurter Zeitung,* there follows a parenthetical remark—deleted in the later reprinting of *Das Ornament der Masse*—which reads as follows: "(Arthur Feiler [politics editor of the *Frankfurter Zeitung*] has commented on the program in a series of articles we just recently published)." See Arthur Feiler, "Autarkie oder Weltwirtschaft?" *Frankfurter Zeitung* 76, nos. 895–897 (December 2, 1931), Reichsausgabe 1–2; *Frankfurter Zeitung* 76, nos. 898–900 (December 3, 1931), Reichsausgabe 3–4; *Frankfurter Zeitung* 76, nos. 904–906 (December 5, 1931), Reichsausgabe 3–4. On Feiler, who emigrated to New York in 1933 and became one of the first refugee faculty members of what was known as the University in Exile at the New School for Social Research, see the privately published tribute by his friends on the first anniversary of his death: *Arthur Feiler, 1879–1942* (New York: New School for Social Research, 1943).

5. Hans Zehrer (1889–1966), German journalist, writer, and editor of the *Vossische Zeitung* from 1923 to 1931. Clandestine editor of *Die Tat* as of 1929, he became its official editor in 1931 and was also editor-in-chief of the *Tägliche Rundschau* from 1932 until 1933, when he was forced by the Nazis to resign both of these last two positions.

6. Hans Zehrer, "Rechts oder Links? Die Verwirrung der Begriffe," *Die Tat* 23, no. 7 (October 1931): 507.
7. Horst Grüneberg, "Mittelstandspolitik, Staatspolitik," *Die Tat* 23, no. 3 (June 1931): 211.
8. Reference as yet undetermined.
9. Josef Nadler (1884–1963), Austrian-born historian of literature, taught at the universities of Freiburg, Königsberg, and Vienna during the Weimar era. His work included a major four-volume study titled *Literaturgeschichte der deutschen Stämme und Landschaften* (Regensburg: J. Habbel, 1912–1928), widely employed by the Nazis, which related the characteristics and overall meaning of literary products to the race *[Stamm]* and to the landscapes that gave rise to them.
10. Zehrer, "Rechts oder Links?" 558.
11. Reference as yet undetermined.
12. Fried, "Der Weg der Reichsfinanzen," 179.
13. Reference as yet undetermined.
14. Horst Grüneberg, "Die Föderalistische Kulisse," *Die Tat* 23, no. 4 (July 1931): 293.
15. Horst Grüneberg, "Mittelstandspolitik, Staatspolitik," 209.
16. Zehrer, "Rechts oder Links?" 510–511. The following citations in the text are all taken from these pages.
17. For examples of the reception of Georges Sorel's work in *Die Tat*, see Zehrer, "Rechts oder Links?" 527–528; and E. W. Eschmann, "Moderne Soziologen II: Georges Sorel," *Die Tat* 22, no. 5 (August 1930): 367–377.
18. Zehrer, "Rechts oder Links?" 532, 559.
19. -h- [unidentified journalistic alias], "Der Fall Charlie Chaplin," *Die Tat* 23, no. 2 (May 1931): 158.
20. First published as a series of articles in the *Frankfurter Zeitung*, this groundbreaking study of the employee class was published as a book by the Frankfurt Societäts-Druckerei in 1930; reprinted in Kracauer, *Schriften* 1, 205–304.
21. Zehrer, "Rechts oder Links?" 556.
22. Georges Clemenceau (1841–1929), French statesman and journalist, consolidated his political power as France's staunchly pro-militarist premier and war minister during World War I. Clemenceau's forceful imposition of his political will, strikingly evidenced in the way he excluded the French National Assembly from the peace negotiations at Versailles, ultimately became the cause of his political demise. The British politician David Lloyd George (1863–1945) had an early career as militarist secretary of state for war before becoming prime minister (1916–1922) during the First World War. His distrust of other commanders and bureaucrats led to his increasing isolation.

23. Johann Jakob Bachofen, *Urreligion und antike Symbole: Systematisch angeordnete Auswahl aus seinen Werken in drei Bänden*, ed. Carl Albrecht Bernoulli, vol. 1 (Leipzig: Reclam, 1926), 182; translated by Ralph Manheim in *Myth, Religion, and Mother Right: Selected Writings of J. J. Bachofen* (Princeton: Princeton University Press, 1967), 213.

24. Bachofen, *Urreligion und antike Symbole* 1, 47.

25. Carl Schmitt, *Die geistesgeschichtliche Lage des heutigen Parlamentarismus* (Munich: Duncker & Humblot, 1923; 2nd ed. 1926), 472; translated by Ellen Kennedy as *The Crisis of Parliamentary Democracy* (Cambridge, Mass.: MIT Press, 1985), 75.

26. Zehrer, "Rechts oder Links?" 544.

27. Ferdinand Fried, "Der Umbau der Welt," *Die Tat* 23, no. 2 (May 1931): 126.

28. Oswald Spengler, *Der Untergang des Abendlandes*, vol. 2 (Munich: C. H. Beck, 1918–1922; rpt. 1980), 1194; translated by Charles Francis Atkinson as *The Decline of the West*, vol. 2: *Perspectives of World History* (New York: Knopf, 1928; rpt. 1992), 507. Cited in Fried, "Die Auflösung," *Die Tat* 23, no. 8 (November 1931): 603.

29. E. W. Eschmann, "Moderne Soziologen III," *Die Tat* 23, no. 2 (May 1931): 141.

30. Spengler, *Der Untergang des Abendlandes*, 466–467; translated by Charles Francis Atkinson as *The Decline of the West*, vol. 1: *Form and Actuality* (New York: Knopf, 1928; rpt. 1992), 363–364.

31. Zehrer, "Rechts oder Links?" 542 (original in italics).

32. [Zehrer], "Wohin treiben wir?" 346.

33. Ibid., 351.

34. Zehrer, "Rechts oder Links?" 544.

35. For Spengler on Caesarism, see *Der Untergang des Abendlandes*, 1101–1107; *The Decline of the West* 2, 431–435. Compare Fried's invocation of Spengler in "Die Auflösung," *Die Tat* 23, no. 8 (November 1931): 601–602.

36. Hans Zehrer, "Glossen zur Zeit," *Die Tat* 23, no. 8 (November 1931): 674–675.

37. Horst Grüneberg, "Mittelstandspolitik, Staatspolitik," 191.

38. Ibid., 194.

39. Ibid.

40. Ernst Wilhelm Eschmann, "Übergang zur Gesamtwirtschaft," *Die Tat* 23, no. 6 (September 1931): 456 (citation in italics). Eschmann, a journalist and later editor of *Die Tat*, also reviewed Kracauer's study *White-Collar Workers* for that journal. See "*Die Angestellten*: Ergänzungen zu S. Kracauer," *Die Tat* 22, no. 2 (1930): 460–463.

41. [Zehrer], "Wohin treiben wir?" 346; phrase italicized in original.

42. Zehrer, "Rechts oder Links?" 559.

43. Eschmann, "Übergang zur Gesamtwirtschaft," *Die Tat* 23, no. 6 (September 1931): 457.

44. Kracauer here mistakenly attributes this citation to Christian Reil, whose article "Die Wahrheit über Frankreich" (*Die Tat* 23, no. 1 [April 1931]: 59–62) begins on the same page as the cited passage. The latter, however, is from an article by Montanus titled "Werkszeitungen als 'weiße Salbe' des kapitalist-ischen Systems," *Die Tat* 23, no. 1 (April 1931): 59.

45. -c- [unidentified journalistic alias], "Ein Wort an Frankreich," *Die Tat* 23, no. 7 (October 1931): 584.

46. Erwin Ritter [pseud. of Hans Zehrer], "Die große Stadt," *Die Tat* 23, no. 8 (November 1931): 633.

Those Who Wait

1. Founded in 1912 by the scientist, editor, and Goethe scholar Rudolf Steiner (1861–1925), the spiritual movement known as anthroposophy is grounded in the belief in a spiritual world at the level of pure thought (that is, independent of the senses)—a world which can, however, be grasped by highly developed intellectual capacities. According to Steiner, man's original involvement with the spiritual world in a dreamlike state has been impoverished by the materi-alism of contemporary culture, with its emphasis on the empirical. His goal, which also informed the pedagogical program of the now widely established Waldorf School system, was to restore this theoretically universal connection to the spiritual by training the intellect to transcend the realm of the material.

2. Founded by the lyric poet Stefan George (1868–1933), the aesthetic formation known as the George Circle sought to respond to a perceived crisis in German culture which it felt was especially manifest in the decline in the literary capacities of the German language. The many writers who belonged to his exclusive personality cult and who contributed to its journal, *Blätter für die Kunst* (published from 1892 to 1919), included Hugo von Hofmannsthal, Friedrich Gundolf, and Max Dauthendey. George's own work, which accorded an almost sacral value to art, attempted to refine German poetry by eliminating impure rhymes and metrical irregularities, and by insisting on carefully chosen vowels and consonants in order to produce a harmonic construct, a symbolic poem evocative of intoxication. This formal poetic rigor, a response to both the positivism of science and naturalism, was coupled with an ascetic Greek humanism which, so George hoped, would ultimately lead to a new social order. His ideal of beauty, informed by a Mallarméan symbolism and close to Jugendstil, inspired everything from the structure of the writing to the external appearance of the books. George's rather Nietzschean view of the spiritual

aristocracy of the poet and his call, in *Das neue Reich* (1928), for the rebirth of Germany as a new Hellas were misread by the Nazis as a premonition of the Third Reich.

3. In the first publication of this essay in the *Frankfurter Zeitung* (March 12, 1922), this word is *"unzugänglich"* ("inaccessible"). In the 1963 reprint and again in *Schriften* 5, pt. 1, 169, it reads as *"unzulänglich"* ("insufficient," "inadequate").

The Group as Bearer of Ideas

1. See, for example, Simmel's work on the group in his 1908 collection *Soziologie: Untersuchungen über die Formen der Vergesellschaftung*, 4th ed. (Berlin: Duncker & Humblot, 1958), reprinted as vol. 11 of Simmel, *Gesamtausgabe*, ed. Otthein Rammstedt (Frankfurt: Suhrkamp, 1992). From this volume, "Die Erweiterung der Gruppe und die Ausbildung der Individualität" was translated by Richard P. Albares as "Group Expansion and the Development of Individuality," in Donald N. Levine, ed., *Georg Simmel: On Individuality and Social Forms* (Chicago: University of Chicago Press, 1971), 251–293; and "Die quantitative Bestimmtheit der Gruppe" was translated by Kurt Wolff as "Quantitative Aspects of the Group," in Kurt Wolff, ed., *The Sociology of Georg Simmel* (Glencoe, Ill.: Free Press, 1950), 87–177.

2. In Jewish mysticism and folklore, certain wise men of Talmudic legend were capable of giving life to a huge manmade effigy of lime or clay by means of charms or groups of letters that spelled a sacred word or one of the names of God. This effigy was the Golem. According to the version of the legend found in the *Sefer Yezirah* (Book of Creation), when these letters were inscribed on a piece of paper and placed in the Golem's mouth or affixed to its head, they would magically cause it to come to life, and it would die just as quickly when the paper was removed. Canonized by Grimm in 1808, the tale was taken up by the German Romantics (Ludwig Achim von Arnim and E. T. A. Hoffmann) and later in Gustav Meyrink's 1915 novel *Der Golem*, as well as in three silent film versions by Paul Wegener. See Emily D. Bilski, ed., *Golem! Danger, Deliverance and Art* (New York: Jewish Museum 1988).

3. Early in his career, Enea Silvio Piccolomini (1405–1464), a renowned Italian humanist, became an official of the Council of Basel (1431–1437), a gathering of bishops whose primary agenda was church reform. His next post as secretary to the antipope Felix V, elected by the remaining bishops in Basel in 1439, led to his excommunication until 1445, when he broke with Felix V. In his subsequent positions as imperial poet laureate and private secretary to Frederick III of Austria, and as bishop of Trieste, Piccolomini worked as a mediator

between the Holy See and the German states. Once elected pope as Pius II (1458–1464), however, he focused his political energies on the organization of a very unpopular and ultimately disastrous Crusade against the Turks who, in the wake of the fall of Constantinople, were threatening to overrun Europe.

4. See Kracauer's early epistemological study of sociology's claim to scientific status, titled *Soziologie als Wissenschaft: Eine erkenntnistheoretische Untersuchung* (Sociology as Science: An Epistemological Study) (Dresden: Sibyllen, 1922), reprinted in Kracauer, *Schriften*, vol. 1 (Frankfurt: Suhrkamp Verlag, 1971), esp. 67ff.

5. The Caudine Yoke refers to a decisive and humiliating rout of the Romans by the Samnites in 321 B.C. that occurred in the Caudine Forks, a series of narrow mountain passes in southern Italy on the stretch of the Via Appia from Capua to Benevento.

6. The tale of the sorcerer's apprentice, which can be traced back to Lucan and was taken up in Goethe's poem "Der Zauberlehrling," is most commonly known through Paul Dukas' 1893 symphonic scherzo "L'apprenti sorcier" and its subsequent cinematic animation by Disney.

The Hotel Lobby

1. Kracauer here and elsewhere uses the anglicism *Hall* instead of the German term *Halle* ("lobby"), which is derived from it.

2. In French in the original. "Face-to-face with nothing."

3. This hallmark phrase from Kant's *Critique of Judgment* is put in quotation marks in the later republication of this essay. See *Schriften* 1, 130.

4. "Soziologie der Geselligkeit," in *Grundfragen der Soziologie: Individuum und Gesellschaft* (Berlin: Göschen, 1917; 4th ed. Berlin: de Gruyter, 1984), 53; translated by Everett C. Hughes as "Sociability," in Donald N. Levine, ed., *Georg Simmel: On Individuality and Social Forms* (Chicago: University of Chicago Press, 1971), 130. Strictly speaking, Simmel's phrase is here used to define not society but sociability.

5. Thomas Mann, "Tod in Venedig," *Sämtliche Erzählungen* (Frankfurt: Fischer Verlag, 1963), 376. Compare the translation by H. T. Lowe-Porter, in *Death in Venice and Seven Other Stories* (New York: Vintage, 1955), 28.

6. Sven Elvestad, *Doden tar ind paa hotellet* (1921), in German as *Der Tod kehrt im Hotel ein: Roman*, trans. F. Koppel (Munich: Georg Müller, 1923).

The Bible in German

1. *Das Buch Im Anfang: Verdeutscht von Martin Buber gemeinsam mit Franz Rosenzweig* (Berlin: Lambert Schneider, 1925). This is the first volume of *Die*

Schrift: Zu verdeutschen unternommen von Martin Buber gemeinsam mit Franz Rosenzweig, 15 vols. (Berlin: Lambert Schneider, 1925-1961). Readers of English should compare the rendering of this first book of Genesis by Everett Fox, titled *In the Beginning* (New York: Schocken, 1983), which is explicitly indebted to Buber and Rosenzweig's translative method. For an extended discussion of the debates surrounding this translation, and Kracauer's critique in particular, see Martin Jay, "Politics of Translation: Siegfried Kracauer and Walter Benjamin on the Buber-Rosenzweig Bible," in Martin Jay, *Permanent Exiles: Essays in the Intellectual Migration from Germany to America* (New York: Columbia University Press, 1986), 198-216.

2. Franz Rosenzweig, *Der Stern der Erlösung* (Frankfurt: J. Kauffmann, 1921). The second edition (Berlin: Schocken, 1930) was rendered into English by William W. Hallo as *The Star of Redemption* (New York: Rinehart and Winston, 1971), following Buber and Rosenzweig's principles of translation (see the translator's preface, p. vii).

3. An institution established after World War I by Rosenzweig where students and teachers—including Jewish scholars such as Martin Buber, Ernst Simon, Gershom Scholem, Erich Fromm, and Nahum Glatzer—studied classic Jewish sources and debated their contemporary relevance. Historical accounts of the Lehrhaus are provided in Nahum N. Glatzer, "The Frankfort *[sic]* Lehrhaus," *Leo Baeck Institute Year Book 1* (London: East & West Library, 1956), 105-122; and in Erich Ahrens, "Reminiscences of the Men of the Frankfurt Lehrhaus," *Leo Baeck Institute Year Book 19* (London: Secker & Warburg, 1974), 245-253. See also Wolfgang Schivelbusch, "Auf der Suche nach dem verlorenen Judentum: Das Freie Jüdische Lehrhaus," in *Intellektuellendämmerung* (Frankfurt: Suhrkamp Verlag, 1985), 33-51.

4. Rosenzweig translated and annotated a volume of hymns and poems by the twelfth-century Spanish Jew Yehuda Halevi: *Sechzig Hymnen und Gedichte des Jehuda Halevi* (Konstanz: Oskar Wöhrle, 1924); a facing-page German and Hebrew edition of the same collection was published by Rafael N. Rosenzweig as *Fünfundneunzig Hymnen und Gedichte* (The Hague: Nijhoff, 1983). In English, there is a translation by Nina Salaman of Halevi's *Selected Poems* (Philadelphia: Jewish Publication Society of America, 1925).

5. Although Buber did not speak Chinese, he did edit a number of collections of Chinese texts; see, for example, *Reden und Gleichnisse des Tschuang-Tse: Deutsche Auswahl von Martin Buber* (Leipzig: Insel, 1910); and *Chinesische Geister- und Liebesgeschichten* (Frankfurt: Rütten und Loening, 1911).

6. *Die Geschichten des Rabbi Nachman: Nacherzählt von Martin Buber* (Frankfurt: Rütten und Loening, 1906), translated by Maurice Friedman as *The Tales of Rabbi Nachman* (Atlantic Highlands, N.J.: Humanities Press International,

1988; reprint of 1956 Horizon Press edition); *Die Legende des Baalschem* (Frankfurt: Rütten und Loening, 1908), first translated by Lucy Cohen as *Jewish Mysticism and the Legends of Baalschem* (London: Dent, 1931), and then newly translated by Maurice Friedman as *The Legend of the Baal-Shem* (New York: Harper, 1955); *Der große Maggid und seine Nachfolge* (Frankfurt: Rütten und Loening, 1922). In 1927 these three volumes were combined as *Die chassidischen Bücher* (Berlin: Schocken, 1927), which was published in the United States in two volumes as *The Tales of the Hasidim*, tr. Olga Marx (New York: Schocken, 1947–1948; rpt. 1991).

7. See Rosenzweig's afterword to his edition of Halevi's *Sechzig Hymnen und Gedichte*, 107–119.

8. When Hebrew ceased to be a living language, the transmitters of the biblical tradition, known as the Masoretes, developed written notations over the course of five centuries to preserve the correct emphasis and phrasings for the reading of the Hebrew Bible. All printed editions of the Hebrew Bible—whose model is the second "Great Rabbinic Bible" published by Daniel Bomberg (1524–1525) in Venice and edited by Ya'aqov ben Hayyim ibn Adoniyyah—constitute a single textual tradition referred to as the Masoretic ("received") text.

9. Reference to the subtitle of Max Scheler's 1921 study of *Vom Ewigen im Menschen* (Bern: Franke, 1954–1968), translated by Bernard Noble as *On the Eternal in Man* (London: SCM Press, 1960), which is discussed in the essay "Catholicism and Relativism," in this volume.

10. In the medieval epic *The Nibelungenlied*, young Siegfried bathes in the blood of a dragon he has just killed, thereby rendering himself invulnerable. Unbeknownst to him, however, a linden-leaf has fallen onto his back during this bath, leaving a spot untouched by the magic blood. This is the only place where he can be—and ultimately is—mortally wounded.

11. The poet, dramatist, and essayist Rudolf Borchardt (1877–1945) translated not only Dante's *Divina Commedia* (Munich: Verlag der Bremer Presse, 1922) but also his *Vita Nova* (Berlin: Rowohlt, 1922). The former is available as *Dantes Comedia: Deutsch*, ed. Marie Luise Borchardt (Stuttgart: Ernst Klett, 1967). On Borchardt as translator of Dante, see George Steiner, *After Babel: Aspects of Language and Translation* (London: Oxford University Press, 1975), 338–341; and Hans-Georg Dewitz, *Dante Deutsch: Studien zu Rudolf Borchardts Uebertragung der Divina Commedia* (Göppingen: Kümmerle, 1971).

12. *Die fünf Bücher Mose, zum Gebrauch der jüdischdeutschen Nation, nach der Übersetzung des Herrn Moses Mendelssohn* (Berlin: Nicolai, 1780). For a discussion of this translation—which was first published in Hebrew characters (and later in German orthography) and was accompanied by a commentary, the *Bi'ur*, that combined traditional exegesis with modern literary aesthetics—see Alex-

ander Altmann, *Moses Mendelssohn: A Biographical Study* (University, Ala.: University of Alabama Press, 1973). A collection of texts by the German-Jewish philosopher of the Enlightenment Mendelssohn (1729–1786) is available as *Moses Mendelssohn: Selections from His Writings*, ed. and trans. Eva Jospe (New York: Viking, 1975).

13. Letter of March 30, 1522, to Georg Spalatin (1484–1545), German reformer, theologian, and supporter of Luther at the court of the Sächsische Kurfürst Friedrich III, in Kurt Aland, ed., *Luther Deutsch* (Göttingen: Vandenhoeck & Ruprecht, 1991), 120; translated by Gottfried G. Krodel in Helmut T. Lehmann, ed., *Luther's Works*, vol. 49: *Letters II* (Philadelphia: Fortress, 1972), 3–4.

14. *Die 24 Bücher der Heiligen Schrift, nach dem masoretischen Texte*, ed. Leopold Zunz, trans. H. Arnheim et al. (Berlin: Veit, 1838). Leopold Zunz (1794–1886), German teacher, editor, and director of the Jüdische Lehrseminar in Berlin, cofounded the important Verein für Kultur und Wissenschaft der Juden (Association for the Culture and Scholarship of the Jews; 1819–1824), which enlisted historical method for the academic study of Judaism both as a challenge to the dominant Christian interpretation and in order to provide a scientific history of Jewish faith, culture, and life for both Jews and non-Jews.

15. Felix Dahn (1834–1912), a German writer, historian, and *Rechtsgelehrter* (professor of law) at the Universities of Würzburg, Königsberg, and Breslau, based his novels on material from old Norse sagas and from the time of the great migrations. Some of the texts from the 13 volumes of his *Kleine Romane aus der Völkerwanderung* (1882–1901) are available in English, including, for example, the anonymously translated *Attila the Hun* (New York: Minerva, 1891). Dahn's biggest success was his vivid depiction of the decline of the Ostgotenreich, *Ein Kampf um Rom*, 4 vols. (1876), translated by Lily Wolffsohn as *A Struggle for Rome*, 3 vols. (London: Bentley, 1878).

Gustav Freytag (1816–1895), a German writer and philologist, published texts in *Die Grenzboten* (1848–1870) that describe the upward aspirations of the middle class, reflecting the author's conviction that the bourgeoisie was to be the basis of a new state. Freytag's sober and pedagogically oriented works, suffused by a belief in progress, were very popular. His three-volume realist novel *Soll und Haben* (1855), translated by L. C. Cummings as *Debit and Credit* (New York: Harper, 1858; rpt. New York: Howard Fertig, 1990), depicted social classes of the time in the manner of Dickens and Scott. The multivolume historical novel *Die Ahnen* (Our Forefathers; 1873–1881), which chronicles the development of the German *Volk* from the time of the Germanen through the nineteenth century, was also popular in the United States. See, for example, the two books translated by Mrs. Malcolm for Holt's Leisure Hour Series, *Ingo* (New York: Holt & Williams, 1873) and *Ingraban* (New York: Henry Holt, 1873).

16. Wilhelm Michel, *Martin Buber: Sein Gang in die Wirklichkeit* (Frankfurt: Rütten und Loening, 1926), 12.

17. Stefan George, *Der Stern des Bundes* (Berlin: Georg Bondi, 1914); translated by Olga Marx and Ernst Morwitz as "The Star of the Covenant," in *The Works of Stefan George* (Chapel Hill: University of North Carolina Press, 1949; rev. ed. 1974), 243–278.

18. Wagner's subtitle and genre designation for *Parsifal.*

19. Martin Buber, *Ich und Du* (Berlin: Schocken, 1922); translated by Ronald Gregor Smith as *I and Thou* (New York: Scribners, 1937), and, more recently, by Walter Kaufmann (New York: Scribners, 1970). See also Kracauer's extended 1923 review essay entitled "Martin Buber," reprinted in *Schriften* 5, pt. 1, 236–242.

20. Emil Kautzsch (1841–1910), a German Protestant theologian, held professorships in Basel, Tübingen, and Halle. A follower of Wellhausen, he edited the *Hebräische Grammatik* by Friedrich Gesenius (revised in accordance with the 28th German edition of 1909 by A. E. Cowley as *Gesenius' Hebrew Grammar* [Oxford: Clarendon Press, 1980]) and also translated and edited *Die Apokryphen und Pseudoepigraphen des Alten Testaments,* 2 vols. (Tübingen: Mohr, 1900; rpt. Darmstadt: Wissenschaftliche Buchgesellschaft, 1975).

21. A reference to the subtitle of Wilhelm Michel's previously cited study, *Martin Buber: Sein Gang in die Wirklichkeit.*

22. Buber and Rosenzweig responded to Kracauer's critique of their translation with an essay, "Die Bibel auf Deutsch: Zur Erwiderung" (The Bible in German: A Rebuttal), which was published in slightly abbreviated form in the *Frankfurter Zeitung* 70, no. 363 (May 18, 1926). This text was reprinted in its entirety in Martin Buber and Franz Rosenzweig, *Die Schrift und ihre Verdeutschung* (Berlin: Schocken, 1936), and is now available in a translation by Lawrence Rosenwald with Everett Fox in *Scripture and Translation* (Bloomington: Indiana University Press, 1994), 151–160. Kracauer's equally polemical response to this rebuttal, entitled "Gegen Wen? Duplik" (Against Whom? A Rejoinder), and published together with Buber and Rosenzweig's text in the *Frankfurter Zeitung,* reads in its entirety as follows:

"Against whom is this rebuttal directed? Against the reviewer? But the reviewer never disputed what the authors prove, with their mass of evidence: the fidelity of their reproduction of the text. On the contrary, from the very start of his discussion he both affirmed and appreciated the fact that 'the writers aspire to *literal translation* and rhythmical fidelity.' Moreover, based on the judgment of informed Hebrew scholars, he gladly confirmed that, in the process, the authors had worked in a 'competent and conscientious way.'

Against whom, then, is the frontal assault of such erudition directed?

Detached, a mere spectator, the reviewer follows a philological bombardment which seems to take place for purely demonstrative purposes, since far and wide there is no antagonist to be seen. But the authors, modifying their pre-positively placed Goethe [Buber and Rosenzweig's rebuttal began with a line from Goethe's discussions with Eckermann: 'I have always found that it is good to know something'], perhaps think it is always good to show one's knowledge.

In their desire to demonstrate that knowledge they seem, in any case, to have forgotten the objections that were in need of rebuttal. What the review objected to was not an arbitrary treatment of the Hebrew text, but rather the under-taking of a literal translation without commentary. Did the reviewer raise any doubts that the surging that brooded everywhere above the waters sought to recreate the original word for word? Did he suspect either the uplifted high-gifts or the 'ruler, you a ruler over us' of being disrespectful of the Hebrew words? What he did was to consider these and the other examples as *German*-language creations, recognizing some of them as posthumous offspring of Bayreuthian poesy. The fact that such formulations, in the combinations favored by the authors, emanate from the archaic climates of bourgeois neo-Romanticism, is a birth defect that the always tiresome appeal to their earlier usage is by no means able to eradicate.

Of course, in order to gauge the transformation that the meanings of the words have undergone, their *sociological* determinations also have to be taken into account. The authors refuse to do so, and not without some contempt. As a result, they claim that contemporary imperatives motivate their adoption of the alliterations; they construe Luther's line about the 'castle and court words' according to their own needs, whereas in reality Luther's move to 'old folk language' *[altvolkstümlichen Wortgut]* is a turn to the profane that goes in a direction opposite to theirs. One recalls the famous passage in the 'Open Letter on Translation': 'For one must not ask the Latin letters how one should speak German, as these asses do, but rather should ask the mother in the home, the children on the streets, the common man in the marketplace. We should listen to their language, the way they speak, and translate accordingly' [Martin Luther, 'Sendebrief vom Dolmetschen' (1530)].

It would be good to know something about things sociological.

Against whom, then, are the objections in the review directed? Against the German linguistic form of the translation and thereby against its *intention*. If the literally faithful rendition of the text gives birth to linguistic excrescences like 'slaughterplace' and 'cultmaiden' *[Weihbuhle]*, then the intention behind this literally faithful rendition is dubious in the sense demonstrated by the review. This 'faithful' reproduction is not at all faithful, because it wants to confer the unmediated power of the original onto words and linguistic configurations that now serve only as signs of a specific period in our past. The reviewer agrees with the authors' opinion that language must 'be completely present, completely for today, completely—spoken.' But *ohnemaß* ('without measure') is not one of 'today's words,' and neither are, for example, the semantic interpretations of the names (Jacob = *Fersehalt*) free of restorative efforts.

The authors have failed to recognize the anachronistic nature of their translation. They obviously enjoy such a happy independence from their time that they believe they can afford to overlook the particular imperatives of our current 'metaphysical and sociological' situation (the adjectives, by your leave, were formulated by the authors). Their detachment from their time may well also account for both their inability to grasp the aesthetic effect of their translative endeavor, and their obliviousness to its reactionary meaning, which the reviewer ascribed to the Germanization fully aware of the literary work and other sundry activities of its authors. It would be good to know something about one's time.

Despite the fact that the rebuttal rebuts nothing, it is not totally useless. It unintentionally supports the reviewer with an accommodation which he never would have dared supply. In its outline it is a commentary which, as such, has the gift of exorcism. By articulating what was meant in and through the terms, it drives the arrogant spirits out of the words that they had possessed. The 'literal' translation, which wants to present the text, blocks one's view of it; the philological exegesis, which would have improved on 'cultmaiden' by employing 'hierodule' instead, opens access to an understanding of it. Did the reviewer deny the legitimacy of a *work of commentary?* Or did he not, on the contrary, draw the conclusion that besides the Luther Bible today only a *critical textual edition* was possible 'which, for instance, would bring Kautzsch up to the current state of modern Jewish scriptural research'? No one would have been more grateful to the authors for their modesty in their sober scholarly work than the reviewer. For he, too, feels that it is good to know something.

In closing, the authors proclaim in an exalted voice that every era stands in an antagonistic relation to the 'word.' But the reviewer whom they accuse of blasphemy claimed nothing other than this. He merely went on to consider, admittedly, how the word would have to be fashioned in *our* time, in order to attack the extant as an instrument of truth. Will the recently deceased German of the translation retain such powers? The reviewer will refrain from giving an answer. He does not want to be suspected of being an Egyptian soothsayer."

Catholicism and Relativism

1. Max Scheler, *Vom Ewigen im Menschen*, vol. 1: *Religiöse Erneuerung* (Leipzig: Der Neue Geist, 1921); reprinted as vol. 5 of Scheler, *Gesammelte Werke* (Bern:

Francke, 1954–1968). The fourth, revised edition was translated by Bernard Noble as *On the Eternal in Man* (London: Student Christian Movement Press, 1960). Scheler originally conceived of the work as three volumes, but completed only one.

See also Kracauer's 1917 reviews of Scheler's *Krieg und Aufbau* (1916) in *Schriften* 5, pt. 1, 23–27; his 1928 obituary "Max Scheler" in *Schriften* 5, pt. 2, 112–117; and his 1932 discussion of *Die Idee des Friedens und der Pazifismus* (1931) in *Schriften* 5, pt. 3, 19–22.

2. The subtitle, "Religiöse Erneuerung" (Religious Renewal), which is also the title of the introductory section of the essay "Problems of Religion," originally designated the first volume of the planned three-part work. Since Scheler never wrote the remaining volumes, the subtitle has been dropped in later editions of the book.

3. *Vom Ewigen im Menschen*, 101–354; *On the Eternal in Man*, 105–356. As Scheler's widow, Maria, explains in an "Editorial Notice" included in the translation, this was the central section of the book, and was placed at the end in the first edition only for pragmatic reasons: Scheler had not yet completed the text when it went to press, and thus the publisher put it at the back in order to proceed with the production of the book. In subsequent editions it forms the centerpiece of the collection which, so the notice explains, was Scheler's original intention. Prior to its inclusion in the book, however, the introductory essay to this section was published as "Zur religiösen Erneuerung," in *Hochland* 16, no. 1 (October 1918): 5–21.

4. *Vom Ewigen im Menschen*, 8; *On the Eternal in Man*, 12. In Scheler's text, the two italicized words are simply in quotation marks.

5. *Vom Ewigen im Menschen*, 8; *On the Eternal in Man*, 13. The emphasis is Kracauer's.

6. A type of philosophical monism developed as a natural-science variant of theistic idealism by the English philosopher and psychologist James Ward (1843–1925). See Ward, *The Realm of Ends, or, Pluralism and Theism* (New York: Putnam's, 1911).

7. Karl Friedrich Hieronymus Freiherr von Münchhausen (1720–1797), a German raconteur known as the "Liar-Baron" for the tales of his exploits as soldier, hunter, and sportsman in foreign lands. A selection of these, attributed to him and published in 1781–1783 as *Vademecum für lustige Leute*, formed the basis for a later, anonymous volume brought out by Rudolf Erich Raspe in London in 1785. It was this collection, and the many later editions that followed the effectively canonical British edition of 1793 titled *The Adventures of Baron Munchhausen*, that came to be virtually synonymous with the genre of the "tall tale."

8. The following note in the first publication of this text was dropped in the 1963

reprint: "An article by Dr. Otto Gründler, 'Die Bedeutung der Phänomenologie für das Geistesleben' [The Significance of Phenomenology for the Life of the Spirit/Mind], which appeared in the October [1921] issue of the journal *Hochland*, demonstrates that in some Catholic circles people have not yet realized the limited significance of phenomenological philosophy or its actual meaning." See also Kracauer's review of Gründler, *Elemente zu einer Religionsphilosophie auf phänomenologischer Grundlage*, introd. Max Scheler (Munich: Josef Kösel, 1922); the review was published as "Religion und Phänomenologie," in *Frankfurter Zeitung* 67, no. 49 (January 19, 1923), Literaturblatt, 1–2.

9. "Reue und Wiedergeburt" (1917), in *Vom Ewigen im Menschen*, 27–59; "Repentance and Rebirth," in *On the Eternal in Man*, 33–65.

10. *Vom Ewigen im Menschen*, 279–285; *On the Eternal in Man*, 284–290.

The Crisis of Science

1. The original version of this essay in the *Frankfurter Zeitung* of March 8 and March 22, 1923, opened with the following editorial remark, which was dropped when the essay was republished: "The essay below had already been completed when the painful report of Ernst Troeltsch's untimely death arrived. The loss of Troeltsch deprives German science of a scholar armed with all the historical, philosophical, and theological knowledge of his time. This was a man who, thanks to his fortunate combination of research and creative gifts, had the rare ability to grasp the larger contexts of European intellectual history without getting lost in the excess of the material. It goes without saying that the scientific achievements of this comprehensive intellect—a spirit that remained lively and stimulating till the very end—are in no way diminished by the following critique of his world view."

2. Ernst Troeltsch, *Der Historismus und seine Probleme*, in *Gesammelte Schriften*, vol. 3 (Tübingen: Mohr, 1922; rpt. Aalen: Scientia Verlag, 1961). The first volume that Kracauer discusses, subtitled "Das logische Problem der Geschichtsphilosophie" (The Logical Problem of the Philosophy of History), was in fact the only volume of the study ever completed. This work by the German theologian, philosopher, and historian Troeltsch (1865–1923) is available in an unsigned typescript translation entitled *Historism and Its Problems*, which was published as such by J. C. B. Mohr (Tübingen) in 1922. The English-language reader can also consult the 1923 text "Ethics and the Philosophy of History," in Troeltsch, *Christian Thought: Its History and Application*, ed. and introd. Baron F. von Hügel (New York: Meriden, 1957), 65–146. The volume contains three lectures written for the University of London which are, as Hügel explains in the introduction, "anticipations of what was to

have been the central theme of the second volume of *The Historical Standpoint and Its Problems*, a volume all unwritten excepting the sketch here presented" (15). Starting with *Protestantism and Progress* (Philadelphia: Fortress, 1986), one of the first of Troeltsch's works to appear in English (in a translation by W. Montgomery in 1912), a number of other works have also been translated, including *The Social Teachings of the Christian Churches*, trans. Olive Wyon (Louisville, Ky.: Westminister and John Knox, 1992); *Writings on Theology and Religion*, tr. and ed. Robert Morgan and Michael Pye (London: Duckworth, 1977); *The Absoluteness of Christianity and the History of Religions*, trans. David Reid (Richmond: John Knox Press, 1971); and *Religion in History*, trans. James Luther Adams and Walter F. Bense (Minneapolis: Fortress, 1991).

3. *Der Historismus und seine Probleme*, 164ff.; *Historism and Its Problems*, 261ff.
4. *Der Historismus und seine Probleme*, 178; *Historism and Its Problems*, 281.
5. *Der Historismus und seine Probleme*, 168; *Historism and Its Problems*, 265–266.
6. *Der Historismus und seine Probleme*, 184; *Historism and Its Problems*, 289.
7. *Der Historismus und seine Probleme*, 178–179; *Historism and Its Problems*, 281.
8. *Der Historismus und seine Probleme*, 565; *Historism and Its Problems*, 883–884. See also Troeltsch's 1920 memorial tribute, "Max Weber," in the collection of his essays and speeches *Deutscher Geist und Westeuropa*, ed. Hans Baron (Tübingen: Mohr, 1925; rpt. Aalen: Scientia Verlag, 1966), 247–252; translated as "Max Weber," in *Religion in History*, 360–364.
9. Max Weber, *Gesammelte Aufsätze zur Wissenschafislehre*, ed. Johannes Winckelmann (Tübingen: Mohr, 1922, 1985). Besides "Science as Vocation" (cited below) a number of the studies contained in this collection have been published in English translation in various volumes, including Max Weber, *The Methodology of the Social Sciences*, trans. E. Shils and H. Finch (Glencoe, Ill.: Free Press, 1949) (this volume contains "The Meaning of 'Ethical Neutrality' in Sociology and Economics," " 'Objectivity' in Social Science and Social Policy," and "The Logic of the Cultural Sciences"); Max Weber, *Critique of Stammler*, trans. and introd. G. Oakes (New York: Free Press, 1977); and Max Weber, *Roscher and Knies: The Logical Problems of Historical Economics*, trans. and introd. G. Oakes (New York: Free Press, 1975).
10. Weber, "Wissenschaft als Beruf" (1919), in *Gesammelte Aufsätze zur Wissenschafislehre*, 582–613; in English, "Science as a Vocation" can be found in *From Max Weber: Essays in Sociology*, trans., ed., and introd. H. H. Gerth and C. Wright Mills (New York: Oxford University Press, 1946), 129–156. Compare also the translation by Michael John in *Max Weber's "Science as a Vocation,"* ed. Peter Lassman and Irving Velody, with Herminio Martins (London: Unwin Hyman, 1989), 3–31.
11. *Gesammelte Aufsätze zur Wissenschafislehre*, 611. Compare also the translations

of this passage in *From Max Weber: Essays in Sociology*, 154; and in *Max Weber's "Science as a Vocation,"* 29.

12. Troeltsch, *Der Historismus und seine Probleme*, 567; *Historism and Its Problems*, 886.

13. Max Weber's "Die protestantische Ethik und der Geist des Kapitalismus" was first published in the *Archiv für Sozialwissenschaft und Sozialpolitik* 20, no. 1 (1904): 1–54; and 21, no. 1 (1905): 1–110. The English translation by Talcott Parsons, *The Protestant Ethic and the Spirit of Capitalism* (New York: Scribner's, 1930; rpt. 1976), is based on a revised edition published just after Weber's death in the *Gesammelte Aufsätze zur Religionssoziologie*, vol. 1 (Tübingen: Mohr, 1920–21; rpt. 1947), 17–206. Kracauer's dating of the original publication as 1901 (added when the essay was reprinted in the 1963 edition) is thus mistaken.

Georg Simmel

1. *Über sociale Differenzierung: Sociologische und psychologische Untersuchungen* (Leipzig: Duncker & Humblot, 1890), reprinted in *Gesamtausgabe*, vol. 2, ed. Heinz-Jürgen Dahme (Frankfurt: Suhrkamp Verlag, 1989), 109–295.

2. *Philosophie des Geldes* (Leipzig: Duncker & Humblot, 1900). The second, enlarged edition of 1907 was reprinted as vol. 6 of the *Gesamtausgabe*, ed. David P. Frisby and K. C. Köhnke (Frankfurt: Suhrkamp Verlag, 1989). It was translated by Tom Bottomore and David Frisby from a first draft by Kaethe Mengelberg as *The Philosophy of Money* (London: Routledge & Kegan Paul, 1978; 2nd enlarged ed. London: Routledge, 1990). *Soziologie: Untersuchungen über die Formen der Vergesellschaftung* (Leipzig: Duncker & Humblot, 1908); reprinted as *Gesamtausgabe*, vol. 11, ed. Otthein Rammstedt (Frankfurt: Suhrkamp Verlag, 1992). Though untranslated in its entirety, many chapters from *Soziologie* are available in English in *The Sociology of Georg Simmel*, ed., trans., and introd. Kurt Wolff (Glencoe, Ill.: Free Press, 1950), 87–408.

3. *Philosophie der Mode* (Berlin: Pan-Verlag, 1905); revised version titled "Die Mode," in *Philosophische Kultur* (Leipzig: Klinkhardt, 1911; rpt. 1923), 31–64, translated anonymously as "Fashion," in Donald N. Levine, ed., *Georg Simmel: On Individuality and Social Forms* (Chicago: University of Chicago Press, 1971), 294–323; "Die Koketterie" (1909), in *Philosophische Kultur*, 104–125, translated by Guy Oakes as "Flirtation," in *Georg Simmel: On Women, Sexuality and Love* (New Haven: Yale University Press, 1984), 133–152; "Soziologie der Geselligkeit" (1911), *Grundfragen der Soziologie: Individuum und Gesellschaft* (Berlin: Göschen, 1917; 4th ed. Berlin: de Gruyter, 1984), 48–68, translated by Everett C. Hughes as "Sociability," in *On Individuality and Social Forms*,

127–140, and also translated by Kurt H. Wolff as "Sociability: An Example of Pure, or Formal, Sociology," in *The Sociology of Georg Simmel*, 40–57.

4. See, for example, *Philosophie des Geldes*, ch. 6, pt. 2 ("Die Arbeitsteilung als Ursache für das Auseinandertreten der subjektiven und der objektiven Kultur"), 645–654; *Philosophy of Money*, ch. 6, sec. 2 ("The division of labour as the cause of the divergence of subjective and objective culture"), 453–463.

5. "Weibliche Kultur" (1902), *Philosophische Kultur*, 268–311, translated as "Female Culture," in *On Women, Sexuality and Love*, 65–101; selections on the miser from *Philosophie des Geldes*, 318–321, translated by Roberta Ash as "The Miser and the Spendthrift," in *On Individuality and Social Forms*, 179–186; "Das Abenteuer" (1910), in *Philosophische Kultur*, 13–30, translated by David Kettler as "The Adventure," in Kurt H. Wolff, ed., *Georg Simmel, 1858–1918* (Columbus: Ohio State University Press, 1959), 243–258; also in *On Individuality and Social Forms*, 187–198.

6. *Kant: Sechzehn Vorlesungen, gehalten an der Berliner Universität* (Leipzig: Duncker & Humblot, 1904); *Die Probleme der Geschichtsphilosophie: Eine erkenntnistheoretische Studie* (Leipzig: Duncker & Humblot, 1892; rpt. in *Gesamtausgabe* 2, 297–421); the second edition of 1905 was translated by Guy Oakes as *The Problems of the Philosophy of History: An Epistemological Essay* (New York: Free Press, 1977).

7. *Einleitung in die Moralwissenschaft: Eine Kritik der ethischen Grundbegriffe*, 2 vols. (Berlin: Hertz, 1892–1893); reprinted as *Gesamtausgabe*, vols. 3–4, ed. K. C. Köhnke (Frankfurt: Suhrkamp Verlag, 1989–1991).

8. "Das individuelle Gesetz: Ein Versuch über das Prinzip der Ethik" (1913), in *Lebensanschauung: Vier metaphysische Kapitel* (Munich: Duncker & Humblot, 1918), 154–245; reprinted in Simmel, *Das individuelle Gesetz*, ed. Michael Landmann (Frankfurt: Suhrkamp Verlag, 1987), 174–230.

9. *Kant: Sechzehn Vorlesungen; Schopenhauer und Nietzsche: Ein Vortragszyklus* (Leipzig: Duncker & Humblot, 1907), translated by Helmut Loiskandl, Deena Weinstein, and Michael Weinstein as *Schopenhauer and Nietzsche* (Amherst: University of Massachusetts Press, 1986); *Goethe* (Leipzig: Klinkhardt und Biermann, 1913).

10. "Michelangelo," in *Philosophische Kultur*, 152–178; "Rodin," in *Philosophische Kultur*, 179–197; *Rembrandt: Ein kunstphilosophischer Versuch* (Leipzig: Kurt Wolff, 1916; rpt. Munich: Matthes & Seitz, 1985).

11. "Der Henkel," *Philosophische Kultur*, 126–134, translated by Rudolph H. Weingartner as "The Handle," in *Georg Simmel, 1858–1918*, 267–275; "Die Ruine," in *Philosophische Kultur*, 135–143, translated by David Kettler as "The Ruin," in *Georg Simmel, 1858–1918*, 259–266.

12. *Die Religion* (Frankfurt: Rütten & Loening, 1906), translated by Curt Rosenthal

as *Sociology of Religion* (New York: Philosophical Library, 1959; rpt. New York: Arno Press, 1979).

13. "Vom Subjekt und Objekt," in *Hauptprobleme der Philosophie* (Leipzig: Göschen, 1910), 86–112.

14. *Philosophie des Geldes*, ch. 6, "Der Stil des Lebens," 591–716; *Philosophy of Money*, ch. 6, "The Style of Life," 429–512.

15. *Einleitung in die Moralwissenschaft*, in *Gesamtausgabe*, vol. 3, 375ff.

16. *Philosophie des Geldes*, ch. 3, esp. 318–321 and 334–337; *On Individuality and Social Forms*, 179–186; *Philosophy of Money*, ch. 3, esp. "The Blasé Attitude," 256–257.

17. The first line of Goethe's late, untitled poem, "Gedichte sind gemalte Fensterscheiben," in Goethe, *Gedenkausgabe der Werke, Briefe und Gespräche*, ed. Ernst Beutler, vol. 1 (Zurich: Artemis, 1949), 569; translated by Joseph Height in *Gold of Goethe: Selected Lyric Poems* (Evanston: Schori Press, 1964), 123.

18. Here, at the end of the paragraph, Kracauer adds a dash of the sort normally reserved for signaling a break in the train of thought *within* paragraphs. The latter type of dash, analogous in function to a paragraph break but less emphatic, here serves to introduce further gradations of semantic rupture in the space of the paragraph break itself.

19. "Der Arme," *Soziologie*, 512–555, translated by Claire Jacobson as "The Poor," in *On Individuality and Social Forms*, 150–178; "Exkurs über den Fremden," in *Soziologie*, 764–771, translated by Donald N. Levine as "The Stranger," in *On Individuality and Social Forms*, 143–149, and translated by Kurt Wolff in *The Sociology of Georg Simmel*, 402–408; "Das Geheimnis und die geheime Gesellschaft," in *Soziologie*, 383–455, translated by Kurt Wolff as "The Secret and the Secret Society," in *The Sociology of Georg Simmel*, 307–378.

20. "Über Kollektivverantwortlichkeit" (1890), in *Über soziale Differenzierung*, 139–168; "Die Erweiterung der Gruppe und die Ausbildung der Individualität," in *Soziologie*, 791–863, translated by Richard P. Albares as "Group Expansion and the Development of Individuality," in *On Individuality and Social Forms*, 251–293; "Das soziale Niveau" (1890), in *Über soziale Differenzierung*, 199–236; "Uber die Kreuzung sozialer Kreise" (1890), in *Über soziale Differenzierung*, 237–257, translated by Reinhard Bendix as "The Web of Group Affiliations," in Georg Simmel, *Conflict and the Web of Group-Affiliations* (Glencoe, Ill.: Free Press, 1955), 125–195; "Die quantitative Bestimmtheit der Gruppe," in *Soziologie*, 63–159, translated by Kurt Wolff as "Quantitative Aspects of the Group," in *The Sociology of Georg Simmel*, 87–177; "Über- und Unterordnung," in *Soziologie*, 160–283, translated by Kurt Wolff as "Superordination and Subordination," in *The Sociology of Georg Simmel*, 181–303.

21. "Das soziale und das individuelle Niveau (Beispiel der Allgemeinen Soziolo-

gie)," in *Grundfragen der Soziologie*, 32–48, translated by Kurt Wolff as "The Social and the Individual Level (An Example of General Sociology)," in *The Sociology of Georg Simmel*, 26–39.

22. "Das soziale und das individuelle Niveau," in *Grundfragen der Soziologie*, 44, translated by Kurt Wolff as "The Social and the Individual Level," in *The Sociology of Georg Simmel*, 37.

23. "Über die Kreuzung sozialer Kreise," *Über sociale Differenzierung*, 237–257; "The Web of Group Affiliations," *Conflict and the Web of Group-Affiliations*, 125–195; "Das Abenteuer," *Philosophische Kultur*, 13–30; "The Adventure," *Georg Simmel, 1858–1918*, 243–258.

24. Simmel's essay "Society" is "Exkurs über das Problem: Wie ist Gesellschaft möglich?" in *Soziologie*, 42–61, translated by Kurt Wolff as "How Is Society Possible?" in *Georg Simmel, 1858–1918*, 337–356. But the passage Kracauer refers to here occurs in "Soziologie der Geselligkeit," in *Grundfragen der Soziologie*, 53; "Sociability," in *On Individuality and Social Forms*, 130. In both cases the phrase is in italics and strictly speaking modifies not society but sociability.

25. "Der Henkel," *Philosophische Kultur*, 126–134; "The Handle," *Georg Simmel, 1858–1918*, 267–275.

26. "Soziologie der Geselligkeit," in *Grundfragen der Soziologie*, 48–68; "Sociability," in *On Individuality and Social Forms*, 127–140.

27. "Die Mode," in *Philosophische Kultur*, 34; compare "Fashion," in *On Individuality and Social Forms*, 297.

28. "Die Mode," in *Philosophische Kultur*, 40; this passage is missing in the edited translation "Fashion," in *On Individuality and Social Forms*.

29. "Die Mode," in *Philosophische Kultur*, 41; compare "Fashion," in *On Individuality and Social Forms*, 302.

30. "Die Mode," in *Philosophische Kultur*, 43; compare "Fashion," in *On Individuality and Social Forms*, 304.

31. "Die Mode," in *Philosophische Kultur*, 52; compare "Fashion," in *On Individuality and Social Forms*, 312.

32. *Philosophie des Geldes*, 12; *Philosophy of Money*, 55.

33. *Rembrandt*, VII.

34. Organized around a series of philosophical topoi, *Hauptprobleme der Philosophie* touches on a wide range of philosophers, including the ancient Greeks, the mystics, Spinoza, and Hegel.

35. [Author's note] In the lectures on Kant, one reads: "The form of his (Kant's) own presentation must be completely destroyed . . ." [*Kant*, 3] in order, namely, for its transindividual content to shine forth for us.

36. *Rembrandt*, 2.

37. *Goethe*, 10.
38. In a concluding note, Kracauer explains: "This study, which was published in *Logos* in 1920, is the introductory chapter of an unpublished book on Simmel." Although the Simmel monograph remained unpublished during Kracauer's lifetime, it will finally be available in its entirety in a forthcoming volume of the Kracauer *Schriften*.

On the Writings of Walter Benjamin

1. In the 1963 republication in book form, the reference to the publisher is replaced by a simple temporal designation: "Recently . . ."
2. Walter Benjamin, *Ursprung des deutschen Trauerspiels* (Berlin: Rowohlt, 1928); reprinted in *Gesammelte Schriften* (hereafter referred to as *GS*), vol. 1 (Frankfurt: Suhrkamp Verlag, 1974), 203–430, translated by John Osborne as *The Origin of the German Tragic Drama* (London: Verso, 1985); *Einbahnstraße* (Berlin: Rowohlt, 1928), reprinted in *GS* 4, 83–148, translated by Edmund Jephcott and Kingsley Shorter as *One Way Street* (London: New Left Books, 1979).
3. Benjamin, *Ursprung*, in *GS* 1, 228; *Origin of the German Tragic Drama*, 47. Material in brackets inserted by Kracauer within the quotation.
4. Daniel Caspers von Lohenstein, "Redender Todtenkopf Herrn Matthäus Machners," from *Hyacinthen*, in *Blumen 1* (Breslau, 1708), 50; cited in Benjamin, *Ursprung*, in *GS* 1, 391; *Origin of the German Tragic Drama*, 215.
5. Compare Soren Kierkegaard, *The Point of View of My Work as an Author*, trans. Walter Lowrie (New York: Harper, 1962), 87. For an overview of Kierkegaard's thematic use of the figure of the *geheime Agenter* or *hemmelige Agenter* ("secret agent") and *Spion* ("spy"), consult the editor's introduction to Kierkegaard's *Philosophical Fragments: Johannes Climacus*, trans. and ed. Howard V. Hong and Edna H. Hong (Princeton, N.J.: Princeton University Press, 1985), XI, n. 9; and idem, *Fear and Trembling: Repetition*, trans. and ed. Howard V. Hong and Edna H. Hong (Princeton, N.J.: Princeton University Press, 1983), 364, n. 10.
6. Benjamin, who had envisioned a collection of his aphorisms as early as 1924, had sent a selection to Kracauer for publication in the *Frankfurter Zeitung*. Kracauer was able to place two groups of aphorisms—"Kleine Illuminationen" (*Frankfurter Zeitung* 70, no. 273 [April 14, 1926]) and "Häfen und Jahrmarkte" (*Frankfurter Zeitung* 70, no. 502 [July 9, 1926])—both of which are reprinted in facsimile in Walter Benjamin, *Briefe an Siegfried Kracauer*, ed. Theodor W. Adorno Archiv (Marbach: Deutsche Schillergesellschaft, 1987), 93–100; see also *GS* 4, pt. 2, 913. In a letter to Kracauer dated April 20, 1926, Benjamin expresses his delight at the publication of the "Small Illuminations" and thanks

Kracauer effusively for having come up with such a perfect title (Benjamin, *Briefe an Siegfried Kracauer*, 17).

The phrase mentioning that some of the texts in *One Way Street* had appeared in the *Frankfurter Zeitung*, and the parenthetical remark set off by commas in the next sentence, were both dropped by Kracauer in the first edition of *Das Ornament der Masse* in 1963. In all subsequent (posthumous) editions, both omissions have been restored by the editors.

7. French in original.

8. Benjamin, "Kaiserpanorama," in *Einbahnstraße*, in *GS* 4, 94–101; *One Way Street*, 54–60.

9. Benjamin, "Tankstelle," in *GS* 4, 85; "Filling Station," in *One Way Street*, 45. Word in square brackets added by Kracauer within the quotation.

10. In the 1963 republication, the following paragraph break is omitted; it is reinserted in all later editions.

11. Benjamin, "Kriegerdenkmal," in *GS* 4, 121; "Monument to a Warrior," in *One Way Street*, 79.

12. Marcel Proust, *Im Schatten der jungen Mädchen*, trans. Walter Benjamin and Franz Hessel (Berlin: Die Schmiede, 1927), reprinted in *GS*, supplemental vol. 2, ed. Hella Tiedemann-Bartels (Frankfurt: Suhrkamp Verlag, 1987); Marcel Proust, *Die Herzogin von Guermantes*, trans. Walter Benjamin and Franz Hessel (Munich: Piper, 1930), reprinted in *GS*, supplemental vol. 3, ed. Hella Tiedemann-Bartels (Frankfurt: Suhrkamp Verlag, 1987).

13. Benjamin, *Ursprung*, in *GS* 1, 212; *Origin of the German Tragic Drama*, 32.

14. Benjamin, "Kriegerdenkmal," in *GS* 4, 121; "Monument to a Warrior," in *One Way Street*, 79.

Franz Kafka

1. Franz Kafka, *Beim Bau der chinesischen Mauer: Ungedruckte Erzählungen und Prosa aus dem Nachlaß*, ed. Max Brod and Hans Joachim Schoeps (Berlin: Gustav Kiepenheuer Verlag, 1931; rpt. Weimar, 1948, and Gustav Kiepenheuer Bücherei, 1982); in English *The Great Wall of China: Stories and Reflections*, trans. Willa Muir and Edwin Muir (London: Martin Secker, 1933; rpt. New York: Schocken, 1946, 1970). Compare also the translation by Malcolm Pasley of virtually the same collection of texts under the title *Shorter Works*, vol. 1 (London: Secker & Warburg, 1973). Since *The Great Wall of China* is no longer in print in the United States, its contents having been absorbed into collections of Kafka's complete stories, the citations below will refer—except in the case of the aphorisms—to the readily available collection *Franz Kafka: The Complete Stories*, ed. Nahum Glatzer (New

York: Schocken, 1983), hereafter referred to as *CS*, and its approximate German equivalent, *Sämtliche Erzählungen*, ed. Paul Raabe (Frankfurt: Fischer Verlag, 1970), hereafter referred to as *SE*. References will also be given to the *Gesammelte Werke*, 12 vols., ed. Hans-Gerd Koch (Frankfurt: Fischer Verlag, 1994), hereafter referred to as *GW*.

Upon its first publication in the *Frankfurter Zeitung* in 1931, Kracauer's essay carried two slightly different titles: in the local Frankfurt edition of the paper it was titled "On Franz Kafka's Posthumous Writings," whereas in the national *Reichsausgabe* it ran as "Franz Kafka: On His Posthumous Writings." The latter subtitle, missing in both editions of *Das Ornament der Masse*, was restored when the essay was reprinted in Kracauer, *Schriften* (Frankfurt: Suhrkamp Verlag, 1990), vol. 5, pt. 2, 363–373.

2. Kafka, *Nachgelassene Schriften und Fragmente*, vol. 2, ed. Jost Schillemeit (Frankfurt: Fischer Verlag, 1992), 136; *GW*, vol. 2, *Beim Bau der chinesischen Mauer*, 245 (Aphorism 100); *The Great Wall of China*, 182 (Aphorism 96).

3. "Forschungen eines Hundes," in *SE*, 334; untitled in *GW*, vol. 8, *Das Ehepaar*, 63; "Investigations of a Dog," in *CS*, 291.

4. "Der Bau," in *SE*, 359–388; *GW*, vol. 8, 165–200; "The Burrow," in *CS*, 325–359.

5. "Der Dorfschullehrer," in *SE*, 252–264; *GW*, vol. 5, *Beschreibungen eines Kampfes*, 154–170; "The Village Schoolmaster [The Giant Mole]," in *CS*, 168–182.

6. Ibid., in *SE*, 263; *GW*, vol. 5, 169; *CS*, 180.

7. "Forschungen eines Hundes," in *SE*, 330; *GW*, vol. 8, 58; "Investigations of a Dog," in *CS*, 287.

8. *Nachgelassene Schriften und Fragmente* 2, 117; *GW*, vol. 6, 231 (Aphorism 20); "Reflections on Sin, Pain, Hope, and the True Way," in *The Great Wall of China*, 165 (Aphorism 17).

9. "Forschungen eines Hundes," in *SE*, 354; *GW*, vol. 8, 92–93; "Investigations of a Dog," in *CS*, 316.

10. Ibid., in *SE*, 341; *GW*, vol. 8, 72–73; *CS*, 299–300.

11. Ibid., in *SE*, 341; *GW*, vol. 8, 72; *CS*, 299–300.

12. Ibid., in *SE*, 341; *GW*, vol. 8, 73; *CS*, 300.

13. "Das Stadtwappen," in *SE*, 306–307; untitled in *GW*, vol. 7, *Zur Frage der Gesetze*, 143–144, 147; "The City Coat of Arms," in *CS*, 433–434.

14. "Beim Bau der Chinesischen Mauer," in *SE*, 296; *GW*, vol. 6, 75; "The Great Wall of China," in *CS*, 244.

15. "Zur Frage der Gesetze," in *SE*, 314–315; *GW*, vol. 7, 106–108; "The Issue of the Laws," in *CS*, 437–438.

16. Kafka, *Tagebücher*, ed. Hans-Gerd Koch, Michael Müller, and Malcolm Pasley

(Frankfurt: Fischer Verlag, 1990), 856; *GW*, vol. 11, *Tagebücher, 1914–1923*, 180–181; "He: Notes from the Year 1920," *The Great Wall of China*, 156.

17. "Der Schlag ans Hoftor," in *SE*, 299–300; *GW*, vol. 6, 83–85; "The Knock at the Manor Gate," in *CS*, 418–419.

18. "Forschungen eines Hundes," in *SE*, 333; *GW*, vol. 7, 62; "Investigations of a Dog," in *CS*, 290.

19. Ibid., in *SE*, 339; *GW*, vol. 7, 69; *CS*, 297.

20. Ibid., in *SE*, 325; *GW*, vol. 7, 50; *CS*, 279.

21. For Kafka's discussion of the *Lufthunde* (aerial or soaring dogs), see "Forschungen eines Hundes," in *SE*, 336; *GW*, vol. 8, 65; "Investigations of a Dog," in *CS*, 293.

22. Ibid., in *SE*, 334; *GW*, vol. 7, 63; *CS*, 290.

23. Ibid., in *SE*, 333; *GW*, vol. 7, 63; *CS*, 290.

24. Ibid., in *SE*, 328; *GW*, vol. 7, 54; *CS*, 283.

25. Ibid., in *SE*, 352; *GW*, vol. 7, 89; *CS*, 313.

26. Ibid., in *SE*, 332; *GW*, vol. 7, 61; *CS*, 289.

27. Kafka, *Tagebücher*, 855; *GW*, vol. 11, 179; "He: Notes from the Year 1920," in *The Great Wall of China*, 155.

28. Kafka, *Tagebücher*, 855; *GW*, vol. 11, 180; "He: Notes from the Year 1920," in *The Great Wall of China*, 155–156.

29. "Eine alltägliche Verwirrung," in *SE*, 303–304; untitled in *GW*, vol. 6, 165; "A Common Confusion," in *CS*, 429–430.

30. "Die Wahrheit über Sancho Pansa," in *SE*, 304; untitled in *GW*, vol. 6, 167; *CS*, 430.

31. "Der Bau," in *SE*, 370; *GW*, vol. 8, 182; "The Burrow," in *CS*, 338.

32. "Der Kübelreiter," in *SE*, 195–196; *GW*, vol. 1, *Ein Landarzt*, 345–347; "The Bucket Rider," in *CS*, 412–414.

33. Kafka, *Nachgelassene Schriften und Fragmente 2*, 123; *GW*, vol. 6, 235–236 (Aphorism 47); "Reflections on Sin, Pain, Hope, and the True Way," in *The Great Wall of China*, 171 (Aphorism 45).

34. "Forschungen eines Hundes," in *SE*, 331; *GW*, vol. 8, 58; "Investigations of a Dog," in *CS*, 287.

35. "Beim Bau der Chinesischen Mauer," in *SE*, 289–299; *GW*, vol. 6, 65–80; *CS*, 235–248.

36. "Forschungen eines Hundes," in *SE*, 341; *GW*, vol. 8, 73; *CS*, 300.

37. Ibid., in *SE*, 341; *GW*, vol. 8, 72; *CS*, 299.

38. "Beim Bau der Chinesischen Mauer," in *SE*, 291; *GW*, vol. 6, 68; "The Great Wall of China," in *CS*, 238.

39. Ibid., in *SE*, 292; *GW*, vol. 6, 70; *CS*, 239.

40. Ibid., in *SE*, 289; *GW*, vol. 6, 65; *CS*, 235.

41. Ibid.
42. Kracauer plays here with two different meanings of the word *Beschwörung:* "invocation" and "entreaty."
43. "Forschungen eines Hundes," in *SE*, 341; *GW*, vol. 8, 73; "Investigations of a Dog," in *CS*, 300.
44. Kafka, *Nachgelassene Schriften und Fragmente* 2, 113; *GW*, vol. 6, 228 (Aphorism 1); "Reflections on Sin, Pain, Hope, and the True Way," in *The Great Wall of China*, 162 (Aphorism 1).
45. Kafka, *Nachgelassene Schriften und Fragmente* 2, 114; *GW*, vol. 6, 229 (Aphorism 6); "Reflections on Sin, Pain, Hope, and the True Way," in *The Great Wall of China*, 163 (Aphorism 6).
46. "Forschungen eines Hundes," in *SE*, 334; *GW*, vol. 8, 64; "Investigations of a Dog," in *CS*, 291.
47. "Zur Frage der Gesetze," in *SE*, 315; *GW*, vol. 7, 108; "On the Issue of the Laws," in *CS*, 438.
48. Kafka, *Tagebücher*, 860; *GW*, vol. 11, 184; "He: Notes from the Year 1920," in *The Great Wall of China*, 159.
49. "Das Stadtwappen," in *SE*, 307; *GW*, vol. 7, 147; "The City Coat of Arms," in *CS*, 434.
50. Kafka, *Nachgelassene Schriften und Fragmente* 2, 117; *GW*, vol. 6, 231 (Aphorism 17); "Reflections on Sin, Pain, Hope, and the True Way," in *The Great Wall of China*, 165 (Aphorism 14).

Calico-World

1. A large forest in the southwestern section of Berlin.
2. Founded in 1917, the Universum-Film AG (UFA) was the largest company in the German film industry until 1945, with studio complexes in the outlying areas of Berlin-Tempelhof and Berlin-Neubabelsberg. Vertically integrated, UFA owned everything from machine shops and film laboratories to production and distribution facilities. It was acquired by the Hugenberg Group in 1927, nationalized by the German Reich in 1936–1937, and dismantled by the Allies in 1945. On the history of UFA, see Klaus Kreimeier, *Die UFA-Story: Geschichte eines Filmkonzerns* (Munich: Carl Hanser, 1992). For more on the studio in Neubabelsberg, inaugurated by the Deutsche-Bioscope Gesellschaft in 1912, see Wolfgang Jacobsen, *Babelsberg: Ein Filmstudio, 1912–1992* (Berlin: Argon, 1992). The "calico" in the title of Kracauer's essay refers to a cloth of thick cotton weave, imported from India and heavier than muslin, which was used in the construction of the film sets.
3. See Part One of Fritz Lang's 1924 film *Die Nibelungen*, titled *Siegfried*.

4. Carl Mayer's 1925 film *Die Chronik von Grieshus* (Chronicles of the Gray House), based on a Theodor Storm story of the same title, conveyed the atmosphere of an evil medieval saga.

5. Ludwig Berger's 1925 film *Ein Walzertraum* (A Waltz Dream), based on an operetta by Oscar Straus, satirized court life in Vienna and was one of the rare German films that met with success in the United States. Berger (actually Ludwig Bamberger, 1892–1969), an art historian from Mainz, had formerly been an opera and theater director who had worked with Max Reinhardt in Berlin, among others.

6. Tempelhof, an industrial area south of Berlin near the Teltow canal and the site of the first Berlin airport (1923), became one of the first "cinema cities" in 1913, when no less than two film studios—the Literaria studio and Projektions AG Union—built film complexes there, to which the National Film AG added a third in 1919.

7. Emil Jannings as Mephisto in *Faust: Eine deutsche Volkssage* (Friedrich Wilhelm Murnau, 1926).

8. The reference here is to Ludwig Berger's 1923 film *Der verlorene Schuh*.

9. Kracauer here plays on the polyvalence of *Objectiv* which means both "lens" and "objective."

The Little Shopgirls Go to the Movies

1. The tenor of the debates surrounding Eisenstein's *Battleship Potemkin* comes across in the polemical exchange between Oskar Schmitz, who denounced the film, and Walter Benjamin, who defended it enthusiastically. See Schmitz, "Potemkinfilm und Tendenzkunst," in Benjamin, *Gesammelte Schriften*, vol. 2 (Frankfurt: Suhrkamp Verlag, 1977), 1486–1489; and Benjamin, "Erwiderung an Oskar A. H. Schmitz," ibid., 751–755. See also Kracauer's highly favorable 1926 review "Die Jupiterlampen brennen weiter: Zur Frankfurter Aufführung des Potemkin-Films," reprinted in Kracauer, *Kino: Essays, Studien, Glossen zum Film*, ed. Karsten Witte (Frankfurt: Suhrkamp Verlag, 1974), 73–76.

2. The *Generalanzeiger* newspapers combined general news and information ("official" marriage, death, and court settlement announcements) with an extensive advertising section. They were nondenominational, more or less politically independent, and flourished in most major towns in Germany starting in the later decades of the nineteenth century.

3. *Don Q., Son of Zorro* (Donald Crisp, 1925).

4. As one of the judges in a 1927 poetry contest organized by the journal *Literarische Welt* (Literary World), Brecht voted for a poem by the cyclist Hannes Küpper, who was not even a participant in the competition. See

Bertolt Brecht, "Kurzer Bericht über 400 junge Lyriker" (1927), reprinted in Brecht, *Gesammelte Werke in acht Bänden*, vol. 8 (Frankfurt: Suhrkamp Verlag, 1967), 54–56.

5. A great admirer of boxing, Bertolt Brecht had planned to write a biography of the former German heavyweight boxing champion Paul Samson-Körner. In the end, he completed only a fragment, which was published in 1926 in *Scherls Magazine*. See "Der Lebenslauf des Boxers Samson-Körner," in Brecht, *Gesammelte Werke*, vol. 2 (Frankfurt: Suhrkamp Verlag, 1967), 121–144. A wide-ranging treatment of the topic can be found in David Bathrick, "Boxing as an Icon of Weimar Culture," *New German Critique* 51 (Fall 1990): 113–136.

6. Kracauer here employs the slang term *Milljöh*, a phonetic rendering of the pronunciation in Berlin dialect of the French word *milieu*, meaning a specific locale or quarter. Heinrich Zille (1858–1929) was a German social caricaturist who captured the poor, proletarian areas of Berlin in striking, sympathetic images and short phrases of typical Berlin dialect. See also his posthumously discovered photographs of old Berlin, *Mein Photo-Milljöh*, ed. Friedrich Luft (Hannover: Fackelträger, 1967).

7. *Die Verrufenen* (Gerhard Lamprecht, 1925).

8. Reference to the title of the important 1903 study by Otto Weininger, *Geschlecht und Charakter: Eine prinzipielle Untersuchung* (Vienna: Braumüller; rpt. Munich: Matthes & Seitz, 1980), available in an "authorized translation from the 6th German edition" as *Sex and Character* (New York: Putnam's, 1906; rpt. New York: AMS Press, 1975).

9. *Das Mäde auf der Schaukel* (Felix Basch, 1926).

10. Kracauer here plays on the near-homophony of *schwül* (sultry, steamy) and *schwul* (homosexual, "gay"), between which, as he puts it, one can hear quartertones.

11. *Hotel Imperial* (Mauritz Stiller, 1927).

12. *Volk in Not: Ein Heldenlied von Tannenberg* (Wolfgang Neff, 1925).

13. *Fridericus Rex:* Part 1, *Sturm und Drang;* Part 2, *Vater und Sohn* (Arzen von Cserépy, 1920–1922).

14. Werner Sombart (1863–1941), *Händler und Helden: Patriotische Besinnungen* (Munich: Duncker & Humblot, 1915).

15. *Der Flug um den Erdball*, Part 1: *Indien—Europa* (Dr. Willi Wolff, 1924).

16. Count Hermann Alexander von Keyserling (1880–1946), *Das Reisetagebuch eines Philosophen* (Darmstadt: Reichl, 1919; rpt. München: Langen, 1980), 8; translated by J. Holroyd Reece as *Travel Diary of a Philosopher*, 2 vols. (London: Jonathan Cape, 1925), vol. 1, 17.

17. *Wien-Berlin: Ein Liebesspiel zwischen Spree und Donau* (Hans Steinhoff, 1926).

18. Haroun al Raschid (763–809) was the caliph of Baghdad during the period

when the majority of the stories that would compose the *Thousand and One Nights* were written.

19. *Her Night of Romance* (Sidney A. Franklin, 1924).
20. *Le Prince Charmant* (Victor Tourjansky, 1925).
21. *Das alte Ballhaus* (Wolfgang Neff, 1925).
22. *Das Mädchen mit der Protektion* (Max Mack, 1925).
23. *Eine Dubarry von heute* (Alexander Korda, 1926).

Film 1928

1. Through the actions of his investment collective, the *Wirtschaftsvereinigung zur Förderung der geistigen Wiederaufbaukräfte* (Economic Association for the Promotion of the Forces of Spiritual Reconstruction), the conservative politician and director of the Krupp industries, Alfred Hugenberg (1865–1951), a bitter enemy of the Weimar Republic and later Nazi finance minister, effectively took control of the nearly bankrupt Universum-Film AG (UFA) in 1927, expanding the group's media empire beyond its holdings in publishing and newspapers. This eventually culminated in the right-wing film monopoly that played a crucial role in the consolidation of Fascism.

2. Kracauer is referring here, respectively, to the 1927 film by Hans Kyser *Luther: Ein Film der deutschen Reformation;* to Otto Gebühr (1877–1954), a German film actor who, following his performance as Friedrich II in the four-part series *Fridericus Rex* (Arzen von Cserépy, 1920–1922), was typecast as the patriarchal Prussian king in *Der alte Fritz* (Gerhard Lamprecht, 1927); and to Karl Grune's 1927 film *Die Jugend der Königin Luise.*

3. *Simplicissimus,* a satirical weekly (1896–1944; 1954–1967) founded by publisher Albert Langen and Thomas T. Heine, was known for its biting political critiques. By contrast, the illustrated, humorous, and much less political publication founded by Kaspar Braun and Friedrich Schneider and known as *Die Fliegenden Blätter* (1844–1944) was famous for its caricatures (by Wilhelm Busch and others) of German bourgeois behavior.

4. The German actor Harry Liedtke (1888–1945) played the role of Armand de Foix in *Madame Dubarry* (Ernst Lubitsch, 1919).

5. Eugenie Marlitt, pseudonym of Eugenie John (1825–1887), a popular German writer, author of serial novels published in the illustrated weekly *Die Gartenlaube,* and later of light romantic novels also highly popular in English translation. See, for example, *Gold Elsie,* trans. A. L. Wister (Philadelphia: Lippincott, 1868); and *In the Schillingscourt,* trans. Emily R. Steinestel (New York: A. L. Burt, 1879).

6. The "Königlich und Kaiserlich" (Royal and Imperial) designation refers to the

Dual Monarchy of Austria-Hungary (1867–1918) under which both the Austrian empire and the Kingdom of Hungary pledged their allegiance to Francis Joseph. The "seventh of October" refers to an event on that day in 1928 when a large and heavily armed contingent from the fascist organization Heimwehr (Home Defense Force) marched through Wiener Neustadt. Units from the Austrian army and from the social-democratic Schutzbund (Defense League) prevented counterdemonstrations by workers' groups in the socialist-controlled capital.

7. Reference to Arthur Bergen's 1927 film *So küßt nur eine Wienerin.*

8. A moralizing film genre, named after the working-class Berlin caricaturist Heinrich Zille, which focused on contemporary social problems such as the social reintegration of ex-convicts (*Die Verrufenen:* Gerhard Lamprecht, 1925) and the care of illegitimate children (*Die Unehelichen:* Gerhard Lamprecht, 1926).

9. Reference to the Carmen Boni film *Lotte hat ihr Glück gemacht / Totte et sa chance* (Augusto Genina, 1928).

10. *Der falsche Prinz: Eine Zeitkomödie in sieben Akten* (Heinz Paul, 1927). Kracauer reviewed not only the film—in the *Frankfurter Zeitung* Stadtblatt of January 1, 1928—but also the book on which it was based. See his 1927 essay "Prinz Domela," reprinted in *Schriften* 5, pt. 2, 75–77.

11. The Saxo-Borussia was a German fraternity founded in Heidelberg in 1820 and composed largely of students of aristocratic background. Although committed to both political and religious neutrality by virtue of its affiliation with the union of university confederations known as the Kösener Senioren-Convents-Verband, antifascist behavior by members of the Saxo-Borussia and other *Korporationen* in 1935 led the Nazis to forbid party members from belonging to any such organizations.

12. Founded in 1928 in response to the perceived mediocrity of commercial cinema, the *Volksverband für Filmkunst* began as an attempt to provide an alternative repertoire of serious cinema programming, with the plan to later expand into production. One of its first projects, a reedited newsreel compiled from extant footage, was immediately banned by the censors. See Kracauer's article on the *Volksverband* in the *Frankfurter Zeitung* 72, no. 325 (May 1, 1928): 1.

13. Kracauer here plays with the consonance of *Dichtung* ("poetry") and *sich verdichten,* which means "to thicken" or "to grow stronger."

14. The *Allgemeiner Freier Angestelltenbund* (General Free Union of White-Collar Workers), established in 1921 in conjunction with the workers' union, the *Allgemeiner Deutscher Gewerkschaftsbund,* was a major voice for the employee class in the Weimar Republic. The ranks of its membership at times numbered over 750,000 before it was dissolved by the Nazis on April 30, 1933.

15. The literary works of Arthur Schnitzler (1862–1931), Carl Zuckmayer (1896–1977), and Hermann Sudermann (1857–1928) were frequently used as the

basis for films in the Weimar era. See, for example, Kracauer's review of Forrest Holger-Madsen's 1928 film version of Schnitzler's *Freiwild* in the *Frankfurter Zeitung* 72 (March 1, 1928), Stadt-Blatt 5.

16. Kracauer here plays with the adjective *groß* ("great" or "large"), which also forms part of the term *Großfilm* (a "major film" or, as it is known today, a "blockbuster").

17. The German film actor, director, and producer Harry Piel (1892–1963) introduced the new genre of the *Sensationsfilm* in the mid-1920s in order to compete with the American "thrillers." The films he directed and produced—such as *Der Mann ohne Nerven* (1924), *Panik* (1928), *Ein Unsichtbarer geht durch die Stadt* (1933)—were often set in artistic and adventurous settings and featured acrobats, trained animals, action scenes, and technical tricks.

18. Thea von Harbou (1888–1954), German author and film director, wrote screenplays for Joe May, F. W. Murnau, C. T. Dreyer, and, above all, Fritz Lang (*Der müde Tod, Dr. Mabuse der Spieler, Metropolis, Spione,* and so on). She was married to Lang until 1933, when he left her, not least because of her explicit Nazi sympathies.

19. English in original.

20. French in original.

21. Fred Majo and Dr. Fritz Wendhausen's screenplay for *Heimkehr* (Joe May, 1928) was based on the novella *Karl und Anna*, by Leonhard Frank.

22. Paul Czinner's 1927 feature *Doña Juana* starred Elisabeth Bergner, Czinner's long-time companion and later wife, with whom he made many films.

23. Vsevolod Illarionovich Pudovkin, *Kino-rezhisser i kino-material* (Moscow: Kinopechat, 1926), translated by Ivor Montagu as *On Film Technique* (London: Victor Gollancz, 1929; enlarged ed. London: George Newnes, 1933), 72. In a note appended to this passage, the English translator explains that the reference to Ruttmann not only is mistaken but was furthermore not in the original text, having been added by the German translators Georg and Nadja Friedland (*Filmregie und Filmmanuskript* [Berlin: Verlag der Lichtbildbühne, 1928]). Indeed, according to the translator Montagu, "the [Ruttmann] instance was repudiated by Pudowkin when brought to his attention" (188).

24. In Henrik Galeen's 1927 film *Alraune*, Paul Wegener (1874–1948) played the role of Professor ten Brinken.

25. The first publication of this text ended with the following afterword, which was dropped in later reprints: "*Afterword:* The press is spreading the news that the *government of the Reich* is playing with the idea of acquiring stock ownership of a large film company in order to have an influence on the production. Besides the economic qualms raised by such a project, would its realization even guarantee the political correctness of future films? It would not."

Cult of Distraction

1. Hans Poelzig (1869–1936) was one of the founders of the modern movement in German architecture. He designed the Grosses Schauspielhaus for Max Reinhardt in Berlin (1919), with its famous "stalactite dome," as well as the "Capitol" cinema in Berlin (1925), the "Deli" cinema in Breslau (1926), and the "Babylon" cinema in Berlin (1928–1929). He also made the Expressionist sets for the second version of Paul Wegener's film *Golem* (1920). For more material on the Berlin film palaces (including extensive photographic documentation), see Rolf-Peter Baacke, *Lichtspielhausarchitektur in Deutschland: Von der Schaubude bis zum Kinopalast* (Berlin: Frölich und Kaufmann, 1982); and Heinz Frick, *Mein Gloria Palast: Das Kino vom Kurfürstendamm* (Munich: Universitäts Verlag, 1986). For information on respective developments in America, see Douglas Gomery, "Towards a History of Film Exhibition: The Case of the Picture Palace," *Film Studies Annual*, part 2 (Pleasantville, N.Y.: Redgrave, 1977), 17–26.

2. Kracauer here plays with the ambiguity of *Betrieb*, which can mean both "enterprise" (business) and "activity" (hustle and bustle, busy-ness).

Boredom

1. Kracauer here plays with the resonance between *langweilen* ("to bore") and *lange (ver)weilen* ("to tarry" or "to linger").

2. In the copy of this article pasted by Kracauer into his scrapbook, this adjective was crossed out in pen. It reappeared, however, when the essay was reprinted in *Das Ornament der Masse*.

3. Kracauer here plays on the resonance between *Funk*, which means "radio," and *Funke*, which means "spark" or "flicker."

4. The semantic fulcrum of this sentence is provided by the ambiguity of *Empfängnis*, which can mean both "reception" (as in a radio broadcast) and "conception" (the result of a sexual—as opposed to radiophonic—dissemination).

5. This English expression, rendered as "surprising party" in the first printing of the article in the *Frankfurter Zeitung*, was subsequently corrected in the 1963 reprinting.

Farewell to the Linden Arcade

1. The Berlin arcade which Kracauer calls the "Linden Arcade" was in fact named the Kaisergalerie and ran from Unter den Linden 22–23 to Behrenstraße 50 and 52, at the corner of Friedrichstraße 164. Opened in 1873, it was "the first independent, so-called modern, purely commercial building." Initially

appointed with elegant shops, cafés, and a concert hall, it was frequented by the urban aristocracy during its first fashionable period, which lasted almost ten years. In 1888, with many of the shops already vacant, the famous Passage-Optikon moved in and immediately changed the character of the space with its motley collection of dioramas, panoramas, souvenir shops, and miscellaneous attractions. At the turn of the century, Friedrichstraße had become the entertainment district, with its concomitant tourism and prostitution, leading to a further "decline" in terms of the class affiliations of the arcade's patrons. Following World War I, the now dingy and rundown space provoked calls for its restoration; instead, it was "modernized" in 1928, reducing the three-storey interior to one storey by means of a vaulted glass roof. It was destroyed by Allied bombing in 1944. For an extensive historical and architectural account of the arcade, see Johann Friedrich Geist, *Passagen: Ein Bautyp des 19. Jahrhunderts* (Munich: Prestel, 1969, rpt. 1979), 132–145, and the English edition "based on a translation by Jane O. Newman and John H. Smith," *Arcades* (Cambridge, Mass.: MIT Press, 1983), esp. 142ff.

2. Kracauer here sets in motion a semantic resonance (which reverberates throughout the entire essay) among the senses of *Passage:* an arcade, a means of passage, a voyage, and finally a site of transition. To mark some of these differences, Kracauer also employs *Durchgang*, or "passageway"; the French adjectival form *passager*, which then means "transient"; and a more musical sense of the term which refers to wares as "passages in the composition of bourgeois life." On the word "passage" and its translation, see Geist, *Arcades*, 3.

3. In fact, Zola's novel was set not in the Passage des Panoramas but in the Passage du Pont Neuf; see *Thérèse Raquin*, trans. Leonard Tancock (Harmondsworth: Penguin, 1962), 31–33. See also Kracauer's 1928 review of Jacques Feyder's film "Thérèse Raquin," reprinted in *Kino: Essays, Studien, Glossen zum Film*, ed. Karsten Witte (Frankfurt: Suhrkamp Verlag, 1974), 136–138. On the Passage des Panoramas, see Geist, *Arcades*, 464–475.

4. For a detailed and humorous description of the Anatomical Museum, see Egon Erwin Kisch, "Geheimkabinett des anatomischen Museums," in *Der rasende Reporter* (Berlin: Erich Reiss Verlag, 1925; rpt. Aufbau, 1986), 165–168, translated in Geist, *Arcades*, 160–162.

5. Under the octagonal cupola in the center of the arcade was the Wiener Café, Berlin's first Viennese coffeehouse. Luxuriously appointed, with reading and billiard rooms, newspapers, and authentic Viennese coffees and pastries, it was a meeting place for the high-class patrons of the surrounding elegant boutiques during the arcade's early years.

6. An 1852 image by Adolf Menzel of a concert given by Frederick the Great in his would-be Versailles "Sanssouci" in Potsdam. See Kracauer's 1930 review

of Gustav Ucicky's film "Das Flötenkonzert von Sanssouci," published in the *Frankfurter Zeitung* the day after the essay on the Linden Arcade and reprinted in *Schriften*, vol. 2 (Frankfurt: Suhrkamp Verlag, 1979), 459–462.

7. The Welt-Panorama, the new name of the famous Kaiser-Panorama (Imperial Panorama) after World War I, was a huge wooden cylinder around which 25 seated viewers looked through peepholes at polychrome glass stereoscopic images of exotic places and current events, all from the extensive collection of August Fuhrmann (1844–1925). Opened in 1883, the attraction—whose program changed twice a week—lasted until 1939. See Stephan Oettermann, *Das Panorama: Die Geschichte eines Massenmediums* (Frankfurt: Büchergilde Gutenberg, 1980), 183–186; and idem, *Das Kaiserpanorama: Bilder aus dem Berlin der Jahrhundertwende* (Berlin: Berliner Festspiele, 1984). In English, see Stephan Oettermann, "The Panorama: An Early Mass Medium" and "The Rise and Fall of the Panorama: The Art Form of an Epoch," *Swissair Gazette* 9 (1986): 15–19 and 24–30.

8. Walter Benjamin, "Briefmarken-Handlung," in *Einbahnstraße* [1928], reprinted in Benjamin, *Gesammelte Schriften* vol. 4 (Frankfurt: Suhrkamp Verlag, 1972), 134–137; "Stamp Shop," in *One Way Street and Other Writings*, trans. Edmund Jephcott and Kingsley Shorter (London: New Left Books, 1979), 91–94. See also Benjamin's wonderful radio lecture "Briefmarkenschwindel," in Benjamin, *Gesammelte Schriften*, vol. 7, pt. 1 (1989), 195–200; in English, "Stamp Scams," trans. Jeffrey Mehlman, *London Review of Books* (September 8, 1994): 16.

9. As described in some detail by the contemporary account of the Linden Arcade in Franz Hessel's *Spazieren in Berlin* (Leipzig: H. Epstein, 1929; rpt. Berlin: Das Arsenal, 1984), the guaranteed similitude offered by the court painter stemmed from the fact that his often life-size oil portraits were based on photographs. An English translation of the relevant section by Hessel can be found in Geist, *Arcades*, 157–158. The entire volume is available in a French translation by Jean-Michel Beloeil as *Promenades dans Berlin* (Grenoble: Presses Universitaires de Grenoble, 1989).

10. Castan's panopticon, initially located inside the arcade, moved to the street corner facing the arcade entrance in 1888. This means that, as of that date, there were no less than two competing panopticon establishments virtually next door to each other. For a historical overview, see P. Letkemann, "Das Berliner Panoptikon," *Mitteilungen des Vereins für die Geschichte Berlins* 69, no. 11 (July 1, 1973): 319–326.

Bibliographic Information

∎∎∎

"Lad and Bull"

raca [pseudonym], "Knabe und Stier: Bewegungsstudie," *Frankfurter Zeitung* 71, no. 726 (September 29, 1926), Feuilleton 1. Reprinted in Kracauer, *Straßen in Berlin und anderswo* (Frankfurt: Suhrkamp, 1964), 132–134; Kracauer, *Straßen in Berlin und anderswo* (Berlin: Das Arsenal, 1987), 97–98; Kracauer, *Schriften*, vol. 5, ed. Inka Mülder-Bach (Frankfurt: Suhrkamp, 1990), pt. 1, 380–381.

"Two Planes"

raca. [pseudonym], "Zwei Flächen," *Frankfurter Zeitung* 71, no. 717 (September 26, 1926), Feuilleton 2–3. Reprinted in *Straßen*, 24–27; *Straßen (1987)*, 19–21; *Schriften*, vol. 5, pt. 1, 378–380.

"Analysis of a City Map"

"Analyse eines Stadtplans," *Frankfurter Zeitung*, 1926 (exact date not yet established). Reprinted in *Straßen*, 16–19; *Straßen (1987)*, 12–14; *Schriften*, vol. 5, pt. 1, 401–403.

"Photography"

"Die Photographie" (Parts 1–4), *Frankfurter Zeitung* 72, no. 802 (October 28, 1927), Feuilleton 1–2; "Die Photographie" (Parts 5–8), *Frankfurter Zeitung* 72, no. 803 (October 28, 1927), Feuilleton 1–2. Reprinted in *Schriften*, vol. 5, pt. 2, 83–98. In English as "Photography," trans. Thomas Y. Levin, in *Critical Inquiry* 19, no. 3 (Spring 1993): 421–436. In Italian as "La fotografia," *La massa come ornamento*, trans. Maria Giovanna Amirante Pappalardo and Francesco Maione (Naples: Prismi Editrice, 1982), 111–127.

"Travel and Dance"

"Die Reise und der Tanz," *Frankfurter Zeitung* 69, no. 198 (March 15, 1925), Feuilleton 1–3. Reprinted in *Schriften*, vol. 5, pt. 1, 288–296. In Italian as "Il viaggio e la danza," *La massa come ornamento*, 69–77.

"The Mass Ornament"

"Das Ornament der Masse" (Parts 1–2), *Frankfurter Zeitung* 71, no. 420 (June

9, 1927), Feuilleton 1; "Das Ornament der Masse" (Parts 3–6), *Frankfurter Zeitung* 71, no. 423 (June 10, 1927), Feuilleton 1–2. Reprinted in *Schriften*, vol. 5, pt. 2, 57–67. Previous English translation by Barbara Correll and Jack Zipes in *New German Critique* 2, no. 5 (1975): 67–76. Anonymous Danish translation as "Massens ornament," in Visuel Kommunikation, ed. Bent Fausing and Peter Larsen (Copenhagen: Medusa, 1980), 2, 331–341. French translation by Ursula Sarrazin as "L'Ornement de la masse," in *Exercices de la patience: Cahiers de philosophie* 7 (1986): 47–57 (volume entitled *Effets de neutre*). In Italian as "La massa come ornamento," *La massa come ornamento*, 99–110.

"On Bestsellers and Their Audience"

"Über Erfolgsbücher und ihr Publikum," *Frankfurter Zeitung* 75, no. 470 (June 27, 1931), Feuilleton 1–2. Also in *Frankfurter Zeitung* 75 (June 27, 1931), Reichsausgabe 469–471, Feuilleton 12. Reprinted in *Schriften*, vol. 5, pt. 2, 334–342.

"The Biography as an Art Form of the New Bourgeoisie"

"Die Biographie als neubürgerliche Kunstform," *Frankfurter Zeitung* 74, no. 477 (June 29, 1930), Literaturblatt 26, 6. Also in *Frankfurter Zeitung* 74 (June 29, 1930), Reichsausgabe no. 475–477, Literaturblatt 26, 18. Reprinted in *Schriften*, vol. 5, pt. 2, 195–199. In Italian as "La biografia come forma d'arte della nuova borghesia," *La massa come ornamento*, 143–147.

"Revolt of the Middle Classes"

"Aufruhr der Mittelschichten: Eine Auseinandersetzung mit dem 'Tat'-Kreis" (Parts 1–3), *Frankfurter Zeitung* 76, no. 917–918 (December 10, 1931), Feuilleton 1–2. Also in *Frankfurter Zeitung* 76 (December 10, 1931), Reichsausgabe no. 917–919, Feuilleton 9. "Aufruhr der Mittelschichten: Eine Auseinandersetzung mit dem 'Tat'-Kreis" (Parts 4–6), *Frankfurter Zeitung* 76, nos. 920–921 (December 11, 1931), Feuilleton, 1–2. Also in *Frankfurter Zeitung* 76 (December 11, 1931), Reichsausgabe no. 920–922, Feuilleton 10. Entire essay reprinted in *Schriften*, vol. 5, pt. 2, 405–424.

"Those Who Wait"

"Die Wartenden," *Frankfurter Zeitung* 66, no. 191 (March 12, 1922), Feuilleton 1–3. Reprinted as the "Erste Gabe des Frankfurter Bundes tätiger Altstadtfreunde" (First Offering of the Frankfurt Association of Engaged Friends of the Old City) by the publisher R. T. Hauser (Frankfurt) as a special bibliophile 22-page pamphlet bound in heavy blue vellum and dated April 12, 1922. Also in *Schriften*, vol. 5, pt. 1, 160–170.

"The Group as Bearer of Ideas"

"Die Gruppe als Ideenträger," *Archiv für Sozialwissenschaft und Sozialpolitik* 49, no. 3 (August 1922): 594–622. Reprinted in *Schriften*, vol. 5, pt. 1, 170–196.

"The Hotel Lobby"
"Die Hotelhalle," the only section from Kracauer's book-length study of the detective novel (written 1922–1925) that was published in his lifetime. Selected by Kracauer in 1963 for inclusion in *Das Ornament der Masse*, it was also included, in revised form, in the posthumous complete publication of *Der Detektiv-Roman: Ein philosophischer Traktat*, in Kracauer, *Schriften*, vol. 1, 103–204. French translation by Geneviève and Rainer Rochlitz as *Le Roman policier: Un traité philosophique* (Paris: Payot, 1981). Italian translation by Renato Cristin as *Il romanzo poliziesco: Un trattato filosofico* (Rome: Editori Riuniti, 1984). An earlier Italian translation by Ursula Bavay, Antonella Gargano, and Carlo Serra Borneto was published as "Sociologia del romanzo poliziesco," in *Saggi di sociologia critica* (Bari: De Donato, 1974), 99–208.

"The Bible in German"
"Die Bibel auf Deutsch: Zur Übersetzung von Martin Buber und Franz Rosenzweig" (Part 1), *Frankfurter Zeitung* 70, no. 308 (April 27, 1926), Feuilleton 1–2. "Die Bibel auf Deutsch: Zur Übersetzung von Martin Buber und Franz Rosenzweig" (Part 2), *Frankfurter Zeitung* 70, no. 311 (April 28, 1926), Feuilleton 1. Entire essay reprinted in *Schriften*, vol. 5, pt. 2, 355–366. French translation by Rainer Rochlitz as "La Bible en allemand: A propos de la traduction due à Martin Buber et à Franz Rosenzweig," *Revue d'Esthétique*, n.s. 12, special issue entitled *La Traduction* (Paris, 1986), 91–97.

"Catholicism and Relativism"
"Katholizismus und Relativismus: Zu Max Schelers Werk 'Vom Ewigen im Menschen,' " *Frankfurter Zeitung* 66, no. 860 (November 19, 1921), Feuilleton 1–2. Reprinted in *Schriften*, vol. 5, pt. 1, 123–130.

"The Crisis of Science"
"Die Wissenschaftskrisis: Zu den grundsätzlichen Schriften Max Webers und Ernst Troeltschs" (Part 1), *Frankfurter Zeitung* 67, no. 179 (March 8, 1923), Hochschulblatt 3. "Die Wissenschaftskrisis: Zu den grundsätzlichen Schriften Max Webers und Ernst Troeltschs" (Part 2), *Frankfurter Zeitung* 67, no. 217 (March 22, 1923), Hochschulblatt 3–4. Reprinted in *Schriften*, vol. 5, pt. 1, 212–222.

"Georg Simmel"
"Georg Simmel," *Logos: Internationale Zeitschrift für Philosophie der Kultur* 9, no. 3 (1920–1921): 307–338. This is the first chapter of an extended and still unpublished book-length manuscript entitled *Georg Simmel: Ein Beitrag zur Deutung des geistigen Lebens unserer Zeit* (Georg Simmel: A Contribution to the Interpretation of the Spiritual/Intellectual Life of Our Time), 1–35. In Italian as "Georg Simmel," *La massa come ornamento*, 37–67.

"On the Writings of Walter Benjamin"
"Zu den Schriften Walter Benjamins," *Frankfurter Zeitung* 72, no. 524 (July 15, 1928), Literaturblatt 61, no. 29, 8. Reprinted in *Schriften*, vol. 5, pt. 2, 119–124; and in Walter Benjamin, *Briefe an Siegfried Kracauer*, ed. Theodor W. Adorno Archiv (Marbach: Deutsche Schillergesellschaft, 1987), 101–106. In Italian as "Sugli scritti di Walter Benjamin," *La massa come ornamento*, 129–134.

"Franz Kafka"
"Zu Franz Kafkas nachgelassenen Schriften" (Part 1), *Frankfurter Zeitung* 76, no. 654 (September 3, 1931), Feuilleton 1–2. Also in *Frankfurter Zeitung* 76 (September 3, 1931), Reichsausgabe 653–655, Feuilleton 10. "Franz Kafkas nachgelassene Schriften" (Part 2), *Frankfurter Zeitung* 76, no. 669–670 (September 9, 1931), Feuilleton, 1–2. Also in *Frankfurter Zeitung* 76 (September 9, 1931), Reichsausgabe no. 669–671, Feuilleton 10. Reprinted in *Schriften*, vol. 5, pt. 2, 363–373. In Italian as "Franz Kafka," *La massa come ornamento*, 175–186.

"Calico-World"
"Kaliko-Welt: Die UFA-Stadt zu Neubabelsberg," *Frankfurter Zeitung* 70, no. 72 (January 28, 1926), Feuilleton 1–2. Initially a radio program for the "Stunde der *Frankfurter Zeitung*" broadcast on January 24, 1926; advertised in the *Frankfurter Zeitung* 70, no. 62 (January 24, 1926): 1.

"The Little Shopgirls Go to the Movies"
"Die kleinen Ladenmädchen gehen ins Kino": a series of eight articles that ran in the *Frankfurter Zeitung* as follows: (Part 1) "Freie Bahn," in no. 187 (March 11, 1927), Feuilleton 1; (Part 2) "Geschlecht und Charakter," in no. 190 (March 12, 1927), Feuilleton 1; (Part 3) "Volk in Waffen," in no. 194 (March 14, 1927), Feuilleton 1; (Part 4) "Die Weltreisenden," in no. 197 (March 15, 1927), Feuilleton 1; (Part 5) "Das goldene Herz," in no. 200 (March 16, 1927), Feuilleton 1; (Part 6) "Der moderne Harun al Raschid," in no. 203 (March 17, 1927), Feuilleton 1; (Part 7) "Stille Tragödien / Hart an der Grenze," in no. 206 (March 18, 1927), Feuilleton 1; (Part 8) "Film und Gesellschaft: Schluß der Serie 'Die kleinen Ladenmädchen gehen ins Kino,' " in no. 207 (March 19, 1927), Feuilleton 1. Reprinted by the *Frankfurter Zeitung* (vol. 71, March 1927) as a separate 12-page booklet entitled "Film und Gesellschaft." In Italian as "Le piccole commesse vanno al cinema," *La massa come ornamento*, 85–98.

"Film 1928"
"Der heutige Film und sein Publikum" (Part 1), *Frankfurter Zeitung* 73, no. 895 (November 30, 1928), Feuilleton 1–2. "Der heutige Film und sein Publikum" (Part 2), *Frankfurter Zeitung* 73, no. 898 (December 1, 1928), Feuil-

leton 1–2. Reprinted under the same title as a 16-page pamphlet (Frankfurt: Frankfurter Societäts-Druckerei, n.d.). Also reprinted in *Die Form: Zeitschrift für gestaltende Arbeit* 4, no. 5 (March 1, 1929): 101–104; and in *Fazit: Ein Querschnitt durch die deutsche Publizistik*, ed. Ernst Glaeser (Hamburg: Gebr. Enoch, 1929); facsimile rpt. with an afterword by Helmut Mörchen (Kronberg/Ts: Scriptor, 1977), 287–305. Slightly edited versions of Part 1 appeared in French as "Le Film d'aujourd'hui et son public," in *Le Monde* 3, no. 86 (January 25, 1930): 6; and of Part 2 as "Le Problème du sujet dans le cinéma allemand," in *Le Monde* 3, no. 88 (February 8, 1930): 8–9.

"Cult of Distraction"

"Kult der Zerstreuung: Über die Berliner Lichtspielhäuser," *Frankfurter Zeitung* 70, no. 167 (March 4, 1926), Feuilleton 1–2. In English as "Cult of Distraction: On Berlin's Picture Palaces," trans. Thomas Y. Levin, in *New German Critique* 14, no. 40 (Winter 1987): 91–96. In Italian as "Culto del divertimento," *La massa come ornamento*, 79–84.

"Boredom"

"Langeweile," *Frankfurter Zeitung* 69, no. 859 (November 16, 1924), Feuilleton 1. Reprinted in *Schriften*, vol. 5, pt. 1, 278–281.

"Farewell to the Linden Arcade"

"Abschied von der Lindenpassage," *Frankfurter Zeitung* 75, no. 949 (December 21, 1930), Feuilleton 1–2; also in *Frankfurter Zeitung* 75 (December 21, 1930), Reichsausgabe 948–950, Feuilleton 15. Reprinted in *Straßen*, 30–38; *Straßen* (1987), 24–29; *Schriften*, vol. 5, pt. 2, 260–265. English translation in Johann Friedrich Geist, *Arcades: The History of a Building Type* (Cambridge, Mass.: MIT Press, 1983), 158–160. In Italian as "Addio alla Lindenpassage," *La massa come ornamento*, 153–159.

Credits

...

Index

■■■